PRACTICAL
Wood
Working
Inside and Outside

PRACTICAL Wood Working
Inside and Outside

Edited by
Alan Mitchell

Windward

First published 1987
by Windward
an imprint of W. H. Smith PLC, St John's House, Leicester

Copyright © 1987   IPC Magazines Ltd

ISBN H/B 0-7112-0470-5
ISBN P/B 0-7112-0469-1

Edited and produced by Quiller Press Ltd,
50 Albemarle Street, London W1X 4BD

Designed by Book Production Consultants, Cambridge
Typesetting by The Burlington Press (Cambridge) Ltd
Printed and bound in Yugoslavia by Mladinska Knjiga

THE FOLLOWING WELL KNOWN DESIGNERS' WORK HAS BEEN INCLUDED IN THE BOOK

Contents

Introduction

Apart from the excellent advice on preserving and finishing by Austin Hilditch of Cuprinol Ltd, this book is composed entirely of a selection of the best projects previously published in *Practical Woodworking* magazine and in writing this introduction I felt it important to first tell you a little about the magazine.

Launched in March 1966, it is a monthly magazine which was conceived to serve not only the dedicated enthusiast but also the less skilled 'Do-it-yourselfer' who simply enjoys occasionally making useful items of wood for the home. The editorial policy therefore has always been to include projects well suited to both accomplished craftsmen and those who are less expert, and when you consider that, according to research, it is read by some 400,000 people each month it is a policy which has certainly paid off over the twenty years or so since its foundation. As you can imagine during such a lengthy period literally thousands of designs have been published and I was delighted when it was suggested that a book should be produced from the best of this material.

This is the book. By a careful process of selection we have maintained the magazine's successful policy of including both simple and advanced projects so whatever your level of skill you will find many useful and attractive items to make for your home. The construction of all the projects is described in detail with stage by stage photographs and fully dimensioned drawings to assist you in the making and ensure a finished result which will give you many years of useful service and of which you can be justly proud.

The projects initially were gathered from a variety of sources; some you may feel have a distinctly continental flavour, these were probably syndicated from foreign publications, some came from regular contributors and some from recognised designer/craftspersons like Lucinda Leech, Jakki Dehn and Ashley Cartwright. These professionals obviously use quite sophisticated woodworking machinery and in some instances you will see illustrations of this being used in the construction of a project, or you may find that they have specified the use of an expensive timber. Don't be put off — if you only possess a basic tool kit, and lack the confidence to start sawing up costly material. There is always a way to achieve a similar result using traditional hand tools (so long as they are sharp) and most of the projects for which hardwood is suggested could also be constructed in readily available pine and would look just as attractive.

Wood is a remarkable material — it is a joy to work, it possesses a unique warmth and beauty and will last indefinitely if properly looked after. This book is about making things from wood which will give pleasure in the making, pleasure in the using and pleasure to one's children, grandchildren and future generations who may eventually inherit what you have made. This I can vouch for as I have experienced it. In my home there are pieces of woodwork which were made by relations who have long been deceased. I treasure them and they often remind me of happy days spent in the company of their makers. I hope you will find the book interesting and decide to make some of the projects which are featured. Who knows, in the distant future a great-great-grandchild of yours may inherit a piece of your work and enjoy the same pleasure that I have experienced.

ALAN MITCHELL, November, 1986

Finishing wood

by Austin Hilditch, Technical Director of Cuprinol Ltd

Finishing wood can be as simple or as involved as you want.

A wide and, in some ways, confusing range of products is available, giving different types of finish and requiring different levels of skill in their use. This chapter gives guidance on achievement of most of the finishes you will want in different circumstances and involves choice between only a few products.

The appearance of the final finished article depends on the wood, on how well it was prepared, on the product used to finish it and on how carefully it was applied. The greater the care, the better the quality but with modern materials a very adequate finish can be obtained with relatively little trouble.

Choosing Wood

All woods can be finished, only with a few, e.g. teak, is it necessary to use a special product.

When using up old timber or refinishing existing articles, choose a finishing system that is going to give best results on such work. When selecting new wood, there are some things to watch for that will affect the quality of the finish and particularly the uniformity of any colouring you apply.

Avoid bluestain and similar defects that will show through the finish (unless you wish to use these as a feature).

Most commercial softwoods contain both sapwood and heartwood. These may be a different colour. Sapwood absorbs liquid more readily than heartwood and so will stain darker. With some timbers, particularly softwood, patches of sapwood will be found, which absorb very much more of the stain than surrounding areas. These areas often occur patchily. They are not usually apparent in new wood when it is dry but they can be detected by wiping the surface over lightly with a rag damped with white spirit. Such variations in absorption do not matter where only a clear finish is to be used.

Different pieces of hardwood, even of the same species, vary in colour. Wood dye can be used to colour these more uniformly but it is better whenever possible to select pieces of closely similar colour.

In selecting wood and in work, remember that deep scratches and other marks take a lot of sanding out.

Preparation — New Work

For many jobs local sanding to remove pencil or other marks and to smooth any rough areas around knots is quite adequate, especially if only a clear finish is to be used. When a dye is used, any roughness, scratches and the like are likely to be emphasised.

Fill large holes, gaps, joints, etc with plastic wood or a wood filler. Use a coloured filler to match the intended colour of the finished work if intending to stain with a wood dye. Use a filler of a colour to match the wood if intending to use a clear finish or to colour with a polyurethane varnish tint.

For ordinary work, sand filler flush, using first, coarse then medium sandpaper. Sand away any local irregularities, marks, etc.

For furniture and other top quality work, sand all over to a fine smooth finish using progressively fine and then flour sandpaper.

Always finish sanding along the grain, removing any deep scores left by earlier use of coarse sandpaper and especially remove any scores across the grain. Hand sanding or use of an orbital or belt sander is preferred, sanding to a flat surface and avoidance of scoring marks across the grain is difficult with a disc sander.

Preparation for Re–finishing or Restoration

Preparation depends on the existing condition of the surface and on the condition to which it is to be restored.

Where the existing finish is essentially sound and the colour is satisfactory, the object of the restoration is to cover surface scratches, restore surface sheen, etc.

Remove dirt, grease and wax from the surface, followed by sanding down lightly with medium to fine sandpaper. Feather-edge scratches and smooth out any irregularities. Removal of wax is particularly important with floors and furniture on which polish has been used.

Wax can be removed by washing down several times with white spirit.

Scratches showing light can be touched up by applying a wood dye or coloured polyurethane varnish locally with an artist's brush. Do this after all other preparation is complete but before applying the final finishing coat. When dry, use fine or flour sandpaper to feather-edge new varnish. Do not use wax based scratch fillers.

When the existing finish is unsound or very badly scarred, or if the colour is to be changed, then the original finish should be removed completely. Sand or use a chemical or hot air paint remover to take off any surface film. Do not use a blow torch because of scorching. Complete preparation by sanding along the grain to a smooth finish.

The original finish is likely to have penetrated somewhat into the wood. If it is intended to refinish with a clear coating only, then provided that the colour is sufficiently uniform this need not be removed. If it is intended to recolour the wood, then use of a polyurethane varnish tint may be the best choice. This requires only the same preparation as for a clear coating, but if it is intended to use a penetrating dye stain then sufficient wood must be sanded away to get below the depth of penetration of the original finish otherwise the dye may go on unevenly. Such a procedure is often impracticable, particularly with veneered items.

Grain Filling

A few woods, of which the commonest are oak and mahogany (including Meranti and other so called mahoganies) have a very open grain. "Mahogany" veneered chipboard is particularly common.

The open grain may be retained as a feature but if a really smooth finish is required a lot of work sanding down successive finish coats can be avoided by use of a grain filler. The grain filler used should be coloured to match the final colour of the work either by using a suitable ready coloured filler or by mixing with stain. Apply by wiping across the grain with a soft rag or pad and when dry (usually next day) sand lightly (with grain) with fine/flour sandpaper.

Staining

The colour of any dye or stain is always "added" to the natural colour of the wood. The final colour is therefore a combination of the two. To ensure that you get the colour you want, try out on a bit of waste wood or a hidden part of the article. Remember that with dyes the colour will look different when the finishing coat is applied so include this in your trial.

Staining can conveniently be carried out with either a wood dye or a polyurethne varnish into which colouring has been incorporated.

Wood dyes penetrate into the timber emphasising rather than hiding differences in grain. Dyes are generally considered to give the best quality of colour.

Polyurethene varnish stains do not penetrate significantly into the timber but form a film on top of it. Hiding of the wood grain and other features is minimal and is of no consequence in many situations but, inevitably, these finishes do not have the full clarity of a dye. They are, however, much more tolerant of variations in the wood. They should be preferred for refinishing work where the old finish cannot be fully removed and for use on wood where the absorption is very uneven. Since colouring and finishing can be achieved with a single product, with less total coats, they also offer convenience.

Wood dyes should be applied uniformly, using a brush or cloth pad. If the first coat does not give a deep enough colour, further coats are best applied before the work has dried. Under no circumstances should more dye be applied than will soak into the wood. A surface film of dye will reduce the adhesion of the finish. Allow dye to dry before continuing with the finishing process.

Dyes are available, which are formulated into water, alcohol (Methylated Spirits) or organic solvent (White Spirit). For most uses, these latter offer greatest convenience. Their medium drying rate makes uniform application easier and they cause no raising of the grain.

Polyurethane varnish wood shades are applied by the same methods as a clear finish (see below). Rubbing down between coats should only be enough to remove any dust or local runs and care should be taken not to sand unevenly through the colour. Products should always be stirred well before commencing application.

With polyurethane tints, the depth of colour can be increased by application of successive coats, often this will result in a complete finish. If the required colour is obtained before a suitable surface finish results, finishing can be completed using a clear coating.

Finishing

Of the range of materials available for final finishing of wood, polyurethane varnishes offer the best quality in all respects. This statement may be challenged by some due to confusion between the properties of these materials and older fashioned oil varnishes. Modern polyurethane varnishes are very flexible in how they may be applied and in the results achieved. The resulting finish depends as much on the application as on the product but always, when finished, the coating is fully transparent, hard wearing and resistant to marring by household chemicals such as water and alcohol.

The most common "standard" polyurethane varnishes are usually described as gloss although these can be applied to achieve not only a full mirror-like gloss but also a low sheen of a type associated with much modern furniture, or indeed a full matt. Other qualities are available designed to give matt or satin finishes.

Application can be by brush or pad, which should be clean and dust free. The preferred method of application depends partly upon personal preferences and partly on the type and quality of the finish required. Use of two coats is generally recommended. One coat is likely to be uneven due to variations in absorption into the wood. For very high gloss finishes additional coats may be necessary. Each coat must be allowed to dry before the next is applied. The drying with most products takes between two and six hours under "average" conditions but may be quicker in very hot weather and will be longer in very cold. Thin coats dry quicker than thick. Always use in a place with good ventilation and minimise dust.

Full Gloss Finish for General Work
(panelling, flooring, etc.)

Use the product as supplied. Apply uniformly, using a paint or polish brush, brushing out as for paint. Take care to avoid runs especially round joints, in corners on panels, etc. Finish each coat off with light brush strokes in one direction only. When dry, lightly sand with fine sandpaper or wire wool to remove any dust adhering to the film and to slightly scar the surface. Apply a second coat in the same manner and continue to build up coats, rubbing down between coats until the required finish is obtained. Mostly, this can be between two and three coats.

An alternative technique is to apply by rag, using a lint-free rag folded as a pad. Dip into the polyurethane and rub uniformly over the surface, finishing off with even strokes in one direction. Carefully applied rag coats give a more uniform finish than brush coats, but they are thinner and additional coats will usually be required. Whenever rags are used to apply this type of product, they should be destroyed or dumped outside immediately after use. They should not be kept indoors since they are liable to ignite if kept in warm conditions.

Full Gloss Finish on Finest Work
(e.g. good quality furniture)

Thin polyurethane with 5–10% of white spirit, apply thinly by pad rubbing well into the grain, wiping across and along but finishing with even strokes along the grain (essentially as in applying french polish). Allow each coat to dry thoroughly, rub down with flour sandpaper or 0000 grade wire wool. Continue to build up coats in the same manner until the desired depth of gloss is achieved.

Carefully applied this technique will give a finish equal to professional french polishing but as each coat is relatively thin more coats will be required than when applied thickly by brush.

Low Gloss or Natural Finish

Use polyurethane clear gloss, apply a thin coat by brush or rag (thinned with white spirit if one of the thicker products is being used), allow the first coat to soak in for a few minutes and then wipe off excess. This may be sufficient, although if a fractionally higher gloss is preferred, or if the first coat soaked in unevenly, a second coat of thinned down material should be applied thinly when the first coat is dry.

A pad of fine wire wool (0 or finer) may be preferred for this application. Where a natural finish is required, a final rub over when the coating is dry with 0000 grade wire wool is recommended.

Matt or Satin Finishes

Use matt or satin quality polyurethanes. Follow the application techniques given above. With these finishes, two coats will usually suffice, only occasionally will more be necessary.

Wax Polishing

A full wax finish takes much time and effort to build up using wax alone. These finishes are then easily marred. A simpler and more serviceable finish can be obtained by first of all applying clear gloss polyurethane as described for a natural finish and applying a conventional wax polish on top.

For most purposes, full finishing with polyurethane to a gloss finish (at whatever level of gloss is required) and use of wax polish only for maintenance will be more satisfactory and more durable.

Teak

Natural oils in Teak, Iroko (African Teak), Apitong, Keruing, Cocus and a few other woods slow the drying of normal finishes. Special finishes – teak oils are produced for use on these timbers to give a matt natural finish.

Teak oil should be applied liberally by brush or pad, allowed to soak in for about 15 minutes and any surplus wiped off. For furniture, rub down with flour sandpaper or 000 wire wool while still wet. Apply a second coat sparingly with a rag pad and allow to dry well before use. Wood finished in this way requires periodic re-oiling.

Exceptionally a gloss finish may be required on these woods (e.g. furniture made from teak veneered ply or chipboard). After initial preparation, wash the surface with white spirit until it no longer feels oily. Once is usually sufficient on this veneer but two or three times may be necessary on solid wood. Allow white spirit to dry. Apply a first coat of polyurethane clear gloss thinly and allow to dry. Drying will be considerably slower than usual – 24 hours or more.

When dry, rub down lightly with flour sandpaper or 00 wire wool damped with white spirit. Wipe off. Apply further coats in this way until a satisfactory finish is obtained. Drying of the second and third coats will be longer than usual but not so long as for the first coat. When proposing to finish in this way, it is a good idea first to try out the finish on a hidden part or waste piece. 48 hours after application of the second coat, push the edge of a coin along the surface to see if satisfactory adhesion between coats has been obtained. If not, further de-oiling with white spirit is necessary. On exceptionally oily woods, gloss finishing may simply not be possible. Note that this test can also be used to see if wax has been removed from all furniture, floors etc. or other wood.

Conclusion

Careful preparation and application is the key to success with any wood finish. Modern polyurethane varnish in combination with wood dyes offer the best route to beautiful, hardwearing and marr resistant finishes.

Products for Wood Finishing

PRODUCTS		USE
Polyurethane Varnish Clear	Gloss Matt Satin	To give a tough durable polish or seal finish to wood. Highly resistant to wear, marking and staining. Use on furniture, panelling, floors, etc. Three grades to give gloss, matt or satin finish.
Polyurethane Varnish Wood Shades		A range of coloured varnishes to colour and finish with a single product. Gives a gloss finish, but can be overcoated with Clear Matt or Satin.
Wood Dyes		A range of penetrating wood dyes to stain indoor wood prior to finishing with Clear Polyurethane.
Plastic Wood Filler		Natural colour wood filler for holes, cracks, etc.
Teak Oil		To give a natural finish to Teak and similar hardwoods – indoors or out.
Cuprinol Exterior Varnish		To give a clear gloss finish to outdoor wood.
Wood Preserver (Light Oak and Dark Oak)		An alternative stain (with preservation) for floorboards and beams.
Wood Stain Sheen for Hardwoods Outdoors		An excellent mid-sheen finish (in 3 colours) for hardwood panelling.
Outdoor Wood Stain – Natural or Sheen Finish		A natural wood finish in a range of colours for softwood windows, doors, cladding, facias, etc.

Wood Working Inside

Select pieces of wood with no natural defects

Child's bed

"Nice and cheerful with some inlay on it" was the brief given to the designer of this child's bed. The design certainly satisfies these criteria while combining economy with space saving.

SPACE is usually at a premium in children's rooms so size was an important criterion here. Economy – always a consideration, posed two challenges. Firstly to use a reasonably cheap material (veneered board), secondly to use this material in an economic way – hence all the main show pieces can be cut from one sheet of board.

Method

All the main pieces are marked out on the veneered board and cut out. I used a portable circular saw with a fine 60 tooth tungsten blade as it gives a good finish and doesn't break out the veneer. Remember to cut the front panel and drawer fronts together so that the grain matches up. I leave cutting the rest of the drawer stuff until the carcase is assembled so that it can be cut to the exact size.

Next cut out the hardwood pieces. I cut the corner pieces in one length as it suited both the plank from which it was cut and made sizing and grooving easier. This was left as a square section to facilitate cramping together. The headboard columns are straightforward enough and all the other pieces were roughed out.

Even after cutting the ply pieces as ac- curately as possible, I always check them for square and correct as necessary. It's far better to do this as you go as it can save a lot of time in the long run. The two ends, back and front panels are then rebated leaving a 9 by 9mm tongue. Then the grooves in the corner pieces 9 by 9.5mm deep are routed out. Remember to stop the grooves on the inside edges of the front corners where the drawer fronts fit (see exploded view).

The main carcase can now be glued up. Assemble the end panels first. When set, the front and back panels can be glued in. I am fortunate to have cramp extensions that will accommodate 1500mm easily, but you could take the sliding feet off two sash cramps and bolt the bars together to gain the required length. Again check for square. Although the structure is quite flexible at this stage it is still a prudent measure.

The front rail, side and middle runners can now be planed up to finished size and cut to final length against the carcase. Rout out the slots in the front rail to take the side and middle runners. Groove the middle runner 15 by 5mm deep and run this through the front rail too. Saw the lap joints on the ends of the front rail and drill for the screws and fit in place. Ensure the screw heads are recessed to the bottom of the grooves so they don't foul the side runner tongues. Now saw the tongues on the runners, cut the lap joints and fit into place. The middle runner will pop into position because the back panel is flexible

USEFUL HINTS

E. A. Hilditch (Technical Director of Cuprinol Ltd)

Selecting Wood

Avoid pieces with too many large or dead knots

Avoid very resinous woods

Avoid wood with splits or normal defects of wood

Avoid signs of decay or surface mould

Avoid bluestain

Cheerful in cherry — the design for this child's bed has a very individualistic touch. It has colourful inlaid shapes to the drawers and headboard, a humourous "ball rolled off" feature and rope drawer handles that won't cause accidents and floods of tears.

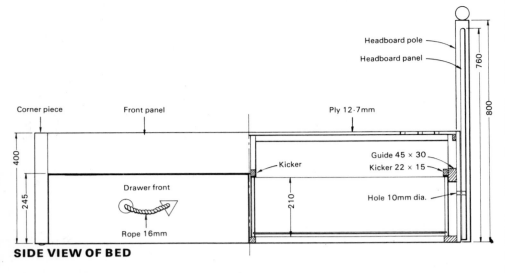

SIDE VIEW OF BED

Corner piece — Front panel — Ply 12·7mm — Headboard pole — Headboard panel

400
245
Drawer front
Rope 16mm
Kicker
Guide 45 × 30
Kicker 22 × 15
Hole 10mm dia.
210
760
800

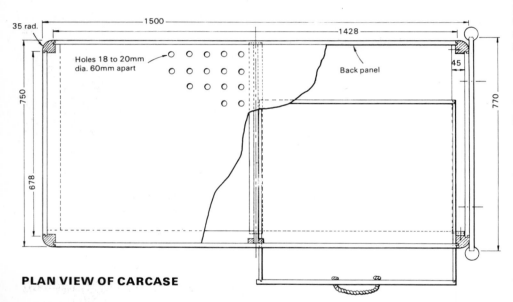

PLAN VIEW OF CARCASE

35 rad.
1500
1428
Holes 18 to 20mm dia. 60mm apart
Back panel
45
750
678
770

enough to allow it. A cramp across here will ensure the joint is properly bedded. Check this runner is square to the carcase so that the drawers will run true.

The glue blocks to hold the middle panel can now be glued and pinned in place and the panel itself glued in.

Drawer guides are next and these are simply glued and cramped in position. The kickers are best left until the drawers are fitted for best results.

Drawers

It is clearly advisable to inlay and drill the drawer fronts before assembly. See headboard section for inlay work.

The drawers themselves are simple tongued and grooved construction. I stopped the grooves short on the drawer fronts so the tongues would not show on the top edge. When marking out these grooves remember to allow for the middle panel in the carcase so that the drawer fronts meet in the middle. The drawer fronts themselves act as stops on the front rail.

Headboard

Prepare the two columns for the lathe and turn down to 45mm diameter. I could just get these onto my Myford lathe. When finished they can be grooved. I made a simple jig from scrap chipboard and softwood battens so that the column was cradled. The battens acted as a guide for the router fence and also made a flat bed for the router base. A light cramp across the battens nips the column and ensures it doesn't move. The groove is 15 by 10mm deep. The end of one column is cut square and drilled to take the 10mm dowel for the ball. The other column is cut at about 80 degrees in line with the groove.

The headboard lipping is glued onto the

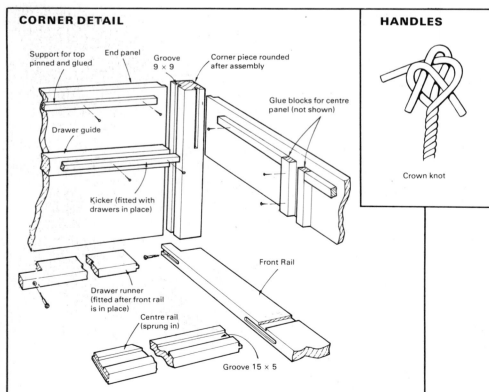

CORNER DETAIL

Support for top pinned and glued
End panel
Groove 9 × 9
Corner piece rounded after assembly
Glue blocks for centre panel (not shown)
Drawer guide
Kicker (fitted with drawers in place)
Drawer runner (fitted after front rail is in place)
Front Rail
Centre rail (sprung in)
Groove 15 × 5

HANDLES

Crown knot

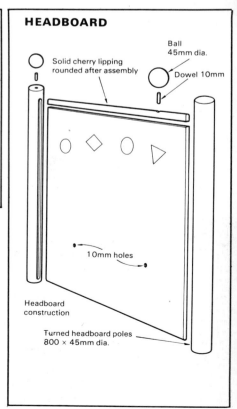

HEADBOARD

Ball 45mm dia.
Solid cherry lipping rounded after assembly
Dowel 10mm
10mm holes
Headboard construction
Turned headboard poles 800 × 45mm dia.

panel and, when dry, drilled to take the dowel for the second ball. The top edge can now be rounded over to suit the round end of the routed slot in the column.

Inlaying comes next. Cut out the required shapes from veneer. These are then arranged on the board and drawn round with a very sharp pencil. The lines are gone over with a scalpel, chiselled out and the remaining waste taken out with an "old woman's tooth", cleaning up with chisel and scalpel. Using veneered board for inlay is ideal as the veneer thickness recess is easily reached. I use hot animal glue for inlay work as it does not leave marks, sets quickly so you can move on to the next inlay, doesn't require cramps so you can see what you are doing, and, if the worst comes to the worst, is reversible. After cleaning up 24 hours later the columns can be glued on. The panel may need to be mulletted in as the 15mm thick panel plus veneers is thicker than the groove allows. At this point I clamped the headboard to the carcase and drilled the holes for the fixing bolts.

The balls were stained with a spirit stain and lacquered before gluing on as the stain has a habit of running. There is no danger of the colours in the veneers running.

Mattress base

Gauge a line right round the inside top edge of the carcase the thickness of the top panel. Glue and pin the baseboard supports to this line. The baseboard can then be laid on the carcase and the cut outs for the corner blocks marked. I found this easily done by drawing round the corner blocks from the inside with a pencil. After cutting and fitting, the ventilation holes can be drilled. All mattresses need ventilation so I drilled $\frac{3}{4}$ in. diameter holes at 60mm centres over the whole surface.

The baseboard can then be screwed into place. I further secured the centre panel to the baseboard with glue blocks.

Finishing

I used an acid-catalyst lacquer brushed on and cut back with 0000 gauge steel wool. This is a very good finish—hard wearing, wipe clean and useful for children's furniture.

The baseboard can be covered with calico or curtain lining. I stapled this in place round the edge and then covered the staples with a similar coloured cloth self-adhesive tape for a neat edge.

The rope handles are now put in. Tie a crown knot in one end. (If you can't make sense of the drawing ask your yacht chandler, they love showing off). Then pass the free end through the drawer front from the inside and back through the other hole and make the second knot; it's more fiddly, but looks good when done.

Materials

I would recommend veneered plywood over chipboard for its greater strength especially when subjected to the rigors of a small child jumping about. I have used English cherry-faced plywood 15mm thick and the design is such that all the pieces that show can be cut from one 8 by 4ft. sheet. The corner pieces and headboard columns are solid cherry and the internal members were cut from some discoloured sycamore I bought some time ago, perfectly good timber, but not nice enough for show work. The mattress baseboard is 12·7mm ply as are the drawer sides. Drawer bottoms are 3·2mm hardboard. The balls were from a woodturner supplier in the East End of London and the rope was from my local yacht chandler.

Cutting List

To suit mattress 1500 × 750mm

From one sheet veneered plywood
8' × 4' 15mm thick

1 off back panel	1428 × 400
1 off front panel	1428 × 150
2 off drawer fronts	700 × 245
2 off end panel	678 × 400
1 off centre panel	720 × 372
1 off headboard panel	770 × 745

12·7mm ply
1 off mattress baseboard	1470 × 720
4 off drawer sides	700 × 210
2 off drawer backs	685 × 210

3·2mm hardboard
2 off drawer bottoms	695 × 675

Solid cherry
4 off corner pieces	400 × 45 × 45
2 off headboard columns	800 × 45 dia.
1 off headboard lipping	770 × 15 × 15

Other timber
1 off front rail	1470 × 45 × 22
2 off side runners	680 × 45 × 22
1 off middle runner	685 × 45 × 22
2 off guides	660 × 45 × 30
4 off kickers	660 × 22 × 15
Glue blocks approx.	7500 × 22 × 15

Other items
2 off machine screws 50mm × M8
wingnuts and washers
4 off furniture domes or castors
Calico to cover baseboard.
Tape
Acid-catalyst lacquer
2 off 45mm balls
Coloured veneer
16mm Polyester rope

Right: view of underside with ventilation holes.

Below: Jig to give support for router when gooving the columns.

Below right: Detail of jointing between ply side and corner piece.

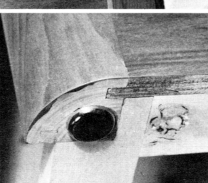

Stage by stage — how to inlay the triangular shapes from marking out to removing the waste, gluing, pressing with a veneer hammer and the finished effect.

Use your loaf

Pine is more popular than ever before for items in the kitchen whether it is for cabinets, cupboards or the various utensils. Here pine is combined with melamine-faced chipboard to provide a bread bin that is both attractive and hygienic.

OUR ANCIENT BREAD BIN had long needed replacing, and for a long time I had mental plans to make a new one out of wood. My ideas were to make the box largely out of solid wood, as the project was planned to be on display in the kitchen and I wanted it to have an aesthetic appeal as well as a functional role. I also wanted it to incorporate modern materials where appropriate.

As I was making the box using a lot of oddments, the wood for the ends needed to be jointed together to gain the required width. I used plain butt joints for this, and placed the work in cramps overnight. G-cramps were also used to ensure the material remained flat while under pressure, and also that adjoining surfaces were dead level. Once out of the cramps, the two pieces were planed and trimmed exactly to the size and shape of the ends shown in the drawings. Wherever possible with identical components, it helps if they can be cramped together, planed and sawn as one.

I decided a piece of white melamine-faced chipboard would be ideal for the base of the project, but in order for all exterior parts of the box to be in pine, this part required a solid lipping to be added to the front edge.

For a job like this, there is little to choose between dowelling the parts together, or tonguing the lipping in place. I settled for dowels, positioning these at about 45mm (1¾in.) centres, and soon had them marked out and bored. Excellent though my dowelling jig is, this type of dowel joint is so simple that the jig is of little advantage. Note how this lipping, although flush with the melamine-faced chipboard on the top, projects on the lower surface by 3mm (⅛in.). This is so that the underside of the lipping would be level with the lower edges of the ends but not the melamine-faced chipboard. Photo 3 shows the parts on the point of assembly, while photo 4 illustrates advantage taken of the saw in my workshop to cut the lipped base to length. The top was, of course, cut to exactly the same length as the base, but the bevel at the front was not prepared at this stage – the sloping edge would have hindered the use of the dowelling jig later.

A piece of pre-finished white hardboard seemed suitable for the back, and therefore the four main parts of the box needed grooving for this. I find a power drill rebating attachment to

1. Boards glued up to provide wider strips.

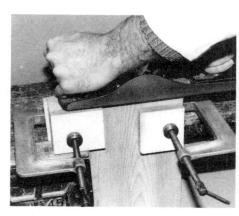

2. Trimming the ends to exact length.

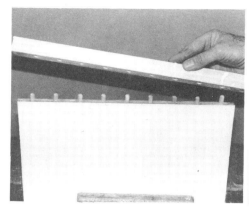

3. Lipping added to edge of the melamine-faced chipboard.

4. The base board is cut to length.

5. Forming the groove for the hardboard back.

be a most suitable way of forming grooves, especially as those on the box sides need to be double stopped. The rebating attachment is no more than a miniature circular saw, and photo 5 shows it in use. Because the blade is so thin, two or three "passes" are required in order to gain the necessary width.

Now I was ready for the main jointing, and for this I made full use of the Record dowelling jig. This really is a superb tool, highly versatile and able to cope with almost any dowelling situation, although in this case the jointing was quite straightforward. Normally for dowel joints I choose a dowel with a diameter of around half the thickness of the wood being jointed, so in this instance the dowels were 10mm ($\frac{5}{16}$ in.). I also find the lip and spur bit used in a power drill to make a good combination with the jig.

With the joints prepared, the front edge of the top needed to be bevelled to conform to the slope on the ends. The job had now reached the stage when some cleaning-up was required, and all surfaces except the outside of the ends were skimmed by plane and

thoroughly glasspapered. I prepared a quantity of dowels with a groove down one side and one end lightly pointed. I also cut a piece of hardboard for the back, and checked very carefully that it would just clear the bottom of the grooves.

Gluing up was quite straightforward. I always make a point of inserting the dowels into the shallower holes first and tapping these down with a hammer until they are fully home. All parts of the joints are, of course, glued, photo 7 showing the last component being added to the remainder. Cramps were added to ensure the ends were tight against the top and bottom as seen in photo 8, the work was tested for being square, and surplus glue cleaned off.

The outer surfaces of the ends had a few shavings removed from them (photo 9) before being glasspapered. Although an orbital sander is most useful for main surfaces, the finishing touches, including glasspapering the arrises, were carried out by hand.

The flap to the box is a piece of 19mm ($\frac{3}{4}$ in.) solid wood. It may be argued that technically

this is not the best of arrangements, but it conforms to the general simplicity of the overall design. After planing to width and cutting to length, both top and bottom edges needed to have bevels formed on them. Indeed, the lower edge required a double bevel, and details of this are to be seen in the cross-sectional drawing. As this part needed no further preparation, it could be cleaned up on all surfaces.

The hinges I obtained for this project are a variation of a butt hinge but made specially for face fixing, and being of brass were particularly suitable. This type of hinge is very simple to fix as no recessing is necessary and it is only a matter of screwing in place.

I was now ready for applying the finish, and decided on three coats of polyurethane varnish so as to completely seal the surface. The first two coats were of gloss, well rubbed down with fine abrasive paper when quite dry. Satin varnish was used for the final coat and this left the surface very smooth with a sheen-like appearance. Screwing the brass knob to the flap then completed the project.

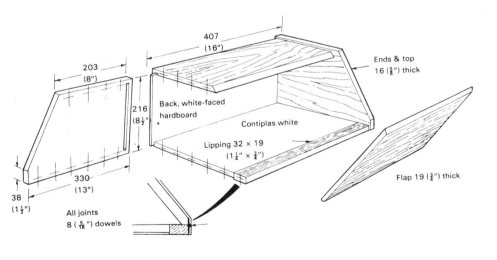

6. Dowelling jig used to form joints.

7. Assembling the box with dowels.

Cutting list

Ends	2 off	356 by 216 by 16mm (14 by 8½ by $\frac{5}{8}$ in.)
Top	1 off	407 by 210 by 16mm (16 by 8¼ by $\frac{5}{8}$ in.)
Base, white melamine-faced chipboard	1 off	407 by 300 by 16mm (16 by 11¾ by $\frac{5}{8}$ in.)
Base lipping	1 off	407 by 32 by 19mm (16 by 1¼ by $\frac{3}{4}$ in.)
Back, white-faced hardboard	1 off	407 by 190 by 3mm (16 by 7½ by $\frac{1}{8}$ in.)

Widths and thicknesses are net; an allowance has been added to lengths. Also required: pair of 38mm (1½in.) hinges; knob; supply of 8mm ($\frac{5}{16}$ in.) dowelling.

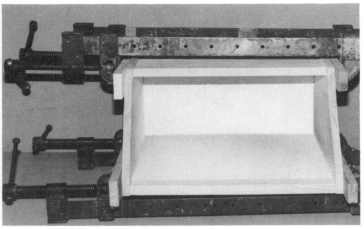

9. Cleaning up the ends with a small block plane.

8. Cramps applied and excess glue removed.

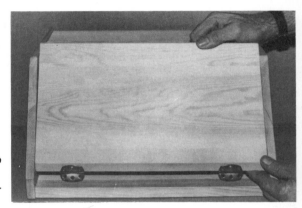

10. Final attention from the orbital sander.

11. Fitting the lid and hinge-ing it to the base.

Make sure wood to be seasoned is surface dry

Christmas cradle

Christmas is a time traditionally associated with goodwill and the giving of presents, but above all it's a family occasion. Even those of you who have no small children of your own can surely find a friend or relative who would accept this lovely cradle as a present to keep in the family for the coming generations. This one is made in pine, but such a charming design would lend itself well to almost any hardwood.

THIS TYPE of cradle is typical of the type found in the large fruit-growing areas south of the Elbe towards the end of the 18th century, and it reflects its creators' closeness to the soil. Decoration is kept to a minimum, and both the materials and the techniques employed are determined by the cradle's practical use.

Exact measuring and cutting and clean workmanship are the most important requirements if the cradle is to look good, and shaping the head and foot of the bed in particular takes a lot of care. This is not really suitable for beginners, but it is ideal for the more experienced as a showpiece for their skills.

You should take time and care when you buy the wood, and only choose well-seasoned pine without knots. If you can't find what you want at your local wood yard, try a joiner's workshop. There you should be able to get the wood planed to size, too. The planing accounts for the small variation in dimensions given for the post sections in the material's list and the drilling guide: the original 50 by 50mm is planed to 48 by 48mm.

The tools required are clear from the photographs: bench circular saw, jig saw and a drill stand—these are essential. You will also need a wood chisel, a plane and a couple of screw clamps. The job has been made easier for the home carpenter in one respect: the panels in the frames are made from 6mm plywood (in the original they were in solid wood, glued into place), and so are the same thickness as the tongues that key the frames together. The grooves in the frame pieces can therefore all be cut to the same width.

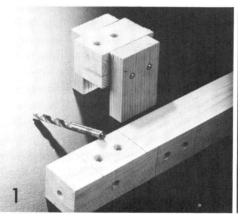

1

A home-made dowelling jig can easily be made up for the alignment of the dowels. Simply line it up with the marks on the timber and use a drill stand to ensure accuracy.

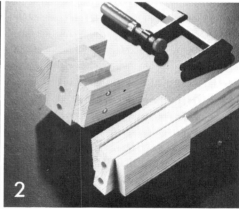

2

The frame ends are also drilled with the same jig, using two similar off-cuts as shown. Simply slip the jig over the end of the frame piece and drill accordingly.

3

The frame sections are grooved continuously on the outside and inside edges (6mm wide, 10mm deep). A jig made up as shown minimises the risk when using a bench saw.

4

The mortise in the posts into which the rockers fit should be chiselled out from either side working towards the centre, having first cut down with a handsaw.

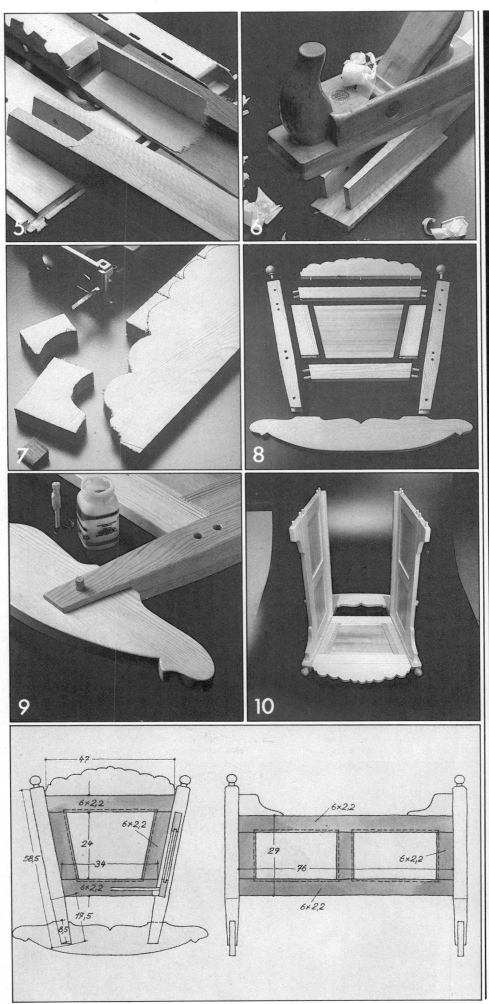

5. To taper the feet on the circular saw you should first make up the jig shown in drawing B. After each stage the shape of the jig is altered by having two wedge-shaped off-cuts glued to it, then the next bevel is cut.

6. A wedge-shaped off-cut fixed firmly under the end of the post makes it easier to plane the surface of the bevelled ends.

7. The shaping of the bed head is done segment by segment. Cut to the deepest point of the curve first and then around it. This way the parts already cut will not get in the way of the work to be done.

8. The individual parts of one of the ends (they are both the same), before assembly.

9. The rockers are fixed into the leg slots with glue and dowels. Use a drill stop to ensure that you do not drill right through and thus ensure that the dowels are not visible from the outside (see main colour picture).

10. When the sides are assembled the head and foot sections can be added. Fit the decorative corner pieces to the sides before assembly.

Drawing dimensions are shown throughout in centimetres.

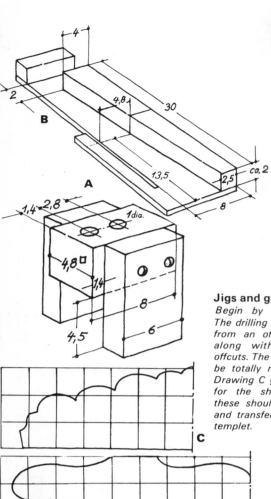

11

A wooden furniture knob from a DIY shop will be sufficient to act as a handle for rocking the cradle. You can, of course, turn up one on the lathe if you have one.

12

The base of the cradle is made in 6mm ply with 30mm holes drilled in it to ventilate the mattress. The knobs on top of the posts are simply furniture handles.

Jigs and guides

Begin by making the jigs. The drilling guide (A) is made from an offcut of the post along with two narrower offcuts. The sawing jig (B) can be totally made from scrap. Drawing C gives the patterns for the shaped parts, and these should be squared up and transferred to card as a templet.

Materials

4 Pine posts	50 by 50 by 585mm
4 Pine knobs	c. 40mm
1 Sheet plywood	10 by 365 by 760mm
Long sides, pine:	
4 Frame pieces, lengthways	22 by 60 by 760mm
4 Frame pieces, upright	22 by 60 by 170mm
2 Frames, centre	22 by 70 by 170mm
2 Base supports	c. 15 by 20 by 760mm
4 Decorative corner pieces	22 by 85 by 160mm

2 Knobs	c. 30mm
4 Panels, pine plywood	6 by 185* by 300*mm
Head and foot, pine:	
2 Frames, horiz.	22 by 60 by 480*mm
2 Frames, horiz.	22 by 60 by 350*mm
4 Frames, vert.	22 by 60 by 270*mm
2 Rockers	22 by 115 by 680*mm
2 Top pieces	22 by 115 by 490*mm
2 Panels, pine ply	6 by 255 by 340*mm

* = Measurement includes allowance for fitting.

USEFUL HINTS

E. A. Hilditch (Technical Director of Cuprinol Ltd)

Selecting Wood

Avoid pieces with too many large or dead knots

Avoid very resinous woods

Avoid wood with splits or normal defects of wood

Avoid signs of decay or surface mould

Avoid bluestain

Tiled top table

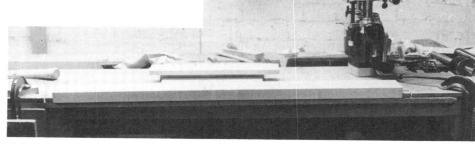

Preparing the colour inlays

THE FIRST thing to do is to cut four strips of sycamore veneer, and if not already dyed soak them for two to three days in a water-based stain. With the table shown, ready dyed pink sycamore veneer was used. However if soaked, leave to dry then glue the four strips together on top of each other with Cascamite glue. It is a good idea to dye the glue with a drop of the stain so that you do not get white lines between the coloured veneers. Put a layer of newspaper on the outside surfaces of the gluing veneers and then cramp all this between two pieces of wood 34 by 2 by $\frac{3}{4}$in. with G cramps. Be careful that the layers of veneer stay on top of each other and do not slide about as you tighten up the cramps.

When glued, clean off the excess glue and newspaper on the veneer with a cabinet scraper, then after planing one edge straight cut on a small bandsaw six strips $\frac{3}{16}$ in. wide.

Solid timber parts

After planing up the solid timber sections, start work on the lipping for the top. Cut the groove for the inlay with a hand router using a $\frac{1}{8}$in. or 3mm cutter making it $\frac{1}{8}$in. or 3mm deep $\frac{1}{2}$in. from the inside top edge of each piece of lipping. You will need to make some sort of jig on your workbench top to hold the timber securely whilst routing out the groove.

Glue the inlay (with Cascamite) in the grooves and tap them in gently with a small hammer. Initially the edges of the veneer inlay may need a final scrape for a perfect fit. When glued, clean off the inlay with a small smoothing plane then set the router up to cut the grooves for the plywood tongues to join the board to the lipping. Put the blockboard tile base in the bench vice, and cut a groove along each edge in the centre 5mm wide and 10mm deep. This will mean doing two cuts, one 5mm deep the second 10mm deep. — you should never make a cut deeper than the width of the cutter. Using the same setting, cut a similar groove in the lipping, making sure you work the router guide off the underside edge of the lipping. Clean all the grooves out with a narrow chisel after routing.

Again using the board, mark off the size and mitres at the corners of the lippings. Cut these just over-size and then carefully plane smooth with a very sharp plane so that the wood does not split out. Butt up and fit the plywood tongues. Clean up the board with grade 100 garnet paper and clean up the lippings with 100 then 180.

Cramp the lipping up to board dry to check corners are a perfect fit — they may need some final adjustment. When ready uncramp two opposite pieces of lipping and glue up with Cascamite. With these correctly positioned do the same with the other two pieces; this stops the lipping moving about too much with the wet glue

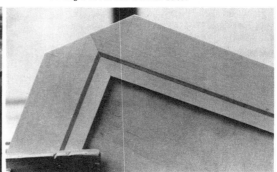

1. The simple jig made up for the routing of the grooves to take the sycamore veneer inlays.

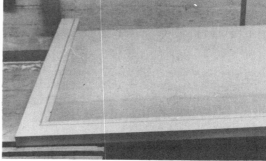

2. Lay the veneer in the groove with Cascamite glue and tap into position.

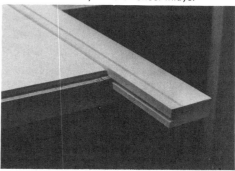

3. The tongue and groove method of fixing the top and outside rails of the table.

4. Planing the mitred edges, a final trim with a very sharp plane and a lot of care.

5. Two sides assembled and tried for fit, all satisfactory at this stage.

6. The final side being tested for fit before the cramping up procedure.

7. All in position ready for cramping, note the marking out for the corner cuts.

8. The cramping up is done with sash cramps, with spacers to prevent bruising.

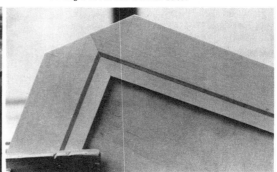

9. The tabletop held in the vice and one of the corners already removed.

and resulting in badly fitting corner joints. Excess glue must of course be wiped off.

Setting the table top aside to cure, you can again use the $\frac{1}{8}$in. or 3mm router cutter to make the grooves down the centre of the outside faces of the legs for the inlay, gluing the strips in as before. It is best not to cut the legs to length until after the inlay is glued in and cleaned off.

When the top is glued scrape off any excess dried glue and sand with 180 and 240 garnet paper. Mark off the corners of the top to be cut off at 45 degrees, saw off, plane smooth and then sand. Clean off the legs, cut to length and carefully plane ends square. You can then mark up for the mortises which should be made $\frac{3}{8}$in. wide and $2\frac{1}{8}$in. long by $\frac{1}{8}$in. deep. Now cut the under-frame to the exact length (i.e. the length of the diagonal of the top, plus $1\frac{3}{4}$in. for tenons and $\frac{1}{4}$in. shadow gap). The tenons on these diagonals are $\frac{3}{8}$in. wide, the full depth of the frame piece and $\frac{7}{8}$in. long. After cutting the tenons, the halving joint in the centre of the under-frame where the diagonals cross over must be prepared.

To fix the top to the frame you will require four 2in. No. 10 screws in each part. Mark the two outer screws to come about $2\frac{1}{2}$in. in under the table and divide the rest of the space equally for the other two. Initially drill a 2in. hole with a Forstner bit $\frac{5}{8}$in. deep where the screws are going to go then drill a clearance hole for the screw through the rest of the timber. This allows the head of the screw to sink further into the member than by just using a countersink bit.

Fit the tenons to the mortises and then glue each half of the underframe to the legs. Check it is square and be careful not to cramp up too tight as the underframe will bow. When dry, clean up the underframe with 100, 180 and 240 garnet paper and join the halving joint.

Turn the table top upside down on the workbench and set the underframe out on top also upside down and cramp it on to mark where the screws are going to go. Take the frame off and drill a small pilot hole, not too deep, where the screws will go. Put a small drop of pva wood glue on the underframe, cramp in place making sure legs are about 3mm from top edge and screw onto the top. Make sure everything is cleaned up and the sharpness of all the edges is taken off by light sanding.

The table needs to be finished before the tiles are stuck in. This can either be done by applying a coat of sanding sealer and then lightly sanding and waxing with prepared beeswax, or for a tougher more waterproof surface use satin polyurethane with two preliminary undercoats of gloss. The first application should be diluted and the second not, but make sure not to apply finish to the surface of the board where the tiles are going to be stuck.

The final coat is satin.

Tiling the top

For the top I selected 25 tiles. These could be all one colour or chequered in two colours. Make sure that there are no odd bits of glaze that need cleaning off the edges that might prevent them from lying close enough together. Put a thick layer of flexible adhesive glue on the board and then scrape into ridges. However, do not put too much glue on the board. Swivel the tiles, pressing them onto the adhesive. You only have about 20 minutes which is not long, so space the tiles carefully and make sure all excess adhesive is wiped off, especially on the edges of the lipping and on the tile tops. Leave to dry overnight or even for 24 hours before applying the grouting. This is mixed to the consistency of double cream and then wiped over the tiles and into the spaces. Ultimately give the surface a final wipe down to clean any excess grouting off.

Materials list

From 1¼in. rough sawn sycamore planks

Lipping for top	4 off	26 by 2⅛ by ⅞in.
Leg	4 off	16½ by 3 by 1⅛in.
Underframe	2 off	39 by 2⅛ by ⅞in.

Blockboard or chipboard for least movement under tiles

Base (18mm board)	1 off	21¼ by 21¼in.

Plywood tongues

Tongues (5mm ply)	4 off	21¼ by ¾in.

Inlay veneers (stained)

Strip	4 off	34 by 2in.

25 CMO8 Cyclamen tiles 4½ by 4¼in. (Cristal range)
Adhesive:
Grouting:

10. The tenons are trimmed up with a shoulder plane after cutting in the normal way.

11. The screws in the underframe are let well in to provide the maximum grip for the top.

12. One of the underframes assembled ready to take its opposite number.

13. After mixing to cream consistency, apply grouting, then carefully remove surplus.

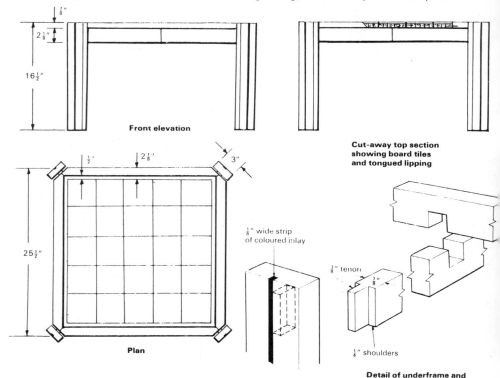

Front elevation

Plan

⅛″ wide strip of coloured inlay

⅜″ tenon

¼″ shoulders

Cut-away top section showing board tiles and tongued lipping

Detail of underframe and leg joints

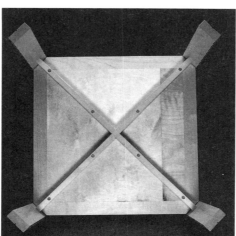

Inlay detail with shadow gap.

Under-structure of the table.

Tiles must be evenly spaced on the top.

Veneered coffee table in ebony

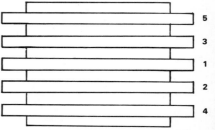

This design for a coffee table makes the most of the stripey ebony veneer while retaining a simple shape and construction.

Design

The design thinking behind this coffee table is to retain a simple shape whilst making the most of the rich stripey ebony veneer. Figured wood is always best on a simple shape, so that the shape does not detract from the visual impact of the wood itself. The construction is box-like in nature using 24mm chipboard lipped at the edges, and with extra thickness to the centre top section provided by the addition of 24 by 12mm battens. This gives a better sense of balance to the design.

Preparation

For the basic preparation you must dimension the board to the sizes shown in the cutting list (note that these allow for 5mm lippings) and prepare suitable lengths of mahogany for the lippings. Start by adding the short mitred lippings to the top. After gluing, pin the lippings in place as this stops any slipping when the cramps are applied. After this apply lippings to the bottom of legs (letting lipping run through as there is no need to mitre the bottom as the end grain of lipping goes against the floor) and then to the long sides of base section. Now plane all lippings flush and to length. You can then mitre the remaining top lippings and apply them followed by the lippings to the legs. While the lippings are gluing the veneer can be prepared.

Preparing veneers

Start by cutting to length allowing a 20mm overhang, then cut to rough width removing any waste, such as sap and big splits. Lay out the veneer to the panel sizes as this gives the opportunity to juggle the pieces around and select for pattern. I chose to mismatch the veneer so the figure looks random, but it could be bookmatched.

Number the veneers so that they can be taped together without confusion in their original pattern. It is advisable not to try and joint too many veneers at one go, in fact I usually joint one panel at a time. Tape together any minor splits on top of the veneer so that it is not on the underneath when pressed. Cramp the veneers between two battens which have been shot square and flat, so approximately 3mm of the veneer protrudes. Carefully plane the veneer to the level of the battens. If the veneer splits or crumbles away tape the edges with Sellotape to hold the grain. Where the veneer has a straight grain, plane with it but this is not always possible with many decorative veneers. Turn the veneers over and plane again.

Lay the veneer out in the pre-marked pattern and tape the joints—first across the grain to pull the joints tight and then down the length. Paper tape can be used but I prefer Sellotape as it has immediate adhesion and you can see through it. The disadvantages are that it is expensive and can be tricky to remove when pressed. If the tape tears the veneer when pulled against the grain it is best to remove it with a warm damp cloth. The same applies to paper tape.

Pressing the veneer

Place the bottom caul (in this case 24mm chipboard) on a pair of carpenter's stools. Don't use blockboard for the cauls as there can be depressions in the board which will give insufficient pressure in patches while pressing. Formica faced boards are ideal because they are flat and do not need plastic sheet or newspaper to prevent the caul sticking to the veneer if glue seeps through.

If using a protective sheet, then plastic sheet is preferable as newspaper absorbs excess moisture from the veneer and is liable to leave the newsprint impression.

Place the taped veneer on the caul inside up, then place the lipped panel on the dry veneer and apply glue to the panel either with a glue roller or serrated spreader to ensure even distribution. Various glues can be used—but not hide glue. I use a waterproof pva for convenience on small panels (and constructional work) and a urea formaldehyde resin, such as Aerolite, on larger surfaces for its economy and slower setting speed.

Now turn the panel over ensuring that it is in the centre of the veneer. Spread glue onto the remaining side and position the other veneer, then cover with plastic sheet and the second caul.

Where small panels are to be veneered, as with the legs, time can be saved by placing one panel on top of another but these must be a caul between panels to allow for any misalignment.

Let the panels stand for a while to allow the glue to become tacky, but not too dry, to reduce the chance of the veneer slipping, and then place battens of approximately 80 by 40mm in section and curved along their length across the cauls with centres spaced about 150 to 175mm apart and with the convex side to the caul.

Cramp another batten, again with its convex side to the caul underneath the central batten. Start with this one in the middle and then work alternatively from each side outwards from the centre to force out any air which might be trapped.

Finally when the glue has set, trim the overhanging edges of the veneer before it is accidentally broken. However do not remove the tape yet as the veneer may have swollen with the glue, and if so the tape will hold the joints together if there is subsequent shrinkage. Also if it is possible, stand the panels "in stick" to allow any moisture to evaporate evenly. It is also advisable to make the panels 1 or 2mm oversize to allow for trimming the veneer.

Jointing the panels

There are basically three ways of jointing the panels: dowelling, tenoning (allow for extra lengths on cutting list) and loose tongues or biscuits, this latter being a variation of the principle used in industry. In this case I used 9mm loose tongues and the grooves for these I cut with an electric router (see drawing).

Joint the base to the legs by running the router with its fence against the panels to cut a groove all the way across the panels, stopping it 15mm short of the ends. If the plywood tongue ran all the way through showing at each end, any movement of the panels might show through at the position of the tongues underneath the crossbanding. However, the tongue must be close enough to the edge of the panel to support the last remaining section of the joint. The grooves in each panel are cut with the same router setting

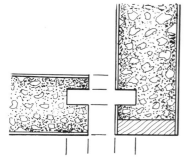

to give a groove 12mm deep.

Joint the top of the legs, but again stop the groove short at each end, and in addition leave a 200mm section in the middle (see drawing). This is to allow for a solid section in the middle of the top which gives strength to the "overhangs."

Mark out the underneath of the table top working from a centre line to give the positions of the grooves where the legs join. Test the marking out by placing the upturned base and legs on the marking out. If correct, joint the underneath with a router by cramping a straight batten across the top and using this as a fence.

Try all the joints up "dry" and make any adjustments if necessary. Sand all the veneered surfaces (except the bottom of the base which can be cleaned up when the job is finished) and give special attention to the insides and underneath the top middle section as it is easier to sand these in flat pieces rather than when assembled.

Assembly

The gluing up of this job is straight-forward using sash cramps. However I would use two of the convex battens from the veneering across the top over the legs so that an even pressure is maintained over the width. Underneath battens and cramping blocks protect the veneer with heavy card to stop even the blocks denting the surface.

Check for squareness and adjust accordingly with sash cramps and of course remove surplus glue. While the top is gluing the crossbanding can be prepared.

When the cramps are removed, cut to length and glue in the mahogany "leading edges" which give the thickness to the middle section of the top. Finally at this stage flush off any joints which may not be quite level and fill any dents and holes.

Crossbanding

Depending upon whether the top is a mismatched or matched pattern can affect the position of the crossbanding. This is a matter of personal preference. With mismatched veneers I prefer to have a random crossbanding so that the veneer does not "continue" over the edge; I feel this has a more "solid look" than having the veneer wrap itself around. However if I was using a matched top I would have the crossbanding follow through as a continuation of the top.

In this case when first cutting the leaves to rough length, allow for two extra thicknesses of top which would be some 100mm on the length of the leaves. The leaves are taped up as one section and the crossbanding cut off each end. With this method they have to follow through.

Glue taped up sections of crossbanding along each end of the top with sash cramps and straight battens. If heavy card is placed underneath the cramping battens it allows for the cramp to pull slightly out of square. Trim the crossbanding and repeat along the sides of the top.

Set out the mitre detail of the leg in pencil and then cut with a knife.

Cut the leg crossband to fit the top joint, letting it overhang bottom of leg. Then hold in position with tape while cramping, then trim. Now mitre the bottom joint then fit and glue in the last section.

Finishing

Carefully remove tape from the crossbanding then scrape and sand to a perfect finish. Very fine sanding must be used as scratch marks can remain visible across the grain. To finish use 240 garnet or 180 silicon paper.

Clean up and sand underneath of the base, check for any dents etc, then give a final fine sand to top and arris edges.

Lacquering depends upon whatever is most convenient and your personal preference. I use a semi-matt pre-catalyst lacquer which is suitable for coffee tables being alcohol and coffee cup proof.

Depending upon the type of lacquer used, it can be either applied by a rubber, brush or spraying. I have tried all of these methods and found it worthwhile investing in a small compressor—the speed and finish far outweighs the cost and unpleasantness of the job. Masks must be worn and follow safety recommendations.

The lacquer is left to cure for a few days, depending upon number of coats, temperature of workshop etc, before cutting back with 240 silicon paper and burnishing with wire wool.

Lastly it can be wax polished, but I do not like to do this, because if the table is damaged, the wax has to be removed before re-lacquering.

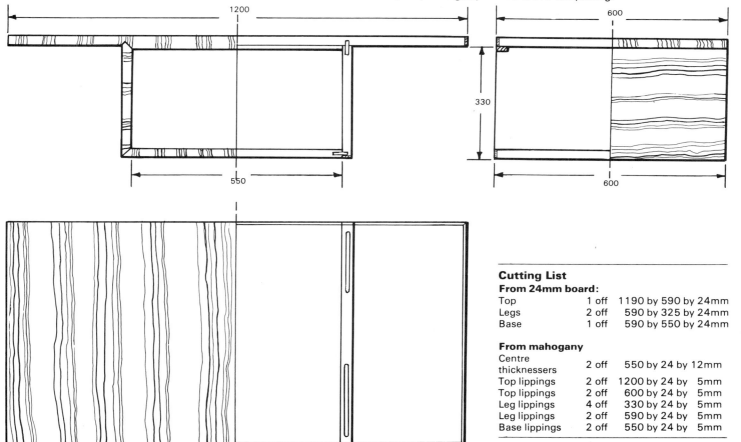

Cutting List
From 24mm board:

Top	1 off	1190 by 590 by 24mm
Legs	2 off	590 by 325 by 24mm
Base	1 off	590 by 550 by 24mm

From mahogany

Centre thicknessers	2 off	550 by 24 by 12mm
Top lippings	2 off	1200 by 24 by 5mm
Top lippings	2 off	600 by 24 by 5mm
Leg lippings	4 off	330 by 24 by 5mm
Leg lippings	2 off	590 by 24 by 5mm
Base lippings	2 off	550 by 24 by 5mm

Cottage style cabinet

Wooden wall cabinets give a warmth and comfort to the kitchen and especially so if they are of a traditional pattern. Here we look at one which is extremely simple to make yet still manages to retain the feeling of solidity we often associate with the country furniture of years gone by. This particular design comes from Germany but it's the sort of piece that can be found in kitchens all over Britain and Europe.

THIS wall cupboard is traditional in concept, although modern in execution. Plywood was not available when this type of furniture was first produced; in those days, the layers had to be painstakingly glued together and built up, a job today's cabinetmaker can happily dispense with. There is enough gluing to be done as it is. The cupboard doors and drawer fronts, cupboard sides and the back wall consist of frames and panels. The frames are joined using mortise and tenon joints; the width of the mortise should be one-third of the frame width, that is, approximately 7mm. The panels are made of 4mm thick plywood veneered in pine, and 3mm thick glass for the doors. The panels are held in place with strips of moulding fixed

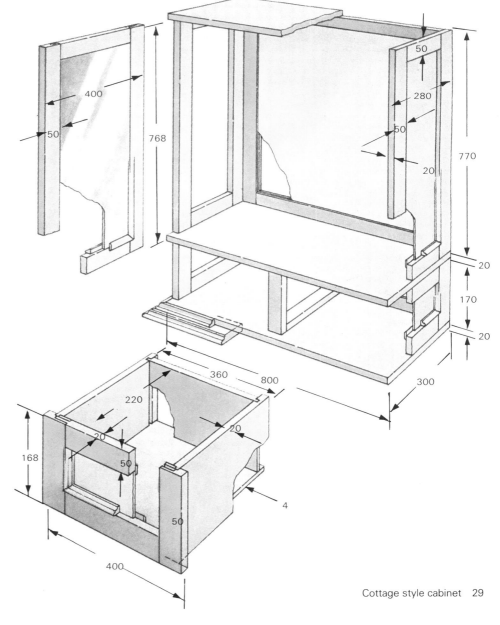

at front and back. Only the back panel is joined by inserting it into a groove in the frame. In this case, the panel is inserted when the frame is glued together. All the other pieces can be assembled when the whole cupboard is put together. Use screws to give extra stability to joints at the back, since they will be invisible but on other parts use glue. The more clamps you have, the quicker the gluing process will be.

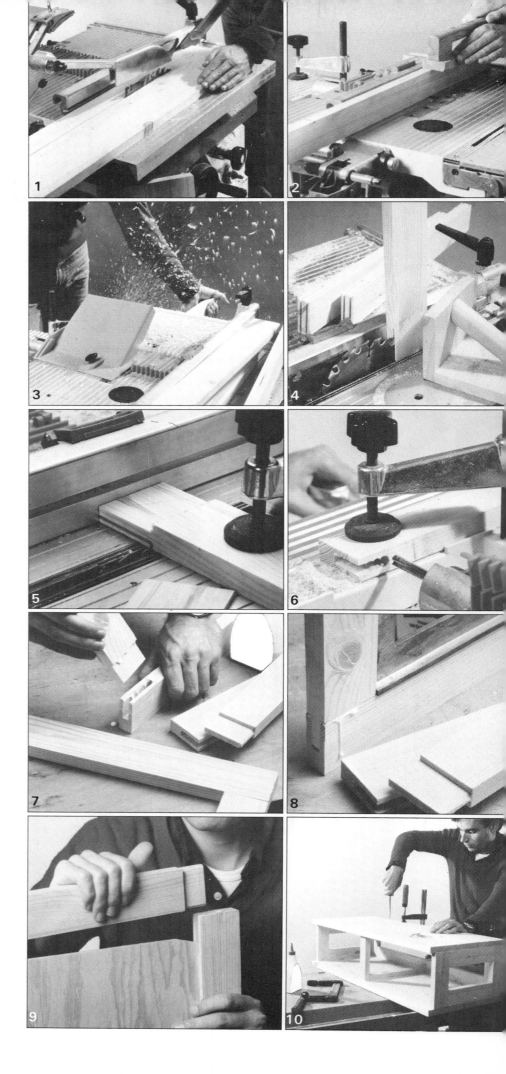

1. *All the frame sections are cut on the circular saw. They are cut 53mm wide and then planed down to the correct size. Use a push stick for the smaller pieces.*

2. *Planing the frame pieces to size on the power planer. This job could of course be done by hand if you don't own this sort of equipment.*

3. *Most universals are extremely accurate when it comes to planing, and a machine such as this one will process wood up to 73mm with ease.*

4. *The tenons are prepared on the circular saw as shown although once again there is nothing here which could not just as easily be done by hand if time allows.*

5. *The tenons are finished off again on the circular saw for convenience. Note the clamping device, the actual wood moves on a small mobile table.*

6. *The hollow mortiser is brought into operation at this point. Start by drilling two holes and then gradually work the groove along its whole length.*

7. *Assemble the frame with woodworking adhesive, applying glue to the mortises and to the tenon shoulders.*

8. *Check for squareness and then wipe off any excess glue which may ooze out of the joints.*

9. *The back panel is grooved into the frame and so must be assembled along with it. Cramp up and allow to dry with the other sections made at this stage.*

10. *The lower part of the cupboard is simply screwed together. The only screw which remains visible is the one which holds the front centre strut in place; countersink the hole, insert the screw and glue in a pellet of the same material.*

11. *The side frames are glued in place; the glued surfaces are sufficiently large for additional screws or dowels to be unnecessary.*

12. *The top of the dresser is screwed in place from above. First join the back panel to the rest of the cupboard. The toothed side supports for the shelves serve as a front support.*

13. *Decorative mouldings can be formed on most universal machines but they are easy to obtain off the shelf from timber merchants. Different patterns from those shown here can be used.*

14. *If you do choose to make your own mouldings you will probably find that it's easier to make them in relatively long runs.*

15. *The decorative top to the cabinet is made from several pieces of moulding glued together and fastened using both glue and nails. The mitres are cut on the circular saw.*

16. *Mark the positions of the hinges and remove the waste with a chisel in the normal manner. Drill pilot holes for the screws. Ensure that the hinges are fitted to the doors before the frame.*

17. *The glass panels are cut 2mm shorter and narrower than the interior of the frames. They are held in place by a flat moulding on the inside and a decorative one on the outside.*

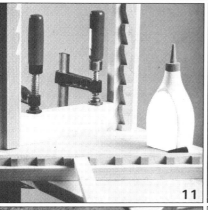

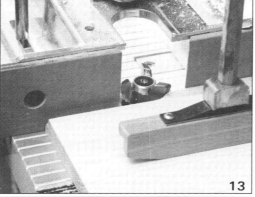

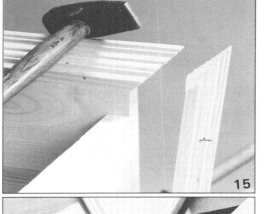

Materials List

20mm thick plywood

Frame pieces (sides)	4 off	770 by 50mm
Frame pieces (sides)	4 off	170 by 50mm
Frame pieces (sides)	8 off	230 by 50mm
Central struts	2 off	170 by 50mm
Central struts	1 off	240 by 50mm
Frame pieces (doors)	4 off	768 by 50mm
Frame pieces (doors)	4 off	350 by 50mm
Frame pieces (back)	2 off	770 by 50mm
Frame pieces (back)	4 off	710 by 50mm
Frame pieces (back)	2 off	170 by 50mm
Frame pieces (drawer)	4 off	168 by 50mm
Frame pieces (drawer)	4 off	350 by 50mm
Drawer sides	4 off	260 by 168mm
Drawer backs	2 off	340 by 140mm

Approx. 8m (continuous) moulding for the cupboard bases; 11m (continuous) flat moulding and 11m (continuous) moulding for the edging of the panels.

4mm plywood (pine-veneered)

Side panels	2 off	640 by 180mm
Side panels	2 off	70 by 180mm
Back panel	1 off	680 by 770mm
Back panel	1 off	80 by 770mm
Drawer panels	2 off	68 by 300mm
Drawer bases	2 off	355 by 340mm

Also required: 3.2m (continuous) toothed battens (shelf supports); 2 panes of glass, 3mm thick 666 by 298mm; 4 furniture knobs; 4 brass hinges; 2 catches; screws; wood glue.

Office unit for the home

With the growing complexity of modern living more people are aware of a need for some kind of office furniture in their own homes. Office desks and filing cabinets are functional but often very unattractive. This design overcomes the problem with simple elegance.

THIS ROLL-TOP OFFICE unit for the home has the air of a beautifully designed piece of furniture from an exclusive shop. It is not, however, too difficult to make, given the right tools. You do however need to have had some experience in making furniture, and to be used to precision work to attempt to make it.

The basic construction of the unit is shown simply in the drawings together with all the dimensions of the various pieces. In the grooves on the side pieces run the two roller shutters: one pushes upwards, the other rolls down to disappear behind the back wall of the unit which also has two grooves. Cross pieces and shelves are fixed with dowels and hold the unit steady and firmly together.

The shape of the unit is determined by the roll-up front: the curved sections at the top and bottom have the same radius of a circle as the grooves to hold the roll-up sections. Again, dimensions for these are given in the drawings.

The most expensive item on the shopping list is the plywood. To keep costs to a minimum follow our cutting guide, or have the do-it-yourself shop follow it when they cut the board for you.

Once you have bought all the material, work can begin at home with cutting the side pieces exactly to size, and working out the centre point of the arcs. The pivot of the circular cutting attachment goes at the centre point, and when you have ascertained the right radius, the groove can then be cut with the router, making a groove 8mm wide. The

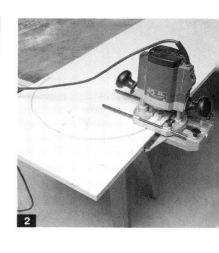

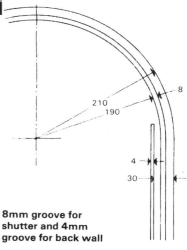

Top left: view of the unit showing fittings.
Bottom left: the elegant shuttered finish.
1. The radial arm will hold the router to the right radius, and is absolutely essential for making this unit. It is the only means of making sure the grooves are correctly positioned.
2. Use a fence on the router to mark out the side grooves making certain that they exactly tie in with the arcs already cut. Time spent at this stage of the work will be well repaid later on.
Right: The drawing shows the dimensions to be worked to on the arc. It is inset from the edge of the board by 12mm and is 8mm wide to take the shutter. Thus the inner radius of the curve is 20mm in from the edge which allows adequate strength to be retained.

210
190
8
4
30

8mm groove for shutter and 4mm groove for back wall

groove is semi-circular in shape at the top, and is worked first; you then make the straight grooves down the side pieces. Make sure that all the measurements are exact and follow them very closely so that there are no hitches between the rounded groove and the straight groove where the shutter might stick. Using a side attachment and the same 8mm router, the long side grooves on the front are made for the roller shutters to go in later. The back wall of the unit also has two grooves made for it, using a 4mm router. You will need the 8mm router again if you are going to have upright shelf divisions between the two upper shelves. The grooves for these should run right up to the back edge and start about 40mm from the front edge. If the front edge of the upright division protrudes slightly, then the groove will be completely hidden.

When you have prepared all the individual pieces as described, and drilled the holes for the dowels, then you can stain the wood. As a contrast to the natural wood colour of the shutters, use a dark stain, such as nut brown, for the main body of the unit. When the stain has been applied and allowed to dry, you are then ready to assemble the unit. First glue together the side walls and shelves and the cross pieces. Now the upright shelf divisions are inserted from behind between the two upper shelves, and the writing area fixed to the sides. The back wall and shutters are inserted from below into the grooves, and finally the strip with the lock and the two half-moon shaped pieces at the base of the side walls are fixed into place. Finish the whole unit with a coat of clear varnish.

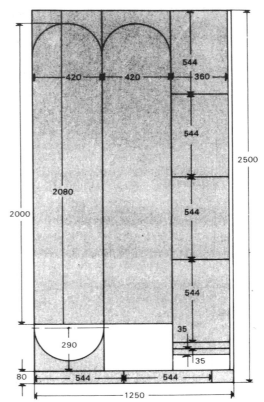

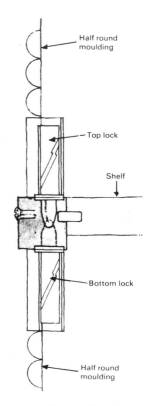

Above: white areas show off-cuts; all shaded areas are integral pieces of the unit with their dimensions.

Above: locking mechanism details. Various makes of this type of lock are available.

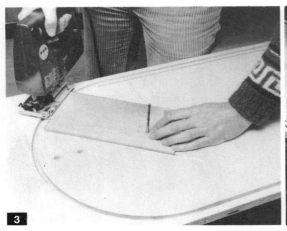

3

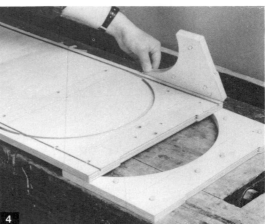

4

5

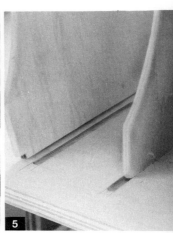

3. Drill a hole at the centre point of the half circle, insert a bit from the drill and with a small board attached to the sole plate of the saw trim up the edge as shown.

4. The half-moon off-cuts are dowelled to the outer bases of the sides. Those on the inner sides will have to be cut out specially for the purpose.

5. The upright divisions add to the usefulness of the cupboard. These are set in stopped housing joints to give a clean and neat appearance to the inside of the unit.

6. Half-round battens are used on canvas backing for the moving shutters.

7. Fix the shutter locking strips and coat up the whole with polyurethane varnish.

8. The handles and locking mechanisms can now be fitted to the two shutters.

9 and 10. After gluing and finishing the upper surface of the unit, the two shutters are inserted in the grooves and pulled round. The half-moon shaped bits previously mentioned are then fitted into position to control them.

11. The strip with the lock set in is fitted over the second shelf from the bottom.

12. The two little pieces of dowel fitted as shown in the photograph are used to ensure that the writing shelf is not pulled out by mistake.

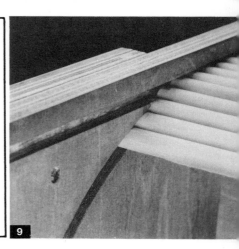

9

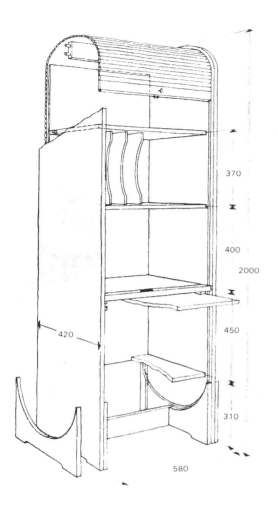

Cutting List

Sides plus half moons	2 off	18 by 2080* by 420mm
Half moons for inside front	2 off	18 by 290 by 420mm
Shelves	4 off	18 by 544 by 360**mm
Cross pieces	2 off	18 by 544 by 80mm
Grooved strips for shelf	2 off	18 by 360** by 35mm
Writing shelf	1 off	10 by 525** by 355mm
Loose shelves	2 off	10 by 544 by 36**mm
Upright divisions	3 off	8 by 370** by 330mm
Back wall	1 off	4 by 1570 by 560**mm
Upper shutter	1 off	7 by 1610 by 560**mm
Lower shutter	1 off	7 by 730 by 560**mm
Handle strips for shutters	2 off	7 by 560** by 38mm
Handle strips for shutters	2 off	10 by 560** by 38mm
Lower handle strips	1 off	10 by 200 by 20mm
Lock strip	1 off	22 by 560** by 25mm
Plates for inside lock	2 off	1 by 90** by 38mm

Also required: 4 chrome handles about 70mm long; 2 shutter locks 15mm; 2 end lock plates; 8 brackets; 1 sheet canvas for upper shutter 1700** by 600mm; 1 sheet canvas for lower shutter 800** by 600mm (cut about 520mm); dowelling; screws; wood stain; undercoat; varnish.

* Includes allowance for sawing out round

** Includes allowance for fitting i.e. measurements take into account the depth of the groove.

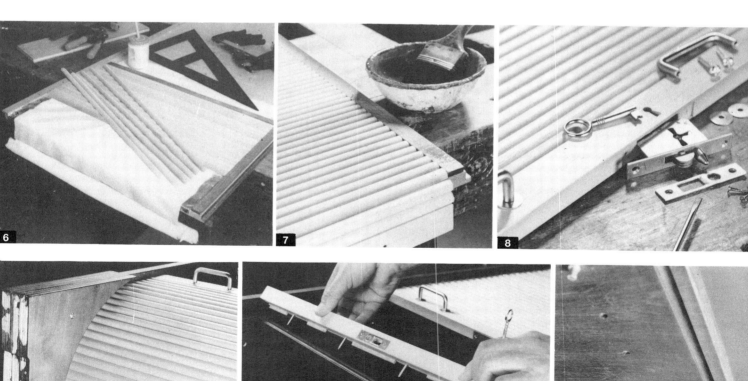

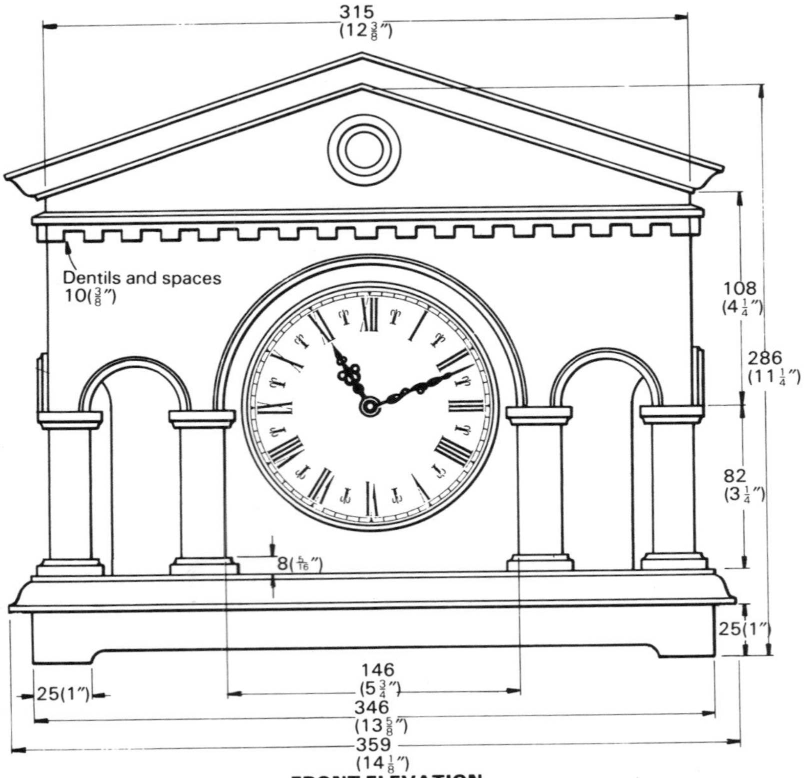
315
(12 3/8")
Dentils and spaces
10(3/8")
108
(4 1/4")
286
(11 1/4")
82
(3 1/4")
8(5/16")
25(1")
25(1")
146
(5 3/4")
346
(13 5/8")
359
(14 1/8")

FRONT ELEVATION

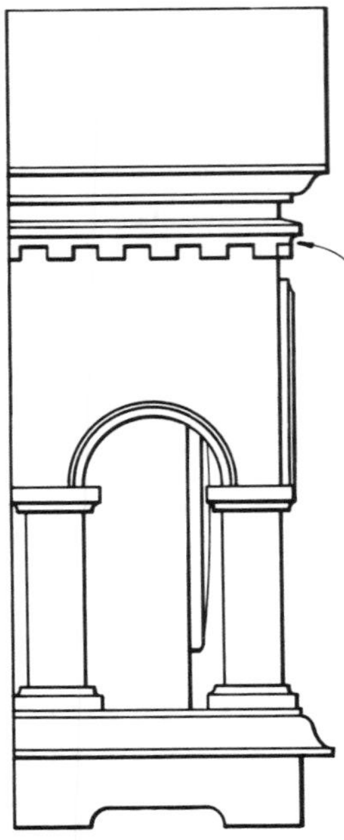

END ELEVATION

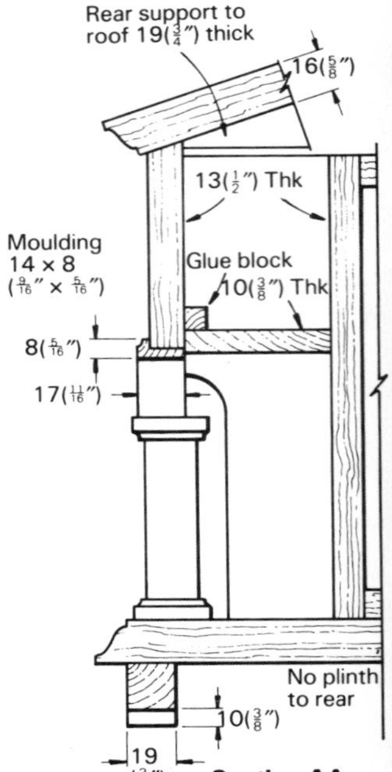
Rear support to
roof 19(3/4") thick
16(5/8")
13(1/2") Thk
Moulding
14 x 8
(9/16" x 5/16")
Glue block
10(3/8") Thk
8(5/16")
17(11/16")
No plinth
to rear
10(3/8")
19
(3/4")

Section AA

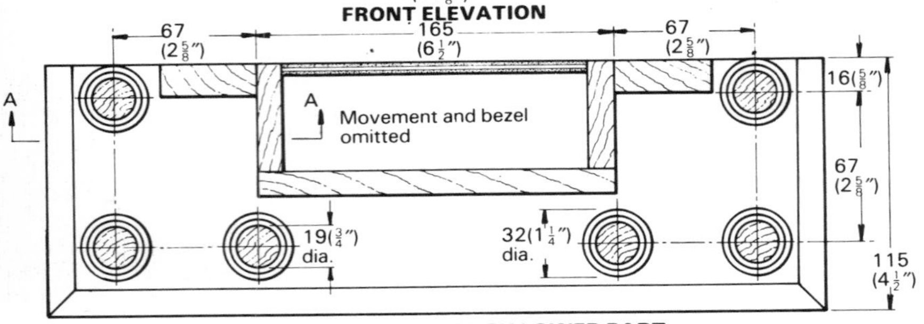
67
(2 5/8")
165
(6 1/2")
67
(2 5/8")
A
A
Movement and bezel
omitted
16(5/8")
67
(2 5/8")
19(3/4")
dia.
32(1 1/4")
dia.
115
(4 1/2")

SECTIONAL PLAN THROUGH LOWER PART

THE DESIGN of this classical clock was inspired by the memory of a marble timepiece.

A clock to suit the face

THE quartz clock movement has revolutionised clock making, especially as far as the woodworker is concerned. Small and compact in size, they are extremely accurate, indeed their time-keeping is usually within a few seconds a year. They will operate for up to a couple of years on one small battery, and have become so popular over recent years that the former mains-electric clocks have become virtually obsolete.

Now to make a clock, rather more than just the movement is required. A face is needed, along with a set of hands, and if these are to be enclosed, then a bezel is required. However, it's the face which determines the size of the clock, and to a large extent its character. This clock design is based on a classical marble timepiece and the final result is a wooden reproduction which is a fairly faithful replica of the original one. It serves as a very good example of how with a little thought and research something rather unusual can be created, even if total originality cannot be claimed.

This one is made in pine, and given a natural finish. The finishing played a rather more significant part in the making of it than is usually the case with most projects, as the majority of the components were finished as they were made. This eliminated the many 'awkward corners' present on completion – it's the corners which always prove difficult whatever finish is being used. The material used for the finishing was a specially formulated quick drying lacquer. I gave a couple of coats of this, using an artist's type of very soft brush about 10mm (3/8in) diameter for the application. When dry, the surface was rubbed down with fine steel wool dipped in soft beeswax polish, with a soft cloth used for the final burnishing.

Although the design as shown incorporates a number of turned parts, it could easily be modified by anyone who wished to make a similar clock, but didn't have a lathe. Dowels could be used for the pillars, and the caps and bases to these could be made square. Alternatively, the pillars could be made to octagonal section. The turned linings to the arches could be left out altogether, and possibly small chamfers worked around the semi-circles. Another option is to experiment with hole saws, as it might be possible to produce something similar with the use of these. Most designs can be adapted to suit both the needs and the resources of whoever is making them, and this clock is no exception.

There are three main assemblies which make up the clock—the base and pillars, the movement housing, and the upper structure. I started work on the base, and prepared a piece of wood to the thickness and length required. At this stage, I left a little extra on the width, in case the moulding process caused any splitting to the rear edge which is the one edge not to be moulded. This is because I used a router for the moulding, where working on end grain can sometimes cause slight damage at the corners. If the end grain is tackled first, any breaking away at the

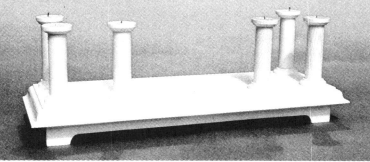

Our classical clock design is based on a marble original but makes an interesting project for the woodworker. Broken down into its three main components, you can see that it is not difficult to make.

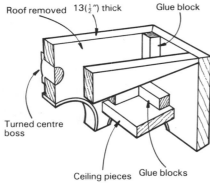

Roof removed 13(½") thick Glue block

Turned centre boss

Ceiling pieces Glue blocks

**ONE SIDE OF UPPER PART
VIEWED FROM REAR**

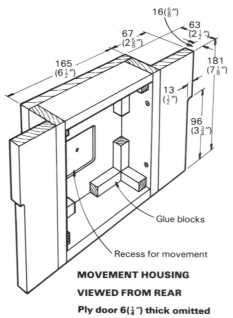

16(⅝")
67 (2⅝") 63 (2½")
165 (6½")
181 (7⅛")
13 (½")
96 (3¾")

Glue blocks

Recess for movement

**MOVEMENT HOUSING
VIEWED FROM REAR**

Ply door 6(¼") thick omitted

corners is removed when the edges are treated, and all is well. If the edges are moulded first, followed by the ends, then the opportunity of righting any slight splitting is lost.

For the actual moulding, I used an ogee cutter equipped with a 'pilot'. The pilot in effect acts as the fence, and I set up my router table for this operation. Even though I was using a powerful router, I formed the moulding in two 'passes', adjusting the cutter slightly for the second pass. Using this technique, splitting at the rear edge had been minimal, but cutting this piece to its final width removed even this and left the corners very clean. Various holes were now bored in this piece for the pillars and the movement houcing, after which it was sanded and finished as described.

The pillars

The pillars, caps and bases are each turned from one piece, and were initially crosscut with a little extra on the length. I used a screw chuck for mounting these on the lathe, and quickly turned them to the profile shown. The upper surfaces on these pillars were sanded and polished along with the main surfaces, and after lacquering the final smoothing was also completed on the lathe. While the classical Greek shape of a pillar shows a slight convex outline with the maximum diameter about one third of the way up, I kept mine with parallel sides. I was, though, careful to check that they were all identical by direct comparison. These were now quickly screwed in place on the base.

The plinths are on the front and ends only, and after preparing to width and thickness they were marked to length showing the cut-outs to the lower edge. The two shorter pieces were marked

from a single piece, and the curved ends to the cut-outs were formed by boring. The two pieces of wood were cramped together, and a 19mm (¾in) hole bored so as to be half way into each piece of wood. The remainder of the waste to the underside of these componenets was removed by saw and chisel, with a gauge line as guide to the extent of the cut-outs. Holes were bored and countersunk for fixing, the parts cut to length with the front corners mitred, and appropriate surfaces sanded. These were screwed to the underside of the base, and in this case the polishing completed once secured in place.

Upper structure

Now it was onto the upper structure, and the material prepared for the main parts of this. The front member was marked to length and showing the sloping top edges to the roof line, along with the cut-outs for the arches. As with the plinth, the two small end components were marked from a single piece, with a total of five arches indicated on the two pieces of wood. For the smaller arches, I had deliberately made the size of these so that they could be made with a hole saw, again cramping the two pieces together so that a full hole centralised on the joint line gave two perfect semi-circles. However, this technique could not be used on the central arch because of its size, and here I used a bandsaw cutting carefully and exactly up to the line.

Next these parts were cut to length, and their upper edges prepared with the slopes to match the roof. Although the front corners are mitred, at this stage they were sawn with their ends quite square. Years ago I made a mitre shooting board enabling mitres to be accur-

ately trimmed by plane, and it was specially intended for mitres of the 'box' type. Although I only use this device from time to time, with a properly adjusted jack plane it produces a perfect 45-degree cut. It only took a matter of minutes to prepare these joints by hand.

Assembling plain mitred joints can often be rather fiddly, especially if the use of pins on the outer surfaces is to be avoided. My method was to first of all secure glue blocks at the ends of the front piece, with one edge of the block exactly in line with the edge of the mitre. Sufficient time was left for the glue to set, when it became fairly straightforward to add the ends as they had something positive to abut against. I was able to cramp these three parts together, although only gentle pressure was needed to ensure good joints.

The roof

The roof was the next to receive my attention, and this was initially prepared in a similar way to the base. One edge and the ends of a piece long enough for the two parts of the roof were moulded again using the ogee cutter, and the mouldings well sanded while the wood was still in one piece. After cutting to provide the two halves to the roof, the mating edges at the 'ridge' were planed to provide what is strictly speaking a mitre, although the angles are not 45 degrees. I used a sliding bevel to check that both pieces were accurately planed, and were identical.

A triangular support piece for the rear of the roof was now prepared, and bored for screws to be inserted from the lower edge. The roof pieces were glued and screwed to this rear component first, before gluing to the rest of the upper assembly. Although I used a number of

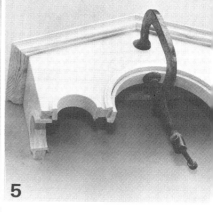

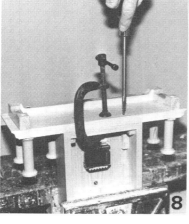

1. Ogee moulding formed on the plinth using a pilot cutter.
2. Smaller arches formed with a hole saw.
3. Arch linings turned using a hollow chuck to form inside.
4. The completed set of linings.
5. Only slight pressure is needed to glue centre linings in place.
6. Dentil mouldings are formed with repeated passes over saw.
7. Tightening the nut to secure the clock movement in place.
8. The movement housing is added by screwing through.
9. Light-weight box hinges are used for hanging the door.

cramps for this, only gentle tightening was needed to ensure the fit was good.

The arches

Five pieces were now cut into discs from which to make the arch linings—unfortunately it was just not possible to make two of these from one turning. The smaller ones were first of all turned on their outer surfaces, complete with rebate and small cove on the outer rim. In order to ensure that the rebated part would be a good fit in the cut-outs prepared to receive them, I used the same hole saw in a piece of scrap wood in which to test the work as the turning proceeded. For the inner part of the turning for these pieces, I had to make a simple holding device. This was no more than a piece turned with a recess in the face, so that the arch pieces were a tight, cork-like fit within this recess. This is a fairly common practice when turning, and this home-made chuck enabled the part completed turnings to have their centre part turned away to give the section shown in the drawings. I used exactly the same method for the larger arch to give me the five 'rings' needed.

These turned components were now cut just over the centre line, so that once fixed in place a small amount would be left protruding on the lower surface for levelling off. These were glued into the semi-circular cut-outs, only the larger arch needed a little help from a cramp to ensure it was properly seated. A little very careful planing was needed once the glue was set in order to level off the lower edge. As with the rest of the project, applying the lacquer and then lightly

abrading down proceeded as each stage was completed.

The dentil moulding adds a lot to the appearance of the clock, and for this I prepared a piece of wood about 356mm (14in) long and 50mm (2in) wide, with the thickness being equal to the 14mm ($\frac{9}{16}$in) dimension of the moulding. The piece was now carefully marked for the cut-outs across the 50mm face of the piece, and what amounted to a series of trenches made by repeated cuts over my small circular saw. Both edges of this strip were moulded on the router table, and a small bevel planed to provide the 'weathering' to the top edge. Now the whole of the strip was well glasspapered, and special attention paid to smoothing the trenches. While still in this form, the work was polished, then a 8mm ($\frac{5}{16}$in) strip sawn off each edge. These pieces were now cut and mitred to length, and secured in place just with adhesive.

Movement housing

The main part of the movement housing is just a rectangular box with the parts glued together and strengthened on the inside with glue-blocks. However, before assembling these parts, a shallow recess was made just where the movement was to be mounted. This was to ensure that the shaft on which the fingers were mounted, and the nut which locks the movement in place, correspond to the thickness of wood through which they pass. Movements may be obtained with long, medium, and short shafts so this point needs careful checking.

After polishing, the plastic clock face was positioned with care being taken

that it was exactly vertical. Then the movement secured in place and the nut tightened. The fingers were added to the shaft, and the bezel fitted which just covered the face. To complete the works, a battery was slipped into place, and I suddenly found that time was catching me up!

The two wings to the movement housing provide the remainder of the back to the clock, and were prepared to the shape shown so as to allow for the rear pillars. They are screwed in place through the movement housing. While a door to the rear of the housing is not essential, it helps to keep the dust out and gives the project a more completed look. A couple of lightweight box hinges were used for hanging the door, with a tiny brass knob and turnbutton to complete this part of the clock. A total of four screws are used to secure the housing to the base, two into the box and one into each wing.

The upper part is not positively fixed to the pillars on which it rests, but I did use the headless panel pins driven part way into the tops of the pillars so that the projecting points would engage in the flat surfaces between the arches. Only at this stage were the two 'ceiling' pieces fixed in the internal angle between the small arches, as it was necessary to make these an exact fit in the spaces to be filled. They are no more than rectangles of wood, held in place by glue blocks.

Suddenly the clock was completed, and three days of intensive work were over. I now realise more than ever just what 'tempus fugit' means!

Sofa bed

WHEN DESIGNING for a particular situation, such as making the most of a small room, then the best solution is often provided by creating a number of items that not only complement each other in style but in function as well.

The sofa bed was made from birch plywood. The size was determined by the 6ft 6in. by 4ft Futon mattress which gives well when bent in the sofa position and look good without any covering. The design

principle is that of a two-box construction, the one box fitting over the other and pivotting back from the sofa position to form the double bed. Full details of this arrangement are given in the drawings.

For the construction of this piece, the first thing to be done is to machine up all the parts for the sides and interior. Sawing down a sheet of ply means that you are often cutting against the grain of the top surface so to prevent splintering of the edges I use a cutting gauge to cut down the marked line before cutting the sheet. With the parts machined up they should be marked for identification and sorted out into the two frames—box 1 and box 2.

Starting with the sides (A, B, C and D), the first joints to consider are the housings for the longer pieces E and F and the stopped housings for H and G. Whilst the joint used here is really a matter of personal preference, I chose

to use a dovetail slot. However if you were to make the bed from solid timber then I would be inclined to opt for through tenons which can then be wedged. Remember though that if you do decide to use tenons you must allow for the extra length when cutting out these pieces. The dovetail slots can be easily cut using a dovetail bit in the router, and the same bit is used to cut the tails. My jig for doing this is shown in the photographs.

With these completed attention can be given to the position of the centre holes "X" and the dowel handle holes "Y". At the same time you can also draw the rounds on the fronts of pieces A, B, C and D. Whilst the pivot holes are only 25mm diameter and are quite easy to drill cleanly, the dowel handle holes are much larger, and to obtain a clean cut hole I decided to use my router. This, however, means that you must make up a jig from 4mm ply as a guide for the router when used with the ring collar. Using an expanding bit I made a number of test holes until I was sure that I had the correct size jig to give a hole in the ply very fractionally

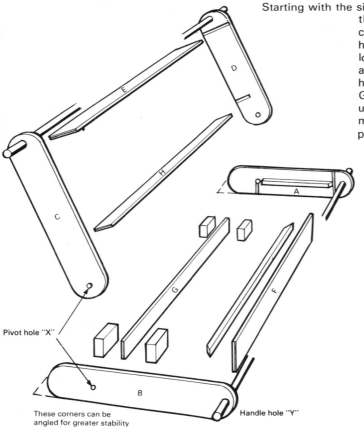

Pivot hole "X"

These corners can be angled for greater stability

Handle hole "Y"

Cutting list

Sides A & B	2 off	988 by 180 by 18mm	Ply
Sides C & D	2 off	805 by 180 by 18mm	Ply
Front piece F	1 off	2004 by 180 by 18mm	Ply
Rear piece E	1 off	2040 by 180 by 18mm	Ply
Centre piece G	1 off	2004 by 115 by 18mm	Ply
Centre piece H	1 off	2040 by 115 by 18mm	Ply
Reinforcement blocks	4 off	115 by 50 by 25mm	Hardwood

Supporting battens

Connected to A & B	2 off	140 by 50 by 50mm	Hardwood
Connected to A & B	2 off	539 by 50 by 50mm	Hardwood
Connected to C & D	2 off	358 by 50 by 50mm	Hardwood
Connected to F	1 off	1980 by 50 by 50mm	Hardwood
Connected to E	1 off	2016 by 50 by 50mm	Hardwood
Dowel handle	2 off	2212 by 45mm dia.	Hardwood
Turned spindles	2 off	100 by 50 by 50mm	Hardwood

Board base for mattress:

Box 1	1 off	1980 by 788 by 18mm	Ply
Box 2	1 off	2016 by 425 by 18mm	Ply

This sofa bed is made out of 18mm ply and the overall sizes are dictated by the Futon mattress used. The pivots and two large dowel handles are stained a vivid red to give colour to the project, and these handles provide the means of support when used in the sofa position with looped webbing stretched between.

bigger than the dowel itself. To locate the jig I took a pair of compasses (set to the size of the jig hole) and drew a circle on each piece of ply using point Y as the centre. I then placed the jig over the ply, lining it up with the drawn circle, before cramping the assembly together with a spare piece of wood underneath. In this manner the holes can be easily and cleanly cut.

For those who may have trouble in finding dowel of this diameter, then I suggest that you consider replacing them with metal rods, such as aluminium, as this can look just as effective.

Before going further with the assembly it is a good idea to cut the rounded ends to the sides—although some may prefer to leave back edges to the sofa support frame squared or angled for extra support if there is the prospect of children climbing on the back and possibly tilting it over. The edges of the ply (although not the joint areas at this stage) can be rounded over using a suitable cutter with the router in the inverted position on a made up worktable.

Part G is too narrow to be drilled for the pivot spindle, so here it is necessary to reinforce the piece with two support blocks at each end. These were thus glued and cramped to the box sides.

It is worth sealing the sides and fronts with polyurethane prior to gluing up the carcases as this makes sanding down afterwards easier, and it is also better for taking off any excess glue when dry. When doing this do remember to mask off the gluing areas.

To hold the ply bed base in place, I used battens screwed and glued to the sides. These are put in after gluing the boxes together, but their positions are marked in before gluing up the carcase—this being the next operation. Ensuring squareness in the assembly is the most important thing here.

When the glue was set, I drilled into part E with a 25mm bit to a depth of 58mm using the hole already drilled to guide the bit in. Next I turned two spindles to fit the pivot hole "X" with a large shoulder on the end the same diameter as the dowel handles. If you don't have a lathe then 25mm dowel glued into a round block will do just as well. Before gluing the spindles in place I waxed the pivot ends of box 2 and also in the pivot hole, this was to ensure free movement and to prevent any glue drying between these parts. Gluing could then proceed with box 2 slotted over box 1, and excess glue being carefully removed.

With the main construction completed I screwed and glued the supporting battens in place. The ply for the base was then cut, fitted and screwed into place on top of the battens and onto parts G and H. It is a good idea to drill holes in the ply bed base to ventilate the mattress.

To take up the gap between the two frames when used in the sofa position a piece of canvas is tacked to the two frames. The best way of fixing this I find is to rout out shallow grooves to take a thin strip of wood and tack through this with the canvas held under the strip.

The large dowel handles were well san-ded then stained and polyurethaned. These were in fact not a tight fit in the holes, but they did not wobble all over the place. They were fixed in position with $\frac{1}{4}$in. dowels, the holes being drilled through the ply into the handles. The dowels were glued in place and the excess was pared off afterwards.

Support for the back frame when it is used in the sofa position is achieved by using webbing stretched from one dowel handle to the other. This is best made after the construction is completed as you can then best determine the angle for greatest comfort and where the loop in the webbing must be made.

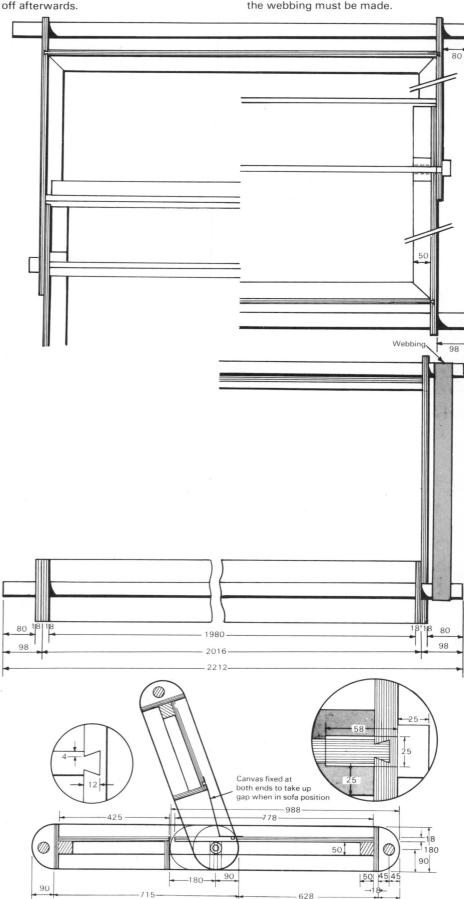

Canvas fixed at both ends to take up gap when in sofa position

1. Cutting the pins to suit the slots with the router used horizontally in a simple jig.

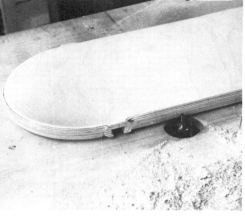

2. Rounding off the edges with the router bit projecting through another worktable.

3. Making test drillings to establish the correct templet size for the dowel holes.

4. The templet is used in conjunction with a ring collar fitted to the router base.

5. Blocks are glued on either side of part G to give correct thickness for the pivot.

6. As both parts are rounded on the edges, the joints must be blended together by hand.

7. The battens which support the ply base are glued and screwed in position.

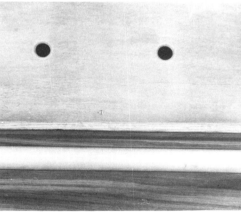

8. Holes to ventilate the mattress are evenly spaced and sanded to avoid sharp edges.

9. The method of fixing the canvas in place is with wooden strips fitted in grooves.

10. The canvas is tacked in position under the strip to give a flat surface.

11. After staining, the handle is fixed in position with a dowel through the ply.

12. The sofa is held in position by webbing straps with loops made in each end.

Culinary capers

Beautiful wood looks good anywhere, and even if you already have a well appointed kitchen why not make these lovely pieces for the home and add a little domestic pleasure.

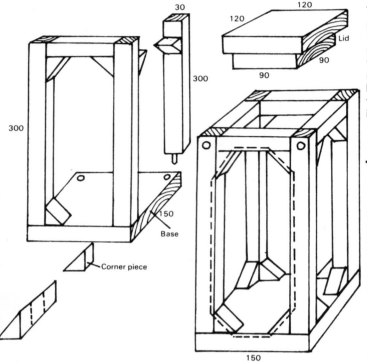

These attractive food containers and the knife holder are made in pine. It has a warm and homely feel to it reminiscent of old times in granny's kitchen although it looks equally good in any modern surroundings. Choose good clean knot-free timber for them and take special care in the jointing and finishing for really attractive results. They can be made in any sizes you want all with the same basic techniques. The chopping board is another simple project but this must be made from a good hardwood such as beech because it will take a lot of hard knocks in its lifetime.

1 The storage containers in photo one are for rice, semolina, nuts or any one of the many household ingredients you choose. The tops and bottoms are cut from 30mm thick timber to give them a nice chunky feel. All the assembly is dowelled together and then stiffened with the triangular corner pieces of the same thickness as shown in the drawing. After assembly (or before if you prefer) a 5mm rebate is milled into the face on each of the four sides to house the acrylic sheet (or a deeper one to take glass). Beading is added to hold the windows in place.

2 Kitchen knives are always best kept out of harms way and what better method than to keep them in a special holder. This one is made from a block of pine 600 by 220 by 30mm sawn in half through the middle. Round off the corners to get a soft attractive shape and cut out the window in the front block with a jigsaw. Both blocks are clamped together to drill for the 15mm corner dowels. When gluing the blocks insert two 15mm strips between them to make the space for the knives. Two rows of 8mm thick dowels are glued in above and below the window to hold the knives in place.

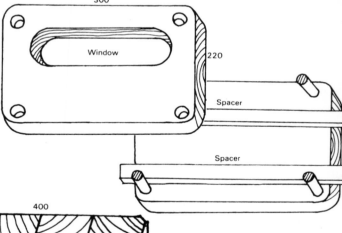

3 400 by 400mm is the size chosen for the chopping block and this is made up from sixteen 100 by 100mm pieces. Use a good durable hardwood. The pieces are stuck together with a waterproof adhesive and when dry a 200 mm groove is cut all the way round on the circular saw. This is to accommodate the metal banding which is secured by nails. Glue in the rope handle as shown, and secure it with wedges driven into the holes.

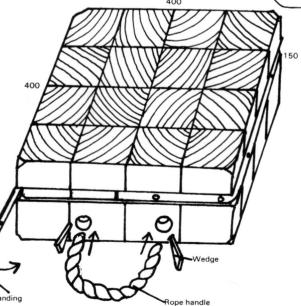

Opposite page
Storage jars in natural pine look really attractive in the kitchen and with good close fitting lids they will keep food fresh and palatable at all times.

Knives will always be readily to hand with this easy-to-build and eminently practical rack. Free standing or wall mounted it's a must for the kitchen.

What better than this sturdy chopping board to make easy work of kitchen preparation. It's simplicity itself to make and adds charm and atmosphere to those everyday chores.

Swinging party bar

Here's something that's a bit of fun to make which will help your parties go with a swing!

WITH THIS MOBILE BAR you will be able to serve drinks to your guests wherever you want with everything to hand. It does not matter where you hold your party — in your dining room, sitting room or even on the patio — you can satisfy your guests' thirsts without having to continually run back and forth. Another advantage of this design is that when the top is opened up, it can service many of the other bar functions, such as a place for food, glasses and even ashtrays. For a stand up party the bar will make a good centre piece, and you can always 'close up shop' as a hint for people who do not know when it is time to leave or when stocks have been severely depleted.

1. This project requires simple and inexpensive materials for the construction with 19mm chipboard being suggested for all the main panels and shelves, and small strips of 10mm thick ply 50mm wide for the retaining strips at the front of the shelves. After buying sufficient material for your needs, as well as the castors, brass rods and fittings, the first step in the construction is to cut all the chipboard and ply components to size.

2. First stage in the assembly is to construct the two parts of the cabinet. Here you can use glue and chipboard screws — these have a double thread all the way up the shank to give a greater hold in this particular material.

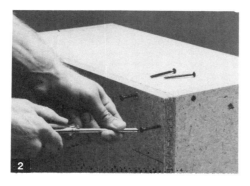

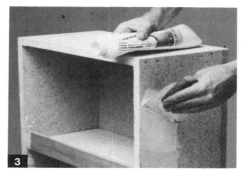

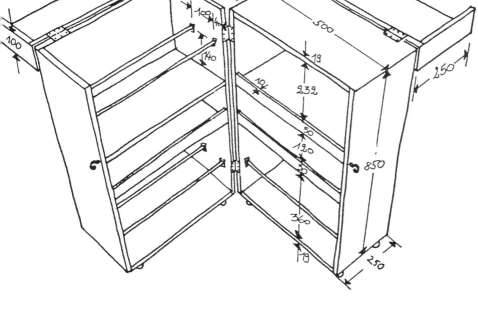

3. Using a plastic spatula work over all the surfaces with a quick drying sealant, taking care to cover all screw heads and blending in at the corners. Applied carefully a smooth and sealed surface will result which is ready for undercoating. Before proceeding to the painting stage, mark out the position of the brass rod holders and also mark and fix the hinges. This is the time to make the trial fitting of the two halves and lids to see that they close correctly. If necessary make adjustments.

4. A coloured acrylic paint applied by brush will give the bar an ideal finish. Not only will it be kick and scratch proof, but spilt alcohol will not stain or mark it.

5. Fix the lids in position and ensure that they open outwards and not inwards.

6. Fix in the internal brass rods to give 100mm spacing.

7. If you feel it necessary to add a lock to your cabinet, then you can either adopt the method shown here which with a large padlock can be made to have a rather humorous appeal, or you can fit a box or drop latch lock.

8. Finally add on the castors by screwing through the plates. A point to note here is that you should make sure that you have the right size castor for your carpet – the deeper the pile the larger the castor. If the castors are too small, the bar will not run smoothly.

At your service

For coffee and Cognac or cakes and ale this handy stand will have a ready use in the comfort of your own home while you relax by the fireside in an easy chair. When finished with it simply folds away to be stored in a cupboard or in the corner of the room.

WE SELDOM see nowadays pieces of furniture which can be said to have charm. Most modern furniture commercially available is either very sophisticated and accordingly expensive, or poor quality, dull boring, and relatively cheap. The portable folding shelf unit we look at here has an old-fashioned appeal but it is really a very practical piece of furniture in the modern world not least because it folds away and thus allows us to make the most of the available space. It manages to retain a charming quality whilst remaining utilitarian, and for this reason it will make a useful addition to almost any home.

This particular one is made in solid ash which adds to its feeling of quality. Needless to say almost any other hardwood could be used or indeed pine of suitable quality. There are small brass brackets linked to the backs of the shelves with screws which are left not quite tight to enable the shelves to fold up. These brackets are handmade in brass (see photo 3), and are very simple to make. Note that the hole nearest the curved end is countersunk from the opposite side (see main colour photo).

1

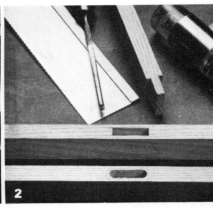

2

The two main uprights are mortised into the base bars in the normal manner to a depth of 25mm. It's probably easiest to mark both mortises together with the two pieces held in the vice. They can be cut by hand or by machinery as shown here.

If you do use machinery for the mortises, square and clean them up with a chisel afterwards. The tenon can be cut by hand (8mm wide by 25mm deep) using an ordinary tenon saw. Once again the shoulders are trimmed with a chisel.

3

4

The 16mm dowelling (248mm) long is let into blind holes drilled 12mm deep in the respective positions (see drawing). The brackets for the shelves are cut from 2mm brass sheet. Clean up the edges and countersink the holes.

The shelves are made up from 16mm ash and cut to squares 220 by 220mm. Mark the centres of each by using diagonals and drill a small hole to take a pivot pin to make life easy when sanding them off to a semi-circle after cutting to shape.

5

Sand off the undersides to a 45 degree chamfer using the same pin assembly to make a clean finish. The tops can be sanded by hand. Lightly recess the ends of the boards for the brackets.

Materials list Planed ash 15 by 30mm:
2 Lengths 900mm, 2 lengths 340mm (uprights and feet)
Planed ash 9 by 16mm:
2 Lengths 600mm, 2 lengths 500mm (shelf supports)
Planed ash boards 16 by 80mm:
3 Metres running length (shelf boards)
Beech dowelling 1200mm by 16mm dia.
To link the shelves to the supports: 8 domed screws (with washers)
24 Countersunk screws for brass brackets and shelves

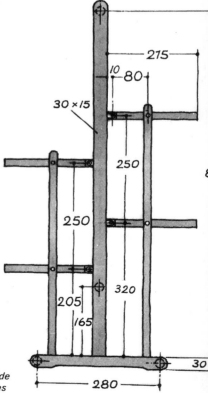

The sketch shows the side view of the unit and gives the necessary dimensions.

The inset above shows the stand folded away ready for storage, a facility which adds considerably to its attraction in today's smaller homes.

The Great Divide

(part 1)

A multi-purpose room divider designed to enhance the character of a room without inhibiting the sense of open space or easy access.

A trend in many modern homes is to have large open plan rooms which serve a double function particularly with one part being used as a sitting room and another as a dining or working area. When this situation is coupled with a need for greater storage and display space, then a series of units specifically designed as a room divider may well help to enhance the character of the room without inhibiting the sense of open space or easy access.

Illustrated below are a number of schemes to show just how versatile such a piece of furniture could be in catering for storage and display as well as providing eating or working space. The final scheme which is illustrated opposite incorporates open and closed shelves, a drawer unit as well as a fold-down table, and these items can of course be rearranged or even omitted to suit your own particular needs.

The construction of the bookshelf and overhead units is described in detail here. The construction of the other two units is described in the following section.

The main colour photograph above left shows the full view of the unit with the integral dining table lowered into position. Bottom far left is the reverse side of the unit showing the area housing the television and stereo unit together with the bookshelves and drawers. The centre photograph shows the table with the legs folded away being set back into the main body of the unit for maximum space saving. Bottom right we see the detail of the drawers with the veneered chipboard fronts and solid mahogany pulls screwed from the back.

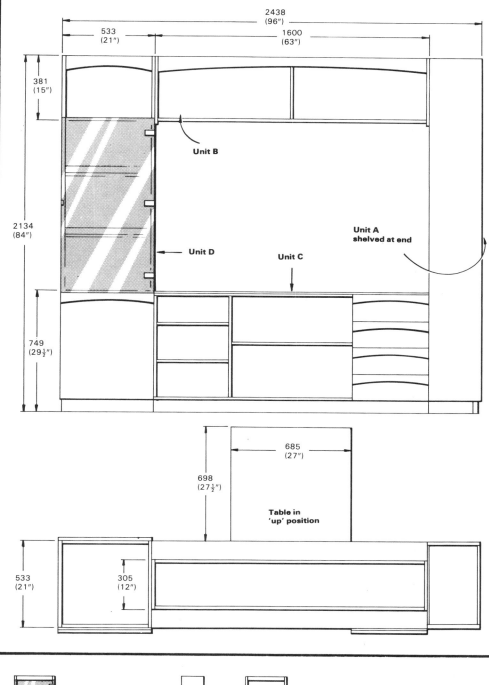

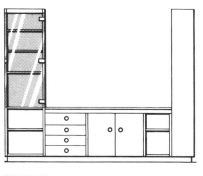

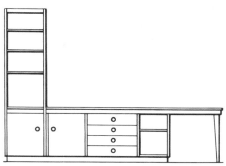

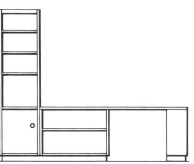

Alternative schemes considered before settling on the design above. The main considerations, apart from general storage and display, were a place for a hi-fi system, a television and a surface for either eating or working at.

Bookshelf unit

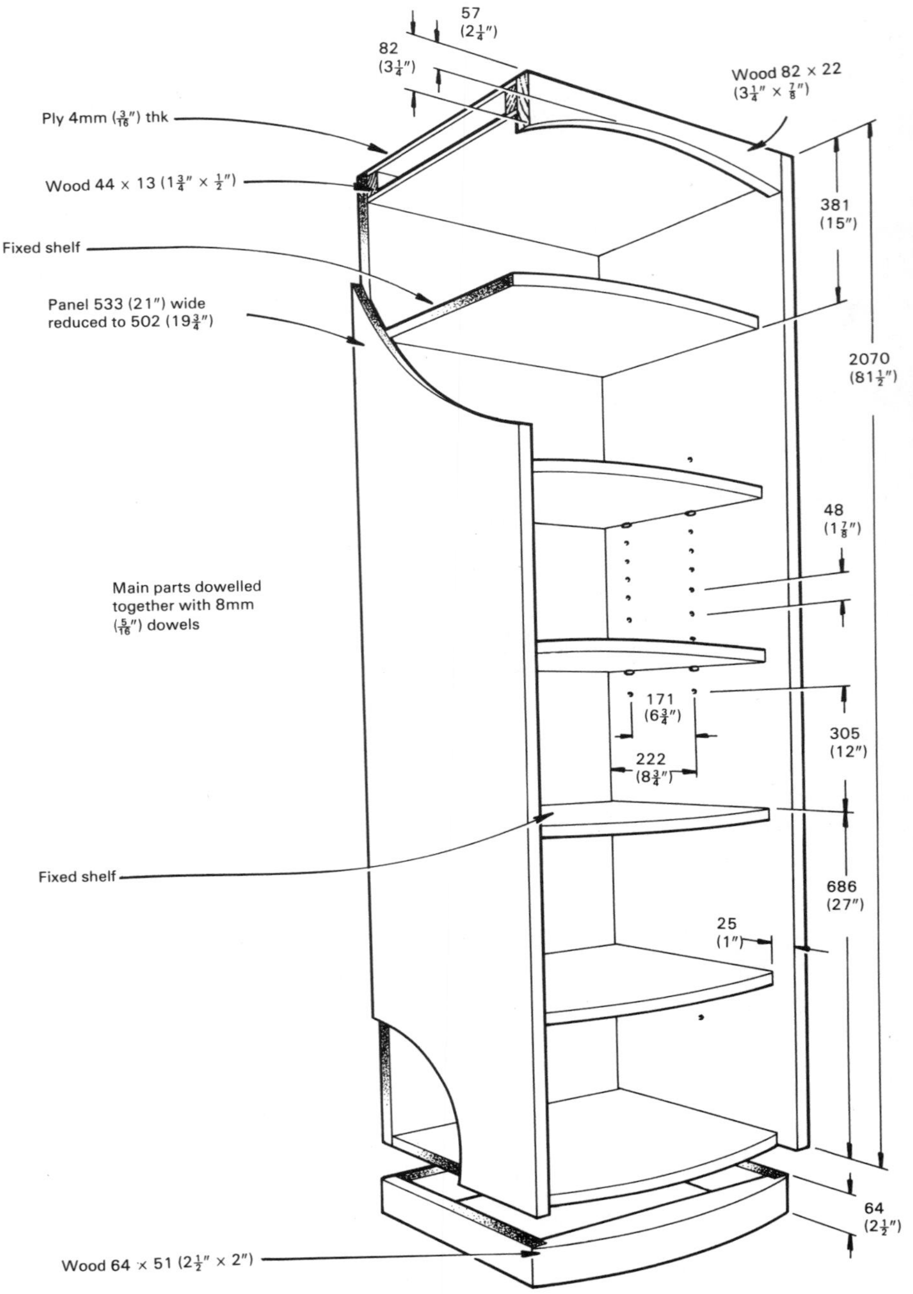

WHILE ALL those who love and work with wood normally prefer to use their basic raw material in its natural, solid form, for a number of reasons most of us also employ man-made boards to a greater or lesser extent. Plywood was the market, followed by block, batten and laminboard. Chipboard followed, then this also became available with ready-veneered faces and edges. Veneered chipboard has now become firmly established as an alternative to solid wood, although nobody would ever suggest that its use is other than limited compared with the versatility of what nature provides almost straight from the tree.

Nevertheless, veneered chipboard for certain uses does have advantages over solid wood. It is readily available, is produced in a wide range of widths, and usually two lengths. In addition, it is reasonably priced, does not have to be seasoned, and does not shrink or swell. It is manufactured with very smooth surfaces, which only require a small amount of sanding to prepare them for the finishing stages.

Because of the basic characteristics of chipboard, this material is at its best when used in relatively wide pieces. As its thickness is standardised at 16mm (or 15mm for the 'Plas' boards), the material should not be used in narrow strips except where additionally supported. Veneered chipboard is used at its most advantageous for cupboards, shelving units, and carcase work where material of fairly considerable width is required. chipboard can also be exploited more fully if used in conjunction with solid wood, and this applies especially to the larger projects.

The multi-purpose room divider described here is the sort of piece which would be at its best in a combined lounge and dining room, or in a flat where one large room has to serve more than one purpose. At the planning stage, four variations were sketched out before settling for the one finally constructed and, as with most projects, the number of alternatives to a basic theme are almost endless. The divider is constructed in four separate units which are secured together, and embraces generous storage and display space including shelves, cupboards and drawers, has accommodation for a TV or music centre, and has a fold-down table with sufficient space for three people. For this project, mahogany faced veneered chipboard was used, with Brazilian mahogany for the visible solid parts.

I commenced work on unit A, which is essentially a tall set of bookshelves. It has two fixed shelves which add considerably to the rigidity, and a series of adjustable ones. First, the two sides were marked out, not just to length, but to indicate the positions of abutting parts and the locations of the supports for the adjustable shelves. As these sides required cutting to length, this was carried out next, and by using a fine-bladed blade in my DeWalt 125, a 'clean' cut was

achieved which needed no further trimming. The shelves were also cut at this stage, and a solid piece prepared for the top front.

Of all the various ways available for jointing chipboard, I invariably use dowelling. It is stronger than mechanical fittings which are screwed in place, and being invisible gives a far neater and more professional appearance. Maybe I'm influenced a little by having in my possession the Record 148 dowelling jig, the best jig by far of the many I've used. For 16mm (⅝in.) veneered chipboard, I use 8mm (⁵⁄₁₆in.) dowels, and usually space these around 50mm (2in.) centres although this is often varied more or less. By using the jig, only minimal marking out is required, the spacing is automatically repeated as often as necessary, and the boring is controlled so as to be quite square to the work. The jig works just as readily on the ends of the work and for this the side guides are quickly added. The solid member at the top is also dowelled. Note that although this piece along with

the shelves are to be shaped, the joints are prepared first as is the usual practice with shaped work.

After toying with the idea of making the back of this unit out of ply, or partly out of ply, I eventually decided that a veneered chipboard panel would be both simpler and better. As well as cutting this down to length, it was also reduced in width so that the overall width of the unit would remain at 533mm (21in.). The back too is dowelled to the sides, here the spacing for them is around 100mm (4 in.), and although the jig was used to guide the drill, it had to be hand held in this instance.

As well as the holes for the dowels, further holes for the sleeves of the shelf supports needed to be bored. For these, I found the Black and decker drill guide to be a useful aid for achieving uniformity of depth.

A feature which was adopted for the divider is the curved edges for most of the shelves, and the door and drawer handles.

Ply 4mm (³⁄₁₆″) thk

Wood 44 × 13 (1¾″ × ½″)

Fixed shelf

Panel 533 (21″) wide
reduced to 502 (19¾″)

Main parts dowelled
together with 8mm
(⁵⁄₁₆″) dowels

Fixed shelf

Wood 64 × 51 (2½″ × 2″)

57
(2¼″)

82
(3¼″)

Wood 82 × 22
(3¼″ × ⅞″)

381
(15″)

2070
(81½″)

48
(1⅞″)

171
(6¾″)

222
(8¾″)

305
(12″)

686
(27″)

25
(1″)

64
(2½″)

To simplify the marking out, a ply templet was made, and the waste cut on a small bandsaw. I knew from previous experience that an excellent way of smoothing curved edges of veneered chipboard is by disc sander, so this was the method adopted. The secret is to keep the board constantly on the move against the disc, and to use only light pressure.

Whenever veneered chipboard is cut, there is going to be an exposed edge showing the core. Edging veneer is available for covering these edges, produced in various types to match the face veneer of the board. The edging veneer has a heat sensitive adhesive ready applied, and is bonded to the veneered chipboard by means of a domestic iron. The iron should be set to medium heat, and it is advisable to place a piece of brown wrapping paper between the iron and the work. The iron must only be moved slowly over the work to allow complete melting of the adhesive and bonding to the edge to take place.

The edging veneer is made about 3mm (⅛in.) wider than the thickness of the board to allow levelling off to take place once bonded in position. A simple tool is available which removes the excess veneer and can be used for the levelling off, or this stage can be completed entirely by glasspaper. Even with the edging tool, a final rub over with glasspaper is worthwhile.

Now although the shelves had been prepared from veneered chipboard panels of the same width as the sides of the unit, that is 305mm (12in.), in fact they needed to be narrower by 6mm so it was simply a case of sawing off this amount. By not reducing the width of the shelves until this point in progress meant that the preparation of the dowel holes was easier, as the same setting of the dowelling jig could be used for both parts of the joint.

The top front member has a similar curved edge to that of the shelves, except that it is concave. After bandsawing to shape, the edge was smoothed with a compass plane.

With the main carcase members now prepared, I gave internal surfaces a light sanding. The shelf support fittings comprise two parts, a sleeve and a stud, the sleeves merely being tapped into the holes to hold them in place. I always prefer to make my own dowels, and grooved a quantity of dowelling prior to cutting to length. It is essential to lightly chamfer one end, and again I use my disc sander for this operation.

It is essential when dowel jointing veneered chipboard to insert the dowels into the shallower holes first, that is those in the face of the board. Dowels were therefore glued into the holes in the sides of the unit. The back was now added to one of the sides, followed by the shelves. Next the second side was lowered into place, before the whole assembly was cramped up. All assemblies must be checked to ensure that all is well, and it is also essential to wash off all traces of glue which exudes from the joints.

The top is of ply, and is in fact a double top. In order to support the ply, strips of solid softwood were prepared to size, and glued and pinned to the four inner surfaces at the upper end. The upper piece of ply was also glued and pinned into place while for the lower one I relied on glue.

1. Cutting to length on the radial arm saw.

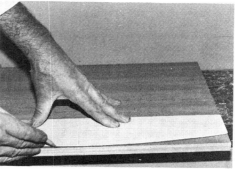
2. Dowel holes prepared in face of sides.

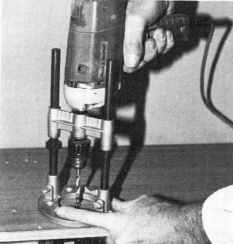
3. Shelf stud holes prepared with drill guide.

4. Curved templet ensures consistency of shape.

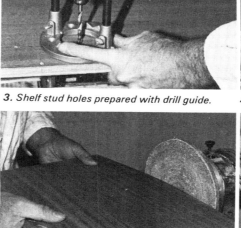
5. Disc sanding follows sawing to shape.

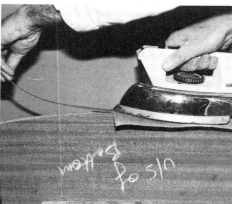
6. Ironing on the veneer edging strip.

7. Excess veneer trimmed with special tool.

8. Reducing the width to suit the unit.

Bookshelf unit *continued*

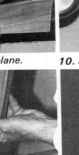

9. *Top rail smoothed with compass plane.*

10. *Shelf support studs and fittings.*

The plinths to the three lower units are set back 6mm (¼in.) from the main surfaces, but in this case the plinth was kept flush with the back as this is where it would abut the centre unit. The curved part of the plinth is of solid material, with the other three from veneered chipboard. To simplify cramping up, the parts were dowelled and assembled before the solid member was shaped. I used screw blocks and glue to secure the plinth to the lower end of the unit.

11. *Assembling the unit—on with a shelf.*

12. *Ensure squareness after cramping assembly.*

Outer surfaces were now glasspapered and the unit prepared for finishing. Because of the combined use of veneered chipboard, ply, and solid wood, I decided to stain the work in order to ensure the slightly varying shades of mahogany would be brought to a matching colour. The 'brown mahogany' stain I used was applied by brush, then the work rubbed over by rag and allowed to dry. This was followed by a coat of slightly diluted polyurethane varnish gloss type, left for twenty four hours then lightly flatted down. The second and final coat was of the satin variety of polyurethane varnish, and this completed the first part of the project.

13. *Softwood strip pinned on at upper end.*

14. *Securing the ply top in place.*

15. *Securing the plinth to the base.*

Overhead unit

For this second unit I decided I would carry out the initial preparation of the veneered chipboard by hand. The panels were marked out to length first by pencil then, after checking, the lines were gone over and squared round to the opposite face using a sharp trimming knife. This lessens the risk of any splintering of the veneer on the underside, even so I used a fine toothed saw and cut just a fraction away from the line. However carefully veneered chipboard is sawn by hand, it should always be trimmed by plane, to ensure it is both dead square and smooth. Whenever possible, pieces of similar length should be cramped together for the planing – not only is this quicker, but it ensures uniformity. It's also wise to check that the ends are quite square, and that the length is exactly as required. As well as preparing the centre division piece to length, this was also reduced in width to allow for the upper solid rails to fit alongside, as shown in the drawings.

A small amount of edge veneering was required, and this was carried out as described previously. At this stage, the top solid rails were planed to size and cut to exactly the same length as the lower main shelf. Now I was ready to proceed with the holes for the dowels, and carried out the minimum of marking necessary before bringing the dowelling jig into use. The holes were quickly prepared, even though the jig did need to be re-set as this stage of the work proceeded.

The top rails also feature the curved lower edge, but rather than make a templet for just a couple of rails, I used a thin lath of wood, and bent this to the required shape. After bandsawing off the waste, a compass plane was used for trimming down to the line. Because this curved edge was relatively flat, I found that my small belt sander was able to give the final smoothing to the edge.

As all the main components were now prepared, I gave all inner surfaces a final cleaning up in readiness for assembling. When inserting the dowels into the holes on the face of the veneered chipboard, I was very careful to ensure the work was fully supported beneath. A long time ago I had a

sad lapse of concentration with disastrous results. I was assembling a chipboard project, and failed to check that the piece into which I was driving the dowels was fully supported on its underside. The result was I drove one of the dowels straight through the board, totally shattering the reverse side. The piece had to be scrapped and a new one made, as well as having to 'reverse' the assembling of those parts which had already been glued together for that stage of the work. However, lessons which are learnt the hard way become engrained in the system never to be repeated – hopefully!

No mishaps this time – first the division was secured to the lower shelf, then the upper rails added, and finally the ends. Cramping is always desirable and usually essential when gluing up an assembly, and although my workshop is well equipped with cramps, I only have one metal sash cramp sufficiently long for this size of work. I overcame this problem by taking the shoes off the cramps, and bolting them together in pairs. After checking the work, all surfaces were well wiped over with a damp cloth.

Only a little levelling off of the outer surfaces was needed once the cramps were removed, and this was quickly achieved with glasspaper. The top to this unit is of similar construction to the first, and therefore strips of wood were secured around the upper inner surfaces. The lower pieces of ply forming the top does of course have to be in two halves because of the division, but the upper piece is continuous. The vertical division had been kept down a little at its upper end to allow for this.

Largely because of the overall size of the whole project, and the limited spare space in my workshop which seems to grow forever smaller, each piece of the divider was put through the finishing process as it was completed. With the staining and varnishing carried out, this part was moved out of the workshop to make way for the next unit. Although all the units are to be secured together on completion with connecting bolts, holes were not prepared for these at this stage.

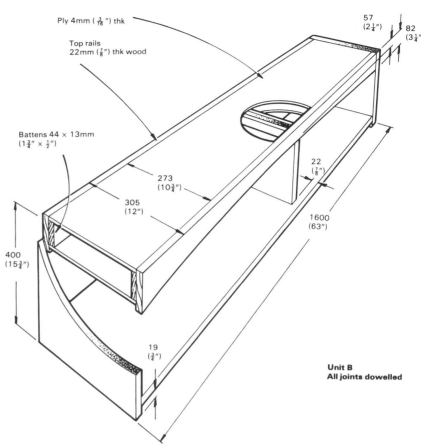

Ply 4mm ($\frac{3}{16}$") thk

Top rails 22mm ($\frac{7}{8}$") thk wood

Battens 44 × 13mm ($1\frac{3}{4}$" × $\frac{1}{2}$")

273 ($10\frac{3}{4}$")

305 (12")

400 ($15\frac{3}{4}$")

19 ($\frac{3}{4}$")

57 ($2\frac{1}{4}$")

82 ($3\frac{1}{4}$")

22 ($\frac{7}{8}$")

1600 (63")

Unit B
All joints dowelled

16. *Cutting to size with a fine toothed saw.*

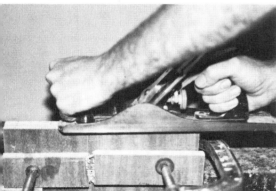

17. *Trimming the ends dead square.*

18. *Checking for accuracy of planing.*

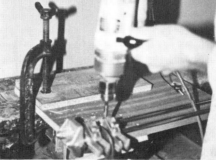

19. *Record dowel jig used for holes.*

21. *Adding the end to the assembly.*

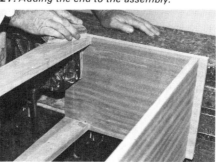

23. *A little levelling is required.*

20. *Curved member is bandsawn to shape.*

22. *Cramps applied and checks completed.*

The great divide

(part 2)

Construction of the final two units completes the four-unit room divider.

WITH AN OVERALL length of 2438mm (96in.), and a height of 2134mm (84in.), the room divider had been designed at the outset to be in four units, each one independent in its construction, but all four to be secured together to form a composite whole. The design of the divider had been based on using mahogany-faced veneered chipboard, as far as possible in its standard widths but cutting down where necessary and combining this with solid wood where appropriate. The divider had been conceived as a multi-function piece of furniture to provide cupboard, shelf and drawer storage, display facilities, accommodation for TV and audio equipment, and a built-in folding dining table. With the first two units completed, I was ready to set about the centre unit which incorporates a variety of features.

First, the four vertical members forming the carcase, the base, and the two solid wood top rails were all prepared to their exact sizes. The base was now marked out showing the cut-out where the table folds, the grooves, and the position of the two middle members. I found a portable jigsaw ideal for forming the main cut-out, while a router provided the means of forming the stopped grooves for the plywood. The router must be used with a batten cramped to the wood in order to guide it, and for chipboard the extra cost of using TCT router cutters is well justified. The carcase was to be assembled using a combination of screws and through dowels, but at this stage only the screw holes were prepared.

All four vertical members needed notches forming at the upper corners to allow for the top rails, and the outer two also needed similar cut-outs at the lower ends for the plinth. These cuts were quickly made on the bandsaw. The grooves in these vertical members for the plywood are all "through" grooves, and so were prepared on a circular saw. All the shelves to this unit are adjustable, the holes for the sleeves of the shelf supports being bored with the aid of a drill

guide. This ensures the holes are true, and that their depths are controlled.

I invariably use beech for drawer runners because of its resistance to wear, and made these sufficiently wide to accommodate the drawer side and the glue blocks beneath the drawer. The runners were prepared with screw holes, glue being used as well when these were secured in place. The top rails required trenches in their inner edges to complete the joint to the veneered chipboard, a stopped groove forming on the underside of one end of these rails to receive the ply back to the drawer section, and screw holes prepared through which the top is later fixed. These two rails also had a small quadrant moulding cut along their outer upper edge, this was formed with a router but using it in a router table. Odd pieces of veneered chipboard were cut down to form support blocks between the base and the ends, these being glued and screwed to the ends between the cut-outs already made for the plinth.

With the inner surfaces cleaned up with glasspaper, I could proceed with the assembling. First, the centre pieces of veneered chipboard were screwed to the base, then the holes made for the dowels. Here I was using the dowels in a rather non-standard way by driving them completely through one part of the joint and into the other, the exposed end of the dowel being of no consequence in this instance. The two ends of this carcase were now added, this time the screws and the dowels were driven in through the ends and into the base. The two top rails were temporarily pinned in place to help with the alignment of the parts so far secured together, and checks were made to ensure the accuracy of the assembly.

The three pieces of plywood which are incorporated in the carcase were now carefully cut to size and slipped into place. Two of these required additional support at the top, and this was simply achieved by gluing small

strips of wood along their upper edges. The top of the third piece of ply engages in the groove on the underside of the top rail, these rails being secured at this stage and again the screw and dowel combinaton was employed.

The plinth is of simple construction, with the strips of veneered chipboard forming this part being glued and pinned in position. As far as was practicable G-cramps were used to hold the various parts forming the plinth tightly in place to the base, and glue blocks were liberally used to further strengthen this part of the unit. Glue blocks used in this way also add considerably to the overall rigidity of the carcase. The kickers to the drawers section were now secured in place. These also serve as an additional way of securing the top, so two sets of holes were prepared in these parts before they were fixed in place between the top rails. The final two drawer runners were made only 13mm (½in.) thick, as these rest directly on the base of the unit to which they were secured. The actual top needed little preparation. It was cut to length and the ends squared up, then simply screwed to the rest of the carcase.

The drawers are of fairly standard construction with a false front. This means that the four sides are of equal thickness, and that through dovetails can be used on all corners. Accurate initial marking out of the length of the wood, and the subsequent cutting always pay dividends in drawer construction, as this minimises the later fitting stages of the work. I always use a cutting gauge to mark the extent of the dovetails which for through joints is equal to the thickness of the wood (photo 6).

While some craftsmen cut the "tails", or "sockets" of dovetail joints first, I've always started by cutting the "pins", which I believe is the way the majority work. I followed normal practice by using a dovetail saw for down the grain, and a coping saw for removing the bulk of the waste. As it is well nigh impossible to use a coping saw with a high

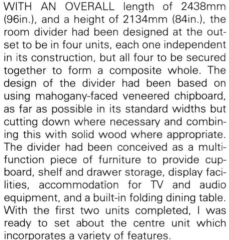

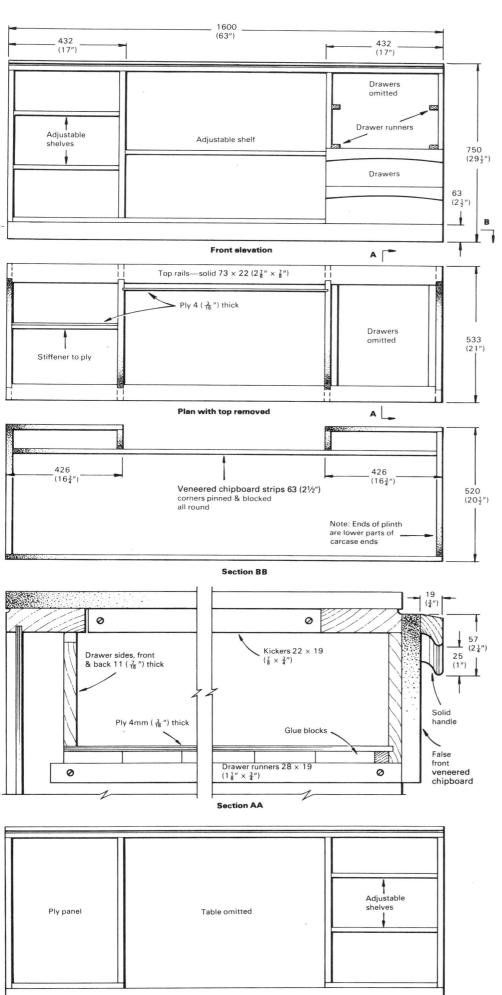

Front elevation

Plan with top removed

Top rails—solid 73 × 22 (2⅞" × ⅞")
Ply 4 (³⁄₁₆") thick
Stiffener to ply
Drawers omitted
533 (21")
A

Section BB

426 (16¾")
426 (16¾")
Veneered chipboard strips 63 (2½") corners pinned & blocked all round
Note: Ends of plinth are lower parts of carcase ends
520 (20½")

Section AA

Drawer sides, front & back 11 (⁷⁄₁₆") thick
Ply 4mm (³⁄₁₆") thick
Kickers 22 × 19 (⅞" × ¾")
Glue blocks
Drawer runners 28 × 19 (1⅛" × ¾")
Solid handle
False front veneered chipboard
19 (¾")
57 (2¼")
25 (1")

Reverse elevation

Ply panel
Table omitted
Adjustable shelves

degree of accuracy, this sawing is made a little away from the line to allow for trimming by chisel.

With dovetail joints, the sockets are always marked out directly from the pins. A sharp pencil is required for this, and it is also essential to make an identification mark on the outer surfaces to ensure that final assembly of the components is as initially marked. Actual cutting of the sockets is essentially the same as for the pins, but the greatest of care is needed at this stage as this determines the quality of the fit of the joint. The grooves for the plywood drawer bottom were formed by circular saw, holes made in the front for securing the false front, and after this all inner surfaces were cleaned up.

With any joint in woodwork, glue is applied to both parts although this does not have to be excessive. A well-cut dovetail joint can normally be assembled by gentle tapping with a hammer, providing of course a piece of scrap is used to protect the work. A little care is needed to follow the current sequence of assembling the four sides, otherwise difficulty will be experienced in adding the final side. Any woodwork assembly needs checking for being square, and drawers especially so, and any glue which exudes from the joints must be wiped off while still wet.

While 'exhibition' standard cabinet work invariably has drawer bottoms of solid wood fitted in the traditional manner, the truth of the matter is that plywood is a far more suitable material to use for this purpose. Thinner ply can be used compared with solid wood, and ply is free from shrinkage problems which means the use of glue blocks can be employed. When I slide the ply into the grooves of the drawer, I add glue to the groove in the front, then by depressing the ply once in place, add a little more adhesive between the ply and the lower edge of the back. I then use round head nails to secure the rear edge of the ply to the drawer back. Glue blocks are added down each side with a couple also positioned at the front, then twenty four hours allowed for complete setting of the glue. The glue blocks not only make the drawer into a very solid assembly, they increase the bearing surfaces on which the drawer will slide and therefore minimise the effects of wear.

The fitting stage of making the drawer is all important if a smooth sliding action is to be achieved. I always start this stage by levelling off the glue blocks on the underside, these always being a little oversize when they are added. Light planing of the sides follows; the drawer must be well supported for this, and the planing carried out towards the centre of the sides to avoid any damage in the area of the joints. Constant checking of the drawer in its allotted aperture within the carcase is essential to ensure that any tightness is being relieved by taking shavings off the right part of the drawer. A sloppy fitting drawer is a real giveaway of indifferent workmanship.

My initial thinking was to have the grain of the drawer fronts running horizontally as would be the case had solid wood been used. However, this idea was quickly changed so that the grain of the fronts would be vertical. This meant that the grain on all

The great divide 57

vertical surfaces to all parts of the divider would then also be vertical, and by cutting the drawer fronts from one piece of veneered chipboard, continuity of the grain pattern could be maintained. The fronts were therefore prepared in this way, with edging trim added as appropriate.

The handles to the drawers are of solid wood, and after initial preparation by planing, the curve to the lower edge was marked with the aid of the templet. After removing the waste by bandsawing, the concave edge was smoothed by compass plane. The finger grip shaping to the lower edge was achieved quite simply by using an ogee cutter in the router which in turn was held in the router table. For any work of this type on a curved edge, it is necessary to use a cutter with a "pilot". As I wasn't happy about using glue alone for securing the handles to a veneered surface, holes for three dowels were prepared for each handle before gluing and cramping in place.

After a little cleaning up to the drawer fronts, including bevelling the top edge of the handles, I was ready for securing them to the drawers. the lowest drawer was the first to have its front added, then I worked upwards temporarily holding them in place with a pair of cramps. I used a couple of steel rules as spacers, and found this arrangement gave just the right amount of clearance.

The folding table to this unit is designed to have its top flush with the main surface so as to maximise its use of providing dining facilities for up to three people. All parts except the top are of solid wood, and it was the upper frame which I tackled first. The four sides of this frame are dowelled together, but before assembling these parts holes needed to be made in them for securing the veneered chipboard top. The three rails which are on edge required the holes to be counterbored, but this was not necessary on the fourth rail positioned on the inner side. With the parts thus prepared, assembly fol-

lowed and the frame was left cramped up for a day. Outer surfaces were smoothed and levelled when dry. The veneered chipboard top required little preparation except cutting to exact size, and edge veneering the exposed surfaces. This was then simply screwed to the frame so that all outer edges were flush.

The legs and leg rail are also dowelled, and after boring these the taper to the legs was formed, and curve to the rail prepared. This gentle curve to many of the solid wood parts, and to the front edges of the veneered chipboard shelves, was a simple decorative feature to give continuity to the four units making up the divider.

Particular care was needed when assembling the legs and rail, to ensure the legs were parallel, the assembly quite square, and also free of twist. When the glue was set, cleaning up both main surfaces was an easy operation using a small belt sander. Outer edges were also cleaned up at this stage, and the simple quadrant moulding formed on all edges of the assembly except the top inner edge where it is hinged. Again the router was used for this, with the work being controlled by the pilot on the cutter. Although a modern high speed router gives a very clean cut to the wood, some glasspapering is always necessary, and for this I used a block shaped to match the profile of the edge.

I used a pair of 75mm (3in.) butt hinges for hingeing the legs to the frame, although back flaps would have given a marginally stronger job. These were fully recessed into the wood, and were first fixed to the legs before locating within the top frame. Three hinges were employed for hingeing the whole table to the rest of the unit; these were recessed into the top frame first, then the corresponding recesses made to the underside of the top rail of the main carcase. To ensure that the legs will lock when the table is in the up position, a couple of stays were used bet-

ween the legs and the underside of the top. However, in order to make sure these stays were working at their most efficient, packing blocks needed to be added beneath the top. These stays snap into the locked position once the legs are lowered, but are easily and quickly released when the table is folded away.

With the bulk of the work to this unit now finished, all that remained of the constructional work was to prepare a series of five shelves. The main part of this preparation was to form the curve to the front edge, and after sawing away the waste the smoothing was completed on the disc sander. Adding the edging veneer to a curved edge in veneered chipboard is just as straightforward as it is to a flat surface, possibly a little more time is required with the iron on account of its limited area of contact because of the curve. Removing the excess trim follows the same procedure, using either a special edge trimming tool or completing the job entirely with glasspaper.

Because mahogany, whether in veneer or solid form, varies appreciably in its colour, I had decided at the outset that staining the work would be desirable in order to achieve a uniform shade. I used a proprietary brown mahogany stain, applied this by brush and then used a rag to remove the surplus. When this was dry, I gave a slightly diluted coat of polyurethane varnish (gloss type) and when dry this was lightly flatted with fine abrasive paper. The final finish is of the egg-shell variety, so a coat of this was applied next which completed this part of the project.

Unit D

The final unit of the room divider is essentially for storage, but mainly it is for display purposes, with this part being enclosed behind glass doors fitted to both sides enabling access to be gained from the front and the back.

The main veneered chipboard parts to this

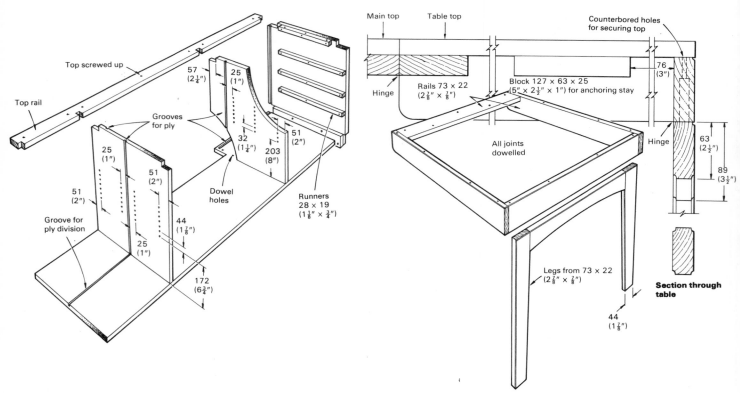

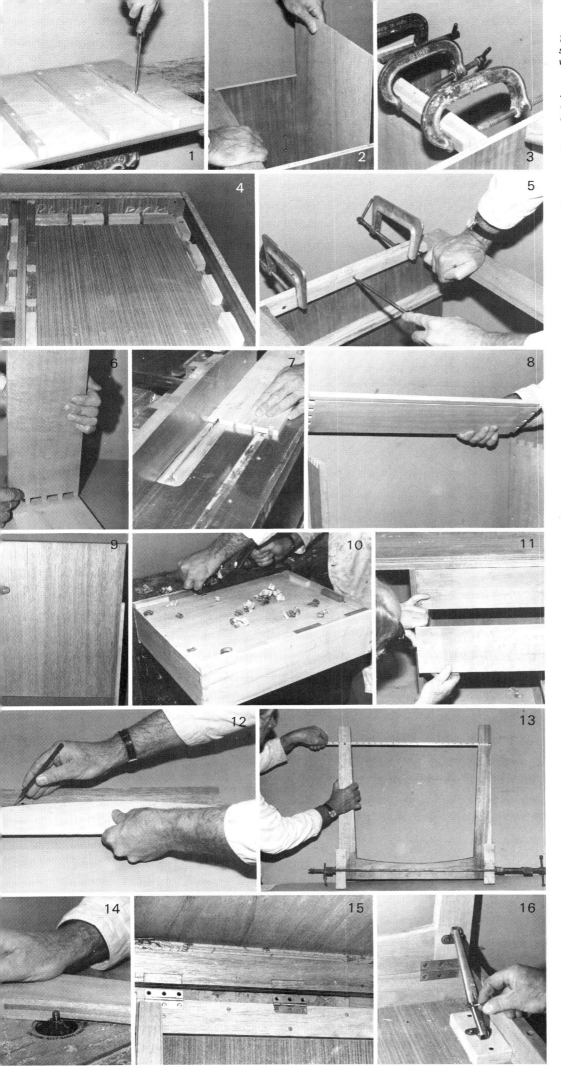

1. The beech drawer runners are screwed to the carcase sides as well as glued.

2. The plywood divisions must be carefully cut to size before sliding into place.

3. A stiffener for the ply division is simply glued on and held in place with cramps.

4. Extra support is given to the plinth by the use of glue blocks added to the underside.

5. The kickers are positioned with cramps before screwing into place. They also serve to secure the top.

6. When cutting the joints, the dovetail sockets are marked out from the pins.

7. The drawer components can be grooved for the plywood bases using the circular saw.

8. Offering up the second drawer side to check that there is a good fit of the parts.

9. Sliding the drawer base into place. The fit should be tight but not so as to cause damage.

10. Levelling off the glue blocks on the underside. These give an extra bearing surface.

11. A final check to test the fit of the drawers before adding the false fronts.

12. The uniform curve to the handles can be achieved with the help of a simple ply templet.

13. It is important to check the legs for parallelism at the gluing up stage.

14. The moulded edges are achieved with a router set up in a table to act as a moulding machine.

15. Three hinges are employed to unite the table with the rest of the unit.

16. Snap stays fixed to the legs and blocks on the underside lock the leg frame securely.

unit were sawn and trimmed to length, and the two upper solid rails also prepared to size. One of the many advantages of using the Record dowelling jig for making dowel joints is that only the minimum of marking out is needed – sufficient to show where one component locates with its neighbour. However, the 533mm (21in.) wide panels I was using were just a little too wide for the largest of the 'rods' available for the jig, thus some improvisation was called for so that the jig could still be used. On the face of the boards, the problem was overcome by simply cramping the jig to the work, while for the holes in the ends of the work two lengths of wood were first bolted to the bush carriers of the jig to enable the cramps to be effective. As both the upper and lower sections of this unit carry a plywood division, a series of both stopped and through grooves needed to be formed. Through grooves were cut on the circular saw, while the router provided the means of forming those which were stopped.

The upper rails were cut and smoothed to provide a concave lower edge as described before, and likewise the holes for the bushes for the shelf supports were also bored as previously described. Two rails were also prepared to the size and shape shown in one of the drawings for fitting beneath the base of the display area, these rails matching similar ones beneath the top of the centre unit. These rails were glued and screwed in place, inner surfaces sanded, and the main components were ready for gluing up.

I followed normal practice of first inserting the dowels into the holes in the face of the boards, then added the cross members to these. Because of the size and relative awkwardness of this stage, I enrolled an assistant to help assemble the parts and position the cramps. Checking the work is an essential part of gluing up, as is removing any surplus glue.

While the ply division to the lower part of the unit had to be positioned within the carcase at the time of the main gluing up, that at the top was added after assembly. After sliding into place softwood strips were added around all the inner surfaces at the upper part so as to support both the "top" and the "false top" as shown in the drawings.

The plinth is essentially a four-sided box with an additional member down the centre, all five pieces of the veneered chipboard being dowelled together with glue blocks added in the internal corners for extra strength. For securing this plinth to the rest of the unit, I decided to use the commercial type of fixing blocks, and soon had the plinth screwed in place. Note that the plinth is recessed on only three sides of the unit, the fourth side is arranged to be flush with the outer surface. This is because of the way in which the units are fitted together, and thus gives the visual effect of continuity to the lower parts of the three units which stand on the floor.

The two doors to the lower cupboard are of course identical, their width being equal to a standard panel of veneered chipboard. All that was needed, therefore, was to cut to length, trim the ends quite square, and veneer the exposed edges. The handles to the doors are of a similar type to those on the

drawers, prepared from solid wood with the lower edge shaped to a concave outline. The router cutter I had been using to create both the finger-grip to the handles and also the quadrant moulding to some of the edges was actually the same cutter. By varying the projection of the cutter above the table, I was able to form just the right cut needed in each case. In fact the cutter I was using was an "economy" one selected from a Black and Decker router cutter kit. This allows for different blades to be fitted to the spindle, the nut which holds the blade in place also serving as the pilot. Although both the cutter and router worked well, I played safe when forming the finger grip and made a preliminary cut before resetting the router for the final shaping. Dowel holes were prepared in the handles and the doors before they were glued and cramped together.

I have been using "concealed" pattern hinges for many years, not only are they very neat and easy to fix, they are also adjustable allowing the door to be aligned to the carcase after hanging. Most variations of this hinge allow for the adjustment in two directions, but not for "up-and-down" adjustment. However, for this unit I was using a type of this hinge I had not used before, and which incorporates the up-and-down movement which was previously lacking, this being a part of the anchor plate of the hinge.

Although these hinges are simple to fit, they do necessitate the accurate boring of a blind hole into which the barrel part of the fitting is housed. A special bit of 35mm diameter is available which is an exact match for the hinge, but it is essential to have some kind of drill stand to enable the boring to be properly completed. The hinges are then

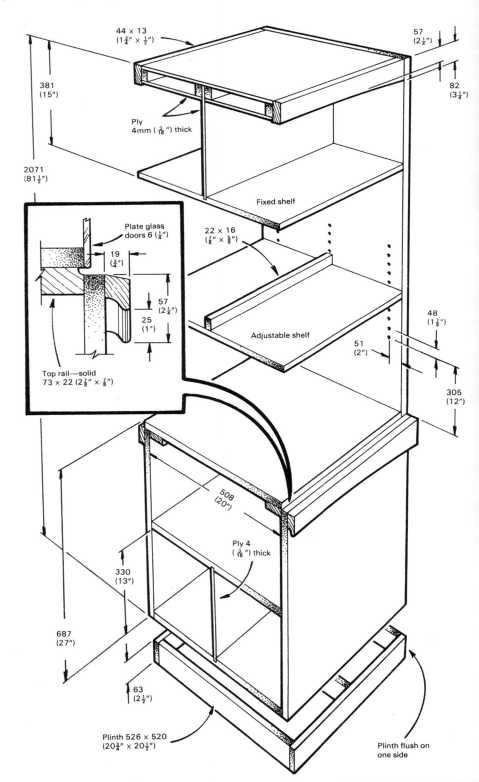

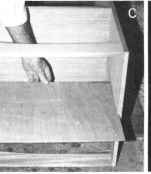

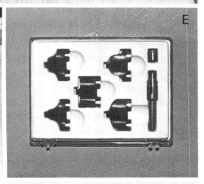

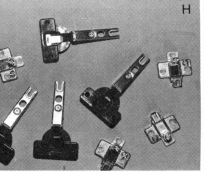

A. As the boards are too wide for the rods of the dowelling jig, it is cramped in place for use.

B. For use on the ends of the boards a length of wood is bolted to the bush carriers then cramped on.

C. Fitting the ply division to the prepared grooves made inside the carcase.

D. In this case the plinth is secured to the main carcase with plastic screw blocks.

E. The selection of profile cutters available in the Black and Decker router kit.

F. Forming the moulding on the underside of the solid wood strip for the handle.

G. Gluing the handle onto the door using scrap wood to protect the wood from the cramps.

H. These concealed hinges are fully adjustable both horizontally and vertically.

I. A good fit will result if the proper milling bit is used in a vertical stand.

J. Marking out the position of the hinge plate with the door offered up to the carcase.

pressed into the holes and secured with a couple of screws. It is best to mark for the anchor plates directly from the parts fixed to the doors, and again a couple of screws hold these plates in place.

The two shelves to the main display area were cut to length, and then reduced in width by approximately 25mm (1in.). The sawn edge required to be veneered, then the sawn-off strip was dowelled down the centre of the shelf as shown in the drawings. The purpose of this is simply to separate one half of the display area from the other, with the option of inverting the shelves should this be preferred.

I had no difficulty in obtaining the smoked grey plate glass doors from my local glass merchant. Not only did I specify the size on my order, I also made a sketch drawing showing the location of the three holes for the hinges. In addition, I submitted one of the hinges to the glass merchant to enable him to check the holes, and I'm glad to say the doors were made in a matter of days exactly to my specification. Fitting first the hinges to the doors, and then the doors to the unit was quite straightforward, the "glass door" hinges I was using being a variation of the pattern used on the doors for the lower part of the unit.

With the actual woodwork completed, finishing followed and this of course was exactly the same as for the rest of the divider. When the final coat was dry, I set

about preparing the holes for the connecting bolts which would hold the four units together. In order to gain maximum accuracy of alignment, each pair of adjoining units were laid on their sides while the holes were actually bored. Four bolts were used for each point of connection.

Little now remained to be done except bolt the units together, and bring the divider into immediate use.

Toddler's toy box

Few things evoke such poignant memories of childhood as a cluttered box in the playroom bursting with colourful games, threadbare teddies, three-wheeled fire engines, and biscuit crumbs. Here's a way to ensure that your children have a few similar memories to look back on in the future.

THIS TOY BOX is made in pine and assembled with glue and dowels. It is quite simple to make and will enhance any child's room; there is plenty of space to tidy away toys, and the box itself is an attractive piece of furniture and fun to play with.

It is best to do all your own cutting but you could get wood cut to size at the timber yard; then the only power tool you need is a drill—you should have access to a stand, though, to ensure that the drilling is accurate.

The drilled holes are an interesting feature of this project since all the pieces (except for the plinth) are assembled with visible dowels. If the holes are not cleanly drilled, the components may not fit properly or will look untidy.

The box is built up from the base, starting with the plinth. The working

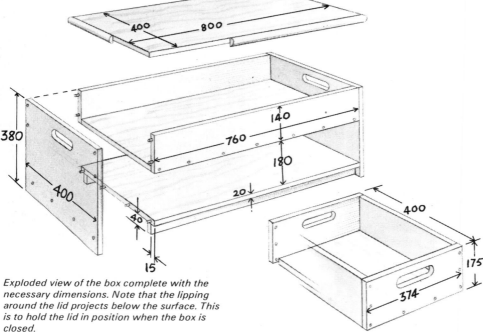

Exploded view of the box complete with the necessary dimensions. Note that the lipping around the lid projects below the surface. This is to hold the lid in position when the box is closed.

Cutting list

3m continuous length half-round moulding
(30mm section) for edge of lid
8mm section dowel rod
19–20mm thick pine
1 lid, 400 by 800mm
1 top shelf, 760 by 360mm
1 bottom shelf, 760 by 400mm
2 side pieces, 400 by 380mm
2 long front and back pieces, 760 by 140mm
2 plinth strips, 760 by 40mm
For the drawers:
2 bases, 360 by 334mm
4 side pieces, 360 by 175mm
4 fronts, 374 by 175mm.

1. All the edges with the exception of those to be glued should be rounded over to avoid splinters. Here we see the plinths being given the treatment.

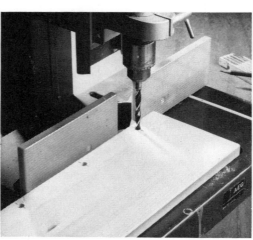

2. Using the drill stand and depth gauge drill the holes for the dowels all at the same distance from the edge of the board. Mark distances from the hole centres.

3. Using the pre-drilled piece as a templet proceed to drill the holes in the mating board. dowel pushed in will prevent any slippage from occurring.

The lid and both the drawers can be removed for maximum play value, and it's all stowed neatly away when it's time for bed.

4. The projecting ends of the dowels are now cut off with a handsaw. This will leave just a small section to be smoothed off with sandpaper, working always with the grain.

5. The best way to cut the grips is to drill out a hole either end of them with a bit or a hole saw and then simply join the holes by cutting with a fretsaw.

6. When assembling the box it's convenient to stand it on its end. Make sure you glue the dowels as well as the edges and do make sure that the surfaces are clean.

drawing gives you all the necessary dimensions.

Attach the plinth with glue, 15mm back from the edge of the box bottom. Do not take the clamps off until the joints are really set, as the glue is the only thing holding it. When set, you should round off the corners with a plane.

The next stage is to assemble the top shelf and the front and back sections. You can follow the procedure in the photographs. Before all the pieces are assembled, you need to prepare the drawers and end pieces. Photo 5 shows you the best way of cutting the hand grips in the ends. The holes for the dowels should be made as for the side pieces: mark the position of the holes; drill using the drill stand with a stop attached; then use the piece you have prepared as a guide to drill the corresponding holes in the piece to which it will be fixed (see photo 3).

A note on fixing the dowels you can either buythem precut, or you can buy dowel rods and cut them too short, if anything make them on the long side — they will have to be sanded off anyway, but do avoid filing the ends in case they snap.

7. One way of cramping the assembly if you have no sash cramps is to use string in the manner shown. Small blocks of wood forced beneath it will give sufficient tension.

8. The edges of the lid of the box are not rounded off but are lipped with a moulding and mitred in the usual way. The moulding should overhang by about 10mm.

9. The moulding is simply glued into position and cramped as shown or in a similar manner. Rub over with sandpaper to get a nice smooth finish.

10. The drawers are built up in the same way as the main carcase and again rubbed down for a smooth finish. A couple of coats of polyurethane completes the job.

USEFUL HINTS

E. A. Hilditch (Technical Director of Cuprinol Ltd)

Selecting Wood

Avoid pieces with too many large or dead knots

Avoid very resinous woods

Avoid wood with splits or normal defects of wood

Avoid signs of decay or surface mould

Avoid bluestain

Traditional Pine Wardrobe

This charming and simple design from Germany is well within the capability of the home woodworker. As a joint project with the family to help with the flower decoration everyone can be involved.

TODAY'S WOODWORKERS have things a lot easier than the master carpenters of the past. When they wanted to make wardrobe frames, floors and shelves they had to plane each piece of wood individually and then glue them together to form a piece of the right thickness. Today, the carpenter can go to the nearest timber yard and choose between ready-made boards in all shapes and sizes if he decides to.

We did the same when we came to build this wardrobe. We cut the inexpensive pine board and ply into frames, bases and shelves with the bench circular saw—as indicated in the cutting list. If you first cut the timber to the length of the longest frame pieces, then you can handle them on even the smallest of DIY circular saws.

The decorative panels at the top and the base can also be made from plywood if you wish. Cut a template half the width of the wardrobe and use it to trace the line of the curves onto the wood. A bandsaw is handy for this but not essential. The cut edges are then slightly rounded with sandpaper. 4mm plywood is used for the panels inside the frames, which are assembled with dowel pegs and glue. The plywood should be cut to size when purchased since the sheets are hard to transport and also to cut up unless you have a full-size circular saw. If you want to finish the wardrobe as quickly as possible, then you can buy veneered wood, but you should take into account that the grain is not always attractive or consistent. We used plain ply and faced it with a fine, specially-chosen pine veneer, because it looks much better.

Particularly decorative points are the mouldings which link the panels with their frames and also those that adorn the top of the wardrobe. These are produced quite simply by gluing existing mouldings together, eliminating complicated milling (you can make up your own designs).

Though the wardrobe is simply constructed, a few tips will help you. The frame for the side panels can be held together after gluing with clamps. It is not so easy with the front and back panels. It helps to clamp one upright to the workbench and then to fix the cross pieces with dowel pegs so that everything lies flat on the bench. The other upright should now be fitted onto the dowel pegs, hammering it in place with a block of wood between the frame and the hammer. Another strip of wood, clamped to the bench next to the second upright, and wooden wedges make it possible to put sufficient pressure on the frame whilst the glue dries. The mouldings which hold the panels in place can be fixed with pins until the glue is dry.

1. The pine boards have to be sawn into different sizes to form the frame pieces. The drawing and the cutting list show you which sizes to use.

2. Beech dowel pegs, 8 by 45mm, hold the frames together. The position of the dowel peg holes can be easily marked with wire nails with their heads clipped off. Knock the nails into one frame piece and push the other against it to make an imprint.

3. The holes, half the length of the dowel peg, are best made with the drill on a stand, but if necessary can be made freehand. Spread glue on the pegs and contact surfaces and then clamp the frame together.

1

2

3

4. The veneer, 35cm wide, should be cut with a veneer saw or a sharp knife, so that the veneer sheets slightly overhang the plywood filling. Trim the edges later.

5. Spread the glue onto the plywood with a toothed spatula. Several sheets can be clamped together at once between two thick boards.

6. Once the glue is dry on the veneered sheets, trim the edges and sand the surfaces. Use the circular saw to cut the sheets to their final size.

7. Rabbeted moulding is attached to the front of the frames and the panels are then dropped in from behind. Battens 20 by 5mm, are screwed on from behind to hold the panels in place.

8. The curves for the mouldings at the top and bottom will be quite symmetrical if drawn using a template. Cut out along the lines with a jigsaw.

9. The door hinges (lift-off hinges) with a decorative top) must be fitted flush into the frame and the door. Mark the position with a sharp pencil and then cut the wood out with a sharp chisel.

10. Use a ratchet screwdriver or drill to join the back wall to the sides, screwing through the rectangular strip glued into the corner. (See drawing). Fix the front in the same way.

11. The base, built around a sheet the same size as the inside measurement of the sides, back and front, is fitted onto the bottom of the wardrobe and fixed with long screws through the rectangular strips.

12. The interior of the wardrobe can be fitted in various ways, either with a clothes rail from side to side or with a dividing wall and shelves.

13. Four different mouldings obtainable from any timber merchant, are simply glued together to form a striking moulding for the top of the wardrobe.

14. The moulding should be carefully measured and sawn in a mitre box. The strips are screwed on from inside.

15. Fitted with dividing wall and shelves, the wardrobe still without decorations.

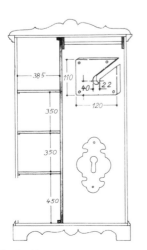

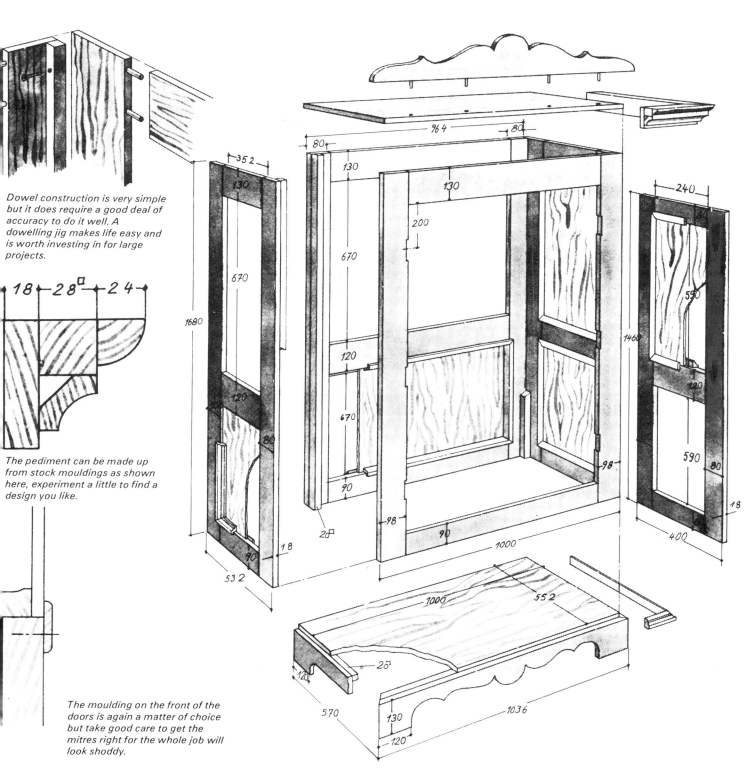

Dowel construction is very simple but it does require a good deal of accuracy to do it well. A dowelling jig makes life easy and is worth investing in for large projects.

The pediment can be made up from stock mouldings as shown here, experiment a little to find a design you like.

The moulding on the front of the doors is again a matter of choice but take good care to get the mitres right for the whole job will look shoddy.

CUTTING LIST

Cross pieces	2 off	804 by 130 by 18mm
Cross pieces	1 off	804 by 120 by 18mm
Cross pieces	2 off	804 by 90 by 18mm
Cross pieces	2 off	352 by 130 by 18mm
Cross pieces	2 off	352 by 120 by 18mm
Cross pieces	2 off	352 by 90 by 18mm
Cross pieces	4 off	240 by 80 by 18mm
Cross pieces	2 off	240 by 120 by 18mm
Carcase sides	4 off	1680 by 80 by 18mm
Carcase sides	2 off	1680 by 100 by 18mm
Carcase sides	2 off	1680 by 98 by 18mm
Door side pieces	4 off	1460 by 80 by 18mm
Plinth front and back	2 off	1036 by 130 by 18mm
Plinth sides	2 off	570 by 130 by 18mm

Decorative top	1 off	1000 by 180 by 18mm
Top and base	2 off	1000 by 552 by 18mm
Partition	1 off	1660 by 513 by 18mm
Shelves	3 off	513 by 385 by 18mm

From 4mm plywood

Back panels	2 off	804 by 670 by 4mm
Side panels	4 off	670 by 352 by 4mm
Door panels	4 off	590 by 240 by 4mm

Also required: *mouldings and batten to suit; pine veneer; glue; screws; hinges; lock; acrylic paint; wax.*

Decorating the Wardrobe

You don't need to be a great artist to decorate the wardrobe with attractive flower motifs, but you should have a flower identification book so that you can trace the flowers true to nature. With a little imagination you can build up bunches of flowers which will fit into the spaces to be decorated: a large one for the doors, a narrow one for the edges and another for the top moulding. Remember, though, that it is better to decorate the wardrobe before it is assembled. It is easier to paint parts of the wardrobe than the finished object.

1. *The flowers, drawings of which you can find in any flower book, are traced and made up into a bunch.*

2. *The design can be traced through, using carbon paper, onto the untreated wood. Hold the paper down with tape so that it won't slip and do not press too hard.*

3. *Paint the design with acrylic paints, starting with the large areas. Cover up the outlines well with paint.*

4. *The fine work comes next, once the large areas are dry. The stems should now be painted in. Add the delicate shading on the petals and leaves.*

5. *To protect the wood and the flower motifs, paint the wardrobe with two coats of furniture wax. The surface can be buffed up with a cloth pad once the wax is dry.*

Suggested flower patterns for the wardrobe decoration.

Welsh dresser

FOR THE CONSTRUCTION of this dresser, extensive use was made of a board product called 'Pinecraft'. This is widely available from D.I.Y. outlets both large and small, and is produced in lengths from 24 in. to 93 in. (305mm to 508mm). Although a manufactured board in one sense, it remains a natural product as the manufacturing merely joints up the wood to gain the widths required, with the final result a board which is accurately sized and finished to a standard thickness of ¾ in. (18mm). On this project, I was in no way attempting to exploit the panel sizes of this product, but really to use it as my main raw material and cut it to the sizes which I needed. The dresser can of course be constructed entirely from the normal pine boarding as available from most timber yards, but in this case a fair amount of jointing up will be re-

quired in order to gain the widths needed for the lower part of this project.

The dresser is made in two separate halves, thus the base part could be used on its own as a small sideboard.

Work started on the front framework to the base, and the material was prepared to the section shown. Positions of the joints of these pieces were squared in and the dowel joints were made with the aid of a Record dowelling jig. Inner edges of the lower part of this frame were cleaned up, and the various members glued and cramped together. Once assembled, the main surfaces were levelled off and made smooth.

The first Pinecraft board was now cut to make the carcase sides. The ends of these two pieces were planed dead square before being reduced

in width from the standard size of 20 in. (508mm). The joint between sides and front is tongue and groove, and photo 1 shows the tongue being formed on the Pinecraft. Small rebating saw attachments for power drills I find extremely useful for operations like this, and the grooves on the inner surface of the front frame can be formed with the same tool.

Although reasonably smooth, a certain amount of cleaning up improves the surface. I followed normal procedure for this, taking off only the minimum of shavings with a sharp and finely set smoothing plane; this was followed by the liberal use of glasspaper. Being a softwood, a scraper could not be used for cleaning up. The next step was to assemble these sides to the front (photo 2).

My intention from the start was to use the Pinecraft as extensively as possible throughout the construction. A strip of this board was now cut to fit behind the lower member of the front frame, then glued and screwed to this lower rail so that it was ¾ in. (18mm) below its top edge. The purpose of this strip was to act as a support for the bottom of the cupboard which, when fixed later, would be level with the rail. By allowing this supporting strip to project below the front bottom rail, it would also serve as a means of holding the shaped plinth. Supports were also needed for the ends of the bottom. Here the Pinecraft was cut with the grain running crossways – that is with the same direction of grain as the sides themselves.

The actual bottom needed little preparation other than cutting and trimming to size. The upper surface was cleaned up, then this part could be glued and pinned in place. Glue blocks added to the underside not only hold this bottom securely in place, but also help to stiffen up the whole job (photo 3). Note that the glue blocks added at the ends are very short indeed – this is to allow for the possibility of movement in the timber and, in particular, shrinkage.

My next step was to prepare a templet for the plinth. In order to ensure that this was symmetrical, the shape was first of all marked out on paper; the paper was then folded on the centre line and the outline cut out. The shaped paper was taped to a strip of thin ply, the waste sawn away and the curved edges trimmed and smoothed. I went to a fair amount of trouble in making this templet, knowing that it would be needed again for the pelmet. A god templet can also be used again on other projects.

A piece of Pinecraft was cut to the width needed for the plinth and then bandsawn to shape (photo 4). Spokeshave and glasspaper were sufficient to finish what the bandsaw had started, and the piece was soon ready for fixing (photo 5). After gluing in place, it was further held by screwing through the piece already added to the carcase. Two small extra blocks at the ends give additional support to the plinth.

My method of supporting the back part of the drawer compartment is rather non-standard, but nevertheless proved to work well. The essence of this is the part referred to in the drawings as the rear frame; this can be seen in photo 6. Five pieces of Pinecraft were cut to the lengths and width required, and two of the shorter pieces bored and countersunk for screws. Initially these pieces were glued and lightly nailed together. One assembled, holed were bored through the joints so that dowels could be inserted from the outside, thus using the dowels as 'pegs'. Three such dowels were glued into each joint – these being 8mm (5/16 in.) in diameter.

Although the rear frame needed accurate location within the carcase, it was quickly glued and screwed in place. A packing strip on the top of this frame brought the upper surface level with the cabinet sides, thus providing support for the top.

For traditional construction involving drawers, three sets of parts are needed to allow the drawer to function properly. These are runners,

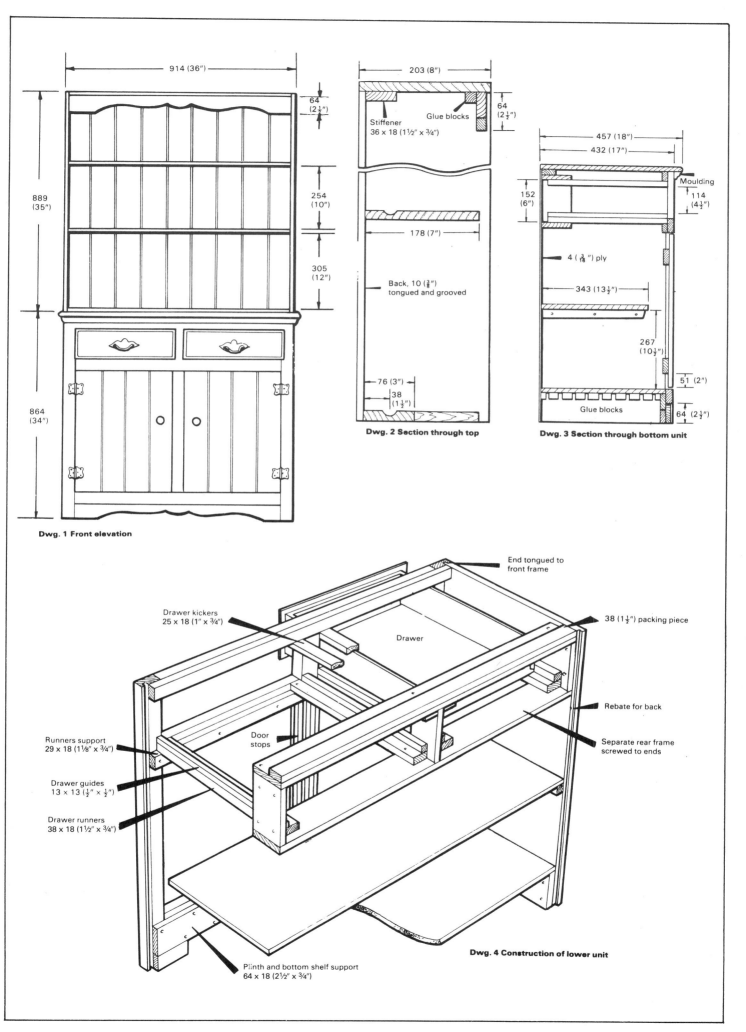

914 (36″)

64 (2½″)

889 (35″)

254 (10″)

305 (12″)

864 (34″)

Dwg. 1 Front elevation

203 (8″)

Stiffener
36 x 18 (1½″ x ¾″)

Glue blocks

64 (2½″)

178 (7″)

Back, 10 (⅜″)
tongued and grooved

76 (3″)

38 (1½″)

Dwg. 2 Section through top

457 (18″)

432 (17″)

152 (6″)

Moulding

114 (4½″)

4 (³⁄₁₆″) ply

343 (13½″)

267 (10½″)

51 (2″)

Glue blocks

64 (2½″)

Dwg. 3 Section through bottom unit

End tongued to
front frame

Drawer kickers
25 x 18 (1″ x ¾″)

Drawer

38 (1½″) packing piece

Rebate for back

Runners support
29 x 18 (1⅛″ x ¾″)

Door
stops

Separate rear frame
screwed to ends

Drawer guides
13 x 13 (½″ x ¼″)

Drawer runners
38 x 18 (1½″ x ¾″)

Plinth and bottom shelf support
64 x 18 (2½″ x ¾″)

Dwg. 4 Construction of lower unit

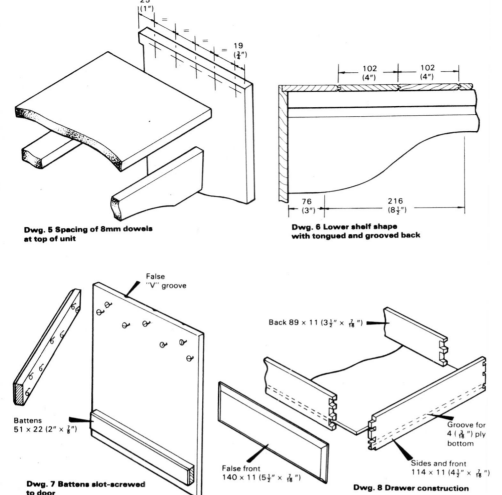

Dwg. 5 Spacing of 8mm dowels at top of unit

25 (1")

19 (¾")

102 (4") 102 (4")

76 (3") 216 (8½")

Dwg. 6 Lower shelf shape with tongued and grooved back

False "V" groove

Battens 51 × 22 (2" × ⅞")

Dwg. 7 Battens slot-screwed to door

Back 89 × 11 (3½" × ⁷⁄₁₆")

Groove for 4 (³⁄₁₆") ply bottom

False front 140 × 11 (5½" × ⁷⁄₁₆")

Sides and front 114 × 11 (4½" × ⁷⁄₁₆")

Dwg. 8 Drawer construction

guides and kickers, and are best if made of hardwood. In order to support the front ends of the runners and kickers, strips were added to the front frame. Guides were glued and pinned to the runners, but the runners and kickers were screwed in place. Note that at the back of these pieces they are in fact slot-screwed. When fixing these I was very careful to check they were parallel in width and height and, because the drawers themselves are comparatively small, only one kicker was fixed to each side.

The top was tackled next. The design of the cabinet allows for this to have a 25mm (1 in.) overhang at the front when cut from a standard 20 in. (508mm) width. Similar overhangs were required at the ends, and the top was cut and trimmed so that the projection of the top was uniform on these three sides. The upper surface of the top was thoroughly cleaned up, and the three projecting edges well rounded. I relied entirely on glue for securing this top, holding it in place with G-cramps (photo 9). For extra strength, small glue blocks were added between the carcase sides and the ends of the top.

Moulding under the top is not essential, but it does add a little to the overall design. An old moulding plane was sharpened and tested, and a piece of straight grained redwood selected for making this part of the job. One of the secrets of producing moulding of this type is to start off with a fairly wide piece of wood, so that it can be easily held in the vice and will not be too flexible. Both edges of the wood were moulded (photo 10), before the material was fed through the circular saw to produce the final section required. After mitring the corners, these pieces were pinned in position.

As the back to the lower unit will not

normally be seen, I had decided at the outset to use 4mm (³⁄₁₆ in.) birch ply for this. This needed little preparation other than cutting to size and adding to the rest of the carcase.

Now it was time to incorporate the shelf in the cupboard section. This was soon cut, trimmed to size and cleaned up. It is supported on battens screwed to the carcase sides, the screws being accommodated in slots because of the different grain directions.

In its original thickness the board was too heavy for making drawers, but when planed down to 11mm (⁷⁄₁₆ in.) it was ideal. The drawers have false fronts, but are otherwise of standard construction. Because of the arrangement of the front, through dovetails could be used throughout with the drawer bottom grooved in. I always add glue blocks very generously to the underside of a drawer; not only do these add a lot of strength, but they also give increased area to the surface on which the drawer runs (photo 13). When the outer surfaces were levelled after assembly, the drawers required very little adjustment before they were a smooth sliding fit within the carcase (photo 14).

False fronts were cut so that they had a 13mm (½ in.) overlap on the drawer, and these too were reduced to 11mm (⁷⁄₁₆ in.) thickness. For decorating the edges of these fronts, a simple quadrant shape was made with the aid of a high-speed router, but an even simpler alternative would be to chamfer the edges. The fronts were screwed to the drawers through holes already prepared, with a little glue added as well. Brass drawer handles were fixed at this stage, although they had to be removed later for the finishing process.

My attention now turned to the doors. Here I

decided to use a single piece of board, but treat it to give the appearance of a boarded door. The two pieces required were cut and fitted to the door openings, and again I used my router to produce the V-grooves down the front. A shallow cut from a circular saw would give a similar effect to this grooving. Because of the nature of **Pinecraft**, the doors needed strengthening; this was provided by adding battens to the back. However, it was again necessary to allow the board to be free to shrink and swell, therefore the battens had to be fixed in such a way as to cater for this. My method was to use "secret screwing." The four battens were prepared to size, and also a card templet of the same width and length as the battens. On this templet were marked the positions of the seven screws needed.

This templet could then be used for locating the positions of the screws in the doors and the slots in the battens, thus ensuring accurate alignment (photo 15). The slots needed with this technique were made in the battens, and when these were finally fixed to the doors, a trace of glue was added to one end of the batten only—nearest to where the hinges would be.

Prior to this I had obtained some decorative brass hinges for the doors and, as they were of the face-fixing type, they were simple to use as recessing was not required. Normally, it is better to fix the hinges to the door first, which is what I did in this case, positioning them to be in line with the battens. By laying the cabinet on its back, it was easy to centralise the door in its opening and screw the hinge to the frame (photo 16). Door stops were necessary to control the closing of the doors; these were added to the vertical framing at the centre and can be seen in the drawings. Because the framing is thicker than the doors, I had to rebate the stops as shown. Glue, plus panel pins, hold them in place.

With the construction of the lower part completed, my attention now turned to the upper section. The six main pieces which form this shelving were all cut and squared off to length. I was careful with the length of the actual shelves, as I wanted the overall width of the top to be the same as the base.

Jointing of the main pieces is by means of 8mm (⁵⁄₁₆ in.) dowels. These joints were quickly and accurately made with the aid of my dowelling jig. Five dowels were used for the top, but only four for the remaining shelves as these are slightly narrower (photo 17). Following the tradition of this type of dresser, I wanted the shelves of the upper section to be capable of holding and displaying plates. This meant the shelves had to be grooved towards their rear edge for the rim of the plate to rest in. My router was employed for this operation, using, in fact, the same coving cutter employed for the front of the drawers. Other methods of producing a suitable groove include using a "round" plane, grooving with plough or circular saw to produce a shallow, square cut, or using a rebate plane at an angle to make a triangular shape of cut.

As the bottom shelf of this part of the job would overlap the top of the base by a fairly considerable amount I decided to remove much of the shelf by shaping it. My bandsaw soon had the waste removed, and the edges were smoothed by spokeshave and glasspaper. Back edges of the sides were rebated in order to receive the back.

Cleaning up followed, after which I was ready for assembling. Although I found it convenient to use a number of cramps, gluing up can be accomplished with only one cramp. providing this is moved quickly from joint to joint. Dowel joints of this type, once cramped tight, are not likely to spring apart again.

The pelmet to the top was cut in a similar way, and using the same templet, to the plinth.

I relied entirely on glue for fixing this piece, adding glue blocks to the inner surface where they would not be seen. As an alternative to rebating the back of the top, a strip of wood was added so as to form a false rebate. This can be seen in the drawings, and it also serves to stiffen up this part of the job.

I wanted to use board again for the back of the upper unit, but could not use the false appearance of narrow boards as had been used on the doors. The alternative settled on was to convert the Pinecraft into tongued and grooved boarding.

The panels were cut down to 108mm (4¼ in.) wide, and reduced to 10mm (⅜ in.) thick. Tongues were formed down one edge, and grooves down the other, and for both these operations I used a small circular saw, The small chamfer which forms the "V" was then planed by hand. The boards were cut to length, and secured with round head nails. I fixed the centre board first, then worked outwards. The last two boards needed a little off their width to enable them to fit properly into the rebates, but by working in this way all the boards were symmetrical with the outer two of equal width.

My original intention was to secure the two parts of the cupboard together with a couple of the connecting bolts made specially for this purpose. However, in practice I found that they were not needed, which means that the lower part can be used on its own at any time without the top being marred by holes.

With all the constructional work completed, I was ready for the finishing process. Hinges and handles were removed, and all surfaces given a coat of gloss polyurethane varnish. This was diluted with about 10 per cent of white spirits and allowed to dry thoroughly. After flatting with fairly fine abrasive paper, a second coat of undiluted gloss was applied. Again this was allowed to dry, then flatted, and the process was completed with a third and final coat which was the satin type of varnish.

Doors were re-hung and the handles re-fixed. Screwing magnetic catches to the doors to hold them closed completed my Pinecraft version of a Welsh dresser.

Cutting List

Front frame stiles	2 off	870 by 48 by 22mm	(34¼ by 1⅞ by ⅞in.)
Front frame rails	3 off	838 by 48 by 22mm	(33 by 1⅞ by ⅞in.)
Front frame centre top	1 off	133 by 48 by 22mm	(5¼ by 1⅞ by ⅞in.)
Front frame centre bottom	1 off	521 by 48 by 22mm	(20½ by 1⅞ by ⅞in.)
Ends	2 off	870 by 435 by 18mm	(34¼ by 17⅛ by ¾in.)
Bottom supports	2 off	114 by 387 by 18mm	(4½ by 15¼ by ¾in.)
Plinth support	1 off	901 by 63 by 18mm	(35½ by 2½ by ¾in.)
Bottom	1 off	902 by 406 by 18mm	(35½ by 16 by ¾in.)
Plinth	1 off	838 by 64 by 18mm	(33 by 2½ by ¾in.)
Shelf supports	2 off	356 by 25 by 18mm	(14 by 1 by ¾in.)
Shelf	1 off	901 by 343 by 18mm	(35½ by 13½ by ¾in.)
Rear frame rails	2 off	901 by 89 by 18mm	(35½ by 3½ by ¾in.)
Rear frame vertical pieces	3 off	171 by 89 by 18mm	(6¾ by 3½ by ¾in.)
Drawer runners	4 off	406 by 38 by 19mm	(16 by 1½ by ¾in.)
Drawer guides	4 off	406 by 13 by 13mm	(16 by ½ by ½in.)
Drawer kickers	2 off	406 by 25 by 19mm	(16 by 1 by ¾in.)
Support strips for runners & kickers	2 off	901 by 29 by 19mm	(35½ by 1⅛ by ¾in.)
Drawer sides	4 off	432 by 114 by 11mm	(17 by 4½ by ⁷⁄₁₆in.)
Drawer backs	2 off	400 by 89 by 11mm	(15¾ by 3½ by ⁷⁄₁₆in.)
Drawer fronts	2 off	400 by 114 by 11mm	(15¾ by 4½ by ⁷⁄₁₆in.)
Drawer false fronts	2 off	425 by 140 by 11mm	(16¾ by 5½ by ⁷⁄₁₆in.)
Drawer bottoms	2 off	400 by 400 by 4mm	(15¾ by 15¾ by ³⁄₁₆in.)
Back	1 off	902 by 781 by 4mm	(35½ by 30¾ by ³⁄₁₆in.)
Doors	2 off	521 by 381 by 18mm	(20½ by 15 by ¾in.)
Door battens	4 off	381 by 51 by 22mm	(15 by 2 by ¾in.)
Door stops	2 off	521 by 19 by 18mm	(20½ by ¾ by ¾in.)
Top	1 off	985 by 457 by 18mm	(38¾ by 18 by ¾in.)
Moulding for top	1 off	2032 by 19 by 19mm	(80 by ¾ by ¾in.)
Upper part			
Ends	2 off	908 by 203 by 18mm	(35¾ by 8 by ¾in.)
Top	1 off	914 by 203 by 18mm	(36 by 8 by ¾in.)
Shelves	3 off	914 by 178 by 18mm	(36 by 7 by ¾in.)
Pelmet	1 off	914 by 64 by 18mm	(36 by 2½ by ¾in.)
Stiffener to top	1 off	914 by 38 by 18mm	(36 by 1½ by ¾in.)
Back (area to cover)	1 off	889 by 902 by 10mm	(35 by 35½ by ⅜in.)

Allowance added to the lengths. Widths and thicknesses are net.
Also required: 2 drawer handles, 2 pair hinges, 2 door knobs, 2 door catches.

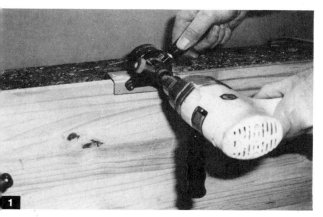

1. Forming tongue along front edge.
2. Ends cramped up to front frame.
3. Glue blocks give extra strength.

4. Bandsaw makes quick work of shaping.
5. Bottom plinth fitted in place.
6. Assembly of rear frame.
7. Screwing frame to back of carcase.
8. Carcase ready for fitted drawers.
9. Top glued up and cramped in place.
10. Preparing moulding for under top.
11. Drawers are through dovetailed together.
12. Sliding drawer bottom into place.
13. Glue blocks added under drawer.
14. Checking for fit in the carcase.
15. Templet used in positioning batten.
16. Hingeing first door to the carcase.

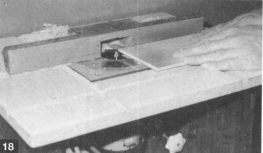

17. Dowel joints prepared in top unit.
18. Forming plate grooves in shelves.
19. Glued, cramped and checked to be square.
20. Adding the boards to the back.
21. Bottom unit used as a sideboard.

Going Crackers

A solid wooden nutcracker is useful at many times, and this one is very easy to use – even little children will be able to crack their own nuts – and it is also a pleasing object to look at. It's made with a deep bowl to catch all the nutshells and stop them spreading all over the carpet.

To make

All the pieces for the nutcracker can be cut from a solid block of wood. You can use various woods but beech or teak are preferable. First cut the templets out of card and then mark the pattern pieces around to find the best way to cut them out.

Before sawing out the various pieces, the bowl-shaped trough should first be drawn on, and then using a chisel with a semi-circular blade, hollowed out. To prevent the wood splintering, first using a straight ended chisel,

make a groove about 10mm deep and 100mm wide across the grain of the wood. Now work with the chisel up to the groove, and even if you handle it clumsily, the splinters will only go up as far as the groove. When the hollow has been made you can then smooth it by hand until it is smooth to the touch. Always work from the edge of the bowl down to the deepest part, and as far as possible in the direction of the grain of the wood. To finish smoothing, use sandpaper wrapped round a ball of wood.

Now saw out the shape, using a fine saw. The hammer of the nutcracker, pieces (c) and

The bowl and pivot post fixed in position ready for the fitting of the hammer.

The hammer assembly showing the pivot pin with its two retaining dowels.

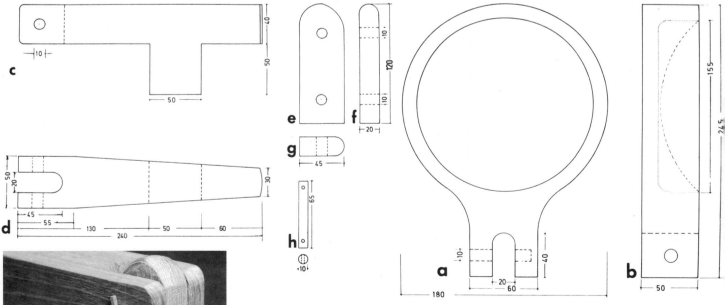

Detail of the assembly at the post end with the retaining pins in position.

(d), is movable, so piece (a) has a vertical support built in to it (piece e). Thus this hinge piece needs a slit in it; bore a hole at the place marked in the drawing using a 20mm drill and then cut out the two straight sides with a fine saw. Piece (e), which is 20mm thick, is inserted into piece (a). Use glue and a 10mm thick piece of dowel to hold it firmly in place.

The hammer piece is glued together, using piece (c) and a 50mm thick block of timber. The hammer, piece (c), has a slit (d), just like the base piece. This controls the vertical strut

(e,f,g) and is inserted into piece (a); test that it moves easily and mark the hole to be drilled at the same time.

Now drill a hole, 10mm in diameter, through the two joined pieces (d and e). Finish the edges with fine sandpaper and smooth the edges of the hammer. The prepared piece of dowel, (h), is now inserted. Using two 3mm thick splints of wood fix the dowel firmly in place. Finally the wood is given a colourless coat of varnish. If you want to stain the nutcracker, do this before applying it.

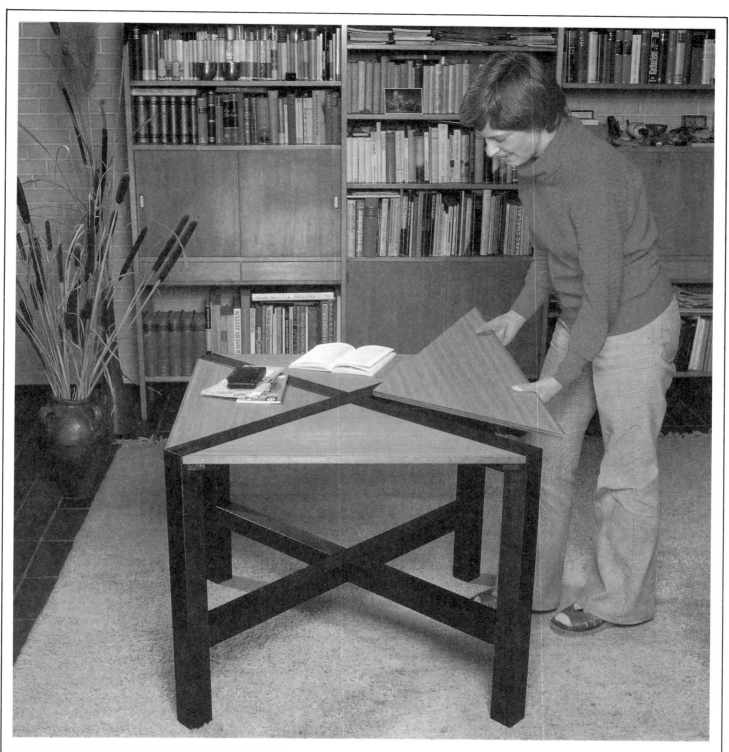

Turning the tables

A bite to eat followed by a few hands of cards is always a pleasant way to spend an evening. Here's a novel idea for a table that will fit the bill admirably. Just flip over the four small tops and there ready to go is a tailor-made card table for an evening's entertainment.

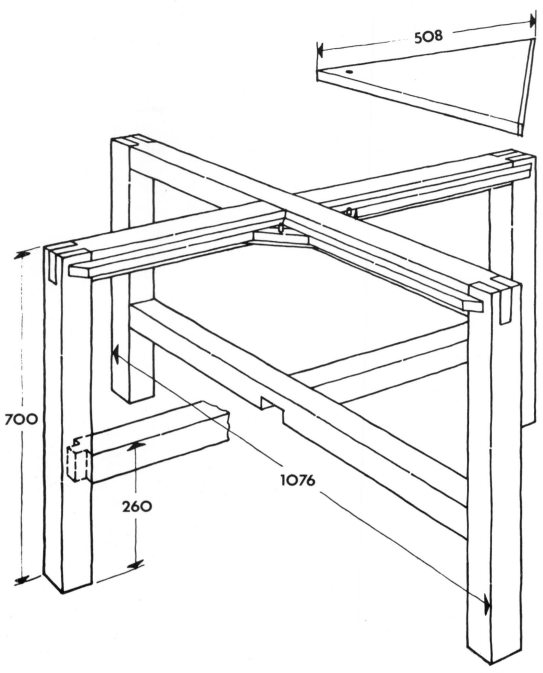

508

700

260

1076

IT TAKES just a second or two to convert this attractive living room table into a practical card table. The top consists of four triangular pieces which are removed and reversed to their felt side. The other side of the top has a mahogany veneer, and the rest of the table, including the legs and supports, is made from pine stained black. For an experienced do-it-yourself carpenter, this table is a piece to be really proud of, and the whole family, whether they play cards or not, will make great use of it.

Firstly you need four 16mm thick triangular pieces of plywood (we used mahogany, as used in boat-building) with sides 701mm and 499mm long respectively. You will also need well-seasoned squared timber, 57mm by

57mm, and some small strips of mahogany, 18mm by 7mm to finish the edges of the top pieces, and a few more strips for supports, as well as 6mm wooden dowels.

The dimension and methods given for the table are the ones we chose to use but they are by no means essential or binding; for example there are many types of man-made boards from which the top can be made and these come in various thicknesses. Readers who use thicker or thinner board will need to set the supports accordingly. Similarly some may not like the endgrain showing on the tops of the legs whilst others may find it attractive. This of course can easily be changed by using a mortise and tenon joint.

1. First cut a halving joint in each of the cross member diagonals. This must be done with a considerable degree of accuracy since any movement at all at these points would affect the stability and the fit of the top.

2. Step two in forming the joint is to cut away the waste with the chisel. Note in the photograph that a series of cuts has been made to allow for easy removal of the waste without the risk of damage to the rail.

3. The finished halving joint. The fit here is of great importance and it is worth spending some time to ensure that it is satisfactory. This same process is repeated for the lower of the two rails.

4. When cutting the joints for the legs and rails be sure to mark the waste areas very clearly. Many a good job has been spoiled by the simple omission of the waste marks and the removal of the wrong pieces.

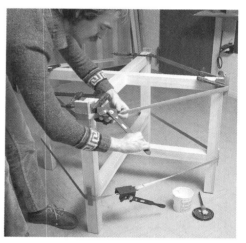

5. The lower rails are fitted to the legs using a true mortise and tenon joint and not the bridle joint as is used for the tops. Again care is needed to ensure that these are a good fit and that the whole structure is stable.

6. The photograph shows a detail of the method that we chose for the clamping up process. Note that the pressure is applied in two directions simultaneously. The joint is cleaned up with a plane later.

7. Here we see a full view of the clamping process with the total pressure being applied to the structure. Readers without these types of cramps will find that making up an ordinary Spanish windlass is equally effective.

8. Detail of the finished top joint after it has been cleaned up with the plane and glasspaper. Remember these joints are fully visible and if well executed will enhance the look of the project considerably.

9. The supports for the table tops are now fixed into position. Note the small angled piece with the dowel inserted. This is used to locate into a mating hole in each of the four table top sections to hold them in position.

10. Having cut and covered the table tops the time has come to fit them. For the sake of a neat appearance a small mahogany bead or lipping is fitted to the outside edge. These can be either screwed or glued.

Bureau in yew

THE COMMISSION for this desk came about through an article in a national paper about my work, after which I received a number of letters. One was from a gentleman who was looking for a piece of 'writing furniture' as he described it. He said that 'although I would prefer a desk, my present small house limits the available space, therefore I am thinking of something in the bureau style'. Lack of space is of course a common problem nowadays, and it was very interesting for me to work on designing a small modern version of a piece which has such a long history.

Initially we discussed possibilities and arrived at dimensions of not more that 3' wide and 1'6in. deep when closed. I think this is about the minimum practical size for this sort of piece. I sketched out ideas of both the upright style of secretaire and sloping fronted bureau, but it was the latter which my customer seemed to favour.

I worked on the idea of combining two contrasting timbers, as a way in which to provide a modern effect, and after some discussion we decided on yew for the main timber, with a small amount of the much darker wenge which is almost black in colour. When combining two different timbers in this way I feel it is generally important to have one predominant one with just a small amount of the other, and here I used the wenge only for the handles, and

the plinth and feet.

I worked out the base first. There are four solid blocks, one at each corner, in wenge, with a rectangular wenge framework between these and the main carcase, with spacers between each to lighten the effect.

Having the principal dimensions fixed the main shape of the carcase was fairly straightforward. 3 large drawers of equal dimensions under the writing surface were indicated, the fronts of these fitting inside the carcase. I considered the possibility of rebating the fall flap over the carcase cheeks as this can make hingeing easier, but this did not look right with the drawer fronts, so I inset it between the cheeks.

It is essential to preserve an uninterrupted writing surface, and I was concerned that a framed up construction using solid timber would provide a groove between frame and panel in just the wrong place for writing in such a small desk, so it seemed a good opportunity for veneering. $\frac{1}{4}$in. blockboard was used lipped and veneered on both sides, using matched veneers and continuing these straight through to the back. Yew veneer is not easy to lay, as it buckles, and damping and pressing was necessary beforehand. I also thought blockboard would solve the likely problems with stability in such a large unsupported area as the fall.

The designer of this attractive desk was commissioned to produce a piece of 'writing furniture . . . in the bureau style' but suitable for the space limitations of a small house.

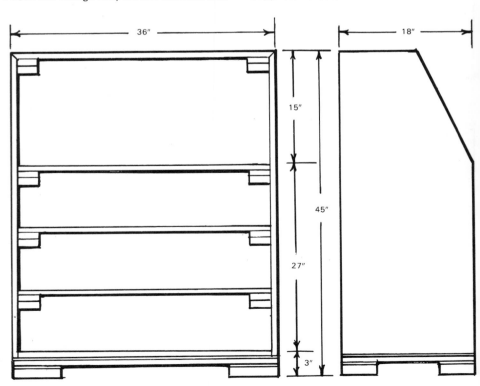

1. Marking out is the first job and we begin with the rail positions of the bureau.

2. Cut mitre in the top and sides and cut the slot for the plywood tongue. Rebate edge and sides for top.

3. Fit the joints and glue up with the cross rails, only making sure that all is square.

4. The top front rail with the moulded curve for the fall swing. Also shown is an oak drawer kicker.

5. The next step is to glue on the top, making sure that the pressure is applied in both directions.

6. For the writing surface, cut the blockboard to size and lip and clean up carefully.

7. Mitre the corners of the rectangular frame with stopped slots for the tongue.

8. Fix the frame to the base rails with screws and spacers and fix feet, again with spacers.

9. Prepare the strip for the handles and rout out the slots for the hand grips as shown.

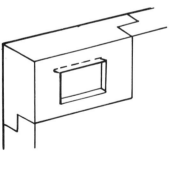

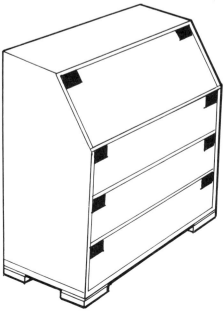

Of course the fall of the writing surface has to be level with the back part when it is open, and with relatively thin material like this, pivot hinges seemed the best solution. This requires an additional bearer rail under the flap, and this must be carefully shaped to receive the swing of the fall.

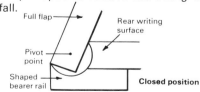

Full flap — Rear writing surface
Pivot point
Shaped bearer rail — **Closed position**

Very accurate marking out is required to position the pivot hinges in exactly the right place to cause the surface to be both level, and with a minimum gap between the two parts when open, and flush with the front rail when closed. Brass stays are added to take the main weight.

The handles were an area where there seemed to be a miriad of possibilities, but it took me a long time to design what I felt would look right. I wanted to keep the lines simple, and the amount of wenge showing a fairly small proportion of the whole. I wanted the handles more or less flush, and certainly not knobs as the whole piece was rather angular in conception. I thought about bands across the top of the drawers, stripes across the middle, and recessed pulls. The drawer fronts being only $\frac{1}{2}$in. was the main limitation of any let in handle.

Since the piece is relatively narrow it is possible to have the handles at the corners, and still be able to open the drawers comfortably and this is what I decided upon. Even having this decision, and having worked out the right sort of size to make them both for use and appearance, there was still several ways of constructing these handles. I wanted them flush if possible, but also had to consider the jointing in of the drawer sides—traditional dovetail method. In the end I made several samples of handles when I had actually got to this stage in the construction, and finally produced this:

The dovetails were then spaced to accommodate this, the top two made

10. The slots are first cut out square, and then worked to the profile shown with the undercut tops.

11. The lower edge of the handles is bevelled to the dotted line shown in the drawing.

12. The handles are glued in position on the corners as shown, note the block to avoid bruising.

13. On the top internal section, cut the base to width and fit inside carcase. Rout the housings for uprights.

14. Cut out the tops of the divisions for two rails. Drill and countersink for attaching to the main top.

15. Glue up the complete pigeon-hole section as shown, and when cleaned up fit it to the carcase.

16. Make up the two small drawers for the central partition, dovetailed in the normal manner.

17. The sides of the drawers are grooved out for the runners to save space.

18. Fit the brass stays for the fall front, having first carefully determined both open and closed positions.

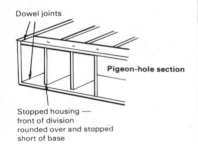

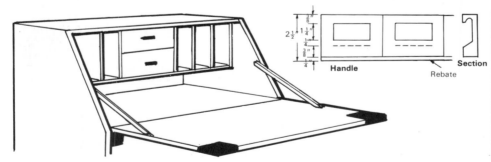

Dowel joints

Pigeon-hole section

Stopped housing — front of division rounded over and stopped short of base

Handle

Section

Rebate

smaller and halved in depth which produced an effect both decorative and practical.

Inside the fall there was to be the usual pigeon holes and small drawers. Here too there is much scope for variation. Because the piece was small I decided to make this as a separate unit and pick it up off the surface to allow the whole writing area to be used. I made two small central drawers flanked by 3 pigeon holes on either side. This section is slot screwed through the top rails to the top. Care should be taken that the depth of this section should not interfere with the closing of the fall stays. The small drawers are side hung.

This is quite a complicated piece of furniture to make, but individuals could make various modifications to suit their own capacity and equipment. It is important that accuracy and attention to detail is preserved, but if achieved this should make what I set out to produce—an heirloom for the future, an aim in which I hope I have succeeded, since my customer's last letter tells me that his grandsons are already debating eventual ownership!

CUTTING LIST

Sides	2 off	42 by 18 in. $\frac{13}{16}$ in.			yew
Top	1 off	36 by 11 in. $\frac{13}{16}$ in.			yew
Rails	4 off	35 by 2 in. $\frac{13}{16}$ in.			yew
Rails	4 off	35 by 2$\frac{1}{2}$in. $\frac{13}{16}$ in.			yew
Drawer fronts	3 off	34$\frac{1}{2}$ by 8 in. $\frac{13}{16}$ in.			yew

Pigeon-hole section

Base	1 off	34$\frac{1}{2}$ by 9 in. by $\frac{1}{2}$in.			yew
Sides and central division	3 off	9 by 9 in. by $\frac{1}{2}$in.			yew
Pigeon-hole division	4 off	9 by 8$\frac{1}{2}$in. by $\frac{1}{2}$in.			yew
Rails	2 off	34 by 1$\frac{1}{2}$in. by $\frac{1}{4}$in.			yew
Drawer fronts	2 off	8$\frac{1}{2}$ by 4$\frac{1}{4}$in. by $\frac{1}{2}$in.			yew
Feet	4 off	7 by 5 by 2in.			wenge
Frame	2 off	36 by 3 by $\frac{13}{16}$in.			wenge
Frame	2 off	18 by 3 by $\frac{13}{16}$in.			wenge
Handles	8 off	3$\frac{3}{4}$ by 2$\frac{1}{2}$ by $\frac{13}{16}$ in.			wenge

$\frac{3}{4}$in. blockboard with 1" width yew lippings to make 1 piece 34$\frac{1}{2}$ by 14$\frac{1}{4}$ and 1 piece 34$\frac{1}{2}$ by 16$\frac{1}{4}$in.

Drawers

Runners	8 off	14 by 1$\frac{1}{2}$ by $\frac{13}{16}$ in.			oak
Sides	6 off	16 by 8 by $\frac{5}{16}$in.			
Backs	3 off	34$\frac{1}{2}$ by 7 by $\frac{5}{16}$in.			
Base	3 off	34 by 15$\frac{1}{2}$ by $\frac{1}{4}$in.			
Back	41 by 34$\frac{1}{2}$ by $\frac{1}{4}$in. birch-faced ply				

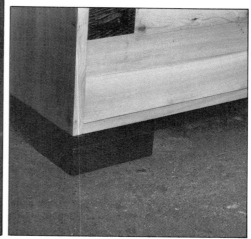

Left: a front view of the bureau showing the beautiful figuring of the yew on the hinged flap. The inset right shows the interesting contrast achieved by using the darker wenge in a sparing but determined manner.

Right: the inside of the bureau showing detail of the writing surface, drawers and pigeon holes traditionally found in writing furniture.

Puzzle pig

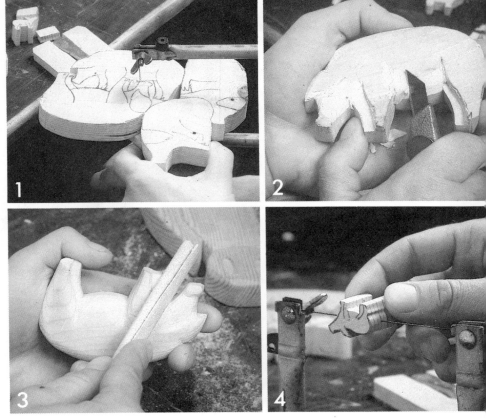

Two things that kids really love are puzzles and animals. Here we combine the two in a charming little project which would make an ideal present. Softwood or hardwood will do or even a mixture of both for some interesting contrasts.

LAY A SHEET of tracing paper over the large photograph of the finished puzzle and reproduce it, overlaid with 10 × 10mm grid. The design can then be easily transferred to the wood and reproduced in any size. Our original is about twice the size of the photograph; so you only need to double the distance between the lines on the grid.

1. After the design has been transferred to the wood (25mm pine) cut out the individual pigs with a fretsaw as shown.

2. Now the pigs can be carved to shape with a knife or chisel. The many edges and corners can be cut cleanly with a milling cutter with a drill and flexible drive.

3. The cut-out shapes should be carefully sanded until they are nice and smooth.

4. The small pigs are cut through the middle to make two of each.

5. Finally the large pig should be backed with a sheet of plywood to which it is screwed or glued. The whole puzzle is then sealed with wax or polyurethane to bring out the grain and to prevent it picking up dirt from sticky fingers.

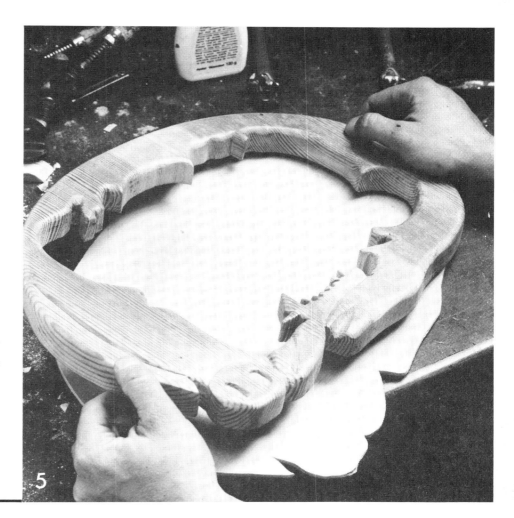

Sideboard from Sweden

Simple pine furniture has grown in popularity enormously in Britain in the last twenty years and many people who previously found it too basic have been won over by its quiet charm and subtlety.

THIS SIMPLE Swedish design for a rustic sideboard is made almost entirely from 16mm pine tongue and groove boarding. The back and the drawer bottoms however are made from 3mm plywood and the drawer supports and runners again in pine.

The back is let in by the simple expedient of cutting away half a groove on the back edges of the boards. In the case of the doors, shelves, top and headboard

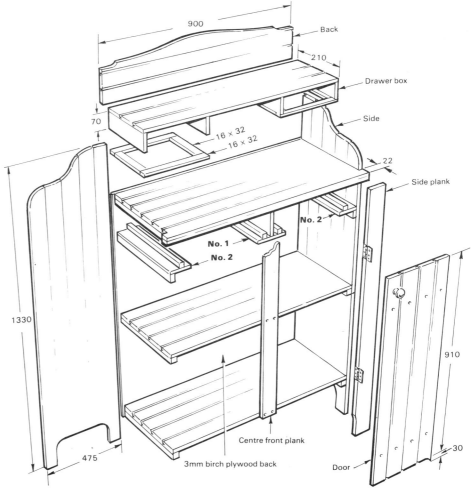

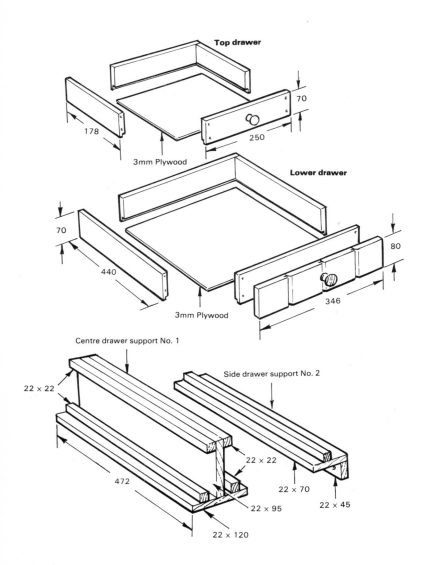

Top drawer

70

178

250

3mm Plywood

Lower drawer

70

80

440

346

3mm Plywood

Centre drawer support No. 1

22 × 22

Side drawer support No. 2

22 × 22

472

22 × 70

22 × 95

22 × 45

22 × 120

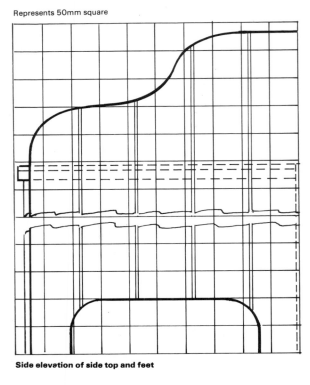

Represents 50mm square

Side elevation of side top and feet

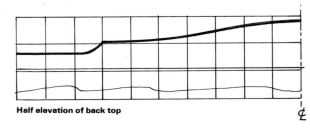

Half elevation of back top

℄

where several boards are joined together these are made up oversize and cut down to correct dimensions later. In this way both the tongues and the grooves on the edges can be lost.

The shaping of the sides and headboard is a simple matter of scaling up a templet from the drawing, marking onto the timber and running around the profile with a jigsaw after the boards are assembled.

In the case of the two main drawers the finish on the front is vertical tongue and groove and it might be just as well to make the doors oversize by just over 80mm and cut the tops of them to give an 80mm offcut which will match up perfectly. The main bodies of all the drawers can be simple butt joints dowelled together. Through dowels on the small top drawers give a decorative effect. Both the doors and the sides of the unit have horizontal battens affixed which not only give additional strength but in the case of the sides serve as positions for the shelves and the drawer runners. These are screwed and glued in position before the unit is assembled. On the face of the unit there are three vertical boards, one either side from which to hang the doors and a centre one which carries the turn buttons for closing them. The result of fitting these verticals is to make it necessary to offset the drawer runners to enable sufficient clearance. Reference to the drawings should make this perfectly clear.

The runners for the top drawers consist of two rectangular frames made up slightly larger than the drawer bottoms (see photograph), and these sit on the main surface of the unit. The actual size is not critical but the visible overlap does give a rather nice decorative effect. On this particular piece the doors are hung with $1\frac{1}{2}$in. brass butts although a more decorative surface fixing hinge could be used to good effect. Similarly the plain turned wooden knobs on the drawers could be replaced with brass knobs or handles if preferred.

A good idea with the finishing is to sand up each of the sections of jointed board before assembly, in this way you can always work on the flat and save a lot of effort. It also ensures that you get right into the corners which gives a professional finish. Two or three coats of polyurethane varnish flatted between coats will give a lasting finish and bring out the colour of the wood.

Incidentally before starting work it's a good idea to store the timber on a flat surface in the house for two to three weeks to enable it to lose the moisture it picks up in the outside air.

Oval dining table in oak

A table designed to cater for
two people at most times and
yet be capable of seating six.

I had been asked to design and make an oval
table to stand in a triangle bay window,
structured in such a way that it could seat
four, or occasionally six, but would normally
only have two people at it. However both of
them wanted to be able to see out of the
window, be near enough together to pass
the marmalade, but with sufficient room to
each read a copy of *The Times*. This table is
the result of that brief.

Basically when you look at the problem,
what it boils down to is the position of the
legs. Normally with an oval table one
would expect to have one person sitting at
each end of the major axis, and for a four
seater the remaining two at each end of
the minor one. But in this case it was
necessary for the people to be placed on
the 'diagonals' as shown in drawing 1.

This meant that the legs have to go on

the axes, as it is not a very large table and
a central pedestal is not practical. From a
visual and practical point of view I wanted
to keep the legs in from the edge, but the
overhang could not be too great or the
stability would be impaired. In my original
design I had 100mm overhang on each,
but later reduced this to 60 in the actual
making of the piece, and the result is certainly very stable.

I used English oak to make the table,
and was fortunate enough to get some
beautiful boards for the top. These were
quarter sawn so had the dramatic
medullary ray figure associated with oak,
but also they were a mixture of light and
brown oak—in the same piece that is. The
dark appeared as a wide streak up the
centre of the tree, and I arranged the timber so that this ran up the centre of the
table top which is very effective. There are
three planks cut into six pieces to make
the top, and I spent hours arranging and
rearranging them to work out the best
combination.

I wanted to keep the design solid but
simple and not too heavy looking. The top
has a plain rounded edge, and this is
echoed on the legs which are rounded
over on the outer corners. The customer
specified a base rail sufficiently high off
the ground that it would not be used as a
foot rail. (They live near a river in Ireland
and have enough mud in the house as it is,
without extra being scraped off on the
table!) Also it seemed a good idea to have

Dwg. 1. Design requirements

space to sweep underneath it. The vertical slats strengthen the base rails and are arranged in two groups of three on the long axis, two on the short. The diagonal bearers under the top make the base framework rigid, and the battens are slot screwed to the top to keep it flat.

Start by marking out and preparing the timber, getting it all straight, flat and to the correct thickness. All the components of the underframe can then be cut to width.

The pieces to make up the top are straight edged and glued up. If you trust your edging, gluing and sash cramps then a butt joint should be adequate. Otherwise dowels may be necessary, but position them carefully so that they will not reappear when the top is cut to shape.

To mark out an ellipse of the correct shape and size (if you are not already acquainted with this geometry) I find the pin and string method easiest. This method is shown in drawing 2. Mark out the long and short axes at rightangles to each other. The length should be marked A-B, the width C-D. Where these cross (i.e. the centre of the table) is E. Measure the length A-E, and draw an arc of this length, centred on C, to cut A-B at F G. Thus C-F and C-G are the same length as A-E.

If you have not done this before, it is really nothing like as complicated as it sounds!

You then knock in three panel pins part way at F, G and C. Tie a piece of string tightly around them, remove the pin at C and replace it with a pencil (photo 1). Move the pencil along, keeping the string taut, and around the other two pins, and the ellipse is drawn. It is advisable to strain the string first as otherwise it may become stretched.

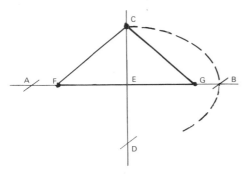

Dwg. 2. Drawing an ellipse

If you are working directly onto the table top you will want to do this on the underneath or the pin holes will show. Alternatively you may wish to make a templet and then draw round it onto the timber. The shape may then be cut out with a jigsaw and cleaned up by hand, or it can be cut with a router. In this case a plywood templet of a quarter of the whole is made, sufficiently smaller to accommodate the router bush, and a small radius grooving cutter is used to cut the shape (photo 2). This reduces the amount of cleaning up necessary, and after it is done the rounded edge may be formed with the correct router cutter, or by hand.

1. Marking out the ellipse with string and pencil technique.

2. A quarter templet used as a router guide.

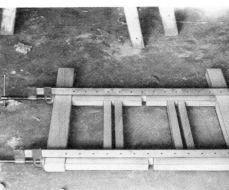

3. Radiusing the outer corners of the legs.

4. Underframe components sized and tenoned.

5. Start by assembling the short leg frame.

6. Joints to accept diagonals and battens.

7. Adding the long rails and vertical struts.

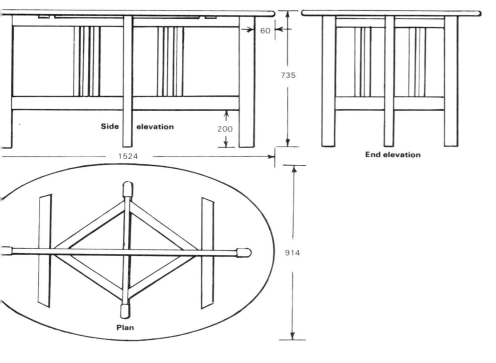

Side elevation

60

735

200

End elevation

1524

914

Plan

Cutting List

Top	1 off	1524 by 914 by 30mm
Legs	4 off	705 by 75 by 45mm
Short top rail	1 off	684 by 65 by 32mm
Short base rail	1 off	684 by 75 by 32mm
Long top rail	1 off	1294 by 65 by 32mm
Long base rail	1 off	1294 by 75 by 32mm
Vertical struts	10 off	385 by 32 by 32mm
Diagonal bearers	4 off	510 by 50 by 32mm
Battens	2 off	630 by 60 by 32mm

8. Adding the legs completes the frame.

9. Pieces drilled for slot screwing.

10. The completed underframe ready to receive the top.

Once all the cleaning up of this edge and of the surfaces is complete the top is ready for finishing.

Construction of the underframe is started with the legs. These should be already cut to width, and may now be cut to a length of 705mm. Two mortises, 16mm wide, 20 deep, are made on the inside face of each leg positioned so that the top rail will be flush with the top and the bottom rail 200mm up from the floor. I generally use the router to take out the main waste and then finish with a chisel. The corners of the outer long edges are now rounded over, shown here using the router again (photo 3). The bottom of the legs should also be chamfered to avoid any breaking out.

The cross rails are now cut to length and tenons made on each end and fitted to the leg mortises. A housed halving joint is cut in the centre of each rail where they cross each other. These must be made so that the direction of fitting is top long rail downwards onto top short rail to facilitate gluing. Following this the mortises for the vertical 'struts' are carefully marked out and cut 20mm square and 10 deep. The verticals are then cut to length and tenoned to fit (photo 4). Note that the mortises here have been masked ready for lacquering. All these components may now be cleaned up, and the long edges slightly chamfered. It is easier to do the finishing and polishing at this stage as long as care is taken to leave the joint areas free.

Start by gluing the short rails to their four verticals, then when this is dry glue two legs onto this short frame (photo 5).

The position of the diagonals may now be marked out onto the long and short top rails, and the two cross battens onto the long rails. These are all half jointed into position, and may now be cut (photo 6). The joint in the short rail could be cut before gluing up, but you may find it easier at the later stage as the long rail can be placed in position temporarily to obtain the correct position and angle.

For the next gluing operation start by gluing and placing the long base rail into the short base rail, then the six verticals, and finally drop the top rail on and cramp. After this has dried the two remaining legs may be glued on (photo 8).

The angle for the end of the diagonal top members can be marked from the actual framework at this point, and after cutting to length they are half jointed at the end and drilled for slot screwing to the top at the centre axis point.

The battens are cut at an angle at the ends (on plan), rounded over, and half jointed in the middle. They are also slot screwed for fixing to the top (photo 9).

Clean up, lacquer, and glue on diagonals with G cramps. Slot the battens into place and turn the whole underframe upside down onto the underneath of the top. Screw the battens to the top and fix the base on by screwing through the diagonal bearers. If using oak be sure to use brass screws as the tannic acid corrodes steel.

Cabinet decisions

Flexibility in furniture is a trend which is increasingly coming to the forefront in the minds of the public and consequently in design. The basic unit or "module" from which various designs can be made up is one form of this phenomenon as indeed was the divan bed which appeared so many years ago. This design is a basic chest or cabinet which is as much at home storing the kid's toys as it is holding exotic cocktails. It is pleasant to look at, easy on the pocket and highly adaptable.

MODERN FURNITURE tends increasingly to be multi-purpose and easily modified. Often a piece has to double as a chest or storage cabinet, or maybe a drinks cabinet or music unit. To this end designs have become deceptively simple requiring the minimum of functional specialisation. This multiplicity of purpose has lead to clean uncluttered lines and uncomplicated construction.

This cabinet is a good example of hybrid furniture and can be used as a bar, chest or music centre according to your needs. In the dining room it would come in handy for storing tablecloths and cutlery to save time constantly running to the kitchen. Alternatively in the kiddies bedroom it could be painted in bright colours and used as a toy cupboard. With a mirror fitted inside one of the lids it would make an ideal beauty cupboard in a lady's bedroom where it could be used for cosmetics and the storage of hair dryers and all the vast array of beauty aids and oddments.

The cut out handles of the drawers add much to the design result but it comes off best if light coloured timber is used. A different veneer such as mahogany or cherry will not give the same dramatic result. In the case of painting, the colour will determine the effect with the lighter shades giving a more pleasing finish.

So, why not have a crack at this "jack of all trades" and make a really flexible piece of furniture to decorate your home. Remember, somebody in the house will always find a use for it and you may find yourself having to make more than one to satisy the family.

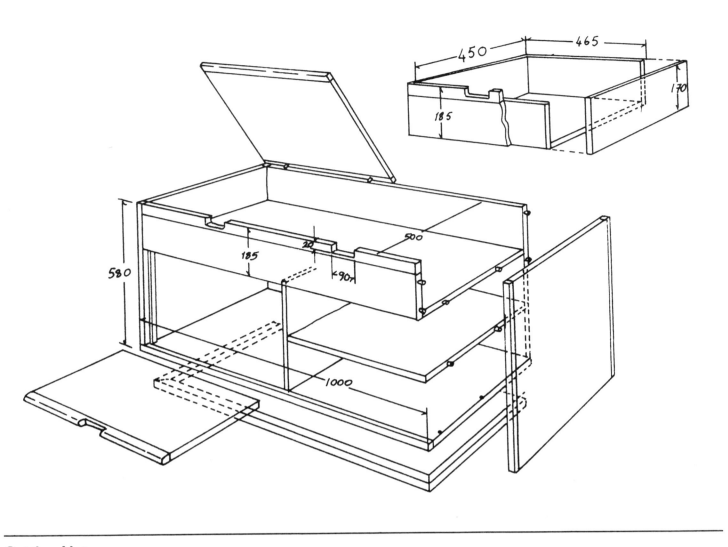

Cutting List

5 ply oak/mahogany 19mm

2 side walls	462mm by 562mm
1 rear wall	962mm by 562mm
1 bottom	1000mm by 462mm
2 lids (top)	500mm by 462mm
1 screen	962mm by 156mm
2 drawer screens	480mm by 156mm
1 lid (door)	480mm by 345mm
1 base	950mm by 25mm
2 base pieces	450mm by 25mm

Strips of oak

19mm by 30mm — roughly 3·5 running meters

19mm by 19mm — roughly 5·5 running meters

19 mm by 5mm — roughly 2 running meters

Guide and fixing strips

Small material

Roughly 75 wooden dowels 8mm
4 Hinges 12mm
2 Supports for lids
1 Lid holder for bottom cupboard
Glue, nails, screws for base.

16mm mahogany

1 middle bottom	962mm by 462mm
1 middle wall	462mm by 375mm
1 running bottom	462mm by 470mm
2 drawer bottoms	420mm by 435mm
4 drawer sides	452mm by 170mm
2 drawer backs	435mm by 170mm
2 drawer fronts (inside)	435mm by 130mm

Left: used as a cocktail cabinet.

Right: to store cutlery and linen.

1. The oak lippings can be cut on a circular saw or perhaps a milling machine. Remember to take small cuts not big hefty ones.

2. For the handle openings first drill two 10mm holes and cut out to shape with a jig-saw as shown. Note material well cramped up.

3. Clean up the handle opening as shown with glasspaper wrapped around a piece of scrap material or with a sanding block.

4. The oak strip will be fitted to the drawer fronts and cupboard with dowel, accuracy at all stages of this procedure is essential. In this case we found it easier to fit the dowels into the carcase first and set the strip to it.

5. For the exposed edges iron-on strip veneer was used. This is an easy operation if you remember to have the iron hot and use the tip for the work.

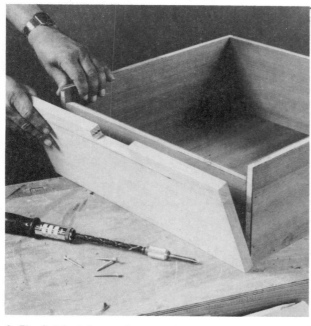

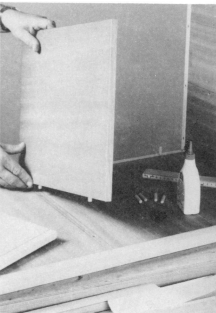

6. The finished drawer front can be fixed with screws, nails or dowels whichever you prefer. Remember of course to fix from behind in any event.

7. The bottom of the chest need only be chipboard or the like, preferably 30mm thick and fixed with screws.

8. The holes in the sides of the unit must be accurately positioned if trouble in the assembly stage is to be avoided.

9. The lid supports or stays can be purchased from almost any hardware shops but are all basically the same as that shown here.

10. The bottom cupboard support shown here is again fairly typical of the types or offer. A brake or damping system is important.

11. The choice of hinges is wide but we used this type because they are neat, inconspicuous, and easy for the amateur to fit correctly.

1

Assembly Sequence

1. The rear wall
2. The side wall fitted.
3. The short centre bottom.
4. The long centre bottom.
5. The dividing wall and the front.
6. The second side wall now fitted.
7. The base and plinth.

2

3

4

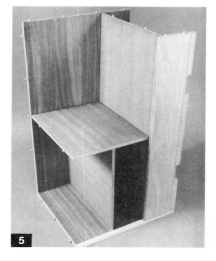
5

6

7

Child's convertible

Whether it's play time or food time, this versatile child's chair quickly converts to suit all occasions. It can be used as a high chair, a rocker or a push-along fun toy. It is simple to change it to the different positions locking the cogwheels in place, and the locking safety 'wedges' through the adjusting pegs ensure that your child cannot trap his or her fingers in the mechanism.

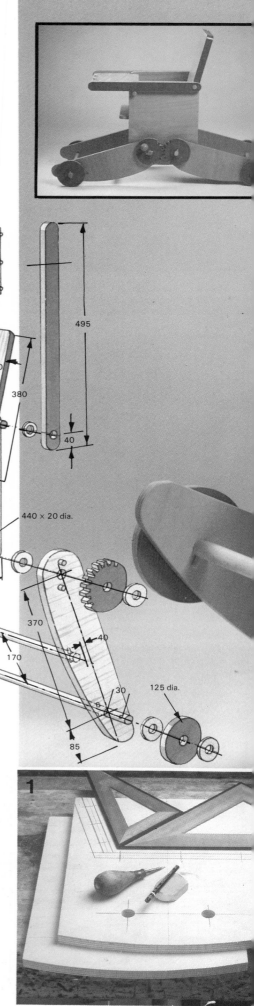

WHILST this rather unusual piece of furniture is novel in its design, it is in fact constructed using techniques from the nineteenth century. The interlocking cog wheels ensure uniform action and easy adjustment allowing the chair to be used as a high chair, a rocking chair and a chair on wheels. The principle material used is 15mm plywood which is strong enough to ensure safety in terms of wear and stress on bearing parts and is durable enough to stand up to the use of several generations of children.

Set in its lowest position, the curved legs and the bottom of the chair sides become a continuous curve allowing any youngster to rock away to his heart's content without danger of tipping forwards or backwards, as the wheels form a safety stop to limit the rocking action. In the middle position the legs are raised clear of the floor with the wheels down, and your youngster can push himself or herself around, piloting the chair by pushing with the feet. Finally, when playtime is over and it's time for the more serious business of eating, a further adjustment will raise the young feet clear of the floor to the correct height for joining the rest of the family at the table.

These adjustments are made possible by the two large wooden cogwheels which are glued firmly to the rockers and also fixed with dowels. These ensure that the legs/rockers are moved simultaneously and offer easy and safe adjustment. To secure the seat in the right position, two round pegs with knobs on the end are fitted through a hole in each cogwheel and through one of the three corresponding holes in the chair sides. They are further secured on the inside with wedges so that there is no risk of the pegs coming loose and the child getting his fingers caught in the mechanism.

The 15mm ply used in the construction is a very durable material and apart from being able to stand up to all the knocks and bangs it will receive, it is particularly suitable for the cogwheels giving greater strength to the teeth than is possible with the short grain of solid timber.

Axles and cross bars are made from 20mm diameter beech dowel, with the retaining peg and dowel joints being of the same material but with smaller diameter.

When fitting the dowel axles, check carefully their true size as it is important to

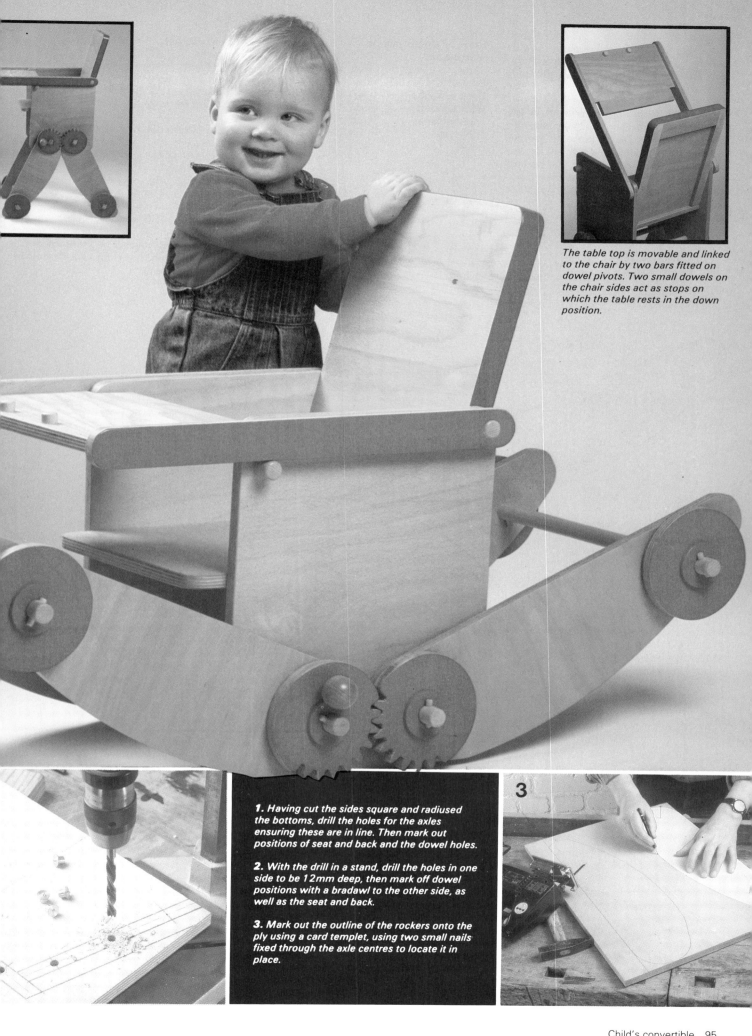

The table top is movable and linked to the chair by two bars fitted on dowel pivots. Two small dowels on the chair sides act as stops on which the table rests in the down position.

1. Having cut the sides square and radiused the bottoms, drill the holes for the axles ensuring these are in line. Then mark out positions of seat and back and the dowel holes.

2. With the drill in a stand, drill the holes in one side to be 12mm deep, then mark off dowel positions with a bradawl to the other side, as well as the seat and back.

3. Mark out the outline of the rockers onto the ply using a card templet, using two small nails fixed through the axle centres to locate it in place.

have a good fit where they have to be glued, as for instance into the cogwheels, and a slightly free fit where parts have to revolve, as with the wheels. If necessary, you can enlarge the holes to give a freer fit with a half-round file or a roll of glasspaper.

The most important components of the chair are the cogwheels. These must be made exactly in accordance with the drawing and glued and dowelled to the leg/rockers. Take great care in making and cutting these, and check that they function correctly in a mock-up situation before fixing to the chair, as the safety of the chair and your child depends upon the teeth biting straight and cleanly into each other.

Materials

From 15mm plywood

Side pieces	2 off 390 by	310mm
Seat	1 off 315 by	280mm
Backrest	1 off 380 by	280mm
Back supports	2 off 380 by	30mm
Back support	1 off 220 by	60mm
Legs/rockers	4 off 510 by	150mm
Table top	1 off 318 by	210mm
Table side bars	2 off 495 by	40mm
Cogwheels	4 off 125mm dia.	

From 4mm plywood

Washers for wheels	16 off	50mm dia.
Washers for table	2 off	35mm dia.

From 20mm dia. dowel

Wheel axles	2 off	448mm
Cogwheel axles	2 off	440mm
Rocker struts	2 off	355mm
Chair body strut	1 off	305mm
Table axle and stops	4 off	35mm

Also required: 2 off 3mm dia. wooden knobs; 16mm dia. dowel for table retaining stops and holding pegs; 8mm dowel for joints; 6mm dowel for wheel retainers etc through axles.

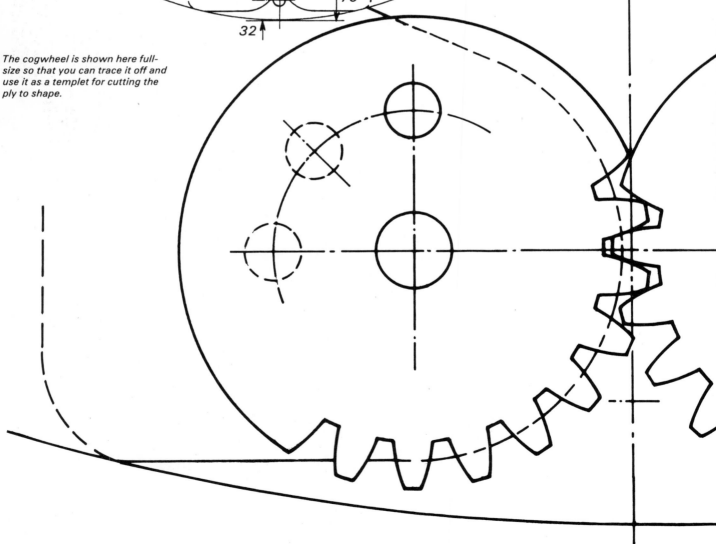

The radius to the underside of the base and the rockers must be made the same to ensure a smooth rocking action. Dimensions show axle and strut positions.

The cogwheel is shown here full-size so that you can trace it off and use it as a templet for cutting the ply to shape.

560

57 57

70

32

4. After fretsawing the rockers to shape, drill the axle holes. A short length of dowel can be knocked through to hold them together for smoothing the edges.

5. With the axles cut to length, hold them in a vice to drill the holes for the safety pegs which are made from 5mm dia. beech.

6. Trace the cogwheel diagram several times onto paper, then glue this onto the ply. Cut the circular form roughly with a compass saw, drill the axle holes exactly and drill holes to form the gullets of the teeth.

7. Wheels are sanded until exactly round by running them round on an auxiliary axle fixed to the bench in front of a disc sander. Teeth are then cut with a fretsaw.

8. The cogwheel must bite cleanly so that the legs move together without sticking. Set them up on one side piece and work over them with a file where necessary.

9. A trial assembly will show if all the pieces fit together cleanly. At this stage mark the positions of the cogwheels on the rockers to ensure correct functioning.

10. Wooden pegs with safety 'wedges' are made to hold the rockers in the right position. Note that the two front cogwheels have only one hole each.

A whale of a time

These exciting toy boxes turn tidying-up into child's play. At the end of the day, teddies, bunnies and other toys simply disappear inside the whale for a cosy night.

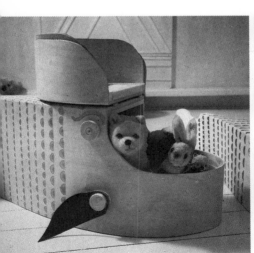

All tucked up and ready for bed the toys are quite happy to spend the night inside a friendly whale. There's bags of room for everybody so the playroom will be left nice and tidy.

Two sturdy hinges hold the whale's mouth in place. The mouth is cut after the assembly to ensure correct fitting, and when folded back it forms a play seat for the children.

The tail fins can be cut from thick leather make them flexible, or from solid timber a carved into shape and glued in place. Do ma sure all the edges are well smoothed over.

TIDINESS is a matter of opinion. Some people believe that tidiness is essential and a way of life, while others dismiss tidiness fanatics as being too lazy to look for things. Since young children usually fall into the latter category, we have designed these whale toy boxes with them in mind. As they are both a toy and a container for toys, they combine usefulness with pleasure.

The basic material for the whales is ⁎mm thick exterior grade plywood, or cardboard which should first be shaped by laying the two sides pieces in the bath for a few hours. Soaking makes the wood more pliable, so that the side pieces can be bent into shape and secured with a 20 degree wooden wedge between the ends. The pieces are then left overnight to dry out, and by the following day they will have taken the correct shape yet will still be flexible enough for the shape of the sides to be corrected. The body is given its stability when the top and bottom pieces are joined to the sides. The container is made more solid by vertical battens reinforcing the sides. Top and bottom pieces are cut from 10mm thick plywood and are fitted to the side walls; the shape of the sides determines the final shape of the fish. As the wooden whales are intended as toys, all edges should be carefully rounded off and all surfaces should be sanded smooth. The number of fish you build is up to you, but as whales are extremely sociable creatures, you should make at least two. Since whales are creatures with a personality of their own, they should look different from one another. This can be done by making them in different sizes, with different fins and different-coloured painted scales.

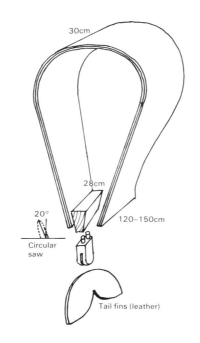

The bent sides of the large fish are 30cm wide. The 20 degree wooden wedge cut on the circular saw has a depth of only 28cm because the top and bottom pieces of the whale cut from 10mm thick ply are fitted over it to come flush with the top surface.

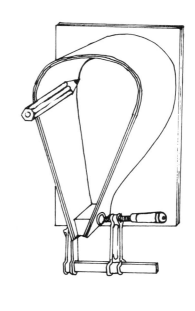

The shape of the plywood top and bottom pieces (placed one above the other) is traced out directly from the bent and dried plywood side pieces as shown. These are glued in place only when the sides are dry.

MATERIALS

Plywood, 4mm thick: 1 piece 300mm wide, 120–150cm long (large fish)
1 piece 200mm wide, 120–150cm long (small fish)
Plywood, 10mm thick: 4 pieces 400mm wide, 700mm long (top and bottom)
Small piece of dowel for eyes, 50mm in diameter
1 pine plank 250 × 180 × 20mm
4m × 20 × 20mm timber
1m × 20 × 50mm timber
Squared timber 50 × 50mm, 400mm long
Thick sole leather for tail fins, paint, masking tape, nails, white PVA glue.

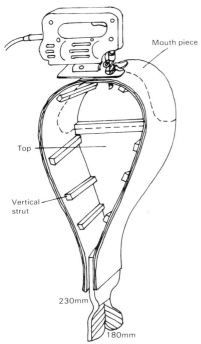

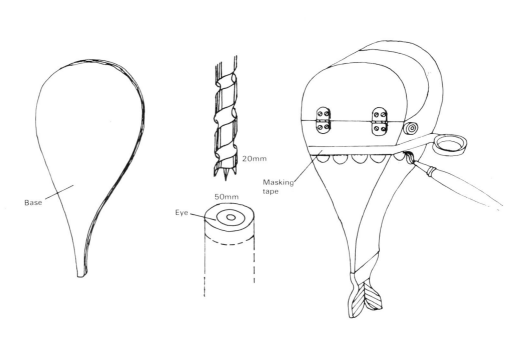

Using a jigsaw the mouthpiece is cut directly from the assembled body. It's very important to mark the strut which takes the hinges on the surface to enable you to make a straight cut along the centre (dotted line).

The eyes are made from pieces of dowel 50mm in diameter. Alternatively they can be cut with a hole saw or something similar. Drill a 20mm hole in the centre for good effect.

Use masking tape to line up the scales on the fish. Make sure you paint the eyebrow line carefully so the whale looks friendly and not like an evil "Moby Dick".

Corner cabinets in pine

Broadly speaking all corner cabinets are the same shape but much imaginative variation can be achieved by using ornamental beadings or the addition of a door. Try out a few experiments for yourself using this basic carcase.

VERY FEW PIECES of furniture so readily enhance a room as a corner cabinet, especially when it contains attractive china or maybe a spray of flowers to set it off to its best advantage. In their various shapes and forms they have been with us since Georgian times sometimes reaching the status of works of art in themselves and at other times being merely functional pieces making the best use of space.

With the growing popularity of pine furniture and the ever present need to utilise space, we thought it might be a good time to look at the basic corner cupboard and to suggest three simple variations of the design. The timber chosen here is ordinary planed deal nominally 4 by 1in. (95 by 18mm) and this is planed up before use. This size is not critical but the greater the width of the material the less work there will be involved in gluing up; similarly it's as well to have the narrow sides in one piece for the sake of appearance. In this case we have settled for 86mm, as shown.

The bottom, top and centre shelf are made up from three boards glued and cramped together and when dry cut out to size as shown in photos 2 and 3. This is a simple operation in each case since the dimensions and the techniques are identical. Be sure to keep good square edges for fitting. The next step as shown in photo 3 is to assemble the main carcase and this entails simply cladding up the back of the cabinet and pinning on the facing boards as shown. Bearing in mind that the cladding on the back overlaps at the corner it should be remembered that one of the back walls will be wider than the other by the thickness of the timber used. Although the front faces are pinned as shown, the back cladding should be screwed and glued for strength. This really completes the assembly of the basic unit. It's as well to sand the shelf, top and bottom as well as the insides before assembly as this is much easier than doing it afterwards. The fitting of the shelf is simplicity itself since it sits

on two small battens fitted at the desired height inside the body or alternatively it could be dowelled from the back.

With this basic carcase to work from we have a choice of the three different units shown, or of course as many variations as your imagination will permit. The most obvious form of decoration will be to fit a form of pediment or ornamentation as shown, along with top and bottom lippings to give a clean finish. Another idea is of course to fit a door. The one shown here is in its simplest form with mitred corners dowelled together instead of the more sophisticated mortise and tenon joints. Each of the four sides must of course be rebated to take the glass. Take care when fitting the retaining beads not to break the glass by using a hammer held on its side as shown. Further decorative beading may be added. Brass hinges and fittings will give the cabinet a graceful appearance and the whole is finished with three coats of polyurethane clear varnish.

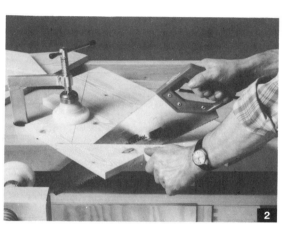

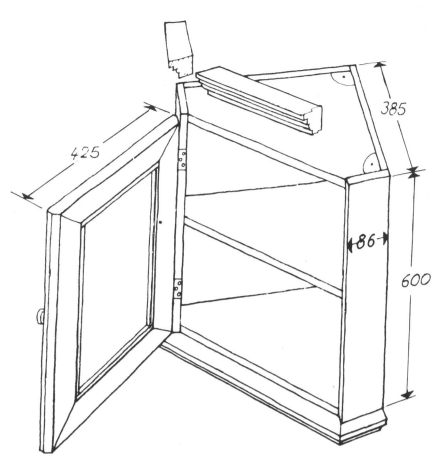

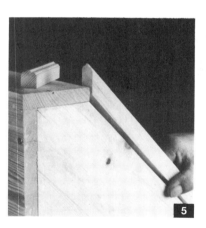

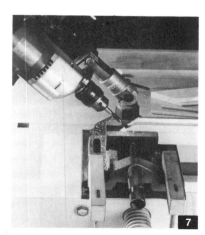

1. First glue and cramp three boards in position as shown.

2. Next cut to shape the top, and repeat for sides and shelf.

3. The main body of the carcase is now ready for assembly.

4. Use an appropriate milling cutter to make the beadings.

5. Fitting the profile edge to give the professional look.

6. Fitting the shelf is a simple matter any way you wish.

7. Drilling mitres for the making of the cupboard door.

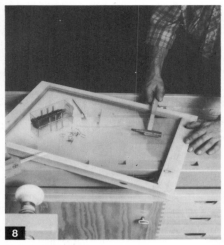

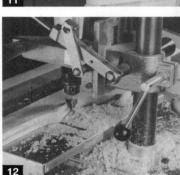

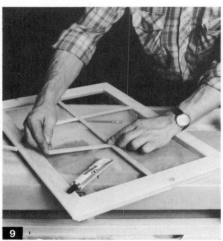

8. Be careful when fitting the glass sprigs.

9. Fitting the decorative glazing bars with glue.

10. Check the door for size and then hinge it up.

11. Cut a decorative pediment from softwood.

12. Milling makes for easy profile cutting in pine.

Preserving wood

Made to Match

A small bedside chest and matching bedhead have been specially designed so that you can choose from a range of wood stains to suit different bedroom colour schemes.

This small bedside chest with bedhead to match was designed to utilise a range of different colour stains. The narrow green stripe breaks up and enlivens the large areas, whilst the darker legs provide solidity and a visual framework. With this striped design, alternative colours could be chosen from the range to suit different rooms. The recessed coloured stripe lies between wider bands of contrasting natural timber which decreases in size towards the top. This gives a feeling of balance to the pieces, and to avoid any sense of heaviness both pieces are suspended from the legs with a 5mm space between.

The chest could be one of a pair for a double bed, and the bedhead could easily be adapted to suit any size of bed. A bed end for the foot could also be made along the same lines.

The timber used is sycamore, a traditional wood to use for staining as it has an even texture and white colour. Here the green and the dark oak (grey/black) finishes were used, together with the natural colour of the timber itself. The striped effect is achieved by staining the components before assembly. Polishing was also done at this stage — a clear lacquer can be used over the finishes, although staining is an adequate finish in itself for indoor work. However, as parts of the pieces are unstained, lacquer and wax were applied to the whole to give a uniform surface.

The bedhead is a straighforward piece of construction, the strips of timber being butt jointed together with battens applied on the back and the whole then suspended from the black ends, or legs, which attach to the bed itself. The chest is a more complicated structure with two mitred

Above: the timber laid out for selection, a process worth taking some time over.

Right: the sides and drawer front for the chest cut from one plank. Cut first to the correct width then cut each into three, noting carefully each piece to ensure they are used with the grain following through to retain the most pleasing pattern.

frames dowelled to three pieces on each side with rails top and bottom, front and back, to form the carcase. The drawers run between these frames and rails, and the top is planted on. The carcase is suspended from four black legs with spacers, and the edges of the frames and the top are stained green.

The back of the cabinet and the drawer bottoms are from birch faced ply. These could perhaps also be stained green. To pull the drawers there is a recess routed into the under edge of the front. (The front projects from the framework.) This means that there is a continuous smooth line round the cabinet uninterrupted by handles.

SPECIFICATION

1. BEDSIDE CABINET/SMALL CHEST OF DRAWERS
2. BED HEADBOARD

Timber: Sycamore

Dimensions:
1. Width— 486mm (19¼″)
   Depth— 400 (15¾″)
   Height— 550 (21¾″)
2. Length— 1370 (54″)
   Height— 950 (37½″)

Details:
1. 3 drawer chest with each drawer divided by recessed green stained strip which accommodates concealed handles. Chest is suspended from 4 black stained square section legs.
2. Bedhead to match chest with natural and green striped main section and black pillar either end to attach to standard sized double bed.

N.B. These two projects provide for differing levels of woodworking skill, the chest being a complicated project and the bedhead relatively simple.

Finish: Wood stain, matt lacquer and wax. and wax.

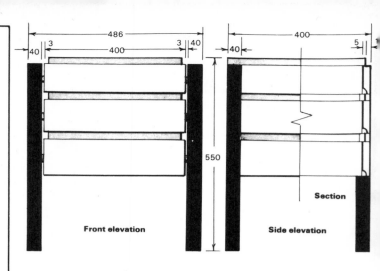

Front elevation

Section

Side elevation

Plan

- Natural
- Black stain
- Green stain

Front elevation

Side elevation

Colour opposite
The headboard and cabinet in use in their natural domestic situation, and the inset shows the cabinet with open drawers showing off the contrasts well. Two cabinets can be made if preferred.

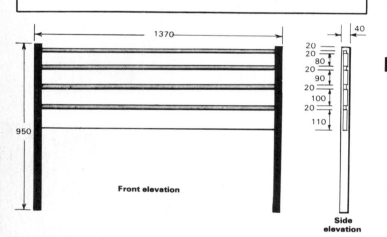
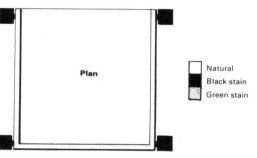

BEDHEAD

1. Components for the bedhead, the narrow strips are thinner than the wide ones (flush at the back and recessed at the front).

2. Narrow strips are stained before assembly. Prepare carefully to make as smooth as possible to enable the wood stain to take evenly. The wood stain is applied with a rubber made from cotton wool and covered with cotton cloth. It is applied thinly in long strokes.

3. The bedhead being glued up (butt joints), the components already sanded and stained. Remove from the cramps and cut to length.

4. Two of the legs are stained black and then three holes are drilled for the 9mm dowels. Three battens with chamfered ends are drilled for slot screwing onto the striped section and for dowelling onto the legs. The dowels are prepared with black rubber spacer rings (tap washers). Something similar could be made in wood.

5. Glue the batten to the leg with dowels and spacers.

6. The batten with leg attached, slot screwed onto the back of the striped section. It's lined up so that the gap between the spacers can be seen right through and the top green stripe projects above the leg to match the chest.

CHEST

7. Make up two frames with the front corners mitred as shown with a stopped tongue and the back rail tenoned into the sides set back 6mm for the back.

8. Glue up the frames and clean up well. Apply green wood stain to the front and sides.

9. Cut the side pieces to width and length. Make up four rails to join the sides at top and bottom, front and back using a mortice and tenon. Set back rails in 6mm and rebate the ends of the side pieces for the back.

10. Drill the top and bottom side pieces centrally and recess for a 12mm plug for suspending the legs. Drill for dowel joint to mitred frames in the edges of side sections. Drill top rails for slot screwing to top. Glue up two top side sections to rails and the same with the base.

11. Use 6mm dowels to join the mitred and stained frames to the two side sections shown in photo 12 and to the two remaining middle side sections.

12. The partially completed assembly.

13. Gluing up the carcase using a lot of cramps to ensure all remains square.

14. The carcase when glued up — mitred frames project from the sides at the front, but will be recessed when the drawer fronts are in position.

15. Components for the drawers. Fit the sides first. Put a 6mm groove in them for the ply base. The joints are made by housings and tenons since the fronts overlap the sides. Top drawer front must project up over the rails, bottom one over the base rail. Fillets must be screwed to carcase top and bottom to act as runners and guides for the drawers.

16. The carcase is attached to the legs by screwing through from the inside with 5mm black spacers. The top of the leg is level with the top of the side. The legs are pre-stained, and the carcase has already been lacquered and waxed.

17. Slot screw through the top rail to attach the top of the cabinet, use an offset screwdriver.

18. The front legs are fixed to come level with the drawers when closed. The screwholes are filled with black plugs.

19. Screw on the birch faced ply back.

The Vienna regulator

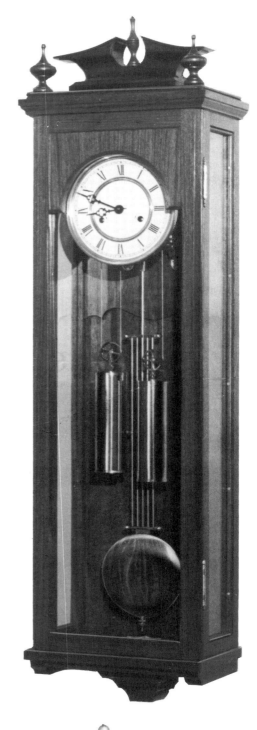

THE VIENNA REGULATOR was developed in the early part of the 19th Century. The high finish to the movement, light weights, and a comparatively heavy pendulum helped to make it a very accurate clock.

The case work of the early Viennese masters was elegant in design, and decoratively restrained. As the German clock industry moved towards modern methods, the popular Vienna regulator was a favourite item for production. The case work however was in typical Gothic style, with much turned work, and intricate carved cresting. It is not a regulator in the accepted horological sense, it is thought to be a courtesy title, probably because of it's accuracy and beauty.

A very fine movement is available today, based on the original movements and an address from which movements may be purchased is given at the end of this article. Unlike the English long-case clock, it appears that very few have survived, at least in this country. A certain amount of reproduction in the Gothic style has occurred in recent years, on a batch production basis.

In designing this case, I have tried to capture some of the grace and elegance of the early Viennese masters, with an individual hand-built model. It's comparative simplicity demands accurate and careful work. The result can be a unique example of Vienna case work in the original style.

The first phase of the work is the main body of the case, followed by the top mouldings and decorative crest, the base and finally the door.

The main members of the body and door are the same section, all in best quality mahogany, $1\frac{1}{8}$ by $\frac{7}{8}$ in. rebated $\frac{1}{4}$ by $\frac{1}{2}$ in. to receive glass and beads. The two back styles are grooved $\frac{1}{4}$ in. deep to receive the $\frac{1}{8}$ in. back panel of mahogany ply, set $\frac{1}{4}$ in. in from the back faces.

The fixing bolts of the movement support bracket require more than the $\frac{1}{8}$ in. back panel, so an extra $\frac{1}{4}$ in. mahogany ply panel is added to the inside to give the required thickness of $\frac{1}{2}$ in. This is 12 in. in depth, and the bottom edge is suitably shaped for ornamentation. This arrangement gives a good solid fixing for the bracker (drawing 1). Top and bottom rails of body and door are mortised and tenoned as usual.

The top moulding (A) is screwed to the top rails of the case body, is mitred at the front corners, and overlaps the front by $1\frac{1}{8}$ in. to receive the door. The second part of the build-up is 2 by $\frac{1}{2}$ in. square edged (B), overlapping the first part by $\frac{1}{8}$ in. all round. The third part (C) completely closes the top, it is $\frac{3}{8}$ in. thick, beaded on all sides and it can be in the solid, or preferably mahogany ply edged with $\frac{3}{8}$ by $\frac{3}{8}$ in. solid to receive the bead. The central platform (D) is 1 in. thick, 4 by 7 in., with a hollow moulded top edge. The central capping (E) is $\frac{3}{16}$ in. thick, $1\frac{1}{4}$ by $6\frac{1}{4}$ in. The broken pediment style crest is mounted on this, it is fitted "dry" on two $\frac{3}{8}$ in. dowel pegs, and is removable. The finials are also fitted in this way.

The pediment piece is cut from a solid block and requires time and patience, but is well worth it. The pediment with it's attendant finials is after all the crown of the case. Having selected a suitable block of mahogany it is advisable to cut the central aperture and the curved ends while it is still in block form, also the curved tops. The shape of the back and front are formed last. Having shaped and cleaned up the main pieces, it is possible to make up the

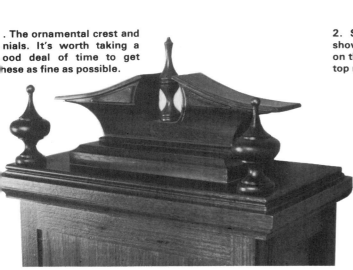

1. The ornamental crest and finials. It's worth taking a good deal of time to get these as fine as possible.

2. Side view of the top showing also the mitres on the glazing bars and the top mouldings.

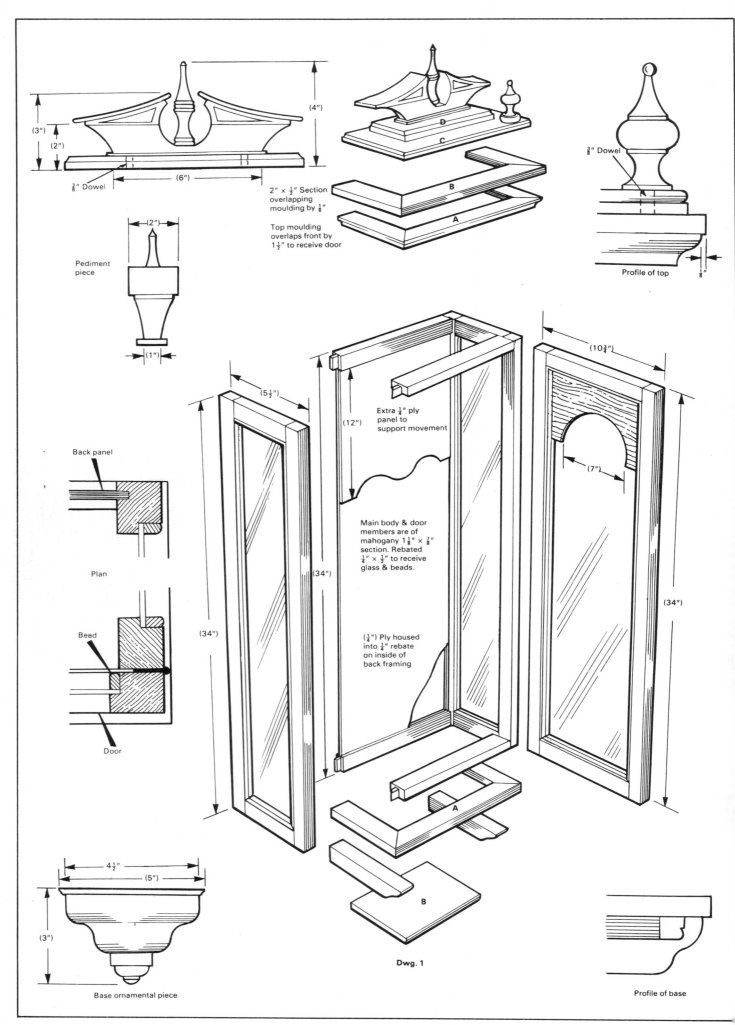

(4″)

(3″)

(2″)

(6″)

⅜″ Dowel

2″ × ½″ Section overlapping moulding by ⅛″

Top moulding overlaps front by 1½″ to receive door

D

C

B

A

¾″ Dowel

Profile of top

(2″)

(1″)

Pediment piece

Back panel

Plan

Bead

Door

(5½″)

(10¾″)

(12″)

Extra ¼″ ply panel to support movement

(7″)

Main body & door members are of mahogany 1⅛″ × ⅞″ section. Rebated ¼″ × ½″ to receive glass & beads.

(34″)

(34″)

(34″)

(34″)

(¼″) Ply housed into ¼″ rebate on inside of back framing

A

B

Dwg. 1

4½″

(5″)

(3″)

Base ornamental piece

Profile of base

top cappings with $\frac{1}{16}$ in. layers of veneers. Using the finished piece as a "Caul" glue up the veneer sections, and cramp them dry to the shaped tops they will eventually occupy. When the glue has set they are preshaped ready for cleaning up. Finally glue and pin into position, remember the cappings overlap by $\frac{3}{16}$ in.

The base is made in a similar fashion. The square edged piece (A) is screwed up into the bottom rails of the case, mitred at the front corners, and must overlap the front of the case by $1\frac{1}{8}$ in. as per the top, to receive the door. The side cheeks are fitted next, made from $\frac{7}{8}$ by $1\frac{1}{4}$ in., the base board (B) is fitted between them, $\frac{3}{8}$ in. mahogany ply, with a solid beading to the front edge.

The door is made with the top and bottom rails, mortised and tenoned as usual into the styles. The glazing occupies the whole space of the rectangle, continuing up and behind the dial mask. This means the mask must be set forward to bring the inside face flush with the rebate. The mask piece is made of $\frac{1}{8}$ in. mahogany ply chosen for grain configuration, and housed beyond the glazing rebate by hand. It is then possible to glaze and fit the beads in the normal way.

The half circle mask should overlap the dial rim by $\frac{1}{8}$ in. In some instances the half circle is left as a bare edge, and rounded over. In this case a rebated moulding is applied and it makes a well finished job. This is obviously a very delicate member to make up. The easiest and most successful way to make it is with veneer strips pressed up in a caul (drawing 2). This is made in $\frac{1}{2}$ in. ply. Glue both surfaces of the veneer strips, adequately, but not excessively. The appropriate inside surfaces of the caul must have masking tape applied. Make the moulding piece oversize and reduce to the required size when it is broken out of the mould. The long tails are the extra required to make the two short returns at (C) and (D) in the caul. These tail ends can be cramped very well with two spring paper clamps.

The base ornamental piece can be cut from the solid, or made up in three pieces. There are many variations of shape for the individual maker to choose from, the overall size however is appropriate for this case.

Glazing the case is a matter for the individual craftsman to decide. The advantages and disadvantages of glass and perspex are well known to us. Glass is heavy while perspex is light and safe. However, working perspex creates static, which attracts the dust,

although once it is fitted and cleaned and the static has dissipated it remains clean, and the safety factor should be considered. The choice rests entirely with the maker, but remember, without man's quest for new ideas nothing would ever have been created.

Polishing? This is even more controversial, I have methods old and new and my own gained over the years. Of course all the old ways we set so much store by were once new.

The hanging bracket is made of 1in. brass strip $\frac{1}{8}$ in. thick. An inverted keyhole type is bored at the upper end, it is housed into the back top rail, and fixed with two screws. A $\frac{3}{16}$ in. metal thread and nut below this comes through the top back rail of the case body, and fixed inside the case it is hidden behind the movement. Here then is a really interesting project which takes us just that little bit further than plain cabinet making yet remains within the compass of the average woodworker who is prepared to take a little time and patience over his craft.

For those interested clock movements and ornamental hinges and fittings for all types of reproduction work can be obtained from A. Brun & Co. Ltd., Airport House, Purley Way, Croydon, Surrey CRO OX7.

3. Side view of movement and fixing brackets. These are particularly ornate and greatly enhance the overall appearance of the high quality case work.

4. The same brackets seen from below. The fixings are simple and elegant as on the original models.

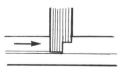

5. The indicator plaque is situated inside on the bottom of the case and must be central with the pendulum when it is at rest.

6. The base ornamentation of the case. As with the pediment time spent here will be well rewarded in the quality of the final article.

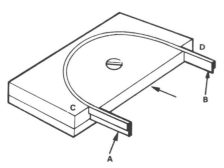

Dwg. 2 Veneer caul

Miniature chest of drawers in pine

A small well-designed set of drawers which will keep the odds and ends of everyday life tidy.

A SMALL SET of drawers like this has many uses around the home, storing and segregating many of the odds and ends of everyday life. The original was made as a present for friends who have placed it in their kitchen to hold items of stationery, string, elastic bands and other paraphernalia without which even the best kitchen cannot properly function.

The original was made in pine and being small it is an ideal way of making something extremely useful yet costing very little. I started by preparing the five main pieces for the carcase (sides, base and two top rails) and these were cut to their exact lengths. A cutting gauge was used to mark out the extent of the dovetails at the top corners, the parts of these joints at the ends of the rails being cut first (photo 1). These dovetailed rails were now used as templets to establish the exact corresponding half of the joint to be cut in the sides, the waste being removed partly by saw but largely by chisel.

The base of the carcase is stop-trenched to the sides, and after marking out with a marking knife and gauge, a small mortise was formed at the front of the trench. Its purpose is to provide a working space for the saw when this is used to cut the sides of the trench. A chisel is the best way of removing most of the waste from the trench, and a hand router provides the means of ensuring the bottom of the trench is level and of uniform depth (photo 2). The small trenches to house the plinth were also cut at this stage.

One of the operations which can be performed on most planing machines is rebating, and photo 3 shows just this stage of the work. I now carefully marked out on the inner surfaces of the sides the positions of the drawer runners. A sample groove of the sizes to be used on the drawer sides made on scrap wood enabled me to prepare the runners so as to fit these grooves with the minimum of clearance. The runners were made of beech, and were bored and countersunk for three screws in each, and the front ends rounded to semi-circles. Even with provision for screw fixing, I find that initial location for components like these is more readily and accurately achieved by panel pins, and these can be spotted in photo 4 which shows one side of the carcase with the four runners in place. Glue of course

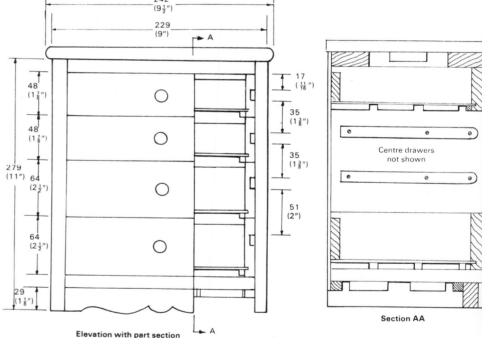

Elevation with part section

Centre drawers not shown

Section AA

Plan with part section

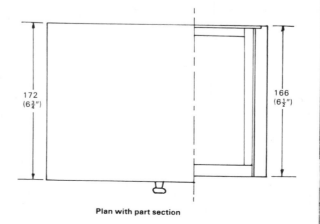

1. Marking joints in carcase sides.

was used as an additional means of fixing.

The front corners of the base were cut so as to fit around the stopped ends of the trenches into which they were to fit, and I was ready for assembling these five main parts. Initially, I relied on glue and pressure to hold the parts together—my fairly large vice and a sash cramp providing the pressure required (photo 5). The work was checked for being square, surplus glue washed off, then left to dry. Panel pins were driven through the lower joints on the underside to provide additional security and complete concealment.

The piece for the plinth was soon prepared to size, and the simple outline shown on the drawings marked out on it. A small bandsaw was used to cut this plinth to shape, although it could have been done almost as quickly with a coping saw. This piece was well glasspapered before being fitted in place (photo 6), cramps being used until the glue had set. A little levelling off and cleaning up of outer surfaces was needed at this point in progress. A shaving or two from the smoothing plane was followed by a thorough smoothing from my orbital sander.

A small overhang is intended at the front and ends of the top as illustrated in the drawings, and the piece for this was accordingly prepared to the sizes required. I managed to find an old "hollow" plane of suitable size in my small collection of such planes to help in rounding the projecting parts of the top (photo 7), but of course a special plane of this type is far from essential for such a rounding operation. Similarly with the glasspapering of these edges, while a rubber with a concave edge makes it that little bit easier to achieve uniformity, a flat glasspaper block carefully used produces just as good an effect. This piece was cleaned up on its upper surface before being added to the main carcase, and for this I relied entirely on glue. I did, though, add a glueblock between top and sides between the upper rails.

With the material prepared for the drawers, the pins for the dovetails were marked out on front and back members. Following traditional practice, those at the front were lap dovetails, and most of the cutting of these has to be carried out by chisel. The waste on the joints on the back can be largely removed by coping saw, using a chisel only for the final trimming.

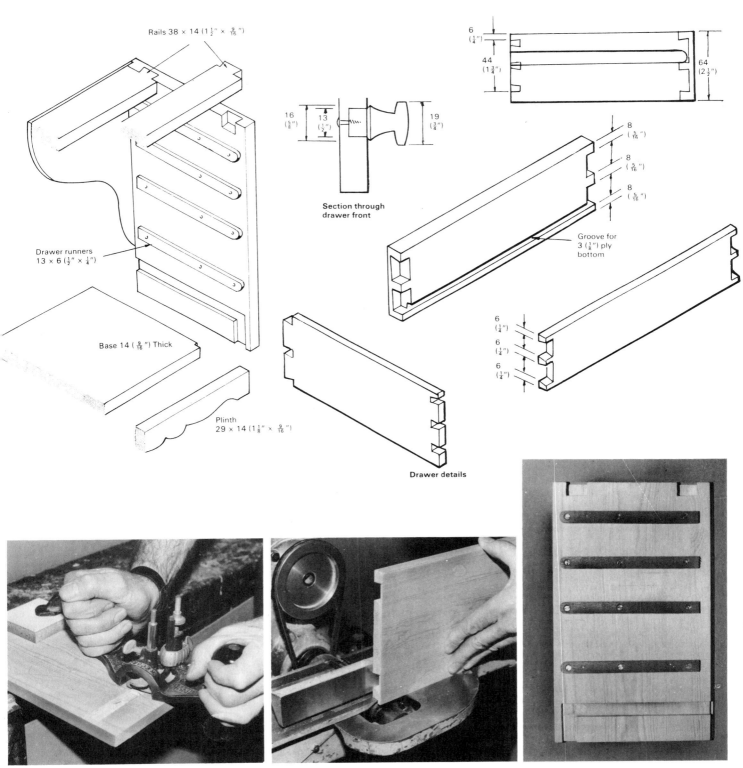

Section through drawer front

Groove for 3 ($\frac{1}{8}$") ply bottom

Drawer details

Rails 38 × 14 (1$\frac{1}{2}$" × $\frac{9}{16}$")

Drawer runners 13 × 6 ($\frac{1}{2}$" × $\frac{1}{4}$")

Base 14 ($\frac{9}{16}$") Thick

Plinth 29 × 14 (1$\frac{1}{8}$" × $\frac{9}{16}$")

2. **Final levelling is done with a router.**

3. **Rebating on a planer for the cabinet back.**

4. **The drawer runners are fixed in place.**

Miniature chest of drawers in pine   111

5. The carcase is assembled as shown and cramped up until the glues dries. Make sure all is square at this stage.

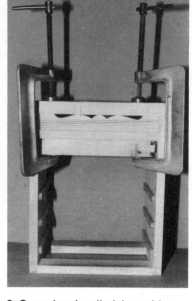

6. Cramping the plinth in position.

7. Rounding the top with a hollow plan

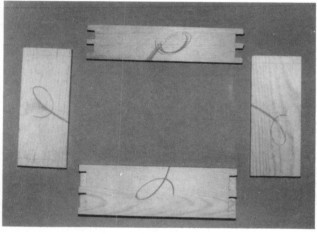

8. The drawer components marked out with facemarks. These are the main guide to the final arrangement in the drawer assembly.

9. Marking out the sockets from the dovetail pins so that the corner joints are perfectly matched.

10. Grooving out on the circular saw.

I am always very careful when dovetailing that the pieces being jointed are properly collated one to the other, and photo 8 shows a stage of the work I always go through. The pieces are arranged as they will finally be assembled, the main guide to this being the face marks which must be consistent in the way they are arranged. Witness marks are then marked on adjacent pieces, these marks being made on the outside so that they will not be removed until after assembly. Thus when the sockets of the joints are marked from the pins (photo 9), there is no risk of finishing up with a drawer that will not assemble because of wrongly matched pins.

The sides and front needed grooving for the drawer bottom, and I knew my circular saw would carry out this part of the work very adequately (photo 10). This completed the initial stages of making the drawers, so all the inner surfaces were skimmed with the smoothing plane, and well glasspapered.

Gluing up a drawer is a straightforward operation, glue being applied to both parts of the joint and a hammer gently used to ensure that parts are well "home". Measuring the diagonals is a simple and effective way of checking an assembly for being square (photo 11), and I took particular care in removing all traces of glue from the inside. The ply for the bottoms was cut exactly to size, and slid into place in the grooves. A little glue was introduced between the ply and the lower edge of the back, but this only after the ply was in place. The ply is sufficiently flexible to allow for this, and the securing was completed by driving in small round head nails into the back. Glue blocks are also added to the underside in order to make the drawer very rigid.

The joints to the drawers were levelled off when the glue had set, and checks made at this stage that the drawers were a comfortable fit within the carcase. Only now did I set about forming the grooves on the outside of the sides, using my electric router set up like a small spindle, with a temporary fence cramped

to the table. The limit of the groove near the front had to be accurately controlled, but this in fact is easily achieved by making clear pencil marks on the fence.

Although the outside of the sides had been carefully planed so as to fit the carcase before the grooving stage, a certain amount of fitting of the upper and lower edges was needed, and vigilance was required so that the gaps between the drawers was both small and uniform. With all the drawers fitted, the fronts were cleaned up and here I was careful to check as I proceeded that all drawer fronts were in line each with its neighbours.

I had deliberately not fitted the back to the carcase at an early stage so as to make the fitting of the drawers that much easier (photo 13). The ply back was now glued and pinned in place (photo 14), and made to protrude at its lower edge as seen in one of the drawings. This was to allow glue blocks to be added all round the underside including adjacent to the ply (photo 15).

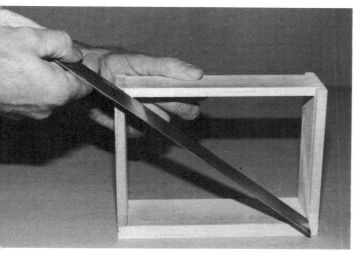

1. Checking the drawer for squareness across the diagonals.

12. Grooving out the drawer on the moulder.

3. Rear view before fitting on the back.

14. The next stage is to fit the ply back.

15. The underside showing the glue blocks.

16. Checking the diameter of one of the knobs.

Some small offcuts of rich dark walnut were used for the knobs, and these were turned up to the section shown. I used a simple homemade gauge to check that the pin part of the knobs was the correct diameter (photo 16), the wood being mounted on a small screw chuck during turning.

Holes were bored part way through the fronts of the drawers, and the knobs were fixed by a little glue and a screw inserted from the inside. With the constructional work completed, I could set about applying the finish. A coat of polyurethane varnish of the gloss variety was applied, and allowed to dry thoroughly. It was then flatted down with fine abrasive paper, and a second and final coat of varnish given. This second application was of the eggshell type, which dried to leave the surface with a satin-line sheen.

Our friends were delighted with their gift. As their kitchen had recently been refitted largely using pine, the nest of drawers blended in particularly well.

Cutting List

Sides	2 off	305 by 166 by 14mm	(12 by $6\frac{1}{2}$ by $\frac{9}{16}$ in.)
Base	1 off	241 by 162 by 14mm	($9\frac{1}{2}$ by $6\frac{5}{16}$ by $\frac{9}{16}$ in.)
Top rails	2 off	241 by 38 by 14mm	($9\frac{1}{2}$ by $1\frac{1}{2}$ by $\frac{9}{16}$ in.)
Top	1 off	267 by 172 by 14mm	($10\frac{1}{2}$ by $6\frac{3}{4}$ by $\frac{9}{16}$ in.)
Plinth	1 off	229 by 29 by 14mm	(9 by $1\frac{1}{8}$ by $\frac{9}{16}$ in.)
Back	1 off	292 by 241 by 4mm	($11\frac{1}{2}$ by $9\frac{1}{2}$ by $\frac{3}{16}$ in.)
Drawer runners	8 off	178 by 13 by 6mm	(7 by $\frac{1}{2}$ by $\frac{1}{4}$ in.)
Drawer sides	4 off	178 by 48 by 10mm	(7 by $1\frac{7}{8}$ by $\frac{3}{8}$ in.)
Drawer backs	2 off	229 by 32 by 10mm	(9 by $1\frac{1}{4}$ by $\frac{3}{8}$ in.)
Drawer fronts	2 off	229 by 48 by 16mm	(9 by $1\frac{7}{8}$ by $\frac{5}{8}$ in.)
Drawer sides	4 off	178 by 63 by 10mm	(7 by $2\frac{1}{2}$ by $\frac{3}{8}$ in.)
Drawer backs	2 off	229 by 48 by 10mm	(9 by $1\frac{7}{8}$ by $\frac{3}{8}$ in.)
Drawer fronts	2 off	229 by 64 by 16mm	(9 by $2\frac{1}{2}$ by $\frac{5}{8}$ in.)
Drawer bottoms	4 off	216 by 178 by 4mm	($8\frac{1}{2}$ by 7 by $\frac{3}{16}$ in.)

Widths and thicknesses are net; allowance added to lengths.
Also required: oddments for glue blocks; hardwood for knobs.

Light design in wood

AN OLD moulded glass bottle, picked up for next to nothing in a junk shop, had such pleasant proportions, that we recreated it in wood, to use as a table lamp base. You can use any sort of bottle you like, and the shape will be enhanced by the colour and grain of the wood. In order that the base and shade should match in design, you should take the bottle along with you when choosing the shade. Only when they are seen side by side can you be absolutely sure.

1. Trace the shape of the bottle onto a piece of cardboard. In order to get both sides symmetrical cut out one half then fold the card down the middle. It can then be cut out and used as a template.

2. The cutting out can be done in the normal way with a Stanley knife or similar instrument. If you want to draw the outline of a circular bottle shine a light behind it and trace the shadow cast into a piece of white paper held stretched across the front.

3. Laminating the body of the bottle from strips of timber will ensure that it will not split at a later date. The centre section as shown is made up from two grooved strips with the grooves facing each other. This provides a convenient channel for the lighting flex without the need for any boring later.

4. Cut the outline of the bottle with a jigsaw or a bandsaw if you have one. At this stage it can be cut out fairly roughly since the final shaping will be done with a plane and sandpaper.

5. Each layer of the base should be glued together well. The layers are cramped up as shown (note that the pressure is applied in two directions at once, this is to prevent the layers sliding over each other whilst the glue is wet. Leave overnight for the glue to dry.

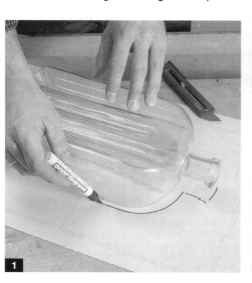

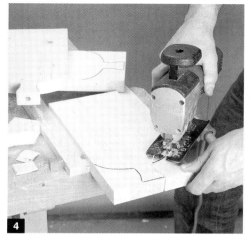

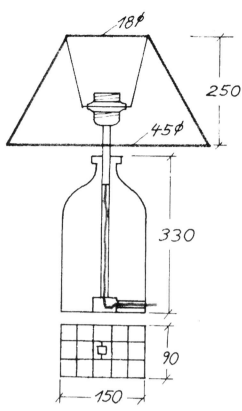

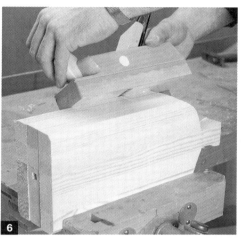

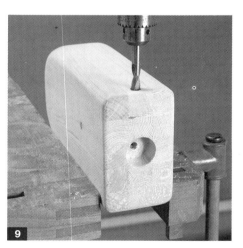

6. Smooth off the arrises with a plane first followed by a rub over with glasspaper. Be sure not to remove too much at a time or this may lead to the shape of the bottle being spoilt.

The neck of the bottle is revealed carefully by cutting away the waste with a handsaw. Again the finish can be put on with either files or glasspaper taking the same precautions as before to ensure that too much is not removed.

8. The fine detailing of the neck being done here with a small hand file. Be very careful when working the short grain on the flange of the neck as this will be particularly susceptible to breakage.

9. With the whole of the body shaped up and sanded work can begin on drilling the holes to take the light flex. An auger or flat-bit is used to make the large hole in the base to enable the flex to turn after it is let in through the side. The actual side hole is drilled out in the normal way as shown in the photograph.

10. All the necessary components ready for final assembly. English readers will note that the fittings shown are not standard and in fact may well not meet British safety requirements. However the equivalent fittings are readily available and if in doubt have a word with your local electrical supplier.

11. The support tube should be fixed in place using ordinary clear adhesive.

Elegant writing desk

Scarcely more than half a square metre is all that's needed to accommodate this charming piece of furniture but its usefulness by far belies its size. Not only will it be a boon to the busy housewife with an ever increasing load of domestic paperwork in the shape of bills, coupons, and leaflets to store, but it is also a really interesting project to make for the home enthusiast woodworker just branching out into cabinetmaking.

This little desk design comes from Germany and was originally made in ash veneered blockboard, ash veneered ply, and used solid ash for the legs and framing. Needless to say it could be made in a variety of materials but some sort of proprietary board would save on the costs.

All the jointing is done with dowels for simplicity and the whole project is well within the scope of the average home enthusiast. A bandsaw would be handy for the shaping of the sides, but this is not essential, and similarly a dowelling jig would speed up the process but one could easily

1. The two end frames and the back rails are cut first and the frames cramped up after gluing. Check the diagonals to ensure all is square.

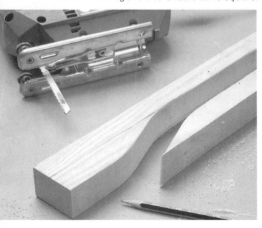

2. The desk frame is left open at the front to allow for sufficient leg room, but decorative curves are fitted either side to soften the line.

3. When the whole frame is assembled, 28 by 28mm strips are fitted to form the inner frame. These protrude 10mm above to create the gap.

manage without one.

Basically the project is an exercise in accurate cutting and marking out and is a good example of the sort of simple design that is enhanced by a workmanlike approach to jointing and finishing.

The solid ash used for the framing will need to be prepared before using and you may find it more convenient to order this from a timber yard already planed and cut to size. Should this be the case have it cut a little oversize in the lengths to avoid any expensive mistakes and to give sufficient for working tolerances.

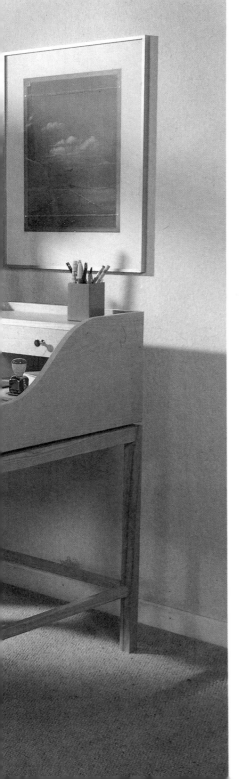

4. Detail of the main carcase showing the inner frame in position to take the main body of the desk. Work can now begin on the upper parts.

5. Since all jointing is done with dowels, some sort of dowelling aid is helpful to ensure the necessary accuracy in the drilling.

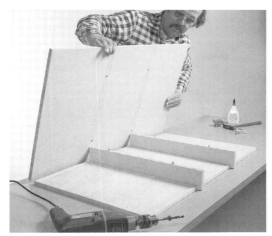

6. The base, partition walls, and writing top ready for gluing up. Note the solid ash lippings glued to the front of the partition walls.

7. The 5 by 10mm grooves for the letter rack are being cut with a router for ease of working, but hand methods can also be used.

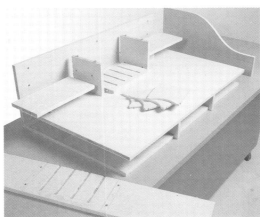

8. The main components of the top of the desk brought together to give some idea of the simplicity of the carcase construction.

10. The sides are the last parts of the main carcase to be attached. Again these are dowelled in position and firmly cramped up as shown.

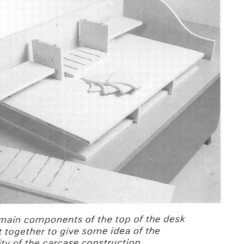

9. When making the sides, an easy way to get a sweet curve is to bend a piece of plastic or card and mark along the line accordingly.

11. The drawer components, with the exception of the front are cut from 10mm ply. The drawer fronts are in the chosen wood

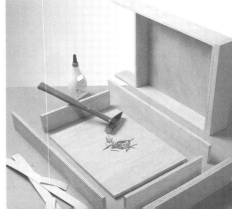

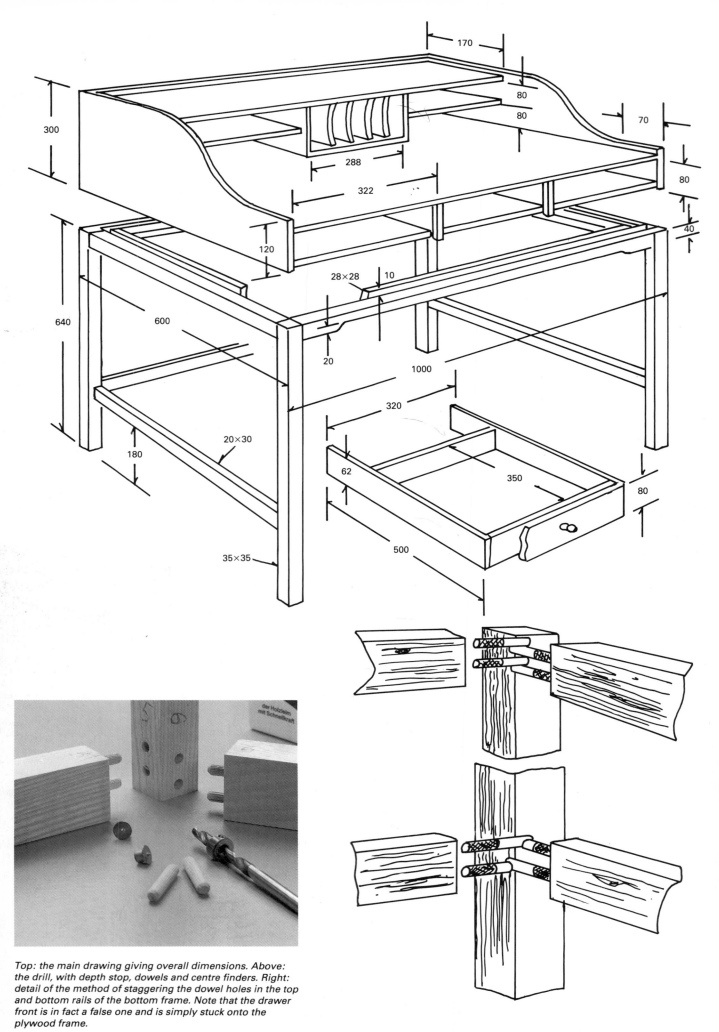

Top: the main drawing giving overall dimensions. Above: the drill, with depth stop, dowels and centre finders. Right: detail of the method of staggering the dowel holes in the top and bottom rails of the bottom frame. Note that the drawer front is in fact a false one and is simply stuck onto the plywood frame.

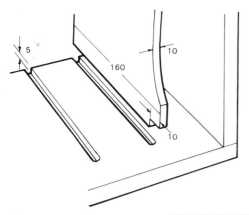

Above: detail of the stopped grooves which accommodate the pigeon hole partitions. Note that the partitions themselves project past the housings.

Right: the finished desk being put through its paces by its new owner. Some idea of the elegance and compactness of the piece can be gained from the photograph.

Detail of the drawer and brass fitting which sets off the pale grain of the timber perfectly.

Begin by making the two ends of the lower frame as shown in the photographs and when cramping up make sure that excess glue is wiped away before it stains the wood. The diagonals are measured to ensure that all is square. When both end frames are dry the cross rails are added and the whole cramped until it is perfectly dry and can be handled. At this stage the inner frame which projects above the top can be screwed into place. Basically this is the bottom part of the desk complete apart from the rubbing down and waxing or varnishing as required.

Reference to the drawings and photographs will give a clear idea of how the upper parts are cut and assembled. You can cut out all the pieces before assembly if you prefer to but the sequence we show seemed to logically dictate itself. Take great care in cutting and dowelling since the finish of the project will depend very much on attention to detail. When cutting the shaped sides you will find it a great advantage to cut both together for perfect matching. The drawers in this case are simply tacked together but you can of course dovetail them in the proper fashion to give that really professional finish to the job. Give all the components a good rub over with glasspaper before the assembly as you will find difficulty working in the many corners. Brass fittings look particularly nice with light coloured woods but this again is very much a matter of personal choice.

Reflections in a bathroom

Although the bathroom cabinet is strictly speaking a purely functional piece of furniture there is no reason why it should not have individual charm. With inexpensive materials and a little forethought this can still quite easily be achieved.

THE CHOICE OF MATERIAL with which the home woodworker can exercise his craft has become increasingly restricted over the past years. There is no great difficulty in getting supplies of softwood for many jobs, but for the smaller articles of household use, and for furniture, the search for suitable material is apt sometimes to become a little frustrating.

Fortunately there are ample supplies of manufactured boards available – the now familiar veneered chipboards sold under various proprietary names. White plastic or melamine-faced chipboard is very clean looking, so that when faced with the problem of providing a cabinet for the bathroom I considered the use of this type of material.

Although in many ways these artificial boards are a good substitute for natural timber, they do have certain drawbacks, perhaps the chief of which is the lack of the one-directional fibrous grain that constitutes the main strength and attractiveness of natural wood. The constitution of these boards affects the ways in which the material can be worked and, consequently, the design and eventual appearance of the articles for which it is used. The result of this is to be seen in the starkly rectangular furniture of today—largely unrelieved by moulding or shaping, which tends to give a somewhat monotonous box-like appearance to much modern furniture.

However, it did occur to me that melamine-faced chipboard, with its clean white surface, would serve admirably for this bathroom cabinet, if its essential rectangularity could be softened by a few curves, and brightened perhaps by a judicious use of colour. It was thus that the design shown in the accompanying drawings and photographs came into being. Since the purpose of this cabinet was to provide accommodation for fairly small articles (classified in the shops as toiletry) it need not be very deep, and it was, in fact, mainly constructed of 6in. (152mm) wide melamine-faced chipboard. The desired relief from the box-like effect was obtained by using an elliptical mirror in one door, by a simple curved shape cut from the lower ends of the sides, and by a modest concession to a traditional feature of cabinets in wood – a cornice moulding.

The dimensions of the cabinet are shown in drawing 1. Although melamine-faced chipboard can be bought in 6in. widths, actually, in his instance, having at hand a 12in. (305mm) board, I cut this in two, producing two boards just under 6in. wide.

A convenient way to cut this veneered chipboard is with a hand electric saw with a fine-toothed blade. This leaves a clean and square edge, which is not produced so easily with an ordinary handsaw or tenon saw. When using the power saw to cut this material one has to be careful about chipping the veneer of the upper surface) this method will leave a clean cut on the underside of the board, where the teeth enter, but this is liable to leave a slightly ragged edge on the upper face, where the teeth break out. Generally this slightly roughened edge may be used where it is not visible, but if both edges are required quite clean then it is best to clamp a piece of thin plywood to the top surface and to cut through this as well as the melamine-faced chipboard. This latter procedure is really necessary when cutting the simple curves at the bottom of the sides. For this a power jigsaw was used. So long as the marked curve is carefully followed it should require no further smoothing and will be ready to receive the "ironed-on" edging strip as a finish.

The bottom of the cabinet was dowelled to the sides; here a dowelling jig was used and a depth gauge on the drill served as a precaution against boring too deeply into the comparatively thin sides (photo 1). The top board was rebated at the ends and screwed to the sides, while the vertical and horizontal partitions were fitted to the cabinet by means of the stopped housing joint shown in drawing 3. The narrow shelf at the bottom is also housed in but will not need to be stopped. A trial assembly of the basic frame components at this stage resulted in the completing of the main carcase shown in photo 2.

Coming on to the finer details, a narrow curtain piece B (dwg. 1) about 25mm (1in.) wide was screwed below the front edge of the top board. After this a simple moulding was prepared as a finish for the top of the cabinet (dwg. 4). On the edge of a whitewood board 22mm ($\frac{7}{8}$in.) thick, two small rebates were cut with a rebate plane. This rebated part was then sawn off (as indicated by the dotted lines in drawing 4) and planed to thickness. After being

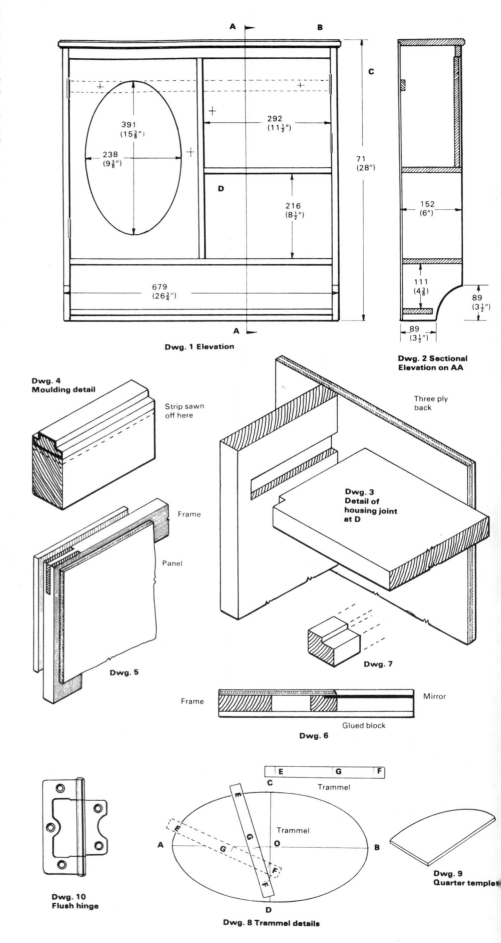

Dwg. 1 Elevation

Dwg. 2 Sectional Elevation on AA

Dwg. 4 Moulding detail

Strip sawn off here

Frame

Panel

Dwg. 5

Three ply back

Dwg. 3 Detail of housing joint at D

Dwg. 7

Frame

Glued block

Mirror

Dwg. 6

Dwg. 10 Flush hinge

Trammel

Trammel

Trammel

Dwg. 8 Trammel details

Dwg. 9 Quarter template

painted white to match the carcase, it was mitred round and pinned and glued in position. Nail heads were then punched below the surface, the holes filled with stopping and the painting completed.

Next came the preparation and the fitting of the doors. The smaller one was a plain rectangular panel of the melamine-faced chipboard. Here the edges were planed so that it fitted easily but not loosely into the aperture. (Remember raw edges will still have to be covered.) When satisfied with the fit the raw edges left by saw and plane were covered with the white plastic strip known as Contistrip. This needs to be stuck down by applying heat with an ordinary domestic flat-iron; it is usually better to cut the strip (with a sharp chisel) to the exact length required before it is ironed on, rather than depend upon subsequent trimming. The plastic strip is wider than the thickness of the board, and needs to be trimmed down so that it is flush with the surface; this can be done by using a small, finely set block plane.

From the sectional elevation (dwg. 2) it will be seen that a three-ply (or hardboard) back is fitted and screwed into rebates cut in the back of the sides. This may be done at this stage.

The next step was the construction of the larger door containing the mirror. This consists of a rectangular frame covered on each side by plywood panels—although the back one may well be of hardboard (dwg. 5). The corners of this frame were connected by open mortise and tenon joints. The door should be made about 3mm ($\frac{1}{8}$ in.) longer and wider than the aperture in the cabinet to allow for eventual trimming and fitting.

The first step is to set out the elliptical opening for the mirror. There are five methods in plane geometry of setting out an ellipse, given its greatest length (major axis) and its greatest width (minor axis). Of these five ways two are the more convenient in practical work—the "pin and string method" (shown in operation in photo 3) and the "trammel method" which is the one recommended here and illustrated in drawing 8. The following is the procedure; set up the axes as shown, AB and CD. Take a straightedge and mark on it the length EF equal to AO. Also mark the distance EG equal to half the length of the minor axis, the point G lying between E and F. This completes the trammel. To set up the ellipse lay the trammel across the axes so that the point F lies on the minor axis and the point G on the major axis. The point E then marks a point on the curve. By varying the position of the trammel so that the points F and G coincide with different points in the respective axes, sufficient points can be obtained to draw the ellipse.

It is not really necessary to construct the whole of the ellipse in this case, one quarter will do. From this a thin templet of plywood or stout card may be made, as shown in drawing 9. Then draw the two axes on the panel and trace round the templet with a soft pencil, reversing the templet where necessary. The ellipse is placed slightly above centre on the rectangular panel.

The opening was cut with a fretsaw, using a fairly coarse blade; any slight errors in the cutting can then be corrected with spokeshave, files and glasspaper. The edges of the elliptical opening were rounded into a quadrant profile. The finished construction (without mirror) may be seen in photo 4. With the shaping completed the front panel may be pinned and glued on to its supporting frame.

The method of fixing the mirror is shown in photo 5. Here it should be pointed out that I happened to have this mirror in stock, as it were. However, it is not necessary to go to the expense of getting the mirror cut to this shape, as a plain rectangular sheet, providing that it covers the elliptical aperture, would be cheaper and the resulting appearance would be exactly the same.

For securing the mirror in position, small blocks were made from a length of softwood rebated to receive the thickness of the glass (dwg. 7). These were of the same thickness as the frame of the door, so that when they were glued in position, and the back panel was screwed or pinned on everything was tight and secure.

The doors were hung with flush hinges of the type shown in drawing 10; these have projecting lugs to position them on the door and are comparatively easy to fit. The doors were slightly recessed into the cabinet—about 3mm ($\frac{1}{8}$ in.). Simple brass pulls and nylon door catches were also added at this stage.

One of the attractive features of the cabinet is that colour was added. The doors were gloss painted a clear yellow and the back of the cupboards treated with a deeper-toned blue vinyl emulsion paint.

The hanging of any wall cabinet always needs to be done carefully so as to ensure that it is quite safe. At the upper back edge of the top two stout metal glass-plates were screwed on and these in turn were screwed into the plugged wall. As an additional safety factor horizontal wood strips (C, dwgs. 1 and 2) were screwed to the back of the cupboards, through which also passed screws into the wall.

To complete the cupboard, it is then a fairly simple matter to fit one or more shelves to the interior of the mirror cupboard. Heights can be varied to suit the particular items that you may have in mind to store there.

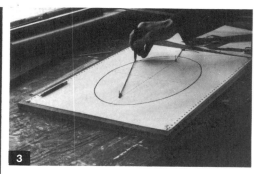

1. Base is dowelled to the sides.
2. Shaped lower ends of the sides.
3. Striking an ellipse with the pins and slack string method.
4. The carcase nears its completion.
5. Securing the mirror in position.

Cutting List

(Sizes in mm and inches)   (No allowance for waste)

Sides*	2 off	702 by 152 by 16mm	(27$\frac{5}{8}$ by 6 by $\frac{5}{8}$ in.)
Top*	1 off	679 by 152 by 16mm	(26$\frac{3}{4}$ by 6 by $\frac{5}{8}$ in.)
Bottom*	1 off	648 by 146 by 16mm	(25$\frac{1}{2}$ by 5$\frac{3}{4}$ by $\frac{5}{8}$ in.)
Lower shelf*	1 off	656 by 79 by 16mm	(25$\frac{7}{8}$ by 3$\frac{1}{8}$ by $\frac{5}{8}$ in.)
Partition*	1 off	552 by 146 by 16mm	(21$\frac{3}{4}$ by 5$\frac{3}{4}$ by $\frac{5}{8}$ in.)
Partition*	1 off	298 by 146 by 16mm	(11$\frac{3}{4}$ by 5$\frac{3}{4}$ by $\frac{5}{8}$ in.)
Curtain piece*	1 off	648 by 25 by 16mm	(25$\frac{1}{2}$ by 1 by $\frac{5}{8}$ in.)
Small door*	1 off	292 by 279 by 16mm	(11$\frac{1}{2}$ by 11 by $\frac{5}{8}$ in.)
Interior shelf*	1 off	337 by 121 by 16mm	(13$\frac{1}{4}$ by 4$\frac{3}{4}$ by $\frac{5}{8}$ in.)
Door stiles	2 off	511 by 32 by 13mm	(20$\frac{1}{8}$ by 1$\frac{1}{4}$ by $\frac{1}{2}$ in.)
Door rails	2 off	337 by 32 by 13mm	(13$\frac{1}{4}$ by 1$\frac{1}{4}$ by $\frac{1}{2}$ in.)
Door panels	2 off	511 by 337 by 5mm	(20$\frac{1}{8}$ by 13$\frac{1}{4}$ by $\frac{3}{16}$ in.)
Cabinet back	1 off	705 by 673 by 5mm	(27$\frac{3}{4}$ by 26$\frac{1}{2}$ by $\frac{3}{16}$ in.)
Cornice moulding	1 off	1092 by 22 by 10mm	(43 by $\frac{7}{8}$ by $\frac{3}{8}$ in.)

* indicates melamine-faced chipboard

Also required: edging strip; flush hinges; door pulls and catches.

Step-up chair

Ideal for almost any room in the house this handy hop-up will earn its keep while making an attractive contribution to the furniture.

FOR ALL THOSE JOBS about the house where you have to reach up high for things on shelves here is the perfect answer: a chair that turns into stepladder when you fold the backrest forwards.

For many people, especially small ones, there are many things around the house that are simply out of reach—whether it is tins on the top shelf in the larder or books from the bookcase when they are beyond reach on an upper shelf. A proper ladder kept in the house would be too cumbersome, but the ideal answer is the chair-steps.

Simple pine is the material to use whether you are going to paint the chair or leave it in its natural state. If you decide on the latter polyurethane varnish should be used to give it a protective finish.

You don't need complicated tools to build the chair-steps a drill for the dowel joints and a sliding bevel to mark the ends of the legs to their sloped shape, plus a pair of clamps with a space of at least 410mm between them to make the actual construction of the chair easier.

Construction

1. The round wood pieces for the backrest, each 270mm long, are glued into 10mm deep holes. The long cross pieces of the backrest are held firmly in place with clamps, then the holes for the dowels are drilled and the pieces all joined.

2. Two boards 120mm wide are glued together to form the seat proper, and then joined to the backrest with dowels. Plane the front edge of the seat so that it joins neatly with the side struts that are set at an angle of 124 degrees.

3. The seat proper and the side struts are joined also with glue and dowel joints. The lower board, which is also the upper step of the steps, is held firmly in place with clamps and then joined with dowels.

4. The side boards of the front part of the chair are also at an angle of 124 degrees to the front pair of legs. This must be bevelled to shape first. Inset the steps to 5mm.

5. The front board of the seat is fixed with two dowels to each side. Clamp together the two side pieces, including cross pieces and steps, without using adhesive, then join the seat on firmly with dowel joints.

6. The holes for joining the lower step are drilled by hand. When you have done this put adhesive on all the joining points and then dowel, again using glue to secure the whole assembly firmly.

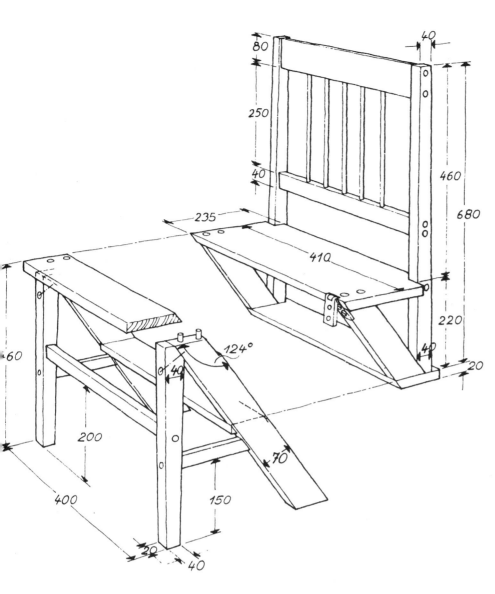

4. Care must be taken to ensure that the slot cut into the supports to take the step is at the right angle and depth.

5. Fixing the front board of the seat into position again using the dowel and glue joint. Note the champher on the front edge.

1. Top left: cut the backrest timbers to size, drill out the holes for the dowel joints and assemble it dry. When satisfied with the fit glue and cramp up.

2. Left: the seat and supporting struts are the next to be fitted and again these are made with dowel joints. Be sure your angles are correct.

3. Above: with the pieces cut and ready glue up in the normal way. When the glue is dry plane off the excess from the dowels flush with the surface.

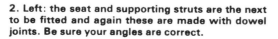

6. When drilling the dowel joints in the treads make sure that they are central or the steps will be weakened.

Round table in end grain

Polished end grain is probably one of the most simple and pleasing techniques used by the woodworker for visual effect. Here we look at a plain table transformed by this basic approach as can be seen above.

IF YOU LIKE natural-looking furniture, you are sure to agree that one of the most beautiful and individual pieces of furniture you can buy is a table in cross-cut pine. Unfortunately, it is usually very expensive. Here we show you how to make one yourself.

You will need twelve metres of planed cross-cut timber to make this solid round table. Pine is the material used for the individual blocks of wood that make up the top and the solid legs.

A little trick is used in the construction of the table; it means you don't have to use very many clamps to build it. The table top is built up of individual square segments, each 90mm in size made up into 360mm squares.

First the wood used to build the table: choose perfectly planed, well-seasoned tim-

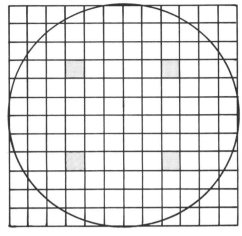

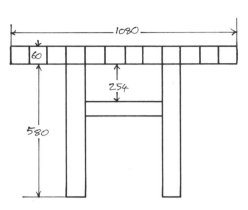

The dark areas of the plan view are the table legs in position where they come through the top. The circle described here is cut from the square top after it has dried completely. Note that in the case of four of the squares little more than half of them is used. The four off-cuts however can possibly be used in some other project given a little imagination.

Side elevation showing the twelve segments of the top diameter when finished.

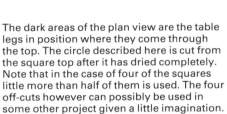

1. After the legs and rails have been cut to size and the mortises chopped out the job of assembling them can begin. Use a good quality woodworking adhesive for the operation.

2. Lay out all the squares on the floor once they have been cut to size, with the legs in position. Ensure that the growth rings run in different directions on each adjacent block when they are assembled.

3. Each of the nine large squares is made up of sixteen pieces as shown in the photograph. Make sure all joining sides are well covered in the adhesive and that the pattern is how it should be.

4. Clamp up the glued squares as shown or with home-made cramps if necessary. In any event it is essential to ensure that the assembly is kept perfectly square while drying.

ber, with few knots in it. The total of 140 blocks, each 60mm thick, which make up the table top should be cut by electric saw. They can be cut by hand; it takes time but is quite possible if you cut a pattern from a spare piece of wood, cutting it exactley to the right depth. Saw the table legs exactly to size for the table shown, in this case 580mm long. All four legs have mortises cut into them, 260mm from the upper end. These are 20mm deep, 30mm wide and 50mm long and each leg has two mortises in to hold the 400mm long rails that are glued into tem later. Draw the mortises onto the wood then bore them with an electric drill to the right depth, using a stop on the drill, and then finish cutting out the wood with a sharp chisel. Do not glue in the rails straight away;

leave them loosely in place so that you can fit the legs into the table-top properly.

First lay out all the blocks and the legs on the floor to test how they will go together. The drawing shows how the leg ends fit into the table top. As you lay them out, make sure that the growth rings in the individual blocks run in the opposite way to the blocks on either side. This will prevent the wood later from "working" in one particular direction and will make sure that the glued surfaces hold well together. A further piece of advice: even unevenly planed blocks will create a beautifully smooth top. Number all the blocks and join them together, 16 at a time, to form the squares as shown.

When you have made all the squares five complete ones and four with a corner mis-

sing to accommodate the legs they are all glued together to form a large, squared top. Again it is best to lay them out to test first on the floor, and then glue all the inner edges, including the struts of the legs, and then insert the ends of the legs into the empty spaces. Use a strong tension strap which will go round all nine squares of the table top to hold it all together firmly whilst the glue dries. When the glue is hard, turn the table over, draw on the circular shape of the top and then cut out with a fret saw. The final procedure is time consuming but essential; start with coarse sandpaper, then finer and finer sandpaper, and use the sanding attachment on your electric drill; sand the top of the table until it is utterly smooth and ready for its final coats of colourless varnish.

A fitting answer

THIS BUILT-IN WALL UNIT is not intended just for a bedroom; it would be useful in any room where there is a need to keep things tidy in a small space. It would go well in a study for instance, as it is book shelves, wardrobe and desk all in one. And what's more, it can be rearranged at will. All the individual parts of the unit are joined together in such a way that the whole unit can be quickly dismantled. The width and number of the units depend on the size of the louvre doors. The height of the room is not decisive and louvre doors can be shortened. If you have to work to size in this way, the long doors remain as they are and the smaller doors at the top of the unit are made to fit. Louvre doors come in various widths and lengths. You should bear this in mind when planning your unit. For the unit shown we used doors 502mm wide; because the doors need extra space to open, each cupboard unit is 520mm wide. All measurements shown relate to doors of this size but individuals may go for different sizes and adjust accordingly.

All the vertical walls of the unit are made from 16mm chipboard, as are the shelves. The top, floor, working surface, and middle shelves of the upper part of the unit are all made of 10mm chipboard.

The construction method for the unit is clearly shown in the drawing. The double floor and shelf pieces join up the unit and make it stable at the same time, and construction of the unit begins with these.

1. Side strips of wood 25mm square are inset to the thickness of the material used for the shelf support and lie between the 10mm thick pieces of chipboard. These floor and shelf pieces are 10mm shorter than the depth of the cupboard because they are finished at the front with a 10mm thick lipping.
2. The pieces are glued and nailed. At the back edge, a piece of squared timber closes up the open end.
3. Slip in the piece of timber used to support the shelf and then bore the holes for the screws that will hold the shelf in place. There are two holes on each side.
4. When fixing the frame together, the supports for the shelf are glued and screwed firmly to the vertical side walls, made of 16mm chipboard, then the shelf is fixed at right angles to it and fixed with small nuts and bolts.
5. The other side is then fixed in a similar manner.
6. Now bore the holes that will hold the unit together, using an angled templet as shown in

the photograph.
7. The angled templet will make sure that the hole you drill is always in the right position, in the long walls of the unit too.
8. The fitments for the doors are now screwed on, although the doors are not put into position until the whole unit is finished.

The unit is now assembled in position. As you do this, make sure that it is about 50mm lower than the height of the ceiling, otherwise it will not join up properly at the top.
9. The outer side wall has already been joined to the floor piece, and the second wall is now being fitted into place. If you tilt the whole thing onto its side, you will find it easy to screw in the lower fixings.
10. With the centre shelf in place, the whole thing starts to become more stable, and the ceiling piece can be screwed into place.
11. Now fix on the back wall of the unit. This is also made from 10mm thick chipboard, and can be screwed or nailed as preferred.

Construct all the upright parts of the unit on the same principle, and then hang the short units on top; this is easy again using nuts and bolts. The nuts can be given little coloured caps to match the unit, so that they do not show.

1

The floor sections are of double thickness with timber battens separating the layers.

2

The shelves are pinned and glued together in the same manner as the floor bases.

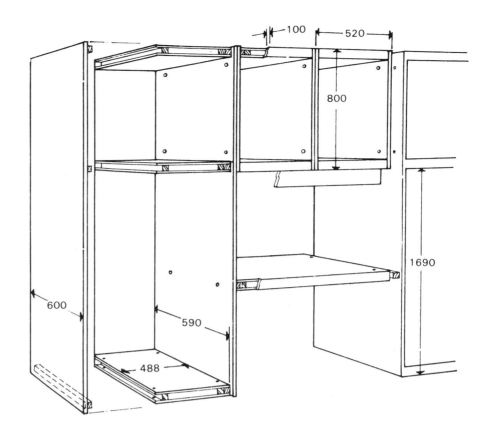

3

Using the drill stand make the holes for the bolts for the shelf fixings.

4

Use long bolts and cappings to join the shelves to the main body of the unit.

5

All four walls of the basic unit are now in place, note the fixing method.

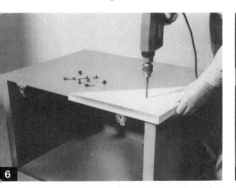

6

Use the angled templet to ensure that the holes are correctly positioned.

7

The templet is also used to determine the hole position in the long side of the unit.

8

Screw the door hinges into place but do not hang the doors until the framework is up.

2. Both upright pieces are now in position, and joined together. They now support one another and so have adequate stability.
3. The stability of the unit is further improved by the placing of the work surface in the middle. The basic construction of the unit is now complete and you can go on building more on to it, as needed. The work surface is joined on in the same way with nuts and bolts.

14. A mirror can be built into the unit as well, if you intend to have the work surface as a dressing table. It is screwed to a piece of hardboard with corner plates. Screw two pieces of lathing to the hardboard to hold the mirror against the side walls.
15. The louvre doors are put into place when the whole unit is finished. They are very simple to hang.

16. The floor of the unit is made of 16mm chipboard. Shelves should not be longer than the length of two doors, otherwise they will bend. The number of shelves you use in the unit will depend on what you need to store. This basic design is capable of a great deal of variation and extension as shown and can of course be added to quite easily as the need arises.

9 The unit is erected in its final position, here the first parts are joined together.

10 The centre shelves are screwed into place, immediately giving it some stability.

11 The back wall is put into position and fixed in place with screws or nails.

12 Fix the upper sections in place and then proceed to join the two sections.

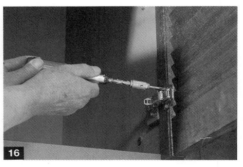

13 With the addition of the central work surface the basics are completed.

14 A mirror may be included if you intend to use the unit as a dressing table.

Top right: The addition of a mirror and a strip light make the unit into an ideal dressing table for the lady's bedroom.
Bottom right: An alternative use of the centre shelf is its adaptation as an office desk. Once again the addition of a strip light on the rear wall might be necessary if the area behind is a little too dark.

15 Hanging the louvred doors should present no difficulty at all.

16 With the doors screwed in position it is an easy matter to adjust their fitting.

Shedding light on veneers

MAKE THIS attractive, slot-together shade out of Oregon pine or any similar veneer. If possible, buy a thick grade of veneer, but if this is not available, buy twice as much and glue two pieces together with contact adhesive. Cut 60 pieces of veneer $1\frac{1}{2}$ by 6in., then cut four slots $\frac{1}{4}$in. deep in each piece with a tenon saw. To make this easier, make a templet by cutting slots in two pieces of $\frac{1}{8}$in. plywood, $1\frac{1}{2}$in. by 6in. as shown. Then sandwich ten to fifteen strips of veneer between the plywood templets in a vice and use the slots in the plywood as a guide for sawing. Slot the pieces together so that each 6in. square is diagonally above the next. Add a dab of glue to each joint as you go along. To support the bulb holder, slot a 6in. square of $\frac{1}{8}$in. plywood between layers near the top and drill a $\frac{1}{2}$in. hole for the wire.

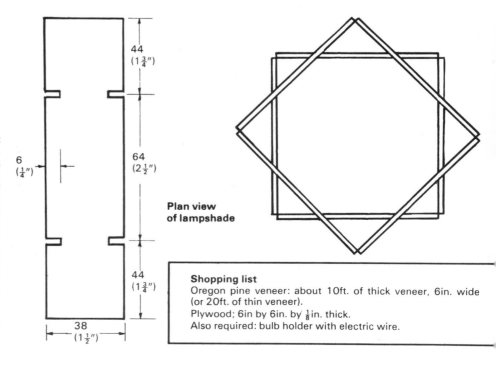

44 ($1\frac{3}{4}$")

6 ($\frac{1}{4}$")

64 ($2\frac{1}{2}$")

44 ($1\frac{3}{4}$")

38 ($1\frac{1}{2}$")

Plan view of lampshade

Shopping list
Oregon pine veneer: about 10ft. of thick veneer, 6in. wide (or 20ft. of thin veneer).
Plywood; 6in by 6in. by $\frac{1}{8}$in. thick.
Also required: bulb holder with electric wire.

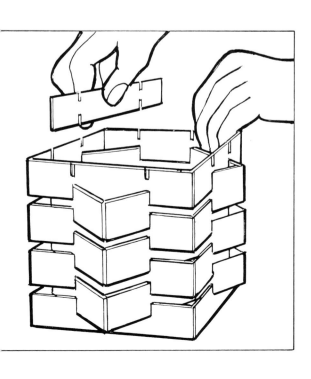

Writing table

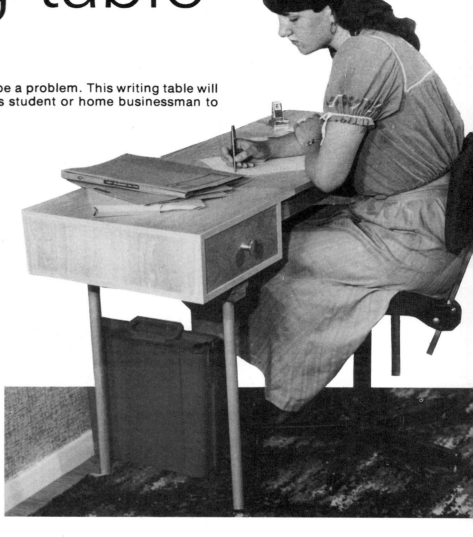

Keeping on top of the paper work can be a problem. This writing table will provide one way of helping the serious student or home businessman to order his or her affairs.

THE SMALL STUDENT'S writing table illustrated here involves full use of modern materials and jointing methods. Attractive grain patterns and the satin finish of pine panels have been enriched by the dark colour of teak drawer fronts, and the whole is set off by the silver sheen of aluminium legs and drawer handles.

Some of my woodworking friends look askance at the use of aluminium in wooden furniture, but I have found the results very satisfying to the eye. The panelling is a pvc veneered chipboard with a printed pine grain. Its hard-wearing surface requires no applied finish and makes a very suitable writing table top.

Constructional methods for this piece of furniture were simple, but a fair degree of accurate working was required to ensure a strong final product. Except for the drawers, jointing depended on accurate screwing of either screws and jointing strips or brass-plated screws into nulon inserts. Suitable aluminium tubing can be purchased from builders' merchants or from hardware stores.

Work started on the carcase with the two drawer compartments. All these parts, except for the front rail, were made from this board, each piece being accurately sawn and planed to size. It is important that the ends of these carcase pieces are accurately square in both directions as the jointing methods employed depend upon squareness for success.

When cutting vinyl veneered chipboard, it is a good idea to cut through the vinyl with a sharp marking knife before sawing. This minimises the risk of lifting the vinyl along the saw cut edges.

Planed chipboard edges, which would have been visible on the finished carcase, required veneering with iron-on vinyl edging strip (photo 1). Cleaning off excess edging strip takes patience, and I recommend a three-stage process: First, chisel away most of the excess (photo 2). Secondly, scrape any remaining edging back to the board surfaces (any scraper is suitable). Finally, sand along the corners with a sanding block tilted at 45 degrees (photo 3).

Four lengths of 16mm ($\frac{5}{8}$in.) square hardwood strips were required for jointing the drawer compartment ends to the table top. Teak was used on this occasion, but any other tough hardwood would be just as good. Each of the strips were planed accurately square to ensure successful corner joints.

Five 5mm ($\frac{3}{16}$in.) holes, drilled and countersunk in each direction along the strips, gave very strong corners (photo 4).

After screwing the strips to the four carcase end pieces, these are screwed in position to the underside of the top (photo 5). Gauge 8 screws, 25mm (1in.) in length, proved suitable. It is advisable to lightly cramp each piece to the top when fitting in position to avoid any movement as the screws are driven home.

Near each end of the bottom pieces, four more 5mm ($\frac{3}{16}$in.) holes were set in 8mm ($\frac{5}{16}$in.). These also required countersinking to receive the heads of brass-plated screws. Each bottom piece was then lightly clamped on the carcase and the insert positions were marked by passing a small drill through each countersunk hole in turn (photo 6).

The carcase bottoms were removed from their temporary positions on the carcase and a 6mm ($\frac{1}{4}$in.) hole bored to a depth of 32mm ($1\frac{1}{4}$in.) at each of the marked insert points. A nylon insert was next hammered into each hole (photo 7) and the bottoms were then screwed to the carcase.

A carcase back could now be fitted. This consisted of a piece of the pine board, sawn and planed to fit uder the top and over back edges of the drawer compartments. It was held in position with screws in nylon inserts set into the back edges of the two drawer compartments. Next, a length of teak 51 by 25mm (2 by 1in.) was planed to fit accurately into the space between the two drawer compartments. This fron rail was securely fastened to the carcase by 16mm ($\frac{5}{8}$in.) square hardwood strips screwed in both directions with 25mm (1in.) gquge 8 screws.

With the carcase completed, attention was given to the leg units. These were designed to give rigid support and also to spread the strain of the legs over as wide an area as possible. Two leg support rails were required, each consisting of a length of 51 by 25mm (2 by 1in.) solid teak screwed to a length of 76 by 25mm (3 by 1in.) teak. To secure these leg rails to the carcase underside, eight 5mm ($\frac{3}{16}$in.) countersunk holes were drilled in the wider pieces of teak.

After marking for the leg positions on the rails, holes to receive the aluminium tubing were bored with the aid of a bench drill stand (photo 9). It is important that these holes are at perfect right-angles to the rails – hence the use of a bench drill stand. A 25mm (1in.) flat bit was used for these holes – after making a number of trial holes to ensure that the diameter matched that of the leg tubing exactly. The aluminium tubing was then sawn to length and glued into the support rails with epoxy resin glue. Wood glues are not suitable for fixing metals in wood. The leg units were now ready for fixing to the underside of the carcase with 38mm (1½in.) gauge 8 screws (photo 10).

The method adopted for running the drawers was slightly unusual, and was devised to overcome two problems. The first of these arose because I wanted to set back the drawer fronts of this table 5mm ($\frac{3}{16}$in.) from the carcase front edges. The second problem was that there were two jointing strips fitted inside the top corners of the drawer compartments. Because of these two difficulties, the drawer boxes were made as shown in drawing 4. Joints used for the

boxes were housing joints, and the runners were glued and pinned to the outside of the drawer boxes to allow free running without fouling the jointing strips.
Construction of the drawers started by planing the fronts from 16mm (⅝in.) thick solid teak to fit exactly into their respective compartments. Then, the drawer sides were planed to slide within the compartments. Drawer backs were next planed to correct sizes, and grooves were cut for the housings – a router, fitted with a

1. **Covering edges with iron-on strips.**

2. **Removing surplus edging from board.**

3. **Sanding corner edges at 45 degrees.**

4. **Drilling four teak strips at once.**

5. **Jointing the table top to an end.**

6. **Marking positions for the inserts.**

7. **Hammering nylon inserts into place.**

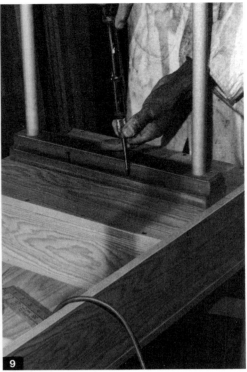

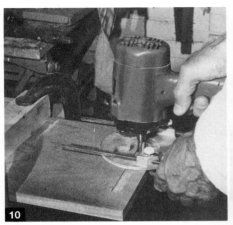

13mm (½in.) tool, was used for this purpose (photo 11). Grooves for each drawer bottom were cut in the front and sides and then all parts were cleaned up by sanding. Drawers could now be assembled and glued together, and runners pinned to the sides after the glue had set. Finally, the drawers were planed for a good sliding fit in their compartments and drawer handles were attached (photo 12).

8. Boring holes in leg support rails.

9. Screwing a leg assembly to carcase.

10. Drawer grooves cut with a router.

11. Testing a drawer for snug fit.

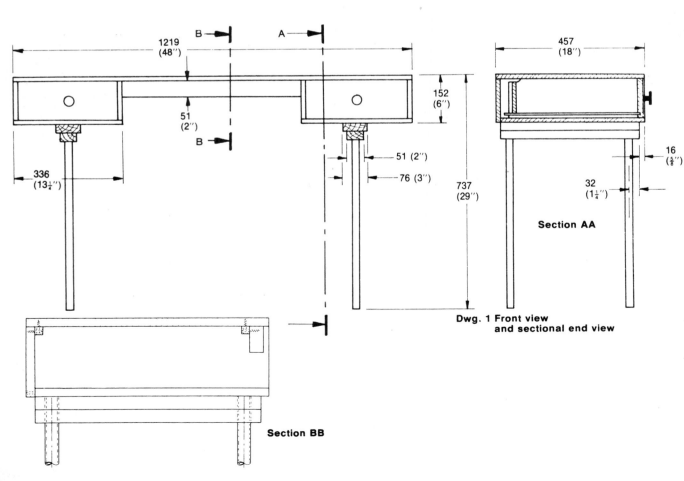

Section AA

Dwg. 1 Front view and sectional end view

Section BB

Several methods of finishing this piece of furniture could be adopted—the easiest being to polish all parts with furniture polish. A number of coats will probably be required for a really good finish.

Alternatively, the vinyl and aluminium parts could be polished with furniture cream and the teak parts given two coats of teak oil. This will result in a darkening of the teak, which you may prefer. A third possibility would be to polish the vinyl and metal, and to apply two coats of polyurethane varnish to the teak parts.

CUTTING LIST

(Sizes in mm and inches) (No allowance for waste)

From 457mm (18in.) Pine board			
Top	1 off	1219mm (48in.)	
Ends	4 off	121mm ($4\frac{3}{4}$in.) reduce to 442mm ($17\frac{3}{8}$in.) wide	
Bottoms	2 off	336mm ($13\frac{1}{4}$in.) reduce to 442mm ($17\frac{3}{8}$in.) wide	
From 152mm (6in.) Target panel			
Back	1 off	1219mm (48in.) reduce to 137mm ($5\frac{3}{8}$in.) wide	
From solid teak			
Drawer fronts	2 off	305 by 121 by 16mm	(12 by $4\frac{3}{4}$ by $\frac{5}{8}$in.)
Leg supports	2 off	425 by 76 by 25mm	($16\frac{3}{4}$ by 3 by 1 in.)
Leg supports	2 off	425 by 51 by 25mm	($16\frac{3}{4}$ by 2 by 1 in.)
Front rail	1 off	548 by 51 by 25mm	($21\frac{5}{8}$ by 2 by 1 in.)
Other material			
Drawer sides	4 off	375 by 121 by 13mm	($14\frac{3}{4}$ by $4\frac{3}{4}$ by $\frac{1}{2}$in.)
Drawer backs	2 off	285 by 102 by 13mm	($11\frac{1}{4}$ by 4 by $\frac{1}{2}$in.)
Drawer bottoms	2 off	285 by 285 by 3mm	($11\frac{1}{4}$ by $11\frac{1}{4}$ by $\frac{1}{8}$in.)
Jointing strips	4 off	425 by 16 by 16mm	($16\frac{3}{4}$ by $\frac{5}{8}$ by $\frac{5}{8}$in.)
Jointing strips	2 off	518 by 16 by 16mm	($20\frac{3}{8}$ by $\frac{5}{8}$ by $\frac{5}{8}$in.)
Jointing strips	2 off	51 by 16 by 16mm	(2 by $\frac{5}{8}$ by $\frac{5}{8}$in.)

Also required: four 585mm (23in.) lengths of 25mm (1in.) dia. aluminium pipe; two drawer handles; 25mm (1in.) gauge 8 countersunk screws; 44mm ($1\frac{3}{4}$in.) gauge 8 countersunk screws; 38mm ($1\frac{1}{2}$in.) gauge 8 countersunk screws; nylon inserts; glue.

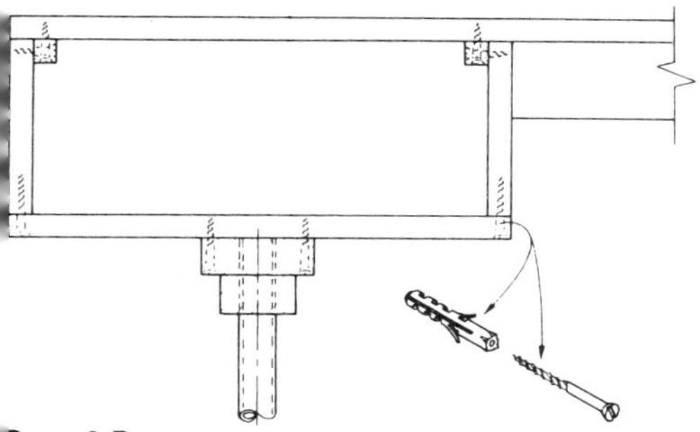

Dwg. 2 Drawer compartments

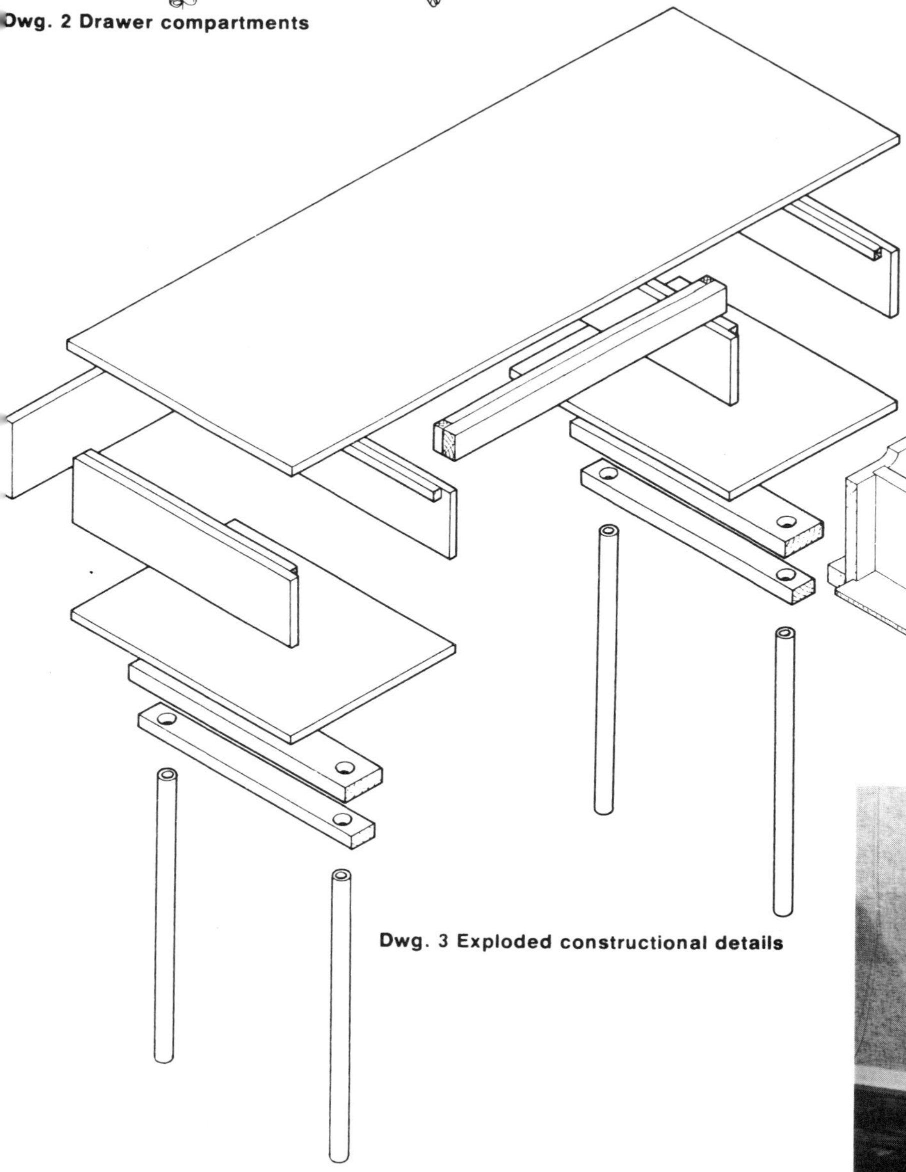

Dwg. 3 Exploded constructional details

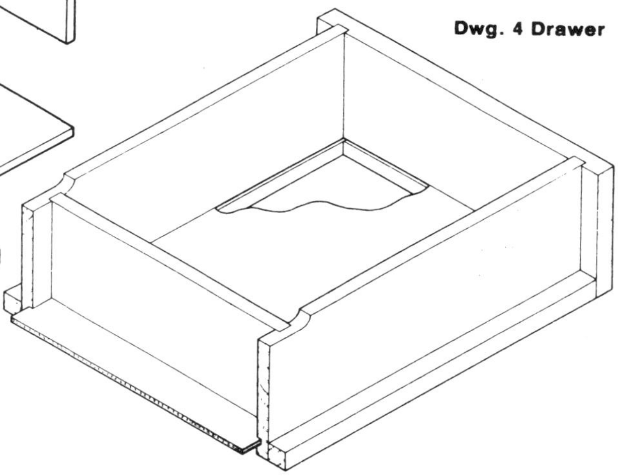

Dwg. 4 Drawer

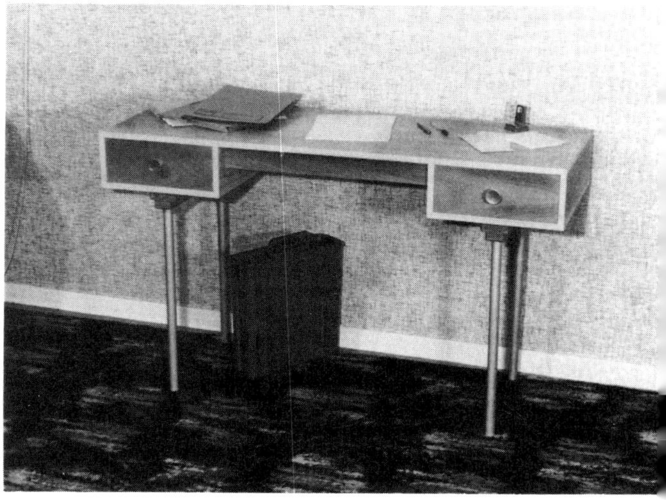

Desk of Drawers

THIS CABINET, come work-desk or dressing table, was designed to suit the needs of my teenage daughter—who would have found her bedroom a little cramped with three separate pieces of furniture. Storage requirements, to fulfil the cabinet function, are satisfied by the three large drawers and, an innovation of the design, the mobile lid helps the unit to fulfil its other two functions.

The lid moves along guides set inside the cabinet. It can be pulled forward to rest at a comfortable angle for writing or drawing and, if pivoted upwards, reveals a tray underneath—above the drawers. This space is intended for the storage of work equipment and/or cosmetics; and, for the benefit of the latter stored items, a mirror may be mounted on the lid underside to allow the unit to be used in its dressing table capacity. When fully pivoted, the lid rests just beyond the vertical.

When using the lid in its forward position as a homework table, plenty of uninterrupted legroom is allowed for by the use of cut-out drawer handles, rather than the protruding type. The lip on the leading edge of the lid is also intended to aid this use for the unit, as it serves to retain books and equipment on the surface.

Construction of the cabinet was designed to utilise standard widths of veneered/melamine-faced chipboard. Although, if using a combination of these two, it should be noted that their respective thicjnesses are slightly different: veneered chipboard being 16mm (⅝in.) thick and melamine-faced chipboard 15mm. As can

be seen in the photographs, I achieved an interesting effect by edging white melamine-faced chipboard with woodgrain iron-on strip. Jointing simply took the form of butt joints, glued and pinned, K.D. fittings and screws – the whole lot being very easy to assemble.

Reference to the general arrangement in drawing 1 will help you to see the layout of the cabinet components. First of all the two side panels were prepared, and the upper and lower rails cut to size. It is a good idea, however, before sawing or planing the board, to scribe the lines with a laminate cutter or Stanley knife in order to prevent the laminate chipping.

These components were edged with the iron-on strip as follows: side panels on the top edge; the upper back rail on one long lower edge; and the top front rail on one long lower edge.

When ironing on the strip it is important to ensure that there is overlap on both sides, to width and to length, and this can then be trimmed flush with a fine abrasive wrapped around a cork block.

The side panel and rail structure was jointed with K.D. fittings as shown (dwg. 2). At this stage the blocks were mounted on the side panels along the centre line of the rails, with the exception of those for the upper back rail. The top edge of these blocks must be at least 76mm (3in.) down from the top edge of the side panels.

Next, the runner guides were prepared. These were to be fixed to the inner faces of the side panels. Full details of their position and

the methods used are given in drawing 2. It is recommended that No. 8 by 25mm (1in.) chipboard screws are used to mount the guides, which should be counterbored to allow the screws to penetrate approximately 10mm (⅜in.) into the sides.

The drawer boxes (dwg. 3) were simply constructed from 12mm (approx. ½in.) plywood, butt jointed, pinned and glued. The back of the boxes were inset by 16mm (⅝in.). Before actually assembling the drawers, I ensured that the clearance holes in the box front had been drilled and countersunk for No. 8 by 19mm (¾in.) chipboard screws, which will later be used to retain the drawer fronts in place.

The 25mm (1in.) diameter finger holes in the drawer sides should also be drilled before assembling the drawer box. These were positioned as shown in drawing 3.

As each drawer box was completed, the drawer bases were glued and pinned in position. Drawer runners were also screwed in place at this stage, along a centre line 60mm (2⅜in.) down from the top edge of the drawer sides. They were secured by screws through from the inside of the drawers.

Drawer fronts could now be cut to length, and the finger cut-outs drilled and shaped. The 25mm (1in.) diameter holes for these were drilled on the centre line flush to the edge at both ends. Then the shape was completed by filing back to 25mm (1in.) diameter arcs either side of the hole. Care should be taken to ensure that the edges are kept square for successful application of the edging strip. The strip

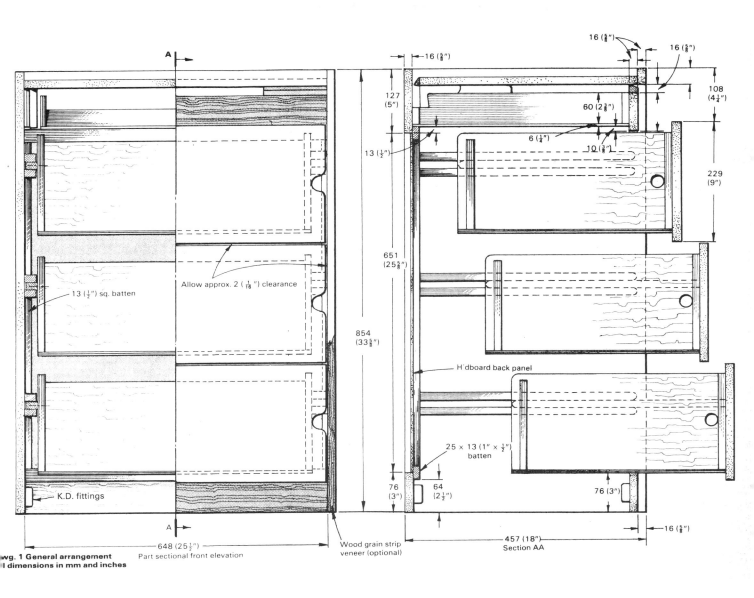

A

16 (5/8")
16 (5/8")
16 (5/8")

127 (5")
108 (4 1/4")
60 (2 3/8")
6 (1/4")
10 (3/8")
229 (9")

13 (1/2")

651 (25 5/8")

854 (33 5/8")

13 (1/2") sq. batten

Allow approx. 2 (1/16") clearance

H'dboard back panel

25 × 13 (1" × 1/2") batten

76 (3")

76 (3")
64 (2 1/2")

76 (3")

K.D. fittings

Wood grain strip veneer (optional)

648 (25 1/2")

457 (18")

16 (5/8")

Dwg. 1 General arrangement
All dimensions in mm and inches
Part sectional front elevation

Section AA

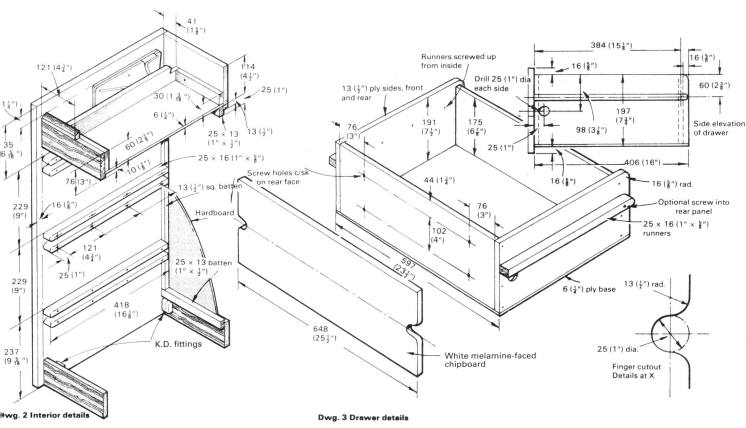

41 (1 5/8")

121 (4 3/4")

114 (4 1/2")

30 (1 3/16")
25 (1")

1 1/4"

6 (1/4")
13 (1/2")

35 (1 3/8")
6 5/8"

60 (2 3/8")

25 × 13 (1" × 1/2")

76 (3")
10 (3/8")

25 × 16 (1" × 5/8")

229 (9")

16 (5/8")

13 (1/2") sq. batten

Screw holes c/sk on rear face

Hardboard

121 (4 3/4")

25 (1")

25 × 13 batten (1" × 1/2")

229 (9")

418 (16 3/8")

K.D. fittings

237 (9 5/16")

Dwg. 2 Interior details

Runners screwed up from inside

13 (1/2") ply sides, front and rear

Drill 25 (1") dia each side

384 (15 1/8")

16 (5/8")

16 (5/8")

60 (2 3/8")

76 (3")

191 (7 1/2")

175 (6 7/8")

197 (7 3/4")

98 (3 7/8")

Side elevation of drawer

25 (1")

44 (1 3/4")

76 (3")

16 (5/8")

406 (16")

16 (5/8") rad.

Optional screw into rear panel

25 × 16 (1" × 5/8") runners

102 (4")

597 (23 1/2")

648 (25 1/2")

6 (1/4") ply base

White melamine-faced chipboard

13 (1/2") rad.

25 (1") dia.

Finger cutout Details at X

Dwg. 3 Drawer details

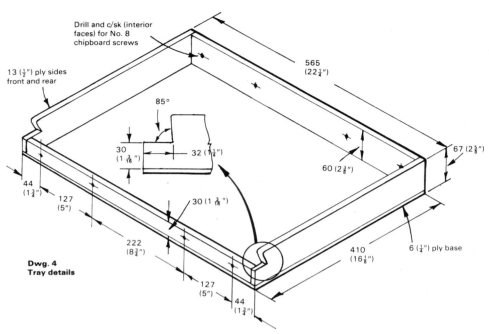

Dwg. 4
Tray details

Drill and c/sk (interior faces) for No. 8 chipboard screws

13 (½") ply sides front and rear

565 (22¼")

85°

30 (1 3/16")

32 (1¼")

60 (2 3/8")

67 (2 5/8")

44 (1¾")

127 (5")

30 (1 3/16")

222 (8¾")

410 (16 1/8")

6 (¼") ply base

127 (5")

44 (1¾")

The other pre-assembly operation was to secure the back mounting battens to the lower edge of the upper back rail, and to the upper edge of the lower back rail. These were secured with No. 6 by 19mm (¾in.) chipboard screws, in such a way that 13mm (½in.) of the 25mm (1in.) width was exposed for back panel fixing.

The basic construction was now ready for assembly with the K.D. fittings. The tray was screwed in position 48mm (1⅞in.) down from the top of the side panels, at this stage, to give the structure extra rigidity. Then, before proceeding any further, I tested the drawers on their runners.

All that remained was to deal with the mechanism of the lid movement, that is the lid runners and guides (dwgs. 5, 6 and 7). Runners were of 19mm section, and this was the result of laminating together 13mm and 6mm plywood—scraps of which were left over from the drawers. However, they could just as well be made from 19mm (¾in.) thick solid material as specified in the cutting list. Holes, for two dowels of 8mm (5/16 in.) diameter were drilled in the position shown, as the runners were to be

was finally ironed on with the toe and edge of an iron. Drawer fronts were then secured to the boxes with an overlap of 25mm (1in.) either side and 16mm (⅝in.) top and bottom.

The tray was constructed from 13mm plywood (dwg. 4) in the same way as the drawer boxes, that is with glued and pinned butt joints. Details of the clearance holes, which should be drilled before assembly, are given in the drawing. These were drilled and countersunk for No. 8 by 19mm (¾in.) chipboard screws.

Sides of the tray were also shaped before assembly, and the shaping consisted of a 5 degree angle towards the front from a point 32mm (1¼in.) from the back, cut down to be flush with the 30mm (1 3/16 in.) width of the tray back. Once the tray frame was complete, the base was pinned and glued in position.

The lid was now prepared to size. I found it easiest to attach the hardwood lipping on the front edge by nails, the heads of which were punched below the surface and filled over with stopper.

To maintain the overall appearance of the cabinet, the face of the lipping can be painted white – if white melemine-faced chipboard is used. Or, it is possible with care, by using a chisel and lighter fuel (for melting the adhesive) to ease off the white melamine surface of a spare piece of melamine-faced chipboard, and use this to laminate the lipping face.

The lid was also lipped at the back, with a 16mm (⅝in.) square hardwood strip planed off at 45 degrees. This was achieved by gluing and nailing the strip in position, leaving the nailheads protruding, and then withdrawing the nails when the glue had set before planing the 45 degree bevel.

There were now two operations to carry out before assembling the basic side panels and rails. First, two blocks of hardwood, which support the lid when it is pulled forward, required fixing in place on the top edge of the upper front rail. These needed only to be glued and nailed in place, but I ensured that all nailheads were punched below the surface to stop the possibility of scratching the lid as it is moved. The angle or bevel on these support blocks was 25 degrees from the horizontal, and it should be appreciated that if you are going to fit a mirror under the lid, it must be mounted between these blocks so as not to foul the forward movement.

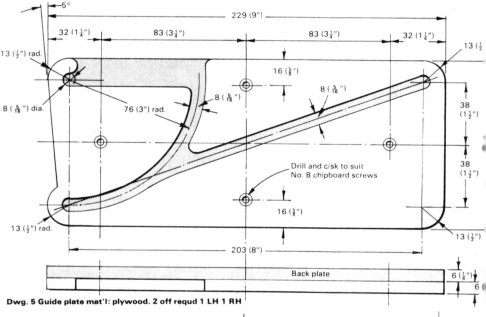

5°

229 (9")

32 (1¼")

83 (3¼")

83 (3¼")

32 (1¼")

13 (½")

13 (½") rad.

8 (5/16 ") dia.

76 (3") rad.

16 (⅝")

8 (5/16 ")

38 (1½")

38 (1½")

Drill and c/sk to suit No. 8 chipboard screws

16 (⅝")

13 (½")

13 (½") rad.

203 (8")

Back plate

6 (¼")

6

Dwg. 5 Guide plate mat'l: plywood. 2 off reqd 1 LH 1 RH

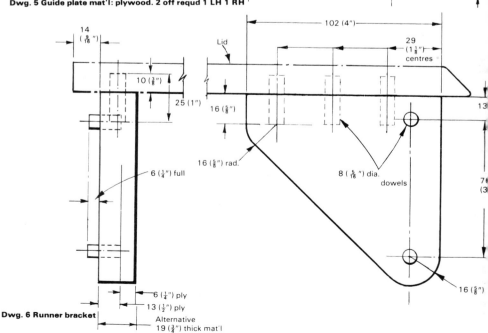

14 (9/16 ")

102 (4")

Lid

29 (1 1/8") centres

10 (⅜")

25 (1")

16 (⅝")

16 (⅝") rad.

6 (¼") full

8 (5/16 ") dia.

dowels

16 (⅝")

6 (¼") ply

13 (½") ply

Alternative 19 (¾") thick mat'l

Dwg. 6 Runner bracket

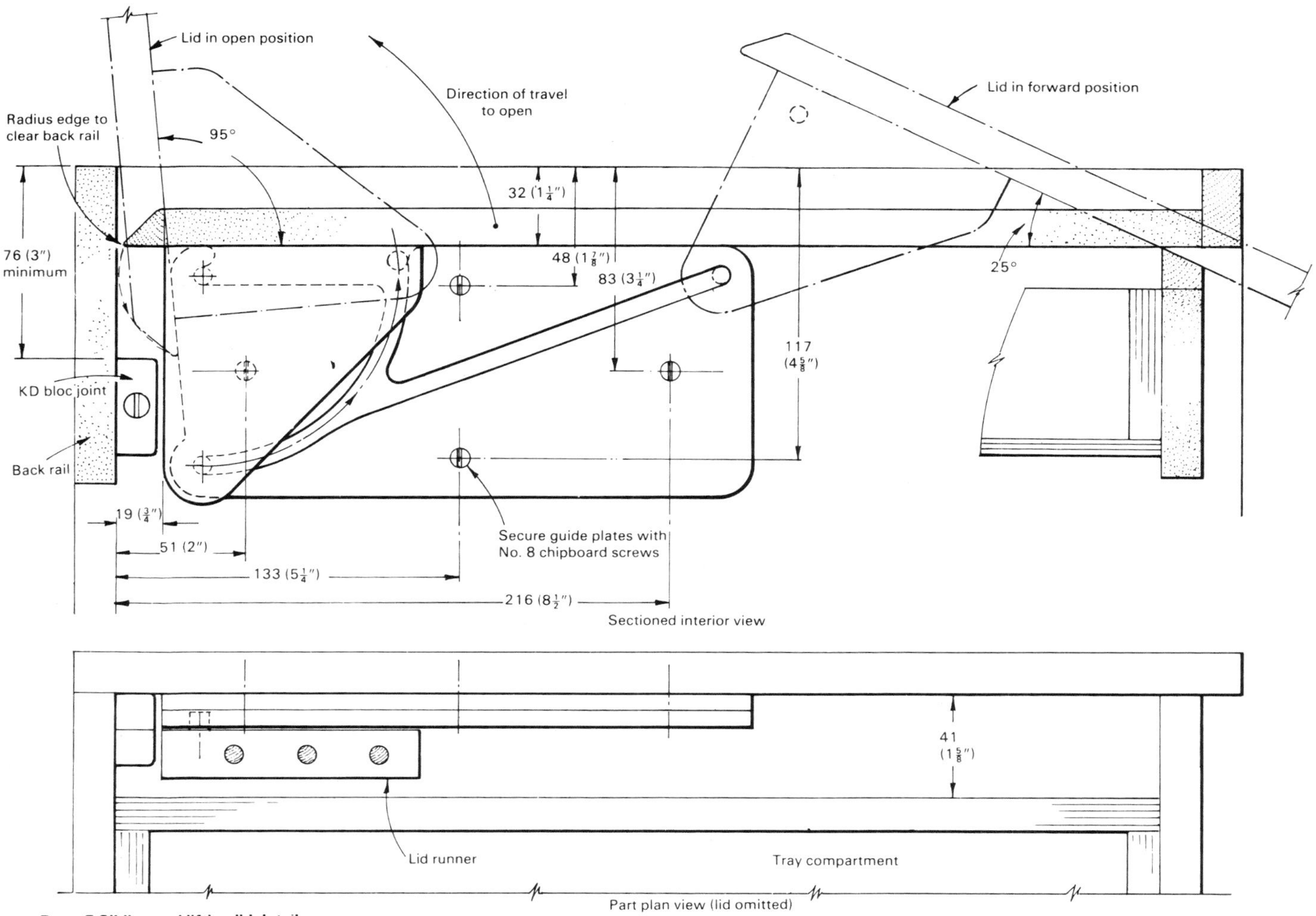

Lid in open position
Direction of travel
to open
Lid in forward position
Radius edge to
clear back rail
95°
32 (1¼")
48 (1⅞")
83 (3¼")
76 (3")
minimum
117
(4⅝")
25°
KD bloc joint
Back rail
19 (¾")
51 (2")
133 (5¼")
216 (8½")
Secure guide plates with
No. 8 chipboard screws
Sectioned interior view
41
(1⅝")
Lid runner
Tray compartment
Part plan view (lid omitted)

Dwg. 7 Sliding and lifting lid details

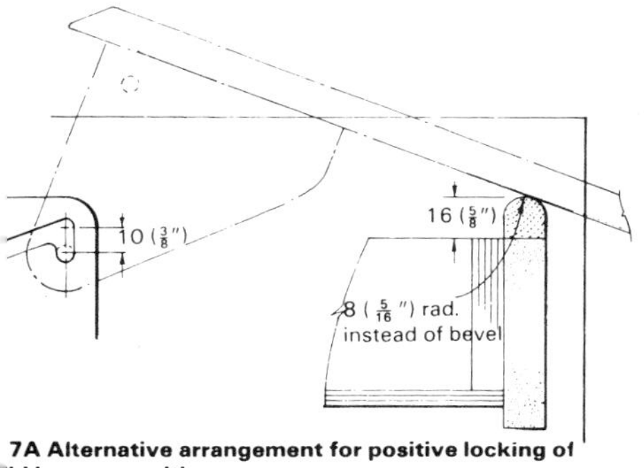

16 (⅝")
10 (⅜")
8 (5/16") rad.
instead of bevel

7A Alternative arrangement for positive locking of lid in open position.

lowel jointed to the lid itself.

Guides were made up in a similar way, as a result of laminating together two 6mm ($\frac{1}{4}$in.) plywood pieces. However, these were not glued together until the inside pieces had had their channels cut out. Channels were marked out by making up a full size drawing and tracing directly from it, and then cutting carefully with a coping saw (or bandsaw if available) working towards holes previously drilled to give the necessary internal radii.

Note that the shaping at the rear of the guides must be carried out on both 6mm ($\frac{1}{4}$in.) pieces and is best done after they are joined. The guides were finally screwed to the cabinet sides with No. 8 by 19mm ($\frac{3}{4}$in.) chipboard screws in the position shown in the drawings.

Slotting the lid in place then completed the unit and it was ready to perform its various duties.

CUTTING LIST

(Sizes in mm and inches) (No allowance for waste)

Sides**	2 off	854 by 457 by 15mm	(33$\frac{5}{8}$ by 18 by $\frac{5}{8}$in.)
Drawer fronts**	3 off	648 by 229 by 15mm	(25$\frac{1}{2}$ by 9 by $\frac{5}{8}$in.)
Lid**	1 off	648 by 406 by 15mm	(25$\frac{1}{2}$ by 16 by $\frac{5}{8}$in.)
Rails (veneered chipboard)			
Top back	1 off	648 by 127 by 16mm	(25$\frac{1}{2}$ by 5 by $\frac{5}{8}$in.)
Top front	1 off	648 by 76 by 16mm	(25$\frac{1}{2}$ by 3 by $\frac{5}{8}$in.)
Bottom back	1 off	648 by 76 by 16mm	(25$\frac{1}{2}$ by 3 by $\frac{5}{8}$in.)
Bottom front	1 off	648 by 76 by 16mm	(25$\frac{1}{2}$ by 3 by $\frac{5}{8}$in.)
Drawer box (plywood)			
Sides	6 off	406 by 190 by 13mm	(16 by 7$\frac{1}{2}$ by $\frac{1}{2}$in.)
Fronts	3 off	572 by 190 by 13mm	(22$\frac{1}{2}$ by 7$\frac{1}{2}$ by $\frac{1}{2}$in.)
Backs	3 off	572 by 175 by 13mm	(22$\frac{1}{2}$ by 6$\frac{7}{8}$ by $\frac{1}{2}$in.)
Bases	3 off	597 by 406 by 6mm	(23$\frac{1}{2}$ by 16 by $\frac{1}{4}$in.)
Tray (plywood)			
Sides	2 off	410 by 61 by 13mm	(16$\frac{1}{8}$ by 2$\frac{3}{8}$ by $\frac{1}{2}$in.)
Front	1 off	540 by 61 by 13mm	(21$\frac{1}{4}$ by 2$\frac{3}{8}$ by $\frac{1}{2}$in.)
Back	1 off	540 by 30 by 13mm	(21$\frac{1}{4}$ by 1$\frac{3}{16}$ by $\frac{1}{2}$in.)
Base	1 off	540 by 410 by 6mm	(21$\frac{1}{4}$ by 16$\frac{1}{8}$ by $\frac{1}{4}$in.)
Lid guides	4 off	235 by 102 by 6mm	(9 by 4 by $\frac{1}{4}$in.)
Lid runners	2 off	102 by 102 by 19mm	(4 by 4 by $\frac{3}{4}$in.)
Back panel***	1 off	651 by 647 by 6mm	(25$\frac{5}{8}$ by 25$\frac{1}{2}$ by $\frac{1}{4}$in.)
Drawer runners*	6 off	406 by 25 by 16mm	(16 by 1 by $\frac{5}{8}$in.)
Runner guides*	12 off	416 by 25 by 16mm	(16$\frac{3}{8}$ by 1 by $\frac{5}{8}$in.)
Lid edging*	1 off	648 by 16 by 16mm	(25$\frac{1}{2}$ by $\frac{5}{8}$ by $\frac{5}{8}$in.)
Lid lipping*	1 off	648 by 32 by 16mm	(25$\frac{1}{2}$ by 1$\frac{1}{4}$ by $\frac{5}{8}$in.)
Lid front supports*	2 off	121 by 16 by 16mm	(4$\frac{3}{4}$ by $\frac{5}{8}$ by $\frac{5}{8}$in.)
Back panel mountings*	2 off	648 by 25 by 13mm	(25$\frac{1}{2}$ by 1 by $\frac{1}{2}$in.)
Back panel mountings*	2 off	625 by 13 by 13mm	(24$\frac{5}{8}$ by $\frac{1}{2}$ by $\frac{1}{2}$in.)

*denotes hardwood **denotes melamine-faced chipboard ***denotes hardboard
(Also required: approximately 300mm (12in.) of 8mm (5/16in.) dowel) eight K.D. fittings; and approximately four metres of iron-on edging.)

It's a frame up

Nothing enhances a mirror more than an attractive frame whether formal or simply fun. Here's a few ideas to play around with.

GETTING IT RIGHT with interior design often takes time and patience, but it is surprising what can be done with decorative mirrors with ornate and colourful frames. Here we look at three fairly simple designs which convert plain glasses into eye catching focal points in the room. The method used for all three is the same although we look at only one in detail here. Once the basics have been mastered the field is open for bags of imagination and artistic scope with your own designs, personal motifs, and themes. The technique will lend itself to formal treatment or equally well to the amusing or lighthearted approach. We found that the use of bold colours tended to set off these particular designs which rely fairly heavily on simplicity for their effect. One cautionary note however, do be careful when cutting the templets because much of the effect depends upon accuracy of fitting especially if you work in solid timber or veneered ply which will only be stained or varnished. The mirror sizes for our three models are 800 by

600mm, 585 by 420mm and 400mm diameter, and the ground plate sizes are 820 by 620mm, 605 by 440mm and 420mm diameter.

The use of the ground plate helps to hold the mirror in securely and the cut outs make the frame. The methods for all three frames are the same.

You begin with the already cut out patterns, mark them out on to 60mm plywood using the same pattern for left and right sides. On all the drawings the patterns are symmetrical, meeting in the middle.

You may find it easier to cut the flowers in pieces instead of one large cut out, but make sure that the top flowers are not joined in the same place as the botton ones. The easiest way is to follow the directions from the photographs.

What the pictures do not show is the mixing of the paints—choose bright colours and have patience and pride with your painting—the effort will be well rewarded.

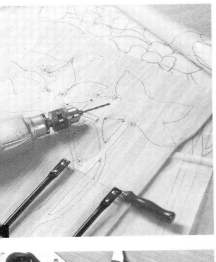

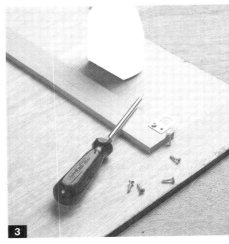

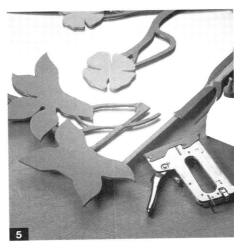

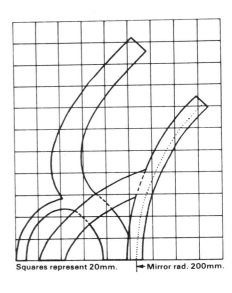

On 6mm plywood make the pattern using
graph diagram, and ⬛ut out with a fret saw,
⬛rst drilling the holes to get the saw
⬛rough.

. After cutting out, smooth edges with
⬛andpaper, especially corners and lay
⬛gether ready for gluing later. Give parts 2
⬛oats of paint including undersides except
⬛r spots to be glued as the under sides will
⬛flect in the mirror.

. Glue a piece of batten across plywood
⬛irror backing and fix 2 mirror plates
⬛aking sure screws are not too long.

. The side batten to hold the mirror must
⬛e 4mm (the same thickness as mirror
⬛lass) the width ⬛d it depends on outlay of
⬛rame and flowers. The battens must lie
⬛ush to the miror and not overlap the
⬛rame, and are best glued and tacked with
⬛vood stapler.

. First layer of Lowers and leaves are glued
⬛ver frame and all pieces to be hidden by
⬛op layer can also be stapled.

. Fix top layer of flowers with glue only.

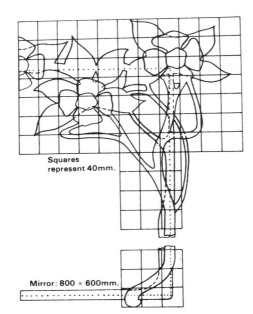

Squares
represent 40mm.

Mirror: 800 × 600mm.

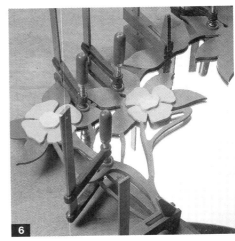

Squares represent 20mm. ← Mirror rad. 200mm.

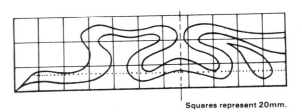

Squares represent 20mm.

Table top trio

Simple eye-catching contrasts have always been the stock-in-trade of the designer especially when they highlight the textures of the materials used and point up the lines of the design. Here we look at an example of this that relies on economy of line and careful choice of materials.

WHY NOT, as a diversion, look at stone topped coffee tables, but really it's no more unusual than the tile topped ones which have proved so popular. The design dealt with here is susceptible to production in many forms and obviously a wooden top would be jusy as easy to fit as any of those shown.

It really is an extremely simple design which relies for its effect on its simplicity of line and deliberate contrasts. Should you decide to give the piece a wooden top choose a dark timber or stain some up to retain the dramatic effect. Also with the wooden top it would be as well to select the frame with the stretcher rails

and not the diagonal variation shown. This will allow for support at the edges of the table. A wooden top can be glued and dowelled in position or glued and screwed from below the rails. The stone ones are simply let into the rebates with no fixing at all. Although stone cannot be worked with the usual woodworkers tools, keen do-it-yourselfers need not shy away from it on principle. Stone slabs, whether slate or polished travertine, can be ordered cut to size. When they are combined with solid wood, stone slabs are excellent for professional looking home-made furniture.

Most people associate stonemasons and

The pronounced grain of the pine leg contrasts with the dark slightly ridged surface of the 30mm thick slate slab used for the top.

stone quarries with monumental masonry or gravestones. But stone merchants also supply the raw materials for many useful things about the house or flat: windowsills, mantlepieces, or attractive tabletops.

This is what inspired us to design this table. One table has a slab of dark grey slate, the other a slab of light, polished travertine (a kind of limestone). Other types of stone are also available: see your local merchant's selection.

The effect is particularly attractive when there is a strong contrast between the wood and the stone top, as can be seen in the photographs. Light natural pine offsets dark

slate, or a dark stained wooden frame sets off the light travertine—choose the effect you prefer. The base is made up of two different corner pieces of planed timber: one is 40 by 80mm (exact dimensions: 38 by 78mm) and the other is 30 by 60mm. A precision mitring saw, as shown in photo 1, is of course ideal for cutting the individual table legs.

The grain of the wood gives additional interest and character to the table, particularly the sturdy table legs. Be careful when gluing the joints that the sections are flush at top and sides. Joints such as these using 10mm thick wood dowel are both simple and strong.

1. The first step is to cut to length the leg pieces. You will need eight pieces of 400mm and eight of 385mm cut off square.

2. Chamfer off the edges of the timber for the desired aesthetic effect and to prevent the timber from splitting at the corners.

3. Glue together the long and the short sections making sure the bottom edges are flush. Then smooth off with a sander.

4. One square piece of timber 40 by 40 mm is used to join together each of the table legs (see drawing for clarification).

5. The rails of the table are held with dowels. These rails are 30 by 60 mm pine and are drilled as shown.

6. With the rails drilled ready for dowelling give them a good smoothing off with the power sander.

7. Pva glue is used here for the joints but any good woodworking glue will be suitable. Coat up the adjoining surfaces as well as the dowels.

8. A close up of the finished leg and rail. The table leg is retained inside the taller or outside leg sections.

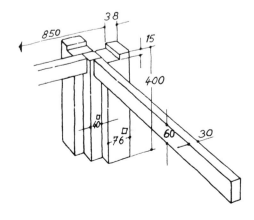

The drawing shows the dimensions for materials when using stone slabs 850mm square. After the glueing, seal the timber with varnish or similar.

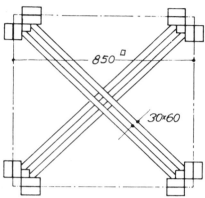

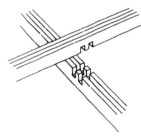

The variation shown here allows for the use of diagonal rails instead of the rectangular ones. Use pieces 30 by 60 mm thick and fix with dowels as before.

Planting an idea

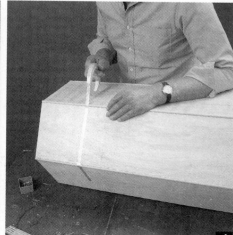

Simplicity is the keynote with this design for indoor plant holders but the overall effect is elegant and fitting for the modern home.

THROUGHOUT THE YEAR we can have a green oasis in the living room, a central display of our favourite pot plants shown off to their best advantage in this nest of holders.

All three of them are made by the same simple method but the effect is obtained by staggering the heights to give a falling or cascading feeling so pleasing with delicate ferns and trailing plants.

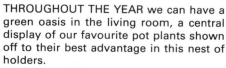

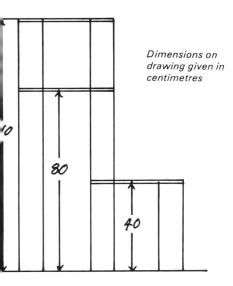

Dimensions on drawing given in centimetres

80

40

10

1. Using a template of paper or cardboard trace out the hexagonal shapes onto 16mm chipboard. Each side should measure 200mm.

2. The sides of the tubes are made in 8mm plywood. Cut them to the sizes you want and glue and tack them in position.

3. The edges are finished off with 6mm dowelling. This eliminates the need to chamfer the edges and produces a clean finish.

4. Bind the dowelling in position at intervals along the tubes until the glue has set. Finish with a light rub over with glasspaper.

The construction method is really simple and almost any timber or man-made board is suitable. Paint them in subdued and subtle colours so they can complement the plants without competing with them. By next spring you'll find they have become old friends and even after days spent in the splendour of the garden and the new growth you'll still appreciate their quiet simplicity at home in the evening.

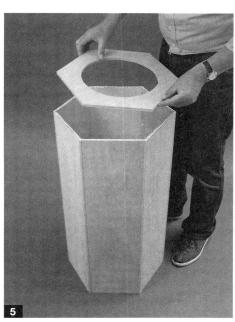

Use 8mm ply for the top hexagons. Mark out round the lip of the pot and cut the hole slightly undersize to prevent it slipping through.

5. Glue and tack the top hexagons in position and again clean up the edges with glasspaper.

6. The finished tubes can be painted in acrylic paint with edges in a contrasting colour if it suits your design scheme.

MILITARY OR CAMPAIGN CHESTS as they are often called have their origins in the time of the Napoleonic Wars around the beginning of the 19th century. It is perhaps slightly ironical that the design features which once made these storage items strong, functional, easy to transport by ship and by land as the officers moved from one campaign to another are the very features which make them so attractive in the modern home today. The flush brass handles and the strengthening corner straps which once gave protection against the inevitable knocks and bangs suffered in transportation now give these pieces a handsome elegance particularly when seen as the contrast between polished brass and the rich colour of mahogany. Another factor about the original pieces is that they were always made to be relatively small, often consisting of two components one sitting on top of the other, and this "smallness" in design is a feature which is well suited to the modern home with its smaller rooms.

In this case the chest shown here is of a design based on the original type, but modifications have been made for ease of construction both in terms of the materials used and methods employed. For the main carcase components 20mm blockboard, veneered on both sides with mahogany, has been used, however veneered chipboard could equally well be substituted for most items. Plywood is used in the drawer construction as well as for the back, with solid mahogany lippings on the front of the carcase. Brass fittings for the corners, straps and handles can be readily obtained from firms which advertise in this magazine.

Military chest

Brass-bound and elegant, this traditional style chest is simple to build and makes an ideal storage unit for clothes and other items.

1. Drawer ledges and runners grooved 5mm by 10mm deep and strips of plastic laminate to give smooth sliding action.

Construction

1. Mark out the components on a sheet of blockboard. With careful positioning most components can be obtained from a sheet 2440 by 1220mm. However ensure consistency of grain direction in the drawer fronts, carcase components and plinth parts.

2. Prepare the five pieces for the carcase accurately to size truing up identical parts together. Where the blockboard structure will show at exposed ends (top and bottom of side panels and backs of top and side panels) use iron-on mahogany edging strip.

3. Jointing of the carcase is by dowelling, using three dowels to each joint. Prepare these with the aid of a dowelling jig and assemble for a "dry run" to check that all is square and that the surfaces meet.

4. After marking out heights of drawer rails on the three vertical carcase panels, prepare the drawer runners and ledges. Initially make 4mm screw fixing holes in the runners 50mm in from both ends, and countersink to a depth of 20mm for screwdriver clearance. Now groove the runners 5mm wide by 20mm deep for their full length taking several passes over the circular saw. These grooves are to take the loose tongues fitted between runners and drawer rails. Ledges are glued and pinned to the runners, but are set in by the thickness of the drawer fronts. Small strips of plastic laminate glued onto the runners will give a better bearing and sliding surface for the drawers.

5. With the runners and ledges glued and screwed into place, the five panels of the carcase can be finally assembled with dowels and glue. Cramp up and check that the carcase is square.

2. Carcase is joined at the corners with blind dowels. Ledges and runners are screwed in position on the carcase walls.

3. Runner is fixed level with the edge. Ledge is inset for drawer front.

4. Loose tongue joint inserted between drawer rail and the runner.

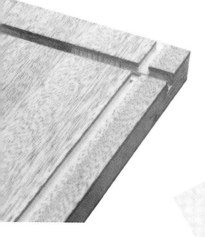

Drawer fronts must be ʒrooved on the circular saw to ƈeive the plywood pieces for ᵉ sides and also the base.

6. Drawer construction—sides and back are from 12mm ply with 5mm ply back pinned to rear.

7. Drawer back supports also act as drawer stops against the back supports.

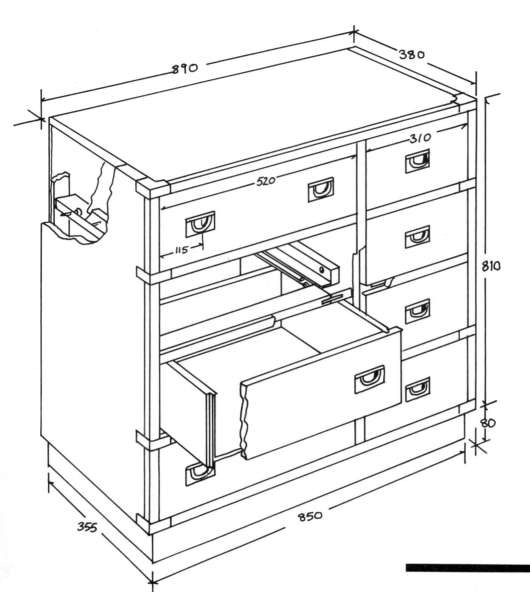

6. Cut the drawer rails to fit between the runners, groove the ends and prepare plywood tongues from 5mm ply. Fit rails into place with glue applied to tongues and grooves.

7. Mahogany strip 20 by 10mm is now glued to all front edges and small brass dome headed screws can be driven in to hold them in place. As these screws are partly decorative space them evenly remembering where the brass angle strips will be applied.

8. The plinth can now be made up, gluing the components together at the corners and using wood blocks behind as strengthening blocks which can be glued on and screwed through. Remember that exposed blockboard ends must be treated with iron-on mahogany veneer. Small blocks are also used to attach the plinth to the carcase—these being glued and screwed from the inside to both parts.

9. The drawer construction shown here is a fairly simple method involving the use of a circular saw for grooving. The veneered blockboard front is grooved to receive the ply base and sides, and exposed blockboard ends are again covered with iron-on edging strip. Sides and back are from 12mm ply while the base is 5mm ply. Although comb joints could be used between back and sides, the simple method shown here uses strengthening blocks which are glued and pinned to the back and sides. The ply base is slid into position and pinned to the back. The brass handles are recessed into the front, and hollows must be gouged out accordingly. Do not fit the handles until after finishing the piece.

10. The final stage of construction is to glue and pin on the softwood back support battens and with these in place, the back itself can be added.

11. All that remains to do is to apply two coats of clear varnish, flatting down between coats, and then add the brass handles and angles and the project is complete.

Cutting list

From 20mm mahogany veneered blockboard

Sides	2 off	810 by 370 by 20mm
Top and base	2 off	850 by 370 by 20mm
Middle wall	1 off	770 by 365 by 20mm
Plinth	1 off	850 by 80 by 20mm
Plinth	2 off	335 by 80 by 20mm
Drawer rails	3 off	440 by 50 by 20mm
Drawer rails	3 off	230 by 50 by 20mm
Drawer runners	12 off	347 by 40 by 20mm
Drawer ledges	16 off	327 by 25 by 20mm

From plywood

Drawer sides	16 off	345 by 177 by 12mm
Drawer backs	4 off	456 by 140 by 12mm
Drawer backs	4 off	246 by 140 by 12mm
Drawer bottoms	4 off	466 by 330 by 5mm
Drawer bottoms	4 off	256 by 330 by 5mm
Carcase back	1 off	850 by 770 by 5mm
Loose tongues	16 off	50 by 40 by 5mm

From solid timber

Mahogany strip	2 off	890 by 20 by 10mm
Mahogany strip	3 off	770 by 20 by 10mm
Mahogany strip	3 off	520 by 20 by 10mm
Mahogany strip	3 off	310 by 20 by 10mm
Back supports	2 off	770 by 30 by 18mm
Drawer strengtheners	16 off	140 by 15 by 15mm

Also required: 10mm dowelling; mahogany edging strip; oddments for glue blocks; plastic laminate for drawer runners; brass handles; corners and angles.

8. Use polished brass corner straps and angle pieces to give the finishing touch to the chest.

Wood Working Outside

If applying finish out of doors, do so when rain is not expected

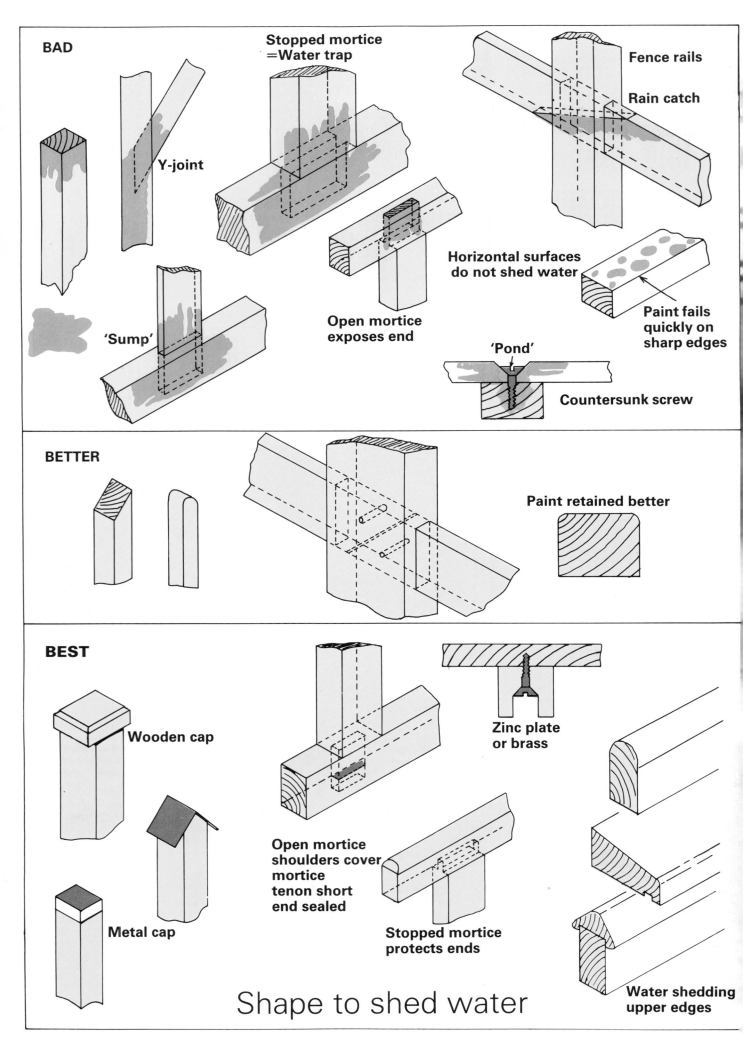

BAD

Stopped mortice
=Water trap

Fence rails

Rain catch

Y-joint

Horizontal surfaces
do not shed water

Paint fails
quickly on
sharp edges

Open mortice
exposes end

'Sump'

'Pond'

Countersunk screw

BETTER

Paint retained better

BEST

Wooden cap

Zinc plate
or brass

Open mortice
shoulders cover
mortice
tenon short
end sealed

Metal cap

Stopped mortice
protects ends

Water shedding
upper edges

Shape to shed water

Making things to last

by Austin Hilditch, Technical Director of Cuprinol Ltd

If you want the things you make to last outside in the weather, you must follow some simple guidelines at the beginning and throughout the job.

  Design it right
  Choose your wood
  Make it right
  Preserve it

You may not be building for posterity, and it is never safe to predict how long anything will last. However, the following 'equations' provide a rough guide which may help you decide what you are going to do.

  Bad design + poor wood = problems within five years

  Better design + normal wood + preservation = 10-20 years, perhaps more.

  Best design + best wood + attention to detail + preservation + maintenance = 25-50 years or more.

Designing and Making

Wood absorbs water. It absorbs it most easily at the ends. When wet, wood swells and is liable to decay.

Simple rules are:
  Avoid water traps ⎤
  Shape to shed water ⎬— to minimise water up-take
  Protect end grain ⎦

  Avoid sharp edges — Finishes fail quickly on them

  Seal water out, not in — Use moisture vapour permeable (microporous) finishes

  Make tight joints — Water gets into loose ones

  Make joints to withstand swelling — e.g. sides of a mortice must withstand swelling of the tenon.

  Use corrosion resistant fastenings and fittings

1. Notice on stack of wood — Chatsworth Estate, Derby. In a balanced natural environment the same amount must rot.

2. Garden seat about 1 hour after rain — water that has run into stopped mortice means wood stays wet longer. Note splitting from mortice.

End grain is most vulnerable. Often, it can be protected by design (See Figure 1), but whenever possible it is best to seal the end grain. A full paint or exterior wood stain system, if used, will seal visible ends but it is well worth sealing end grain inside joints. There are very few materials available in shops that will do this effectively, the best is an old-fashioned lead primer — if you do not want to use lead, use a two-pack epoxy adhesive such as Araldite. Most other glues, even those recommended for outdoor use and other paints are inferior for this purpose.

  Mild steel rusts quickly in wet wood. Rusting may be accelerated by acids in some woods e.g. Western Red Cedar. First the wood near the nail or screw is stained black. Later the wood may be damaged or the fastening fail. Use copper, brass, aluminium, zinc plate or galvanised iron. If you must use mild steel fittings, coat all round with a corrosion resisting paint.

Choose Timber

Decide the type

Timber from different types of tree differs considerably in appearance, workability, durability, ability to take in a preservative, or retain a finish, availability and cost.

  Table 1 will help you select timber for your job. For outdoor work, you should either select timber that is very durable, and be prepared to cut out and waste any sapwood or one that can readily be treated with a preservative.

Selecting Timber

When you go to buy timber, select the pieces for yourself. This is worthwhile with all timbers, but it is most important with ordinary softwoods. Do not select pieces with too many large or dead knots, resin pockets, or that are exceptionally resinous, or split or have any of the other "normal" defects of wood.

  Avoid any sign of decay or surface mould.

  Avoid bluestain. This shows through and spoils the appearance of transparent finishes and even where opaque finishes or paints are to be used, it is still best to avoid it, since it often coincides with increased permeability.

3. Garden seat on patio – water soaks up end grain.

4. Summerhouse mounted clear of ground with waterproof felt below wood.

Sometimes, green timber is kept wet for a long time before being sawn and seasoned. During this time it becomes infected with bacteria which make it much more permeable, so that it will absorb twenty or more times as much water as normal wood. Such timbers are best avoided out of doors. Water gets in so easily that decay is an even greater risk than usual. Paints fail sooner and if you treat it with a preservative, it will absorb a very large amount. This will take a long time to dry and may add to painting problems.

This type of defect is very difficult to detect, since the colour and appearance are normal. Avoid any timber with yellow or other coloured stains, for although this is not necessarily indicative of high absorption, it often coincides. The only way you can really detect these areas of high absorption (often called ponding), is by rubbing the surface with a rag, wet but not soaked, with white spirit. Ponding usually occurs in odd patches and these will show up a darker colour than the rest.

Why wood needs Preserving

Wood is a plant material and like all such materials, some organisms can feed on it.

The main organisms feeding on wood are the fungi, and the grubs of some insects. Fungi cause decay (both wet and dry rot). Bacteria invade it and sometimes cause a little damage. Algae and lichen both grow on it and can spoil its appearance.

In a completely natural environment, such as a forest, it is essential that dead trees are broken down. Unfortunately, fungi and destructive insects do not see any difference between wood used by man and dead trees.

Fungi need water and air to grow, therefore if wood is kept dry it will not rot, but this is not possible all the time in any outdoor situation. Timber that is wet for as little as two months in a year, is likely to decay. Spores are everywhere. Studies have shown that when new wood is put out of doors, bacteria get into it within a very few days, moulds and mildews, only a few days later. Decay fungi are found within a month.

The most destructive fungi for outdoor wood are the wet rots. (Dry rot only occurs in buildings.) A large number of individual species make up the wet rots. All belong to the same class as the common mushroom (Basidiomycetes), and can produce large fruiting bodies which may be seen as mushroom or bracket shaped growths on old tree stumps.

Outdoors, decayed wood is usually soft and pulpy. Water oozes out if pressed and while decayed wood retains the main outlines of the original wood for quite some time, it has no strength and will shrink very considerably when it dries out and will eventually crumble away. Sometimes during dry periods, decayed wood may be seen to crack across and along the grain in a cubicle fashion. (More frequently seen indoors than out). When this type of

cracking is seen on the surface, but the wood is sound two or three millimetres down, then decay is most likely to be by a type of fungi of a group known as the soft rots. These act more slowly but are ever present in the soil and will destroy timbers resistant to wet rot. Wood decayed by wet rot is most usually dark brown or black, sometimes called brown rot, but some of the wet rot fungi cause the wood to turn lighter, almost white. These are known as the white rots.

Sometimes a few black, brown or white strands may be seen on the wood surface, but usually with wet rot there is no obvious sign of fungi, just the progressive deterioration of the wood.

Wood is liable to decay at moisture contents above 20%. (For wood, moisture content is always measured on the weight of the dry wood, so this means 100kg of oven-dry wood plus 20kg water), but wet rot will only flourish at moisture contents above about 30% and growth is fastest around 60-70%. To get this wet it must be in contact with liquid water. This of course is available in profusion from rain, dew, soil, damp concrete, masonry and especially from any pools that form on it. Water needs a little time to soak deeply into the wood. In the soil, it has all the time it requires, but where the main source of water is rain, then how much soaks in and how wet the wood gets is very dependent on whether the structure sheds or retains this water (Figure 1).

Commonly, an individual piece of timber will be part wet, part dry. For example, a fence post, even in dry weather, will be wet below and just above the ground, but dry higher up (getting wet quicker and staying wet longer near the top end). A garden chair will stay wet where rain runs into the joints, but soon dries after rain elsewhere. Very simply, the wet bits decay and the dry bits stay sound. This factor may help your understanding of which parts are most likely to decay, but it is not of much consolation, a chair rotten at the joints is only good for firewood.

When wood is exposed to the weather, it will deteriorate, even if not wet enough for long enough to decay rapidly. Deterioration is less spectacular, destruction is slower, but the appearance changes rapidly. With almost all woods the surface will soon go grey.

This change in appearance is due to changes at or near the surface of the wood, due to a combination of things. A chemical breakdown due to the action of sunlight, particularly ultra violet. Physical breakdown due to the stresses and strains set up by repeated swelling and shrinking caused by continual cycles of wetting from rain or dew followed by rapid drying under the influence of wind and hot sun, and continual exposure to extremes of temperature fluctuating hourly, daily and seasonally. When cold showers and hot sun follow each other, temperature changes at the wood surface might be as much as 50°C. There may also be corrosive action and disfigurement by atmospheric dirt and assault by micro-organisms blackening the surface. Here, the quickest developing, most obvious organisms are the spoiling moulds, mildew and sapstaining fungi. Algae usually take a little while to appear, but may be seen well within a year. Green algae are particularly common and obvious where the wood is shaded from direct sunlight, especially northern aspects (southern aspects in southern hemisphere) or if overhung by trees.

Posts and any timber buried in the ground, or used in flower tubs and the like, is nearly always wet and is always surrounded by lots of fungi. Decay is certain. Softwood sapwood lasts 2-5 years. Preservation is essential, preferably by a long soak. Timber laid on, but not buried in the soil, is not very different.

After rain, there are usually pools of water on stone or concrete paths or patios. Timber standing on them will soak this up. Decay in this situation may be slower than in soil, but effective preservation is still necessary.

Timber above the ground, open to the weather, is mainly wetted by rain, sometimes by fog or dew, but it is also dried by the sun and the wind. Decay of the mass of timber is therefore very dependent on how far the structure retains the water falling on it, so that it can soak in. Many items from garden chairs to fences, will decay first at the joints. Coatings that are impermeable to water vapour – as are traditional paints – can hasten decay by preventing wood from drying.

Insects such as the common furniture beetle will attack wood outdoors – their natural habitat is dead wood on trees – but usually only occur in articles that are very old.

Preserving

The basic principle of preserving wood is to put sufficient preservative chemical into the wood to prevent fungal or insect attack. The wood into which the preservative has penetrated forms a toxic barrier or "cordon sanitaire" around the wood in the centre of the piece. Thus it is essential that all surfaces of the wood are treated.

The more preservative that gets into the wood and the greater the depth of penetration, the greater will be its effect. Thus the effectiveness of a preservative treatment depends on the method of application and on the composition of the preservative.

Because of the conditions to which outdoor timbers are exposed, more preservative must be applied than when treating timbers for use inside buildings.

For home use, in treating timbers for out of doors, the only preservatives that should be used are those in which the carrier liquid is organic. Organic liquids, as used for example in Cuprinol Wood Preservatives, penetrate much more quickly than others, so that deeper penetration is obtained. They also have the advantage of not causing any swelling and of drying out relatively quickly.

General instructions for Preserving Timber

Timber should be fully worked, dry and free from bark (including inner bark), paint, varnish or other surface coating. It must be treated freely on all surfaces. The more preservative you get into the wood, the more effective it will be.

Brush Treatment

At least two coats must be given. The second and subsequent coats can be applied as soon as the preceding coat has soaked in and must be applied before it is dry. A large brush is best and the preservative should be flooded onto the wood in a flowing coat, not brushed out like a paint. Penetration of the end grain is most important. Only treat end grain by brush if there is no alternative, then dab repeatedly until no more soaks in. Preferably, even if the rest of the article is being treated by brush, treat the end grain by standing in preservative in a bucket, tank or even old paint tin, (the deeper, the better).

Spraying

Flood the surface of the wood with at least two coats as in brushing. When applying a preservative (as opposed to a paint or wood stain), the object is to get as much preservative onto the wood as possible. A low pressure garden-type spray is better than a paint spray. Whichever type is being used, adjust pressure and nozzle to avoid production of an atomised mist and/or bouncing of liquid off the wood surface. Both are wasteful and inefficient and the former may allow excessive drift onto the operator and surroundings.

When spraying out of doors, do not let any of the spray get onto plants and if a garden sprayer is used, it is best not to use the same sprayer for applying pesticides to plants. (If you do use the same one, clean out immediately after use and clean very thoroughly.) If the sprayer you use has previously been used for garden pesticides, make sure that no water remains in it when using for wood preservatives. Some preservatives will cause staining of plastic sprayers.

Dipping

This is in every way the most effective of the simple methods of treatment and should be used whenever possible. The longer the dip, the more preservative will be absorbed and the more effective the treatment. For outdoor timbers, at least ten minutes immersion for permeable timbers, three or more times as long for timbers that absorb preservative less readily.

This period is normally satisfactory for outdoor timbers that are not in contact with the ground or constantly wet conditions.

For fence posts and other timbers in contact with the ground, soak for at least one hour, if possible up to twenty-four. If it is not possible to soak the whole length of the timber, the part going into the ground and some 150-300mm (6-12 inches) above this should be given this prolonged treatment, the top end a 10 minute dip and the remainder thoroughly brushed.

Cutting timber after treatment will remove much of the preservative value, and will often completely nullify it by exposing untreated wood below. Therefore, make your article before preserving the wood. Fit all joints, make bolt holes etc., then knock down and preserve. Remember to allow the preservative to dry before re-assembling if glues are to be used. If cutting or drilling after assembly is unavoidable, then the cut areas must be retreated.

General

Wood preservers are supplied ready for use and must not be heated or mixed unless this is specifically recommended for the product concerned. Containers should be kept stoppered and if preservative is left in buckets or tanks for any length of time, these should be covered. Brushes, sprays etc., may be cleaned with paraffin. Always read the instructions first, particularly if you intend to paint or finish your article. Some preservatives sold for outdoor timbers are not suitable for over-painting. Where a product is recommended for over-painting, treated timber must be allowed to dry thoroughly before painting, staining or varnishing.

When it is intended to use the treated timber in a closed area like a greenhouse, or in very close contact with plants, such as seed boxes or plant tubs, then allow to dry most thoroughly before using. Never do the treatment inside a greenhouse while there are plants in it. Note that some wood preservatives are unsuitable for these uses, even when dry. Again, find out by reading instructions.

5. Weathering of exposed end grain.

Application Rate

It is essential to apply enough wood preservative if it is to do its job. The more you apply, the longer and more certain the results. Skimping on the preservative is "saving a penny to lose a pound". The more severe the conditions the treated wood must withstand, the more preservative you will need. Typical rates of application that should be aimed at for most Cuprinol wood preservers are shown in Table 2. These must be achieved on all sides and ends of the timber. The treatments shown will achieve these rates of application on most common timbers e.g. European Redwood. For timbers that are more resistant to treatment, the severity of treatment must be increased, say three times as long. Rough sawn timber absorbs more than planed timber (about twice).

Retreatment

Where exterior timbers are fully exposed to the weather, there will be some small but progressive loss of preservative and checks or mechanical damage are liable to occur. Periodic retreatment is therefore advisable. With fences, sheds, and the like, this must be carried out where they stand. The time should be chosen so that the timber is dry and if, as is often the case in such situations, there are plants nearby, extra precautions are called for.

Wood preservatives for home and garden use, use an organic solvent as carrier for the wood preservative chemicals. These solvents have an effect on plants similar to that of tar oil winter wash, in that while they are relatively harmless to bark and harder woody stems, they cause severe scorching to leaves and other delicate tissues. In treating a fence or shed by brush and especially by spray, care must be taken to avoid getting any preservative onto nearby plants that may be harmed. If treatment is carried out in the spring or summer, climbing plants should be loosened from the fence and brushing should be carried out carefully to avoid splashing. If spraying, when some spray drift cannot be avoided, it is best to protect plants with plastic sheeting. Fences etc., should be allowed to dry for a few days before refixing plants.

Alternatively, carry out treatment in the late autumn or winter (provided you can find a long enough dry spell). At this time of year annual plants will have died down, leaves will have fallen off deciduous plants, harder woody plants are unlikely to be harmed. Should you have any more delicate plants to which a tar oil winter wash would not be applied, take precautions recommended for summer. Avoid getting any onto the leaves of evergreens.

Even then, it is sensible and economical to avoid getting much onto the plants and dripping too much onto the soil. Note that while the above comments apply to preservatives such as the Cuprinol S range, other preservatives may contain active ingredients which are harmful to the plants, applied at any time of the year. You should avoid getting these onto the plants or into the soil near the roots (the most common preservative chemical that is harmful to plants is pentachlorophenol).

Many water-based products are available for the decoration and protection of fences. These are less harmful to plants at the time of application (generally), but are primarily intended for colouring. Few, if any, provide any real protection against decay.

Wood with bark on

Wood preservatives will not penetrate through bark, so that wood with the bark left on cannot be properly preserved. However, for appearance, wood with the bark on is often used around the house and garden. Stand cut ends in preservative for as long as you reasonably can. If you are using wood with the bark on as posts, cut the bark off the part that will be below the ground and soak this. If you are making plant boxes with offcuts of logs with bark on one side, then soak for as long as you can so that preservative can penetrate through from the side without bark. Preserving timber with the bark on is always unreliable, but I soaked the wood for some plant troughs as described, in one of the Works vats of Cuprinol Wood Preservative Green for a fortnight — they lasted nearly 20 years.

6. Fungal fruiting bodies at base of fence post.

7.

7 and 8. Decay in various types of fence.

Table 1 Choosing Timber

Timber type	Natural Durability		Absorption of Preservative		Paint Holding	Work-ability	Weight kg/m³	Availability Group	Comments
	Sapwood*	Heartwood	Sapwood	Heartwood					
Softwoods									
Baltic Redwood/ Scots Pine	Perishable	Non-durable	Permeable	Moderately resistant	Good	Good	510	1	Commercial timber typically high proportion sapwood
Radiata Pine	Perishable	Non-durable	Permeable	Moderately resistant					
Jack Pine	Perishable	Non-durable	Permeable	Moderately resistant					
Whitewood / Spruce/Fir	Perishable	Non-durable	Resistant	Resistant	Inter-mediate	Good	470	1	Bad choice for ground use
Hemlock	Perishable	Non-durable		Resistant	Inter-mediate	Good	490	2	
Red Cedar (Western)	Perishable	Durable		Resistant	Good	Soft	370	2	Usually little, if any sapwood in cut timbers. Stained by iron
Larch	Perishable	Moderately durable	Moderately resistant	Resistant	Poor	Good if not too many knots	590	4	
Douglas Fir / Oregon Pine	Perishable	Moderately durable		Resistant	Poor especially on Plywood	Not as good as other Softwoods	530	1	Much used in external ply
Hardwoods									
Teak / Iroko (African Teak)		Very durable		Extremely resistant	Very poor	Hard	640	3	
Oak – European / Japanese	Perishable	Durable	Permeable	Extremely resistant	Poor	Hard	670-720'	3	Stained by iron. Japanese oak often contains much sapwood.
Oak – American White		Durable	Moderately resistant	Extremely resistant	Poor	Varies	750	3	
American Red	Perishable	Non-durable		Moderately resistant			770	3	Porous
Meranti / Luan	Perishable	Non-durable to moderately durable	Permeable to moderately resistant	Resistant to extremely resistant		Fairly good	510-670	3	Commercial timber from many species – very variable
Elm – English / Dutch	Perishable	Non-durable	Permeable	Moderately resistant	Poor	Moderate	550	2 or 3	Take care to select sound timbers in areas where available from trees killed by Dutch Elm Disease

Availability and Cost of Timbers

Group 1. Freely available most temperate regions usually main constructional and general purpose timbers. Lower price range. Use of specific timber varies locally – Baltic Redwood in UK, Scandinavia and parts of Europe. Fir or Spruce, parts of Europe and Canada. Radiata Pine, Australia and New Zealand. Jack Pine and others in parts of USA and Canada.

Group 2. Generally available, but less widely than Group 1.

Group 3. Available from specialist stockist – even more expensive.

Group 4. Widely used for fence panels. In UK not widely available in larger sizes. Cheap.

* Sapwood almost always present in softwoods. Is also susceptible to fungal staining. Sapwood often absent in sawn hardwoods – if present also susceptible to staining.

9. Wet rot in fence rail.

10. White strands of a wet rot – only sometimes seen.

Finishing

Using a finish protects the surface of the wood and gives you an appearance to your liking. Even if you do not particularly want to change the appearance of the timber, you still need to use a finish to protect the appearance, for outdoors, unprotected this will change quite fast.

Recently, many new products have become available for finishing outdoor wood. You now have a choice of both traditional and new finishes. This choice is shown in Table 4.

In choosing a finish, you should consider:

(1) Appearance
(2) Protection provided
(3) How long it will last
(4) How easy to maintain
(5) Cost

You must decide your own order of importance, it may well be different for different jobs. For example on something that you have spent a lot of time and money making and is not going to use much finish, then the cost of the finish will be of little or no importance, but on a long fence that will need a lot of finish, cost may be your first consideration.

In finishing, wood is different to any other material. Weather is very bad for finishes. The properties of wood (particularly swelling and shrinking) place the strain on the finish outdoors. You must select a finish that is specifically intended for use on wood out of doors.

Whatever finish you select, it will give best results if it is applied correctly. To some extent the different finishes, exceptionally even different makes, are slightly different in the best way to use. You should always read the instructions on the tin. The comments below are just as a general guidance.

Wood should be seasoned and surface dry. No finish should be applied during or soon after rain. Water-based finishes are a little more tolerant of damp surfaces than those that are oil-based, but only a little so and both types are best applied when it is dry.

Applying the finishes out of doors, do it when rain is not expected until after the finish is expected to be dry. Water-based finishes may be washed off by rain before they are dry. Oil-based products will be less effected but even here the surface may be marred by rain immediately after application. Gloss finishes may lose their gloss if they get wet from rain, fog or dew, before they are dry – so be cautious about using a gloss paint in the late evening, even in the summer.

The time any finish takes to dry is partly dependent on the weather. Figures quoted by most manufacturers relate to "average" drying under "good" conditions, say dry weather with temperatures 15-20°C. Oil based products may take three or more times as long to dry at temperatures between 0 and 5°C, while water-based products will generally not dry satisfactorily at temperatures below 10°C or when it is very humid. This type of finish should not therefore be used out of doors in the colder part of the winter.

The rougher the wood, the longer a finish will last. This even applies to paints, although for obvious reasons you are unlikely to want to put a traditional three-coat paint system on rough-sawn timber. With wood stains, especially on cladding, sheds and the like, if you have the choice of using rough-sawn timber, you should consider it very seriously, not only is rough-sawn timber cheaper, but wood stains will last two or more times as long as on prepared timber. There is even a small difference between planed and sanded surfaces, so that unless you need to sand to remove or feather-edge stubborn old finishes, save yourself the trouble.

When re-finishing, all finishes will look or last better if dirt is cleaned off the old surface. The only type of finish that you should even consider applying without cleaning down, is the penetrating coloured wood preservatives such as Cuprinol Exterior Browns or Creosote.

When an old finish is unsound, or has weathered unevenly, it will mostly be best to remove it. For paints this will need the use of chemical or hot air paint strippers, but for those stains that fail by erosion and not by flaking, and for most Red Cedar finishes, adequate cleaning down will result from just scrubbing the surface with a hard bristle brush, detergent and water. Hose off, and allow to dry. Scrub along the grain. On soft timbers such as Western Red Cedar there may be some roughening – do not worry, this will improve the retention of the finish. Do not use a wire brush. This is too rough and may leave iron stains on the wood.

If you are selecting your finish for performance then some indication of the intrinsic weather-resistance of the different types

11. Decay of bottom of shed (from inside).

Table 2   Application Rates

Description	Hazard	Example	Treatment	Minimum rate of application
Exterior Timbers not in ground contact	Decay and/or insect attack	(a) Timberrs of small cross section e.g. fence panels, shed walls	Dip 3 minutes Brush/Spray – 2 applications	1 litre per 8 sq. metres (1 gal. per 400 sq. ft.)
		(b) Timbers of large cross section, e.g. exposed framing timbers, decking etc.	Brush/spray – 3 applications Steep 10 minutes to 1 hour according to species, exposure etc.	40 litres per cu. metre (¼ gal. per cu. ft.)
Exterior Timbers in contact with ground	Severe decay and/or insect attack	(a) Large section- fence posts, gates etc.	Steep 1 hour minimum according to species and size	
		(b) Small section- garden stakes, window boxes	Steep 15 mins. to 1 hour	
		(c) Very thin – seed boxes	Dip 5 minutes	

Table 3   Cuprinol Wood Preservatives

	Exterior Chestnut/ Golden Brown	Green	Clear	Red Cedar
	General purpose preservative for outdoor use, in 2 shades of traditional brown. Not paintable.	General purpose preservative giving maximum protection in ground. Coloured but not suitable where decorative colour required.	General purpose. Colourless. Preferred for over-painting or staining.	Combined preservative and stain, primarily for Western Red Cedar.
Posts or other timber in or on ground	✔	✔	✔	
Sheds – not to be painted	✔			✔
– to be painted or stained			✔	
Fence panels	✔			✔
Fence rails – to be painted			✔	
Green houses – inside or outside		✔	Clear S	✔
Garden furniture				✔
Other rough sawn – not to be painted	✔			
Other timber – to be painted, stained, finished			✔	

12. Algal growth on shed.

13. Blue stain shows through varnish.

of finish is shown in Table 4, but if you have first selected your finish because of your personal preferences on appearance, there are still differences between different products and while to a large extent you must rely on manufactuers' claims, the three principal factors for consideration are –

(i) Elasticity or Flexibility of the Finish

Wood swells and shrinks as its moisture content changes. It does this repeatedly. Under the variations of outdoor weathering, the difference between maximum swelling and maximum shrinkage is only about 2%, but unless the finish can match this (both to start with and after a long period of weathering) then the finish will crack.

(ii) Moisture Vapour Permeability

Sometimes referred to as MVP and confusingly also termed porosity, microporosity, breathability. It is very desirable that a finish minimises the extent to which rain can get into the wood through the film, but no matter how good the finish is in this respect, some water will still find a way into the timber, perhaps through end grain and joints. It is even more important that the finish does not seal in this moisture. If it does, then the wood will be more likely to decay and the adhesion of the coating may be adversely affected.

(iii) Fungicidal

Paints and stains can be damaged by fungi growing on the film or on the surface of the wood below the film. Many fungi causing the worst damage to paints are not the same as those causing decay, and in an outdoor situation the best service is likely to be obtained from finishes containing a fungicide. Here be very careful in how far you accept manufacturers' claims.

The use of a finish containing fungicide effective against moulds, mildews and similar types of growth is almost a must but no finish will serve as a substitute for initial treatment with a proper wood preservative. Many wood stains are formulated to contain fungicides known to be effective against decay. These however, only penetrate fractionally into the wood, they can be very useful in reinforcing or even restoring the preservation of timbers that have long been exposed to the weather, but they are not effective as a total protection against decay unless backed up with an initial preservative treatment.

Conclusion

Unless it is made from wood of the highest natural durability, all wooden structures and articles should be protected from decay with a wood preservative. If you also want things to go on looking "cared for", then protect the surface from deterioration with a finish.

If you want to maximise the life of anything you are making then design and make it to last as well.

Table 4   Outdoor Finishes

Type of finish	Example	Main uses	Coverage M²/Lt/coat () coats recommended	Maintenance* cycle (approx)	Maintenance	Comments
Traditional paint system	Brolac, primer undercoat, gloss	House timber, some garden furniture Primer Undercoat Gloss	Planed 11 (1) 14 (1) 16 (1 or 2)	4-5 years	Clean down, lightly sand surface and remove loose paint. Spot prime bare wood. Undercoat and apply 1 coat of gloss paint.	Completely hides surface. Long lasting, excellent protection against weather. Impermeable retains water in wood. Flexibility decreases with age, fail by cracking and flaking.
Moisture vapour permeable or microporous paint	Berger Cuprinol Wood Paint Sheen (Oil) Matt or Gloss (Water)	House timber 1. Wood Paint Sheen 2. Wood Paint Matt 3. Wood Paint Primer + Wood Paint Gloss	Planed 12 (2) 10 (2) 10 (1) 16 (2)	5-6 years 5-6 years 5-7 years	Clean down, remove any loose paint. Spot "prime" with Wood Paint Matt or Sheen or Wood Primer Paint as appropriate. Finish with 1 or 2 coats of Wood Paint.	Appearance similar to ordinary paints, but are more permeable, allowing water in the wood to dry out. Water borne paints generally retain flexibility better and last longer, but should not be applied outdoors in winter.

(Table 4 continued)

Type of finish	Example	Main uses	Coverage M²/Lt/coat () coats recommended		Maintenance* cycle (approx)	Maintenance	Comments
Wood stain	Berger Cuprinol Wood Stains Natural Sheen Hardwood Sheen	House timber, especially cladding and window frames	Planed 20(2 or 3)	Sawn 10(1 or 2)	3 years 4 years 4 years	Clean down, remove any loose Wood Stain finish. Spot prime with Finish and apply 1 or 2 coats. Avoid more than 3-coat film thickness.	Transparent and semi-transparent, allowing wood to show through. Excellent permeability and flexibility. Fail by erosion enables easy retreatment. Many products (inc. all Berger Cuprinol) contain fungicide).
Cedar treatment	Cuprinol Red Cedar	Cladding sheds and greenhouses of Western Red Cedar	Planed 2(2)	Sawn 6(1)	approx. 2-3 years	Clean down and apply 1-2 coats of Cuprinol Red Cedar Preserver	Stains and Preservatives specifically formulated for use on Western Red Cedar.
Teak oil	Cuprinol Teak Oil	Teak garden furniture	Planed 20 (1)		1 year	Clean down. Apply further coat with brush or cloth.	Specific product for dressing Teak or Iroko (African teak) which do not accept paints or similar finishes. Some Teak oils are mainly intended for indoor use. These are thinner. (Manufacturers' instructions seldom clear.)
Coloured wood preservative	Cuprinol Exterior Brown	Fences, Sheds	Planed 8(1 or 2)	Sawn 5(1)	3 years	Brush or clean off surface dirt and re-apply 1 coat.	Primarily preservative product, brown tone colour. Penetrates well, easily applied and re-applied.
	Creosote	Fences, Shed	6 (1 or 2)		1-2 years	as above.	Similar to above but with colour variations between suppliers. Strong smell, oily, cheap.
Water-based timber stain	Cuprinol Timbercare	Rough sawn only Fences	10 (1 or 2)		approx. 2-3 years	as above.	Cheap, easy to apply, Good colour. Only suitable for rough sawn timber. Protection against decay negligible (despite some manufacturers' claims). Ideal finish fencing pre-treated with preservative.
Varnish	Cuprinol or Berger Exterior Varnish	Doors, furniture.	17 (3 or 4)		approx. 2 years	Clean down surface. Remove any loose varnish. Lightly rub over with sandpaper. Patch prime bare wood. With varnish, apply 1 or 2 coats overall.	Very popular. Very good when new. Will maximise visibility of wood grain and texture. Relatively poor durability. In exposed situations 4 coats only lasts 1½-2 years. Regular maintenance essential–performance improved by precoat wood preservative or fungicidal containing stain.

() Number of coats recommended
* For inland parts of U.K. repaint or stain can usually be carried out with minimal preparation. In sheltered places or if stripping of old coating acceptable, maintenance period may be up to double stated figure.

Chelsea Garden

The furniture in the setting for which it was designed.

For some years now we have been involved in the Chelsea Flower Show which takes place during May. We feature here the *Popular Gardening* garden designed by Geoff and Faith Whiten in which we took responsibility for the furniture. Here are photographs of the patio garden which was awarded the Banksian silver-gilt medal, along with details of the items designed by Ashley Cartwright and pictures of some of the other gardens of interest.

Later (see page 164) we will look at the construction of the tree seat. Here we focus on the garden table which like all other projects was designed by Ashley. Tim Wells is the craftsman who made the table and the benches, while Gordon Warr made the tree seat and screen.

Top: *The table and benches made in oak pick up the design theme of the other pieces.*

Middle: *The angled uprights of the screen with the curving motif create a fascinating background. (see page 171)*

Bottom: *The tree seat in elm, made by Gordon Warr. (see page 164)*

Other gardens of interest featuring wooden structures in their design.

1. The Daily Express garden
With the sand pit at its centre, this garden was created with the young family in mind. Rustic poles are used to provide walls and edging to the different levels and the steps which are formed from log slices.

2. Daily Telegraph and Sunday Telegraph garden
As the winning entry in their own design competition, this garden features a pergola with an oriental character—shelter being provided by the canvas stretched between the posts.

3. The Amateur Gardening garden
This Victorian villa garden from our sister magazine was awarded the gold medal.

Garden Table and Benches

Simplicity of construction was one of the aims when designing the oak garden furniture described here. An important consideration is the relationship between the table and benches which have the appearance of being a unit.

The relationship between the two benches and the table was a stimulating structural and visual problem. The canting in of the legs at 45 degrees produces a stiff structure and this when repeated on the benches satisfies not only the problem of stability but of visually integrating the benches and table. The angle at each end of the bench directs the user towards the table. The bench top is in three pieces — two of which are the outer planks which provide most of the surface area. The thin piece along the middle is a plank which has been used on edge to tie the end supports together and which is seen at the end of the bench cut through at 45

Construction sequence for benches

1. Prepare cutting list.
2. Bandsaw the timber to size, marking out to make best use of boards.
3. Plane and thickness the timber.
4. Dimension to size where appropriate.
5. Prepare mortise and tenon joints.
6. Shape the ends of the legs according to a prepared templet.
7. Cut cross halvings between beam and cross rails.
8. Cut and fit central support bracket.
9. Glue up the assembly so far.
10. Place planks onto structure and mark the positions of the fixing brackets.
11. Cut the ends of the planks and notches to the correct angles and plane.
12. Remove arrises from the edges.
13. Paint in the details.
14. Complete the assembly.

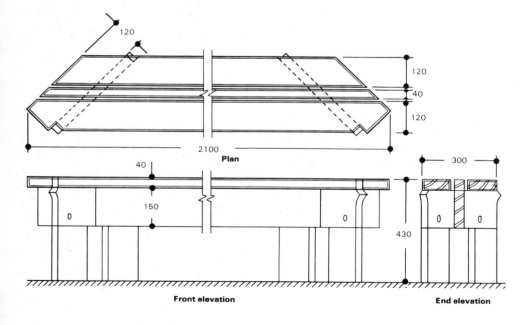

120

120

40

120

2100

Plan

40

150

0

0

300

0 0

430

Front elevation

End elevation

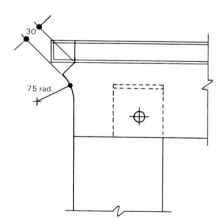

30

75 rad.

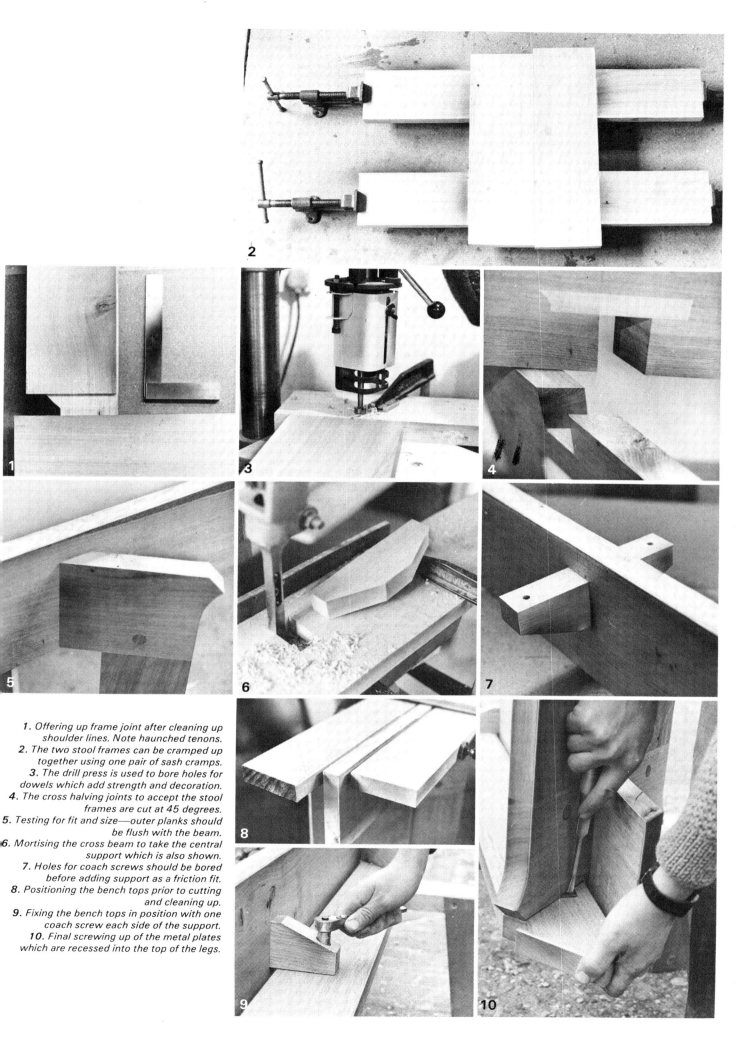

1. Offering up frame joint after cleaning up
   shoulder lines. Note haunched tenons.
2. The two stool frames can be cramped up
   together using one pair of sash cramps.
3. The drill press is used to bore holes for
   dowels which add strength and decoration.
4. The cross halving joints to accept the stool
   frames are cut at 45 degrees.
5. Testing for fit and size—outer planks should
   be flush with the beam.
6. Mortising the cross beam to take the central
   support which is also shown.
7. Holes for coach screws should be bored
   before adding support as a friction fit.
8. Positioning the bench tops prior to cutting
   and cleaning up.
9. Fixing the bench tops in position with one
   coach screw each side of the support.
10. Final screwing up of the metal plates
    which are recessed into the top of the legs.

Garden Table

This interesting garden table was based on the dining table shown above.

The starting point for the structure of the table was a dining table made in sycamore some two years ago which subsequently received a Design Centre selection approval. Because the legs are opposed to each other at 45°, the overall structure of the table can be fairly simple. The dimensions of the table are just over a double metre square and the under-structure being two chevrons which are halved together.

As long as the dimensions of the table are based on a square or a double square the jointing will all be at right angles. This is good for the making process and for the overall rigidity of the piece. The top planks of the table are of sufficient thickness that they merely need attaching to the legs

without further complicated stiffening underneath.

The four main joints between the legs and cross structure are haunched mortice and tenon joints, with the connections in the middle of the table made by 2in. back flap hinges or similar right-angled metal sections screwed from behind.

When preparing the drawing I considered cutting notches across the table to reflect the understructure, perhaps you might like to try the idea.

The table was made from 2in. English oak but of course wych elm, iroko or teak would be ideally suitable exterior timbers to use. The complete project was finished with a Cuprinol wood preserver.

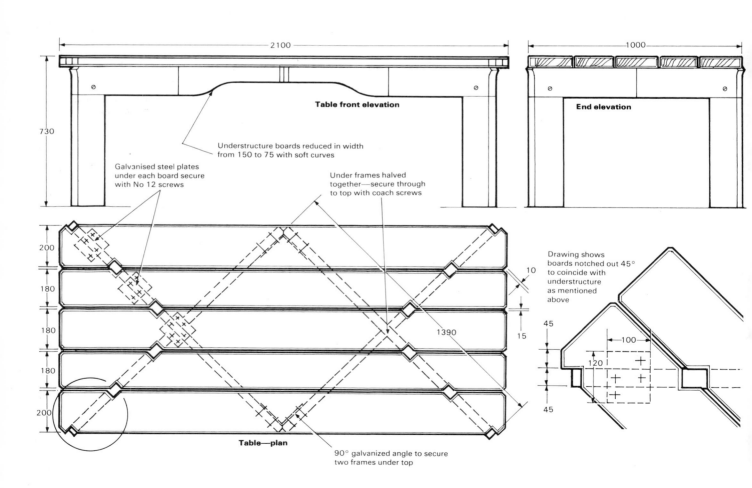

2100

Table front elevation

End elevation

1000

730

Understructure boards reduced in width from 150 to 75 with soft curves

Galvanised steel plates under each board secure with No 12 screws

Under frames halved together—secure through to top with coach screws

200

180

180

180

200

10

1390

15

Drawing shows boards notched out 45° to coincide with understructure as mentioned above

45

45

100

120

Table—plan

90° galvanized angle to secure two frames under top

1. The seasoned English oak ready for conversion.

2. A portable saw was used for the rough sawing.

3. Preparing the timber on the bandsaw.

4. Morticing the rails of the table.

5. The tenons are quickly cut on the bandsaw.

6. Offering the joint to the tenon after cleaning.

Sketch of table showing alternative treatment

7. Table legs being cramped up prior to assembly.

8. Dowel holes being drilled on the drill press.

9. The top boards are planed to a good finish.

10. The top boards are cut to width on the dimension saw.

11. The dowels are inserted with glue prior to planing off.

12. A template is used for leg details which are then sawn.

13. A detail being drawn on the table top prior to cutting.

14. Wood preserver being applied.

The Tree Seat

Based on a floral design, this tree seat is made of elm which if treated with preservative should last for many years. The method of construction is described in detail.

This seat was featured in the Practical Woodworking exhibit at the Chelsea Flower Show

An overall impression of the garden.

THIS TREE SEAT is based on a floral design, circular on its outer edge but with the inner aperture of a more decorative scalloped outline. The sixteen segments are of identical size, and are secured together in pairs around a leg. Fixing the legs to each pair of segments to make up one petal of the flower is achieved by the use of angle iron, and angle iron fabricated into a square is also used for linking together all eight petals.

I obtained a supply of elm for this project, sawn to a thickness of 1½in. and 2in. As is normal with home-grown hardwoods, the planks had been sawn through and through, were waney edged, and both the lengths and widths were random. The consequence of buying timber prepared in this way is that it is necessary to obtain rather more than the net amount needed in order to ensure that the actual material required can be cut.

My first task was to prepare a templet for one of the segments, and for this I used a piece of hardboard. In effect, a full-size drawing was made on the hardboard, using a long lath of wood to act as a beam compass. The templet was made an exact replica of one of the segments except for

The tree seat assembled round a sapling.

the cut-out for the leg, and here I simply bored a small hole at the centre of what would be a 50mm hole for the radiused edge of the leg.

I could now use this templet to roughly mark out the 1½in. planks in order to give maximum economy, with one or two large knots being avoided. Initial cutting of the planks was achieved by chainsaw, before bandsawing the rest of the outline. At this stage, I kept well clear of the lines, so that there was a fair amount of waste included.

Now the sixteen segments could be planed down to the finished thickness of 30mm, and one edge planed quite true. Next, the templet was used again to establish the exact shape required, with one edge of the templet kept flush with the planed edge of the wood. The bandsaw was used to cut the shaped ends of the segments, but not the straight but tapering edge, nor at this stage the rounded corners. For the straight cut I used the circular saw, first of all making a very simple cradle in order to hold and guide the segments. The advantage of using this compared with the bandsaw was that the edge produced was perfectly straight, and uniformity of size and angle was also assured.

Rounded corners were marked out and the waste removed. Smoothing of these corners and the concave narrow end was done by a combination of disc and drum sanders. The curved outer edges of the segments were left as from the bandsaw in order to provide a little 'texture' to these parts.

The cut-outs in the segments had to correspond exactly with the legs, so I now turned my attention to preparing these parts. They were planed to the exact sizes shown on the working drawings, and carefully cross-cut to the finished length of 430mm. The semi-circular edges to these legs can be formed almost entirely by hand planing, but I decided I would bring my spindle into use for this, and invested in a pair of cutter blanks to grind up to suit the job. Although it took me about an hour to grind the cutters, it was really time well

spent as once set-up in the machine all sixteen edges were prepared in a matter of minutes. I did, though, plane a large chamfer on the corners first to lessen the amount of wood to be removed by the spindle. A few rubs with some coarse glasspaper was all that was needed to give me well rounded edges.

The templet was again placed on the segments in order to mark out the hole which would be the first stage of forming the slot. I simply used a bradawl through the small hole already made in the templet for this purpose in order to give me the centre for the larger hole. I had already checked in a piece of scrap that the hole saw I had would produce just the size of hole I needed, indeed I had also confirmed that the rounding of the legs would match the hole! With the holes bored, I was ready for removing the rest of the waste to complete the slot. The blade of my circular saw was adjusted to give me a depth of cut of 65mm the distance from the edge of the wood to the centre line of the hole, and two cuts over the saw were all that were needed to remove the rest of the waste to the slot. To complete this part of the work, the outer corners were radiused and smoothed on the sander.

Apart from the bolt holes needed for assembling, only one stage required to be carried out. All sharp corners had to have a small chamfer formed on them, and a router is an ideal way of carrying this out especially on shaped work. Router cutters with 'pilots' on them do not require a separate fence—the pilot in effect acts as the fence, and allows the router to work around the edges of intricately shaped outlines. By setting up the router in a router table, all that was required was to feed both sides of the segments past the piloted chamfer cutter. Both the top and lower end of the legs were similarly chamfered.

I had no difficulty in obtaining a supply of 40mm by 40mm angle iron, ordering sixteen pieces to be cut to 300mm for the leg supports, and two lengths of 1,800 for the inner frame. This inner frame has to be formed in two parts to enable the seat to be constructed in halves so that it can be assembled around the tree. The leg brackets needed a total of six holes drilling in each, four for screwing to the underside of the segments and two for bolting to the legs. Centre punching of the metal is a necessary pre-requisite to drilling, after which the corners of the metal were rounded over by file. There was a little more preparation needed for the two parts of the inner frame. One half of this is arranged with the flange of the metal facing inwards, the other with the flange fac-

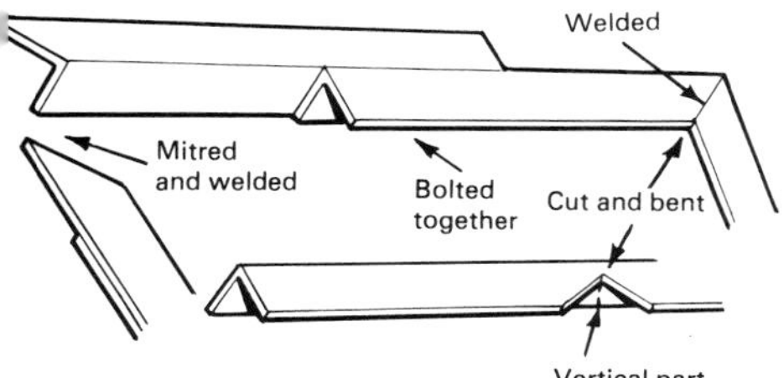

Elevation

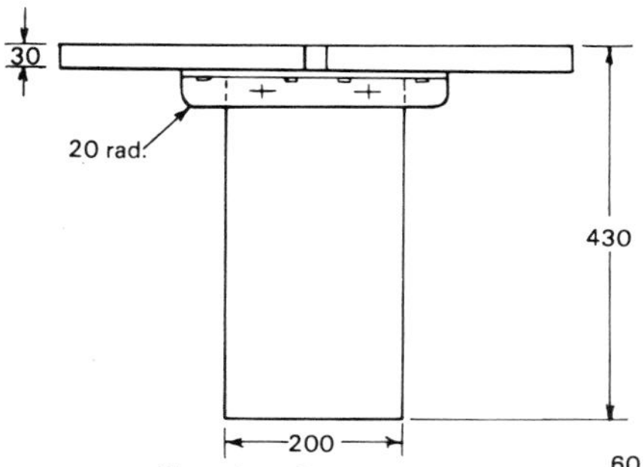

Elevation of one segment

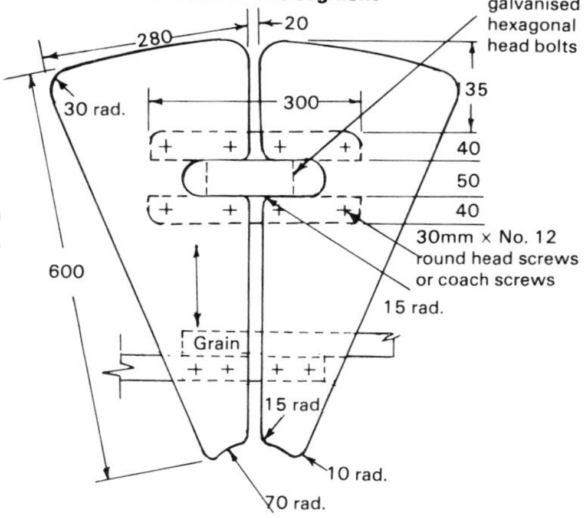

30

20 rad.

430

200

Plan

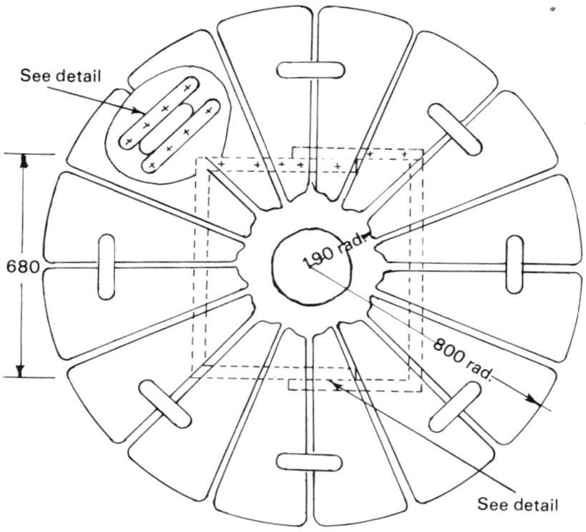

See detail

680

190 rad.

800 rad.

See detail

Angle iron frame details

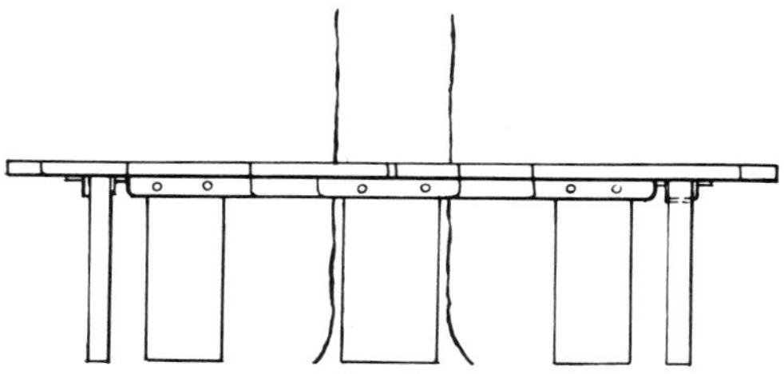

Welded

Mitred and welded

Bolted together

Cut and bent-

Vertical part not cut

Plan of one segment

280

20

30 rad.

300

35

40

50

40

600

Grain

15 rad.

15 rad.

10 rad.

70 rad.

60 × 10 dia. galvanised hexagonal head bolts

30mm × No. 12 round head screws or coach screws

15 rad.

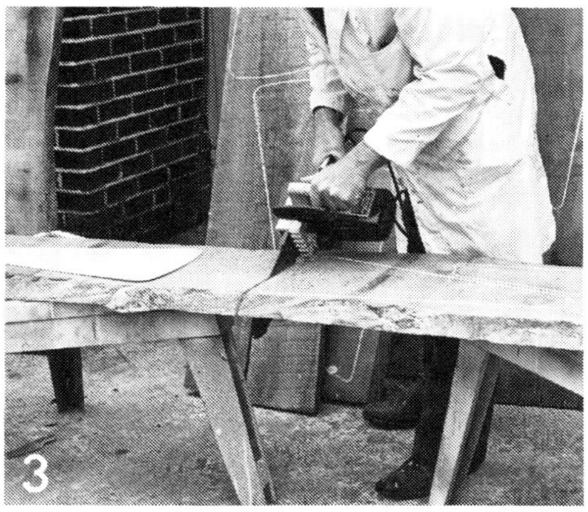

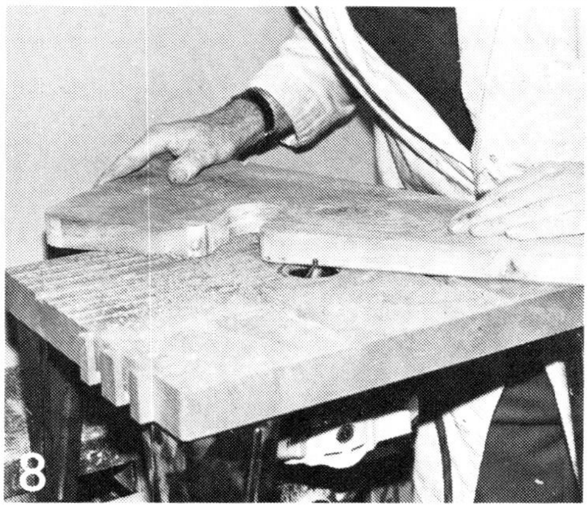

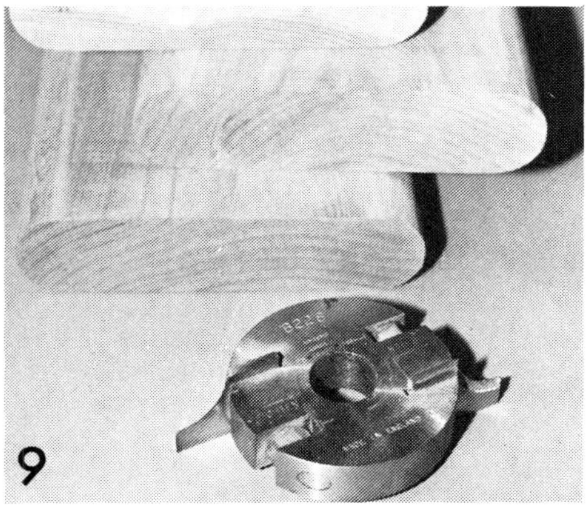

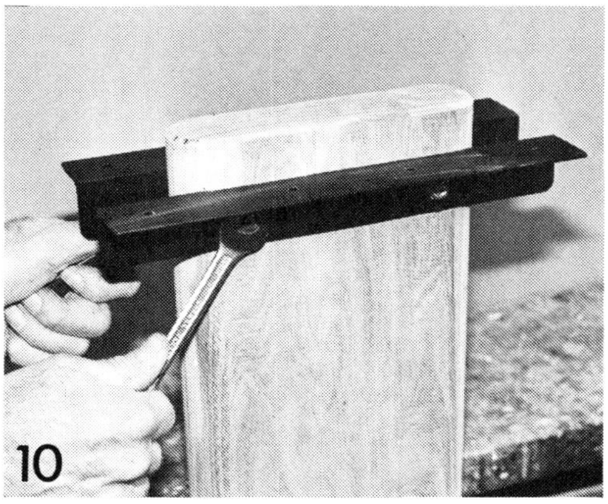

3. Initial cutting of the elm boards.

4. Preliminary bandsawing of a top member.

5. Smoothing inner end of top segment.

6. Hole saw used to partly form the slot.

7. Completing the slot on the saw.

8. Edge chamfer formed with a router.

9. Spindle cutters for shaping leg edges.

10. Angle iron supports are bolted on.

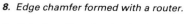

ing outwards. On the piece with the flange on the inside, a vee-shaped piece was cut out of the flange at the two corners, enabling me to make a right-angled bend without cutting the metal completely through. With the metal held in a fairly large engineer's vice, I had no difficulty in forming a bend with the cut-away vee part closing together to form a mitre. An exact fit of the 45 degree cuts was not necessary as the corners had to be welded.

I could not follow the same method of only partly cutting through the metal in order to form the corners of the second half-frame. Because of the flange being on the outside of this half, this part was in fact made from three separate pieces. The ends of the metal forming the two corners were simply sawn through at 45 degrees.

A small amount of excess length needed to be cut off the overlapping ends of the two halves to ensure all were the correct length and that the right amount of overlap had been established. Only at this stage were the holes prepared for the bolts which would secure the two halves together. First, the holes were drilled in one part of the overlaps, then this was G-cramped to the second part. By drilling through the holes already made in one of the pieces, those in the second part were produced in exact alignment. Care at this stage was very important, as proper assembly of the whole of the seat depended on the accuracy of these bolt holes.

Now although I've never done any welding in my life, I have had a little experience of both brazing and silver soldering. My limited experience of these processes have taught me how important

it is to have parts to be secured together properly held in their correct relationship prior to applying any heat. This temporary holding of the parts exactly as they are to be fused together is really the most important stage of the job, and makes the rest of the process much more straight-forward.

I therefore first bolted the overlapping angle iron together, then further held the metal in place by using a series of G-cramps. The frame was cramped to a hefty piece of wood passing across the centre, this largely to keep the frame flat. Cramps and wood were also used at the corners to ensure these were correctly aligned. I constantly measured the assembly to ensure it was parallel in both directions, and also quite square. Fortunately, I have a young friend who is a welder, and it took him only a matter of minutes to complete my preparation of the frame.

Before I proceeded further with the project, I gave all the metal components three coats of paint. The first was a metal primer, and this was followed by a couple of applications of matt black.

Now I was ready to start the assembling, and the first stage was to bolt two of the brackets to each leg. The brackets were carefully cramped to the wood so that their upper surfaces were exactly 30mm from the top of the leg, this corresponding to the thickness of the segments. I then used a hand-held drill to bore the holes in the wood, using the holes in the metal as the guide. Bolts 10mm in diameter had been obtained for securing these parts together, and these were soon in place and tightened up.

Next, each of the legs had to be assembled to a pair of segments to make up one of the eight units forming the seat. By having the three parts inverted on a flat board, and with a cramp positioned either side of the leg to pull the segments together, I found this stage easier than anticipated. Careful adjustment of pressure on the cramps ensured that the gap between the segments was parallel, after which it was simply a matter of inserting the screws.

An area of my workshop was cleared and swept clean so that the eight assembled petals could be laid out upside down and carefully spaced so that all the gaps were uniform. The inner frame was lowered into place, carefully centralised and the holes marked out on the metal for securing to the wood. With the last set of holes drilled in the steel, I was ready for the final stage of the assembling. Although the drawings indicated ordinary woodscrews were to be used for this, I decided that coach screws would make an even stronger job. As these were inserted constant checks were made to ensure that the final assembly was as intended.

Suddenly the project was completed—or nearly so. The inner frame was un-bolted to separate the seat into two, and taken out of the workshop for preservative treatment. A couple of generous coats of preservative were applied, with extra applications being given to the end grain.

Now I was ready for the last lap, to re-assemble the seat around a smallish tree in my own garden, and to seek the approval of my wife. I am happy to say that both the designer and I were given full marks.

11. Cutting out waste prior to bending to form corner of the inner frame.

12. Drilling bolt holes in the angle iron after centre punching the locations.

13. Frame securely held using clamps and bolts prior to welding joints.

14. Coach screwing the petals to the inner frame—note that spacers can help.

15. The finished seat showing the full richness of the elm grain and colour.

16. Underside of one of the half assemblies showing leg supports and main frame.

17. Applying a generous coat of Woodplan Double Action Timber Preservative.

18. The seat is simple to assemble, positioning each half and then bolting.

19. Chamfering is also applied to the top of the legs so there are no sharp edges.

20. The inner ring shaping further reflects the floral theme of the seat design.

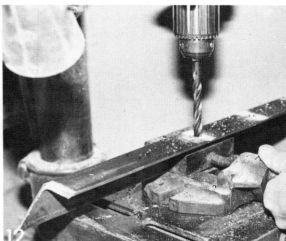

16

17

19   20

A selection of front gates showing how they enhance quite modest houses and create the mood and setting for the rest of the property.

Making an entrance

Individuality seems nowadays to be a rare quality amongst people, and standardisation of much of the hardware of everyday living tends also to press for bland conservatism. Here we look at a few ideas for making things just that bit more interesting.

FIRST IMPRESSIONS count for a lot and if you really want to impress your visitors how about a new garden gate this summer. Remember it is not only the first thing they see but also the last as they leave the house, and lasting impressions are as important as the first.

The system we have used here is a sandwich technique where the horizontal slats are held in position in three layers of wood. You can make up many designs this way and several alternatives are shown using the same basic approach. The drawing shows the construction of the frame and the slats let in position. The timber used here is 20mm thick (just over $\frac{3}{4}$in.) and when screwed and glued in a three-part sandwich it forms an extremely strong structure. Obviously individual gates will be made up to suit existing openings or new specifications, and thus the measurements given here serve only as an example of fairly common sizes.

In the case of the gate post we have taken a central core of impregnated timber 100 by 100mm (about 4 by 4in.) and clad it all round with a timber to match the gate. This not only gave us a good match but produced a feeling of solidity and substance. The post incidentally is let into the ground 700mm (about 2ft. 4in.) and obviously it's unnecessary to clad it all the way down. The drawing makes this clear.

So why not nip outside your own front door, look at the gate and fence and ask yourself what would I really like to see there to set off the house to its full advantage. Maybe some of our examples will give you an idea and modifications to any of them are quick and easy. Incidentally a few simple hand tools will cover most of the work but if you do want a lot of fancy curves a jig-saw or bandsaw would be handy.

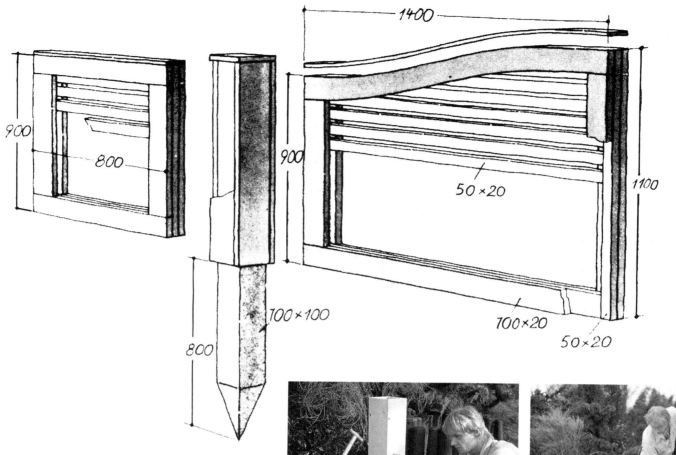

900

800

100 × 100

800

1400

900

50 × 20

1100

100 × 20

50 × 20

2. Ensure that the post is upright in both planes or this will lead to fitting and closing problems later.

3. Prepare a mix of about 5 to 1 sand and cement, fill in the hole and leave for at least 24 hours.

. That section of the gate post which remains above ground is clad up in timber to match the gate to be hung.

4. Mark out the desired curve on the rail with a templet and cut out with a jigsaw as shown.

5. With the gate frame on the ground join the sections together and screw and glue.

6. Before actually gluing the frame together particular attention should be paid to ensure the angles are perfectly correct.

7. Overlay the framework with the 5mm planks gluing and tacking them to the inner surface.

9. The upper edge is fitted with a capping to keep away the worst of the wet weather.

8. The other half of the frame is now placed on top and screwed and glued in position.

10. A galvanised striker plate firmly set in cement is advisable.

Heavy-duty fittings will be necessary since the form of construction leads to the gates being solid and heavy. The three photographs show some of the types that were used in this case.

Screen for the Chelsea Show

Continuing our selection of garden furniture projects designed by Ashley Cartwright for *Popular Gardening* magazines' garden at The Chelsea Flower Show, Gordon Warr describes here the painted oak screen which he constructed to the designer's specifications.

THIS ITEM I made to Ashley Cartwright's design for the Chelsea Flower Show, it's a large screen, to be installed between two walls built of stone. Both oak and elm are excellent native timbers for use out-of-doors, they have a long life even when left in their natural state, so when treated with preservative their longevity will be extended even further.

I obtained a supply of oak for the screen, and as with the elm I had used for the tree seat, this was purchased as through-and-through sawn stock. This means that the lengths and widths are random, and that both edges are waney. A consequence of this is that a lot of offcuts are created, and therefore it is essential to obtain a generous supply of material in the first place. Careful planning of the require-

ments against the variously sized planks ensured that the timber would give the most economic yield and initial cutting was carried out with my portable circular saw. The timber was both so bulky and heavy that this preliminary work was completed in the driveway.

With all the material now cut with at least one straight edge, the wood was brought into the workshop and the saw on my combination machine was put through its paces cutting the oak to width. Now I was ready for facing the wood on the planer of the same machine, but because of the length and weight of the oak wood, I recruited one of my sons as an assistant.

Over many decades of woodworking, I have equipped my workshop with a num-

1. Intial cutting with the portable saw.
2. Facing the prepared oak on the planer.

ber of small machines, so I'm now able to carry out a wide variety of operations with the assistance of power. Of all the functions I can now carry out on one or other of the machines which are squeezed into my modest-sized workshop, it's the ability to thickness which saves me the most time, and which still excites me. I think the latter stems from the fact that thicknessers have power feed, and therefore the planing is carried out-'automatically'.

I've no idea just where the oak I was using was grown, except that it is home produced. What I do know, though, is that one or more of the trees from which it was sawn must have stood in the way of a marksman and his quarry. For while planing up the timber, I lost count of the number of lead shot pellets I uncovered embedded in the oak, fortunately they are so soft that the blunting effect on the cutters is only slight.

When the timber had been first cut from the planks, I had left a little waste at the ends to allow for more accurate cutting later. The next step, therefore, was to cut the nineteen fins to their exact length, and here I was able to bring my DeWalt radial arm saw into use. First, one end was squared off on the machine, then by rigging up an extension to the fence and to which I fixed a 'stop', all the pieces were sawn to identical length without the need for any marking out.

The fins are all held within a frame, which is simply mortised and tenoned together at the corners. First, the upright members of the frame were marked out while held together in the vice, at this stage it was only a matter of squaring the lines across to indicate the shoulders of the tenons. There was rather more marking out required for the horizontal members, for as well as pencilling in the limits of the mortises, the trenches for the fins

had to be correctly spaced out. The centre fin is fixed at right angles to the frame, the remaining nine on either side are evenly spaced and set at 45 degrees to the frame. I found a pair of engineer's dividers helpful as a simple method of gaining uniformity of spacing to these fins. Completion of the marking out of the trenches was achieved by try square and gauge, while a mortise gauge was used to indicate the thickness of the corner joints.

While my combination woodworker has mortising facilities, the top and bottom members of the frames were so long and heavy that they were really too large for the machine. However, it did not take too long to cut them by hand, although I did use a power drill to first of all bore out the bulk of the waste. This was followed by chiselling and using saw and chisel to form the haunch.

Now the DeWalt 125 is not just a radial arm saw, but with appropriate attachments can carry out a whole range of operations. One such attachment is the dado head or cutter. The dado cutter will form grooves and trenches (dado is American terminology, where the radial arm saw was first introduced in 1922),

and is adjustable to give varying widths of cut. The same cutter can be readily used for cutting tenons, although a series of 'passes' will be required for all but the smallest of tenons. This was the method I used for removing the waste from the tenons on the uprights to the frame, the width to which the cutters are set are not critical for this operation.

I decided that reducing the width of the tenon to form the haunch to this part of the joint was easiest carried out by hand, so after marking out in pencil the waste was simply sawn away. As the joints were to be secured together by draw-boring, holes were bored in preparation for this through the mortised members, leaving the final stages for this part of the work until the frame was assembled.

The DeWalt came into its own for cutting the trenches in the upper and lower parts of the frame. However, because the wood had to be stood on edge on the machine, a temporary fence was secured to the table to ensure proper support. After cutting the centre trenches, the arm of the saw was swung 45 degrees to one side while half of the trenches were cut, then to the other side for the remain-

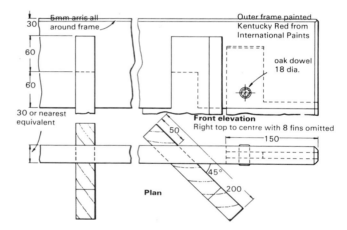

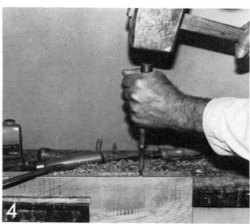

3. Spacing out the fins with dividers.
4. Paring the mortise after boring out waste.
5. Saw and chisel used to form haunch slot.
6. Tenons to uprights cut using dado attachment.
7. Reducing the tenon to form the haunch.
8. Sawing the trenches at a 45 degrees angle.
9. Paring with a chisel to remove the waste.
10. A few persuasive blows to achieve the fit.
11. Marking through the hole onto the tenon.
12. Dry assembly allowing joggles to be saw off.
13. Forming the chamfer with a router cutter.

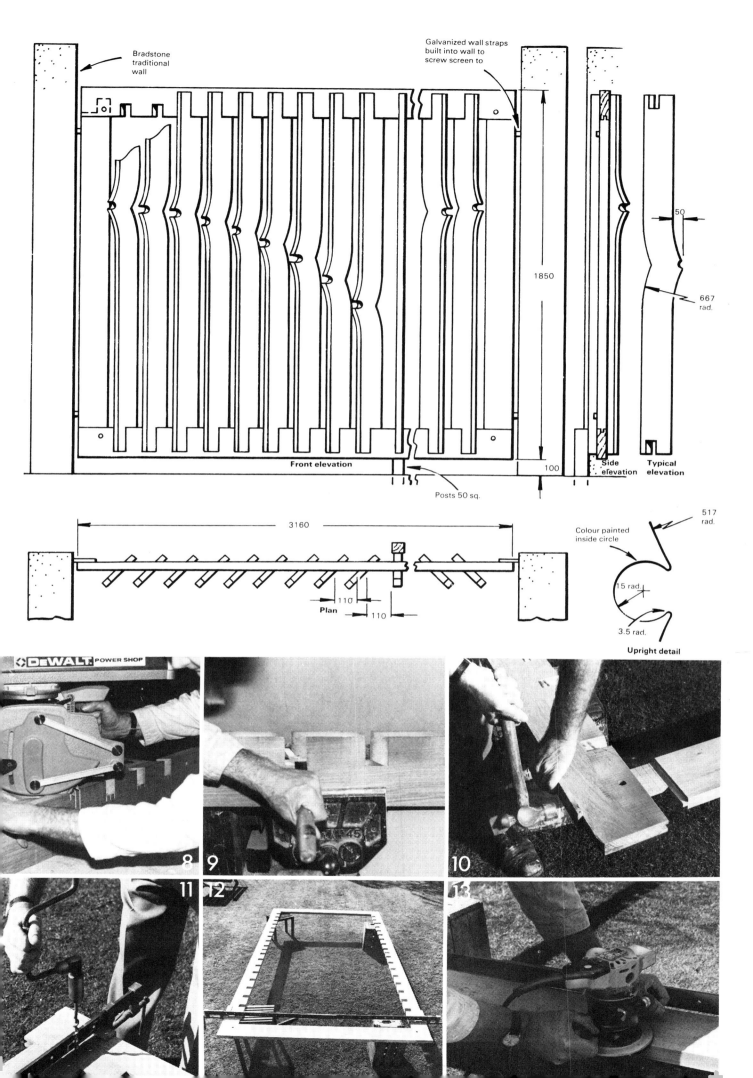

Bradstone traditional wall

Galvanized wall straps built into wall to screw screen to

Front elevation

1850

100

50

667 rad.

Side elevation

Typical elevation

Posts 50 sq.

3160

110

110

Plan

517 rad.

Colour painted inside circle

15 rad.

3.5 rad.

Upright detail

D-WALT POWER SHOP

8 9 10

11 12 13

der. In fact only the limits of the trenches were cut on the radial arm saw, the waste then being removed by chisel.

Now I just do not have enough space in my workshop to assemble a frame over three metres by two (10ft.6in. by 6ft.0in.), and still leave room to move around, so it was into the back garden for the next stage. I had taken the pecaution of chamfering the ends of the tenons to aid their entry, and persuasive blows from a heavy hammer soon had the parts fitting together as planned. By bolting a couple of sash cramps together, I was able to use these to ensure that all joints were tight.

Only at this stage were the holes prepared in the tenons for the pegs. The method is to mark the tenon through the hole already made in the mortised member, then separate the parts. The hole in the tenon is bored around 1·5mm ($\frac{1}{16}$ in.) nearer to the shoulder than the position first marked, this is so that the peg will very positively draw the parts together— hence the name "draw boring". Only four pegs were required, but as these needed to be of oak I decided the easiest way of making them was on my lathe. They were turned to a length of 75mm (3in.), with one end well tapered.

At this stage the pegs were only partly inserted to ensure that all was well, then the joggles at the ends of the mortised members were sawn off. A small chamfer had to be formed around the edges of the frame, an ideal instance for the use of a router fitted with a 45 degree cutter. As the cutter I was using incorporated a pilot, this part of the job was both quick and easy to complete.

The frame was now given a couple of coats of clear wood preserver.

Although this part of the project was to be painted, the preservative is an additional protection for long life. Only when the preservative had been completely absorbed and the surface dry was the paint applied. The paint is a new type of micro-porous paint which allows the wood to breathe. A primer is not required, and excellent coverage is gained with just a single coat. The paint will not crack or peel, is highly resistant to fading, and allows the timber to breathe. I found application to be very easy, and was able to use a large brush for this. The paint dries in about two or three hours.

Now my attention returned to the fins, and I set about marking out the joints at the ends with try square and gauge. The waste to these joints I had to cut by hand, first sawing down the grain at an angle, then removing the bulk of the waste with a bow saw. A little careful chiselling was needed to complete these joints.

All the fins required to be shaped, the height at which this shaping occurs varies so as to give a 'sweep' effect to both halves of the screen. It was therefore necessary to make a template for the profile needed. This was made out of hardboard, and included the centre for the hole which is a part of the shaping on the front edge. Using the template was straightforward enough, with a bradawl being used to mark through for the centre of the hole needed. It was the hole which was first made, followed by bandsawing to remove the remainder of the waste. A little hand work with chisel and glasspaper was needed to form the small radiused ends between the hole and the curved front edges. With the main work to the

fins completed, the router was again brought into use to form a small chamfer on all edges. With all cutting and shaping completed, the fins were given a couple of coats of the preservative, but of course these parts were not painted.

Now although all the parts had been tested individually to check the fitting of the joints, the real test had yet to come, — would all the components fit together as planned by Ashley Cartwright, the designer? I had kept my fingers very tightly crossed throughout making this screen, as the possibilty of error was fairly high. No two fins are quite the same, the main shaping to the front edges being at varying heights with the angled joints being set in opposite directions for each half.

I first temporarily secured the lower part of the frame so that it would not tilt, into which all the fins were located, then added the end members of the frame. Positioning the last component was a little tricky, nineteen half laps and two mortise and tenons all had to be located at the same time. Earlier attention to detail and patience at this final stage paid off, I managed to get all vertical members located into the top of the frame and breathed a sigh of relief that no adjustments were required.

Now it was all dismantled, loaded into a van along with other items and a course set for the Capital. Re-assembling the screen at Chelsea was easy, this time I had no less than the Editor himself to give a hand! The walls of textured stone had already been built on the garden setting where this magazine was involved, and happily the screen fitted perfectly into its allotted space between the stonework.

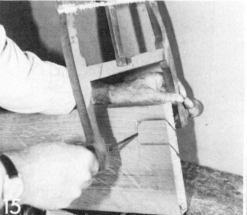

14. Applying micro/porous paint to the posts – note the chamfered edges to the tops.
15. Initial bowsawing of the fin joint before cleaning up with a chisel.
16. A hardboard templet should be made and used to ensure exact repetition of shape.
17. Bandsawing to the marked outline.

18. No primer is needed with this micro-porous paint.
19. The centre fin is secured from the rear with a coach screw.
20. Assembling the fins within the frame.
21. Gentle persuasion to ensure all is home.
22. The trial assembly works well.
23. Shaping detail—note arris on all edges.

18

19

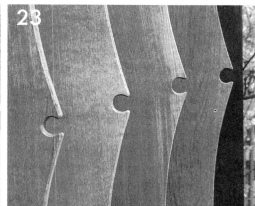
20

21

22

23

Toolstore and Playhouse

For the 1985 Chelsea Show, Lucinda Leech turns her attention to two areas often not given much thought to in a small garden — a toolstore and playhouse for children. These matching projects have similar design features to the central arbour and were made using lauan and ply provided by The National Hardwood Campaign and The Timber Trades Federation.

Artists' impression of the overall garden design

THE playhouse and toolstore were originally designed to echo the theme of the central arbour in our woodworker's garden at the Chelsea Flower Show. However, they would look just as good, either singly or as a pair, in any small garden. The arched hoops on the roof would look very cheerful with nasturtiums or other climbers growing over them from pots placed on the roof.

The toolshed is frequently a very ugly item in many gardens. This one is intended to be an attractive feature, and whilst it would not be large enough to house a big lawnmower or other major equipment, it is quite adequate for the tools needed in a small town garden.

The playhouse has stable type doors with a counter on the lower one to increase the play value for such games as 'shop'. Small furniture could be made to go inside and this could be painted in cheerful colours. At the Flower Show we used miniature flowers in the window boxes as these appeal to children. When planting these it is better to use small plants in individual pots so that they may be easily removed for watering, and may also be changed over during the season.

The construction of the toolstore and playhouse is basically the same, apart from the double doors and windows in the playhouse, and the internal fittings of the store. The timber used was lauan (Philippine mahogany) to match the arbour, and Cascamite was used throughout as a waterproof glue suitable for external use.

Laminated roof sections

Make up a former 50mm high from scrap wood or build up from chipboard, and attach it securely to the baseboard. The shape is a semi-circle of radius 425mm with a straight section of about 50 to 75mm at each end. As with previous projects you can use construc-

tional laminates or prepare your own to make the four curved components; these should finish, after cleaning up, at 34 by 25mm section. For further details on the laminating process consult the August issue where it is described at greater length in the article on the chaise longue.

Front (door) frame

Shape the front uprights from 80 by 34mm section timber with angled ends and rebate for the door, and groove for the ply walls using a tilt arbor saw or a router *(see Drawing 1)*.

Front rails

Prepare the bottom rail at section 60 by 25mm, top rail 40 by 25mm. The shoulder length in both cases is 492mm plus a tenon of 18mm each end.

Cramp the two front uprights together with face A uppermost. Mark out a total height of 1200mm, the rail positions and the mortises for the rails. Cut these at 18mm deep. Leave the uprights over-length at this stage. Cut the tenons on the end of the rails to fit. Glue up the front frame. Note the offcuts from the uprights being used, reversed, as glueblocks to aid cramping pressure on the awkward shape. Cut off the excess when dry.

Back frame

Prepare uprights at 40 by 35mm section, the base rail 40 by 25mm and the top rail 35 by 25mm. The shoulder length of the rails is 540 plus a 15mm tenon each end. Mark a total height of 1182mm (to allow for the thickness of the ply) on the wider face of the uprights. Mortise for the top and bottom rails which should then be tenoned to fit.

Glue up the back frame, and when dry trim off the excess length at the ends. Draw up the base plan full-size on a spare piece of ply or card. Place the back frame vertically on the drawing and mark the

Toolstore & playhouse   177

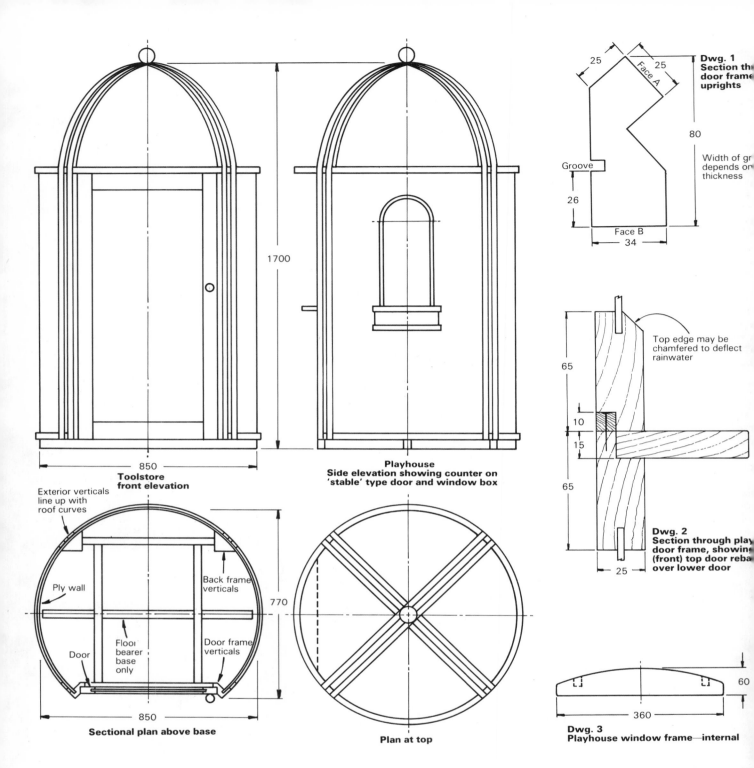

Dwg. 1
Section th[rough]
door frame
uprights

25 · 25 · Face A
80
Width of gr[oove]
depends on
thickness
Groove
26
Face B
34

1700

850
Toolstore
front elevation

Playhouse
Side elevation showing counter on
'stable' type door and window box

Top edge may be
chamfered to deflect
rainwater

65
10
15
65

Dwg. 2
Section through play[house]
door frame, showing
(front) top door reba[te]
over lower door

25

Exterior verticals
line up with
roof curves

Ply wall

Back frame
verticals

770

Floor
bearer
base
only

Door

Door frame
verticals

850
Sectional plan above base

Plan at top

60
360
Dwg. 3
Playhouse window frame—internal

Cutting list

Front uprights	2 off	1200 by	80 by	34mm
Back uprights	2 off	1180 by	40 by	35mm
Top front rail	1 off	528 by	40 by	25mm
Base front rail	1 off	528 by	60 by	25mm
Top back rail	1 off	570 by	35 by	25mm
Base back rail	1 off	570 by	40 by	25mm
Top cross rails	2 off	594 by	30 by	21mm
Base cross rails	2 off	594 by	40 by	30mm
Floor bearer	1 off	830 by	40 by	35mm
Cover strip	1 off	635 by	70 by	18mm

Door—toolstore:

Stiles	2 off	1170 by	65 by	25mm
Top rail	1 off	434 by	65 by	25mm
Base rail	1 off	434 by	80 by	25mm

Door—playhouse:

Top stiles	2 off	530 by	65 by	25mm
Bottom stiles	2 off	640 by	65 by	25mm
Top rails	3 off	434 by	65 by	25mm
Bottom rails	1 off	434 by	80 by	25mm
Counter	1 off	335 by	70 by	15mm
Exterior vertical strips	6 off	1180 by	34 by	26mm

Playhouse:

Window frame—internal	4 off	360 by	60 by	30mm
Window frame—sides	4 off	300 by	25 by	20mm

Also required:
Laminates 28 off 1500 by 35 (cut to be 40) by 3·5mm
2 circles 18mm shuttering ply 840mm dia.
1 circle 18mm shuttering ply 900mm dia.
1 sheet 4mm ply (or hardboard) for wall
Door panel (toolstore) 1 off 1054 by 434 by 4mm ply
Door panel (playhouse)1 off 430 by 434 by 4mm ply
Door panel (playhouse)1 off 520 by 434 by 4mm ply

Also odd bits of ply etc for window boxes and frame, and
clear plastic for windows.

curve on the back corners of the uprights. Saw off the waste at the correct angle, on a tilt arbor saw if possible, then plane by hand to give the slight curve.

Cross rails

Cut two base rails section 40 by 30mm, two top rails 21 by 30mm with a shoulder length of 570mm plus a 12mm tenon each end. Mortise the front frame for these rails 15mm from the joint and allowing for the thickness of the floor and ceiling ply. When it is placed on them, the top of the ply should be flush with the top of the door frame cross rails. Mortise the back frame 39mm from the joint. The rails should be flush with each other as the ply fits over all of them at the back. Tenon the ends of the rails to fit.

Make a 35 by 40mm section bearer for the floor, to cross the centre of the base parallel with the door frame. Half joint it onto the two cross rails and glue it to them. Glue up the whole framework—i.e. four cross rails to the door and back frame.

Ceiling and floor

Mark out two circles radius 420mm on 18mm shuttering ply marking the door frame position as on the full-size drawing made earlier. On one circle also mark the position of the back uprights to be cut out for the base.

Cut out, clean up and give the two pieces two coats of International Paint floor paint—in this case Denim blue. Drill and countersink to screw and glue the ceiling piece on the top of the completed framework, and the floor onto the base of

the frame. Fill the screw holes and paint over. Drill and countersink the top piece for screwing up into the roof in the centre plus about four fixings nearer the edge.

Walls

The walls may be made of hardboard which bends easily, but this will not be completely durable for outside use, so 3 or 4mm exterior grade ply is preferable. However, this must have laminates of equal thickness and not be of solid core construction or it will not bend adequately.

Measure the circumference of the ceiling accurately and add the depth of the groove twice. This should be the same as the measurement at floor level, of course. The ply should be cut to this length carefully. The width should be 1160mm in the centre rising to 1180mm at each end to allow for an 18mm fall in the roof from front to back. Paint the inside face of the ply—we used a mixture of 1·5 Alaska White to 2 parts Virginia Green Ranch Paint to produce a soft blue/green.

Put the Cascamite in the groove of the door frame, along the edge of the floor and ceiling ply and on one back upright. Slot one end of the ply into the groove and bend it round the structure, aligning it carefully top and bottom. Pin it onto the ply and the uprights to hold it in position. Spread more glue as it goes round. Finally slot it into the other groove and work the ply tight into it by pinning—this whole manoeuvre is definitely a two person job! The G cramps in Photo 11 are holding blocks to stop the ply bowing out of the

groove. Once the glue is dry plane the top of the ply to the 18mm fall front to back.

Cut out a cover strip for the top of the door frame to fill the gap of section 70 by 18mm. Cut the ends to shape to match the door frame and plane the top at an angle to match the fall of the ply. Glue and pin it over the door frame.

Roof

Cut out a complete circle of radius 450mm from 18mm ply. Treat all components with two coats of International Paint Double Action Timber Preservative, including the laminated sections. When completely dry, paint the outside of the walls and the roof with Virginia Green Ranch Paint. However, if the piece is to be left outside for any length of time it would be advisable to felt the roof instead.

Cut four pairs of slots 34mm wide by 25mm deep in the edge of the roof circle. These may be marked out by placing the roof in position on the main structure, matching up the centres and marking on the roof the position of the door frame, face 'B'. This is the first of the slots, the gap between it and the next is 20mm. The remaining two pairs are diagonally opposite.

From the original former, mark the centre and the finished length of the laminated components. Mark 10mm on either side of the centre at the top of each piece to give the 20mm gap, and then cut a pair of halving joints 34mm wide in each—two removing the top and two removing the bottom face.

Drill and counterbore for plugs 9mm up

1. Laminates for curved section glued up and cramped round former screwed to baseboard.
2. Uprights for the front door frame are easily shaped with a tilt arbor saw.
3. Cramp the two uprights together for measuring and cutting to size.
4. Cramping up the door frame using the offcuts to aid cramping pressure.
5. The rear frame in cramps—the excess lengths are cut off afterwards.
6. Cross rails prepared to size with tenons and trenches formed.
7. The completed framework around all other parts are fitted.
8. Ceiling and floor are formed from 18mm shuttering ply and shaped to fit.
9. The ply rounds are glued and screwed in place and the holes subsequently fitted.

from the ends of the laminated pieces to screw to the edge of the roof. Clean up the curved pieces and glue the four top halving joints. Glue and screw the laminated components into the slots in the roof. Plug the holes and cut the ends off flush. Cut a thin edge strip 18 by 3mm and pin and glue this round the edge of the ply. Fill the pin holes and treat with preservative.

Fix the roof in position by screwing up through the ceiling from the inside.

Paint a toy ball green to match the outside and glue to the apex of the roof arches.

Exterior

Cut six uprights of 34 by 26mm section to length for the exterior vertical strips. Screw them on from the inside to line up with the base of the floor arches. Fill the screw holes and repaint inside.

Doors

Prepare the material for the door —stiles and top rails 65 by 25mm section, base rail 80 by 25mm (playhouse two centre rails also 65 by 25mm). The height is 1170mm.

The playhouse has two doors—top 530mm high and lower 640mm high. The rails have a shoulder length of 410mm plus a tenon each end of 12mm.

Use the saw or router to groove all door components centrally in the face edge 12mm deep and 4mm wide. Open out this groove to 9mm wide with the router to make the mortises for the top and bottom rails. Tenon the rails to fit.

Cut 4mm ply panels to size, treat with preservative and paint to match the walls.

Glue up the doors and fit them. The toolstore door is hung normally on a pair of hinges with a knob and ball catch fitted. All exposed wood is treated with preservative.

The top playhouse door has a 10 by 10mm rebate cut with a router along the internal face before hanging. The lower door has a 10mm strip glued and pinned to the top of it at the back to act as a stop. The front face of the lower door has a rebate cut centrally 335mm long by 15 by 15mm. Into this a counter of 335 by 70 by 15mm is glued, with its front edges rounded over (see *Drawing 2*). A bolt may be fitted inside the lower door and a ball catch on the top one.

Playhouse window

Cut out a newspaper templet 255mm wide by 300mm high with a semi-circular arched top. Fix this onto the outside of the playhouse with masking tape, 340mm from the door frame and 150mm down from the top. Draw round it, remove the templet and cut out the shape with a jigsaw.

Use the templet again to cut out two 'window frames' from 4mm ply, 25mm wide and the internal shape to match the window opening. Clean these up and paint them cream. To make the internal frame, cut out four pieces 360 by 60 by 30mm. Cut the internal curve of the wall on one of the long edges. Round off the inside corners and edges (see *Drawing 3*). Glue in position on the inside of the window opening, one level with the

bottom of the window, one immediately above it. Glue in a vertical on either side between them of 25 by 20mm section, to form an internal rectangular frame for the window area.

Cut out two pieces of 2mm clear plastic, using the outside of the external ply frame as a templet, allowing an extra 120mm straight section below. Drill and countersink the ply frame and drill the plastic, to screw through the ply, the plastic and the wall into the internal window frame. Fill and paint over. Run a mastic bead around the outside to waterproof the joint.

Window boxes

Make up a base of 300 by 110mm from 9mm ply. Cut out a curve to match the wall along the back edge. Butt joint the sides and front, also made from 9mm ply and 120mm high, fixing them with glue and pins. Use a strip of thin ply to bend round to make the back, fixing it with a block at the corners. Fill and paint cream. Pin and glue narrow strips of solid wood to the top and bottom edges, mitred at the corners. Drill a couple of drainage holes in the base. Screw the window boxes into position over the extension of the plastic.

Inside the toolstore

Shelves may be made with the backs cut to fit the internal curve. They may be fixed onto blocks attached to the uprights. Hooks may be attached to the ceiling for hanging hoses etc., and wooden brackets also fixed to the ceiling to suspend garden tools from.

10. The walls of ply or hardboard must be bent round and pinned in place.
11. G cramps and blocks hold the ply in the groove and prevent it from bowing out.
12. The cover strip is planed to give a fall to match the ply.
13. Applying the Virginia Green Ranch Paint to the outside walls.
14. Thin edging strip is glued and pinned to the edge of the roof to conceal the laminations.
15. The lower playhouse door is rebated to receive the play counter.
16. The thin ply external window and one of the internal shaped cills.
17. Internal verticals are glued to the walls using cramps to apply pressure.
18. The completed window box should be postioned over the projection of the window plastic.

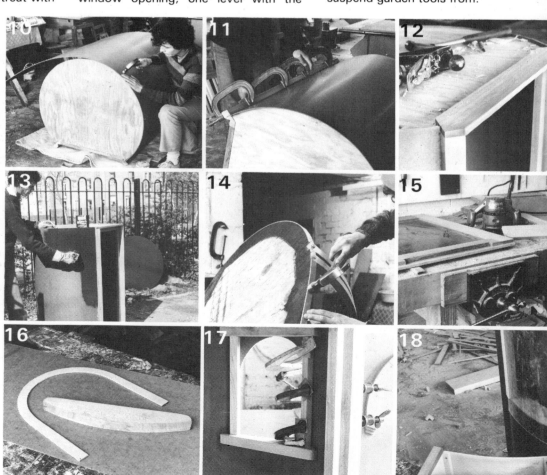

Chaise Longue

IF this summer is anything like the last one, most people will try and find at least some time to lounge around in their gardens in the sunshine. However, most of the commercially available sunloungers, though comfortable enough for the purpose, are not exactly aesthetic to look at. This piece of furniture is intended to be pleasing to the eye even when you are hard at work on the mowing. You will see that the flat area available by your right arm is quite adequate for that well-earned pint, and thus it encourages you to collapse in to it when you have finished the work!

The chaise longue is, of course, designed to go with the table and chairs which were displayed on the front deck at our 'Woodworker's Garden' at the Chelsea Flower.

The laminating process may seem complicated at first, but once the former has been made it may be used again if required. It is fairly cheap to construct and you may even have suitable pieces of chipboard lying around in the workshop. Laminating is an easy method of making curves, although you must buy in enough

Cascamite as there is a large glue area in each piece. The other problem in any small workshop may be a shortage of cramps. G or sash cramps may be used, but as both of these are so expensive now I hope you can manage to borrow extra if you need them.

For this Chelsea project we were fortunate to be given some lovely American oak by the Timber Trades Federation which laminated well and should prove to be durable for outdoor use. However, I think it is best to store the piece inside in winter, if possible, where it can double as indoor furniture if you have the space.

You may like to experiment with the angle of the back in a mock-up to make sure that you have optimum personal comfort, and I trust that members of your family can be persuaded to agree on the angle so that you do not end up having to make one for each of them!

Construction

The laminating process for the curved components takes some time as allowance must be made for the Cascamite to set before each piece is taken off the

Do not apply finish during, or soon after rain

Cutting list

Laminates	56 off	1870 by 50 by 3mm
Under frame horizontals and uprights	14 off	510 by 75 by 30mm
Short uprights	2 off	300 by 75 by 30mm
Base rail	1 off	980 by 75 by 30mm

1580

720

890

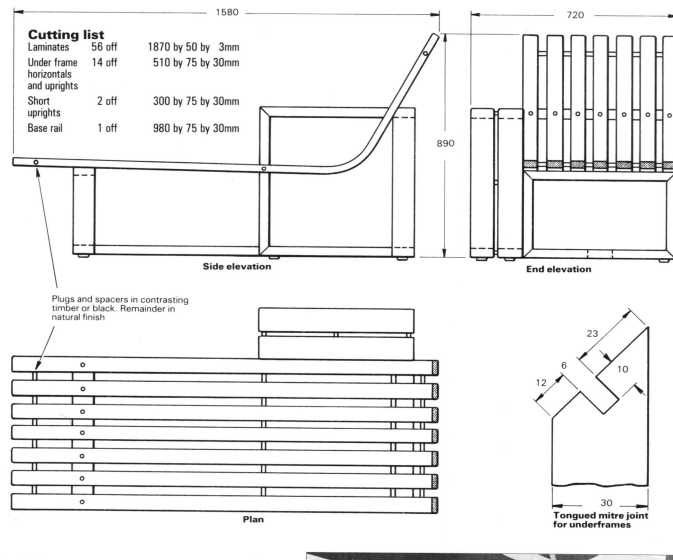

Side elevation

End elevation

Plugs and spacers in contrasting timber or black. Remainder in natural finish

Plan

23
6
12
10
30

Tongued mitre joint for underframes

Baseboard

Straight sections fixed to board

Loose curved block

Curved section fixed to board

Laminates

Curved components former

Loose straight blocks

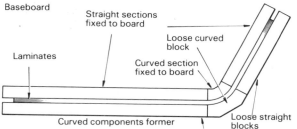

1. Three layers of chipboard glued and screwed to the baseboard make the former.

2. Preparing the laminates on a circular saw – a finger plate could be used to reduce vibration.

3. The former is greased with a candle and an extra precaution is to tape newspaper inside.

4. Use three cramps on the middle section, and start cramping from the middle.

5. A large number of cramps are required but not necessarily as many as this.

former. Accordingly, it is best to begin with this part of the project.

To prepare the former a rigid baseboard is required, and 18mm chipboard may be used for this. The laminate and the former should be made at least 5mm over width to allow for cleaning up afterwards.

Draw the side elevation of the seat component full-size on to the baseboard. Prepare two pieces for the straight sections approximately 50 by 55mm section, by 650mm and 1200mm long (this allows for extra length) and a block approximately 200 by 100 by 55mm high for the curved section. For these either use softwood or glue and screw together three layers of 18mm chipboard. Mark out and cut the internal curve for the seat on the block using a bandsaw. Clean this up ensuring that it is smooth and at right-angles to the face.

Glue it in position on the baseboard, screwing it up from underneath, then do the same with the two straight sections which should extend approximately 50mm beyond the ends of the finished component. Sand or trim where the pieces meet to form a smooth curve.

Prepare two straight lengths the same as the two fixed ones to use as outer blocks on the straight sections, and a further block from which to make the external curved former. This should be accurately marked out from the internal curve with the thickness of the laminate taken into account and it should be cut out carefully with three straight faces on the outside to take the crampheads.

3mm constructional laminates may be purchased and sawn to width or the laminates may be prepared either on a bandsaw, or as in this case on a circular saw, although this does mean a high wastage through loss from the saw kerf. If the saw is a tilt arbor it is a good idea to make a ply finger plate with the narrowest possible slot to reduce vibration when cutting such thin pieces.

Try to cut sufficient laminates for one complete seat section from one block, and keep them in the order in which they were cut to glue them up. Thus the laminates for one seat section would be prepared from a block originally 1970 by 55 by 50 allowing for a kerf of approximately 3·5mm. The two outer faces of this block should be cleaned up and sanded before it is cut into strips. These, then, remain on the outside and inside of the curve and save having to clean them up after shaping.

Prepare the former by greasing it with a candle. This should be done between each gluing operation in addition to scraping off any old glue which may have dripped on to it. A spare laminate may also be greased on both faces to act as a pad between the laminates themselves and the outer blocks. Newspaper may be taped to the internal face of the former as an extra precaution.

Mix up plenty of Cascamite with a slightly higher proportion of water than usual to ensure an even spread. Place a stack of eight laminates on the bench and spread glue on one face of seven of them and re-stack making sure they remain in the same order. Lay the stack on the former, place the padding laminate on the outside, and start to cramp up from the centre of the curve. Use three cramps on the curved section so as not to put excessive pressure on the middle of the loose block, and once it has begun to pull round place the outer straight blocks in position and start applying pressure to them. Tighten up fully from the centre outwards. (It is probably not necessary to use quite as many cramps as I have shown in the photo!)

Depending on weather and temperature of the workshop, allow around eight hours before removing the component. It is a long process as you need to make seven of these!

The laminated sections should now be cleaned up to exact width. This may be done by planing by hand or by cutting on the circular saw, which requires some care. To do this cut them to approximately 53mm, working with the edge which was against the baseboard on the mould against the fence of the saw, then feed them through again at a setting of 50mm with the sawn edge against the fence. Care is necessary because of the pieces being curved and thus difficult to manoeuvre. Clean up the sawn edges by hand with a smoothing plane.

Mark the position of the back frame on the laminates. This may be done by aligning a straight piece of wood against the lower outer edge and measuring up from it to the position shown on the drawing. Drill a clearance hole for a No. 8 screw in the centre of the section where the laminate will cross the frame.

Framework

Plane up all the timber to 30mm thickness, then cut all the components to 75mm width from a straight edge. Excluding the base rail, the remaining pieces should be cut to length at an angle of 45 degrees. This may be done by hand or

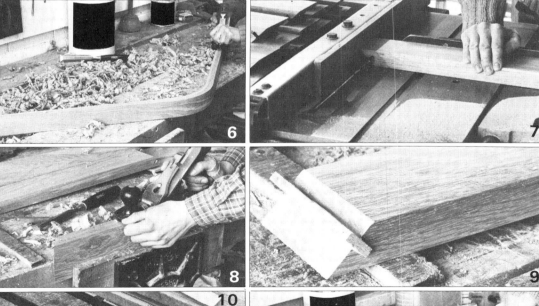

6

8

9

10

11

6. The laminated sections must be cleaned up to exact width either by planing or sawing.

7. Cutting the slot in the mitre with guard removed to take the jointing tongues.

8. The component pieces to the frames receiving a final cleaning up with a plane.

9. The tongues are glued in with Cascamite and allowed to project either side.

10. Cramp up the frames in both directions and check for squareness.

11. Drilling pilot holes for the No. 8 fixing screws on the angled face of the large frame.

machine. Cut a slot 10mm deep across the mitre for the loose tongue, as shown in drawing. If your saw is a tilt arbor, set it to 45 degrees to cut the pieces to length then reverse the components and use the same setting to cut the slot after winding the blade down until it projects sufficiently to give the 10mm depth. Use the rip fence, or a stop on the sliding table if you have one, to keep the piece in the correct position whilst feeding it in with the cross-cut fence. It should then be moved along to widen the slot to 6mm. However, it is necessary to remove the top guard for this operation so care must be taken if it is done in this way. The same job may be done by hand using a tenon saw and the waste taken out with a chisel.

Make solid tongues 20mm long, 85mm wide and 6mm thick. The grain runs in the short direction for strength. Then clean up all components.

Mix up some Cascamite and spread it on one face of each joint and in the slot. Push the tongue into position, allowing it to project on each side and glue the remaining area. Place the other component onto it. Cramp up with two sash cramps in each direction and check the frame carefully for being square. Once the glue is dry, trim off the excess tongues, clean up the joints and lightly chamfer all edges and corners.

On the small frame, plane the top face to a drop of 1·5mm from front to back. On the large back frame, saw and plane an angle of 120 degrees to the horizontal on the inside vertical edge of the top. On this angled face mark the centre of the areas where the laminated sections will cross it and drill for No. 8 screws.

Cross rail

Make a mortise 50 by 12mm in the centre of the inside face of the base of the small frame and the back frame. Cut the base rail to length and tenon the ends to fit. Cramp up dry and place a laminate in position, screwing it temporarily to the back frame. Mark the position for screwing to the small frame. Remove the laminate from the frame and square this position across onto the other laminates and drill clearance holes. Drill pilot holes in the small frame.

Glue the frames to the base rail checking carefully that it is square. The two outside laminates may be screwed on to help hold it square.

When the glue is dry, screw all the laminates in position and square across to mark the ends and the position of the spacer rods. These are 60mm from each end and one at the point where the side frame vertical meets the laminate. The side frame will need to be placed in position for this and the remaining rod positions in the two arm frames may also be marked.

Remove the laminated sections, numbering them for reassembly later, cut them to length and drill three 6mm holes in each in the centre of the thickness at the marked positions. Clean up and chamfer the ends and edges.

Drill 6mm holes in the side and back frames for the rods.

Prepare 24 spacers 26mm long 15mm in diameter with a 6mm hole bored in the centre of each. These may be turned in a contrasting wood or made from dowel and painted.

Mask the areas on the frame and the laminates where they will cross and treat all the pieces with two coats of clean wood preserver.

When this is completely dry, apply three coats of exterior varnish, cutting back lightly between coats. Allow the last coat to harden, then reassemble.

Threaded rod

Cut M6 threaded rod to the length taken from the piece itself at the point where the holes are drilled through —wedge the spacers in position temporarily to measure the exact length which should be approximately 10mm less than the actual width to allow for the plugs. Drill a 15mm hole 5mm deep in the outer two laminates at the rod position to accept the contrast plug. Drill for a 12mm plug on the top face of all the laminates where they are screwed to the frame.

Put a washer and nut on the end of the threaded rod. Place it through the first laminate and lay it on its side. Thread on three spacers and push the next laminate section down onto it. Repeat for all sections. Thread a washer and nut onto the other end of the two rods, align the spacers if necessary, and tighten up using a small socket. Glue and screw to the frame.

Align the two arm sections with rods and spacers, tighten up as before. Glue in contrasting plugs in face and sides, clean up and varnish over.

Cushions

A shaped cushion may be made for the head and neck which should fit over the top of the laminates and a matching one may be made for the small of the back if required.

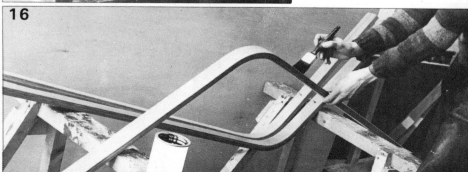

12. The base rail is tenoned to fit the mortises in the centre of the two support frames.

13. Cramping up the base rail and using the outer laminates to hold the assembly square.

14. Squaring across the ends of the rails prior to cutting them to length.

15. With the position of the laminates marked off, the frame is treated with two coats of wood preserver.

16. The preservative treatment is followed up by three coats of exterior varnish.

Chelsea Chairs

Another project from our Woodworker's Garden at the Chelsea Flower Show is a pair of chairs suitable for more formal eating than the usual 'al fresco' sandwich. Here Lucinda Leech details the construction and suggests a technique for repetitive profile shaping with a router.

AS our garden at Chelsea was designed to be used as an 'outside room' I felt it appropriate to have chairs which could be used for slightly more formal eating than the usual sandwich in an easy chair, and thus they also provide a contrast to relaxing in the chaise longue which will be featured in the next issue.

With this in mind the proportions of the chair are much the same as for an ordinary dining chair, and they are intended for use with a 28in. table such as the one shown last month. It would be quite possible to use the chair inside the house too, although the sturdy construction and the slatted design using small components is ideal to combat the effects of our normal variable weather outside.

I have used American oak, which is very suitable for outdoor work, but other timbers suitably treated would also be durable. The construction is fairly traditional and the profiled router work is an interesting technique to add to your repertoire. It is not as complicated as it sounds in the description and could prove useful in other woodworking situations. On the other hand it is quite possible to make the shaped pieces in other ways if necessary.

Construction

The first thing to do is to prepare the oak boards by rough cutting to manageable sizes, straight edging the boards, machining flat and planing to the correct thickness.

Front legs

After cutting the pieces selected for the front legs to width (keeping them parallel), mark out for length. You can then mark out the mortises on two adjacent faces at the top and one for the lower rail 150mm up from the base on the inside. As the legs are tapered and the lower mortises are square to the original faces, these should be cut before the taper is made. All the mortises finish 12mm deep and 12mm wide so that the shoulders on the sides are 4mm each and on the top and bottom should be 2 to 3mm.

One quick way of removing the waste from the mortises is to use a router, and in this case I used a Makita 3608B to remove the main waste and followed this

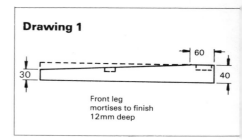

Drawing 1

Front leg
mortises to finish
12mm deep

by squaring out with a chisel. Remember though that the lower mortise needs to be cut deeper due to the taper (see drawing 1).

The taper to the front legs is on the inside face only and begins 10mm below the top rail continuing down to the base where the leg should be 30mm square in section. Remember that the bottom edges which are in contact with the ground should be chamfered to reduce any risk of damage due to pulling up the chairs and so on.

At this stage the legs can be cut to length at the correct angle before cleaning up and lightly rounding over the sharp edges. For best results oak should always be finished directly from the smoothing plane or scraper rather than from sanding.

Back legs

For the back legs it is better to make a full-size templet marking on the positions of the seat and mortises and squaring these across from the front straight edge of the ply. After marking out from this templet you can cut them out on the bandsaw and clean them up in pairs with plane and spokeshave. This is a time-consuming operation and it is difficult to ensure accuracy, so if a number of chairs are to be made then ideally you should use a spindle moulder running against a guide templet. Having no spindle moulder I adapted this technique for use with a router.

To make the templet guide take a piece of ply approximately 1100 by 300mm with a straight edge. Note that the thickness will be governed by your particular router guide although in some instances this may be adjustable. My Makita model is fixed and needs 9mm ply for the guide. Line up the previously made full-size templet on the larger piece of ply with the front edge on the straight one,

then draw round this and square the positions of the mortises and ends across (drawing 2).

Put a long reach router bit in the router and attach the bearing guide. Now measure the distance from the outer edge of the guide to the cutting edge—I will call this Xmm. Mark this distance inside the line you have on the larger piece of ply and parallel to it. Cut out the guide to this line. Repeat the process for the back edge on the other side of the ply taking care to align the mortise positions. The guide should remain overlength so that you can pin it to the workpiece and it should be wide enough so that the G cramps holding it will not foul the base of the router.

At this stage you can mark out the shape of the legs on the timber using the full-size templet, and then cut out the

front edge on the bandsaw about 2mm from the line allowing waste at each end. Now pin the templet guide to the timber through the waste Xmm back from the finished edge aligning it at the top and bottom. Bear the router guide against the ply templet and cut to shape using the long reach bit (drawing 3). You can then repeat the procedure for the back edge.

The final cleaning up of the back legs

should be done in pairs, so drill through the waste of one leg and pin it to the second one. Run over the faces with a smoothing plane and spokeshave to remove any ripple marks left by the router.

To mark out the mortises, take the original full-size templet and mark out the positions from this, squaring across onto the front edges. For the lower rail to be parallel to the ground, the lower mortises

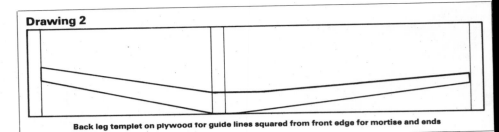

Drawing 2

Back leg templet on plywood for guide lines squared from front edge for mortise and ends

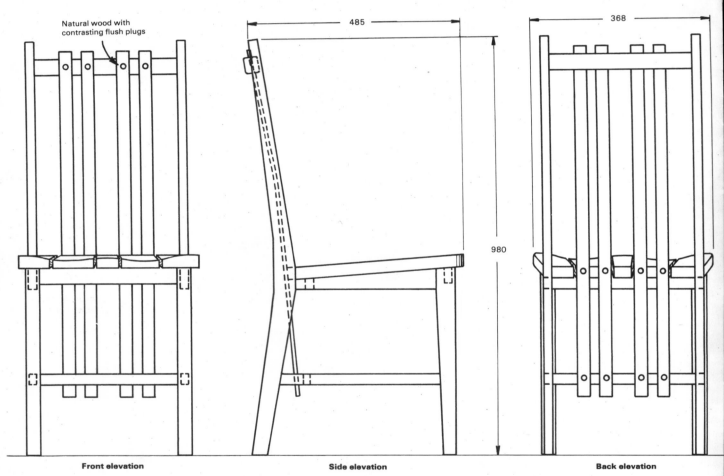

Natural wood with contrasting flush plugs

485

980

368

Front elevation

Side elevation

Back elevation

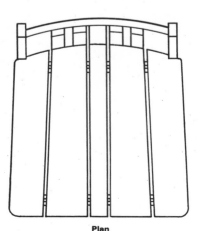

Plan

Cutting list

Seat	1 off	406 by 395 by 30mm
Back legs*	2 off	980 by 100 by 24mm
Front legs*	2 off	440 by 40 by 30mm
Top side rails	2 off	334 by 50 by 20mm
Lower side rails	2 off	377 by 30 by 20mm
Front seat rail	1 off	344 by 40 by 20mm
Back seat rail	1 off	354 by 30 by 20mm
Top back rail	1 off	352 by 60 by 40mm
Lower back rail*	1 off	354 by 60 by 30mm
Back splats	4 off	850 by ** by 30mm

* These are shaped components and may be cut more economically (if timber dimensions allow) by fitting around each other

** See instructions in text

must be cut at an angle (78 degrees), so a square should be set up and the work held in a vice at the correct angle before working the mortises by hand.

Mortises for the seat rail are at right angles to the face at that point and may be cut using the router and squaring off with a chisel as before.

Prior to sawing off the legs to the

correct length and angle, mark the positions of the top back rail. Note that for the setting out of these mortises you must square onto the inside from the front edge. These may then be cut as before.

Rails

Start by cutting all the rails to width keeping the top rails parallel at this stage. Mark and cut the tenons on each end of the top side rails, then fit to the front and back legs using cramps in a dry assembly. Now line up the lower cross rail in position under the frame ensuring it is parallel with the top rail. You are now able to mark off the length and the shoulder angles onto the rail and use these marks to transfer the positions onto the other rail for cutting the joints. Now taper the top side rails.

After tapering the top side rails, cut a

mortise 30mm back from the shoulder for the cross rails. With this preparation work done, you can clean up the rails and then glue up the side frames with Cascamite using wedge-shaped blocks to assist in pulling up the lower rails.

Now cut the seat cross rails to length, but remember that the back one will be longer than the front one because of the shoulder on the front leg. Do not bevel the rails at this stage but leave them square so that they project above the seat frame. Cut the tenons on each end then cramp up in a dry assembly so that it is possible to obtain the exact dimensions of the curved rails. Make a ply templet of the curve for these rails. Mark the shoulder length square from the face edge on the wood, then lay the templet on aligning the shoulders and draw round it.

Drawing 3

Router bit
Router guide
Router base
Plywood guide
Workpiece

Router guide used to cut back legs and splats

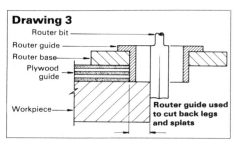

1. Using a small router to remove the bulk of the waste from the mortises.

2. The mortises in the front leg should be made prior to tapering and cutting to length.

3. Using a ply templet to mark out the back leg shape onto the timber.

4. Cutting to shape on the bandsaw allowing 2mm waste for final finishing by router.

5. With the templet pinned to the waste, bear the router against the guide to cut the edge.

6. To cut the angled mortise, cramp the leg at an angle in the vice and use a square for reference.

7. The completed back legs prior to chamfering off the bottom edges and cleaning up.

8. Lining up the lower rail to mark off the length and shoulder angles.

9. Gluing up the side frames and using wedges to assist in the clamping.

10. The cross seat rails—note that the rear rails are slightly longer than the front ones.

11. Marking out the curved rails with a ply templet—these can be cut in sequence.

12. The back splats can be cut in sequence to save timber and part-shaped by router.

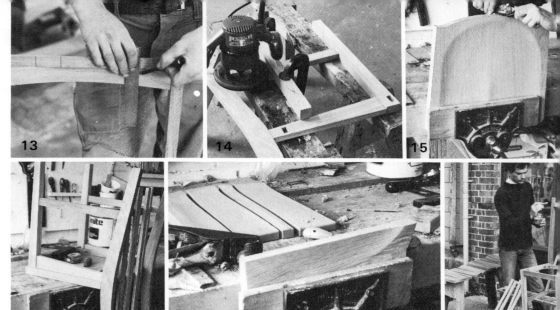

13. Marking off the splat positions from the top rail onto a measuring stick.

14. An improvised fence used as a guide for cutting the mortise for the curved rail.

15. Cleaning up the back of the seat with a spokeshave prior to cutting into segments.

16. Screw the whole seat in place so that after cutting the segments will locate exactly.

17. After cutting the seat into sections clean up the edges with a plane.

18. Mask off the gluing areas before applying varnish to all the component parts.

It is more economic in material to cut the rails in sequence but traditionally each component should have its joints complete before the curve is cut. This is not possible if the curves are fitted into one another, and it is still possible to cut the joint after the curve has been made, especially if the top and bottom shoulders of the tenon are cut first. Bandsaw the convex edge first and clean it up with a spokeshave before cutting the other as this is easier. Cut the remaining shoulders of the tenon.

Back splats

The front edge of these may be shaped with the router in the same manner as the profiling of the back legs. This is economical on timber as they may be taken in sequence from a 30mm thick plank. This should be prepared overlength to allow for pinning the guide.

The ply guide should be prepared in much the same way as before, also overlength. Mark the end of the back splat on the guide and match it up with similar lines squared across the plank itself. The plank should be cut about 2mm from the line on the bandsaw and the ply guide pinned and cramped in position Xmm back from the finished edge as before, and the router run against the guide. Again the long router cutter will be required to reach the full depth of the splat.

Once the front edge is clean, use a marking gauge adapted to it for the back edge. This is cut on the bandsaw and cleaned up by hand since there is insufficient area on which to bear the router base. If preferred the back edge may be routed and the front edge done by hand, or of course the whole thing may be cut out and cleaned up by hand. The process is repeated for the remaining splats.

Position of lower back rail

To establish the position of the lower back rail again you need to cramp up the side frames to the seat cross rails in a dry assembly. The other component which must be considered in the positioning is the seat, so make up a ply template for this and cramp it in place. Now you should

mark the positions of the splats on the top rail; to do this make a measuring stick cut to the same shoulder length as the top rail with the spacing of the splats marked on it. Now place this between the shoulders and square down onto the rails, and repeat onto the seat templet and lower rail. Square a line across the face of the back splats 25mm down from the top. Align this with the top of the rail and G cramp in position. You can then line up the splats at seat level and offer up the lower curved rail against the splats and the lower side rails. Position it so that the rail is equidistant from the back leg at each end and mark the position of the tenons. Dismantle the frame, and mortise the lower side rails. Mortises should not normally be made to fit the tenons—usually it is the other way round—but any small variation in the splat profile will alter the position of the rail so that it is necessary to fit the rail and make the mortise at this late stage.

If a router is used to make this mortise, a piece of thin scrap wood should be used to bring the base up level as the back leg projects above the rail.

Clean up the rails and glue up the frames with Cascamite. When dry, plane off the top and back cross seat rails to the correct angles.

Seat

Glue up a suitable blank preferably with only one joint down the centre, then carve out the required shape and clean up using abrasive discs in the drill followed by orbital and hand sanding. Draw round the templet and cut out the curves and side taper on the bandsaw. You can then clean up with plane, spokeshave etc. Use a tenon saw to cut out the back of the seat round the back legs—note this should be parallel to the front edge and not square with the side.

Corner blocks

These should be small to avoid them showing through the gaps between the seat sections. Drill and countersink them so that they can be screwed to the rails and also vertically to the seat. Glue and

screw them to the rails. Always use brass screws in oak as the tannic acid causes steel to corrode. Work which is to be left outside should use brass screws anyway as steel will rust. However beware of brass sheering—use a steel screw of the same size first to cut with the stronger thread into the timber. Screw the seat temporarily in position.

G cramp the splats in position again and mark and drill a clearance hole in the centre at seat level. Screw to the seat. Realign and fix similarly to the top and bottom rail, marking off the splat positions on the seat. Mark off top and bottom of the splats so that you can then remove them and cut to length.

Mark out the sections of the seat allowing a 6mm gap between pieces—these should line up with outer edges of splat pairs. Mark the centre of the three middle sections on the front and back rail.

Remove the seat and drill a clearance hole vertically through the rails at this point, countersink underneath. Screw the seat back through the corner blocks and rails as the seat will then go back exactly in position after it has been cut up. Remove the seat and cut it into sections as marked. Clean up the edges with a plane. Clean up all components and mask the back splats and rails where they cross. Now give all components two coats of clear wood preserver.

When this is quite dry, apply three coats of exterior varnish, sanding lightly between coats. Now you can counterbore the back splats for ½in. contrasting timber plugs. Follow this by gluing and screwing the back splats to the rails and screw to the seat. It then only remains to glue in the plugs and, when dry, clean off and touch up with varnish.

Further projects from this Chelsea Garden continue on page 194

Garden Runabout

HIS GARDEN RUNABOUT is a toy for outdoor use intended for youngsters who are past the toddling stage and have plenty of energy, zest and imagination. The design is based around rubber-tyred plastics wheels of 152mm (6in.) diameter, but secondhand wheels of around this size would be equally suitable. Certain parts are made of plywood, and for these an exterior grade was used.

After determining sizes and methods of construction, some preliminary full-size drawings were made (photo 1). Work actually started by cutting out the ply base. This is no more than a rectangle of material, with edges and corners well rounded. Various holes were needed in this piece—ten down the centre for the chassis member and three on each side near the back for the rear axle blocks. Two holes were also made at each end for fixing the ends of the truck, and accordingly these holes were made at a slight angle. A third hole for a centre screw was made later, once the chassis had been added.

The chassis was the next part to be prepared, and for this a piece of straight-grained softwood was used. I used glue when fixing this, as well as screwing through from the top of the ply. An offcut of hardwood provided material for the rear axle blocks. Holes for the axles were bored in these blocks in the positions shown; note that the dimension here is fairly critical if the truck is to ride level. The blocks were initially shaped, as shown in the drawing and as also seen in photo 2, and then glued as well as screwed to the base. Because of the importance of these axle blocks, I used cup washers under the screw heads rather than countersink the screws. The washers effectively increase the size of the head of the screws, thus helping to spread the load more evenly over surface of the ply base.

As I didn't have any 19mm (¾in.) ply in the workshop, but did have some 10mm (⅜in.), I decided to laminate two pieces of this thickness together to provide material for the ends of the truck. After gluing together, the sandwich was trimmed to size, top corners

CUTTING LIST

Base	1 off	857 by 343 by 13mm	(33¾ by 13½ by ½in.)
Chassis piece	1 off	851 by 114 by 19mm	(33½ by 4½ by ¾in.)
Ends	2 off	362 by 286 by 19mm	(14¼ by 11¼ by ¾in.)
Slats	4 off	940 by 70 by 19mm	(37 by 2¾ by ¾in.)
Rear axle blocks	2 off	197 by 108 by 38mm	(7¾ by 4¼ by 1½in.)
Front axle support	1 off	349 by 83 by 25mm	(13¾ by 3¼ by 1in.)
Front axle blocks	2 off	95 by 51 by 25mm	(3¾ by 2 by 1in.)
Front link piece	1 off	273 by 114 by 25mm	(10¾ by 4½ by 1in.)
Handle sides	2 off	832 by 44 by 22mm	(32¾ by 1¾ by ⅞in.)
Handle	1 off	413 by 25mm dia.	(16¼ by 1in. dia.)
Cross dowels	2 off	152 by 19mm dia.	(6 by ¾in. dia.)

Allowance added to lengths, widths and thicknesses are net.
Also required: 4 off 152mm (6in.) dia. wheels, axle rod and hub caps; approx. 203mm (8in.) of 6mm (¼in.) dia. axle rod and hub caps; cup washers; turntable.
Wheels, hub caps and axle rod obtainable from: W. Hobby Ltd., 62 Norwood High Street, London SE27. Turntable obtainable from: Woodfit, Whittle Low Mill, Chorley, Lancs.

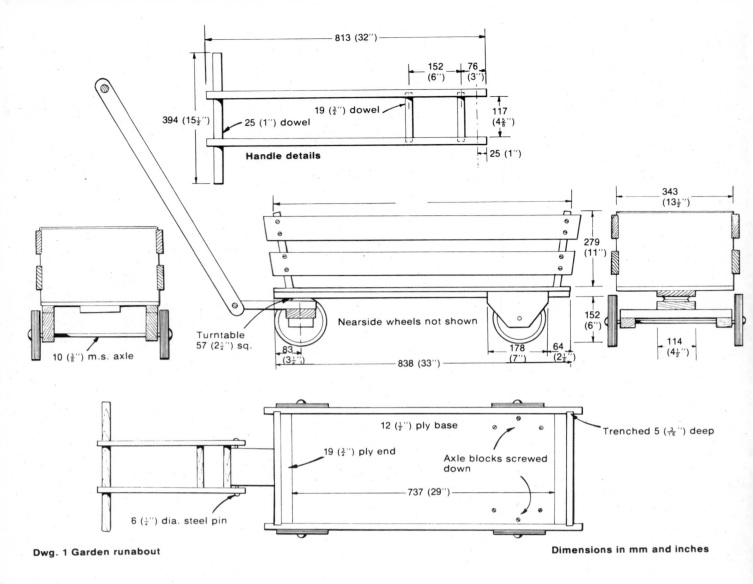

Handle details

813 (32")
152 (6")
76 (3")
19 (¾") dowel
117 (4⅝")
394 (15½")
25 (1") dowel
25 (1")

343 (13½")
279 (11")

152 (6")
Turntable 57 (2¼") sq.
Nearside wheels not shown
83 (3¼")
178 (7")
64 (2½")
114 (4½")
10 (⅜") m.s. axle
838 (33")

12 (½") ply base
Trenched 5 (³⁄₁₆") deep
19 (¾") ply end
Axle blocks screwed down
737 (29")
6 (¼") dia. steel pin

Dwg. 1 Garden runabout

Dimensions in mm and inches

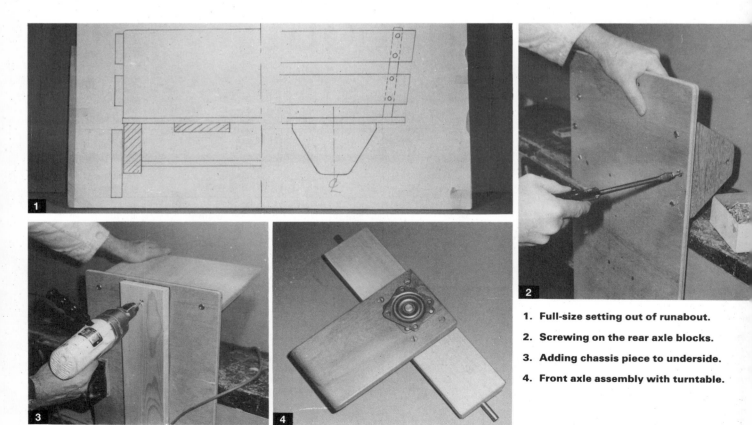

1. Full-size setting out of runabout.
2. Screwing on the rear axle blocks.
3. Adding chassis piece to underside.
4. Front axle assembly with turntable.

well rounded and the lower edge planed to a light bevel. When screwing these pieces in place, I was careful to pre-drill for the screws—to prevent any splitting of the ply. Only at this stage was the hole made in the chassis and ply base so that a screw could pass through both and into the ends. Photo 3 shows this stage and again cup washers were used with the screws.

Now my attention turned to the front axle assembly. The cross member was made first, then the small axle blocks were prepared to size. These were bored for screws and for the axle and when fixing— with the help of a little glue—the axle itself was inserted so as to ensure the accurate alignment of the parts being fixed together.

The piece which links the axle to the handle was made next. After boring holes for the pivot pin at the front and for the screws, the front end was rounded. This component was now added to the axle assembly.

At the outset it was decided to use a small turntable on which to mount the front axle to the body; the purpose of this was to give a smooth and easy turning action. The turntable was first fixed to the axle assembly using 2BA engineers' screws and nuts to secure it. These have an approximate diameter of 4mm ($\frac{3}{16}$in.) and provide rather more strength than woodscrews. The work at this stage can be seen in photo 4.

Next to be tackled were the four side slats. These are trenched to the ends. Here I felt it would be sufficiently accurate to mark the position of these trenches directly from the job. Two slats were laid in position, their spacing checked, and the position of the tuck end pencilled onto the inner surfaces of the slats. Trenches were gauged in to be 5mm ($\frac{3}{16}$in.) deep, and cut by saw and chisel (photo 5), finishing off with a hand router. Two holes were bored in each trench for screws, the waste at the ends cut off on the splay, and they were screwed to the body. Although the slats were fixed in place at this stage, they were removed later on for finishing operations.

The handle was quickly constructed. Two pieces of straight-grained material were prepared for the side parts and, after marking to the overall length, the centres for the various holes needed were positioned on the wood. These holes were bored to the sizes shown and, although the 19mm ($\frac{3}{4}$in.) holes are indicated as ''blind'', it would make very little difference if these were bored right through.

Ends of these pieces were rounded, and the dowel for the actual handle cut to the required length. It is important when assembling the handle to check that the inside distance between the side pieces is approximately 3mm ($\frac{1}{8}$in.) greater than the width of the linking part of the front axle assembly to which it is to connect. Glue, plus a panel pin through each end of the dowel, were used for securing the parts together.

With the constructional work now completed, I was ready for applying the finish – a combination of preserver, paint and varnish. All surfaces were given two coats of clear wood preserver. The four side slats were unscrewed and given three coats of varnish, while the remainder of the job was given the standard painting process of primer, undercoat and gloss. Knowing the attraction of bright colours, I used a combination of blue and orange.

A piece of axle rod provided the pivot to connect the handle to the front axle, and this and the wheels were held in place with snap on hub caps. Re-fixing the varnished slats then completed the project.

Wheels, axle rod and hub caps are obtainable from: W. Hobby Ltd, 62 Norwood High Street, London SE27 9NW. The turntable is obtainable from: Woodfit, Whittle Low Mill, Chorley, Lancs PR6 7HB.

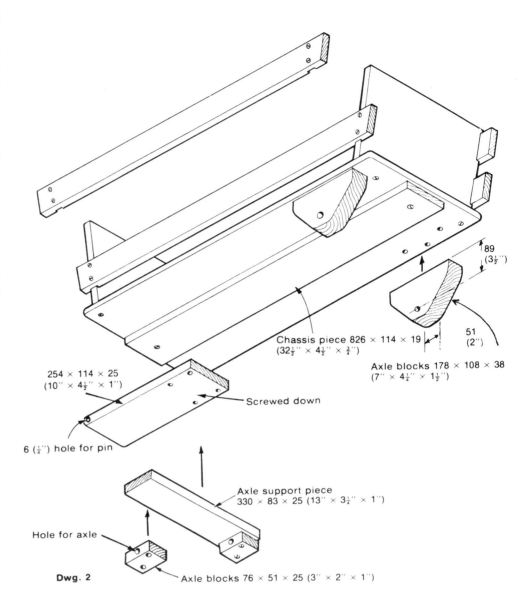

89 ($3\frac{1}{2}$")

51 (2")

Chassis piece 826 × 114 × 19 ($32\frac{1}{2}$" × $4\frac{1}{2}$" × $\frac{3}{4}$")

Axle blocks 178 × 108 × 38 (7" × $4\frac{1}{4}$" × $1\frac{1}{2}$")

254 × 114 × 25 (10" × $4\frac{1}{2}$" × 1")

Screwed down

6 ($\frac{1}{4}$") hole for pin

Axle support piece 330 × 83 × 25 (13" × $3\frac{1}{4}$" × 1")

Hole for axle

Dwg. 2

Axle blocks 76 × 51 × 25 (3" × 2" × 1")

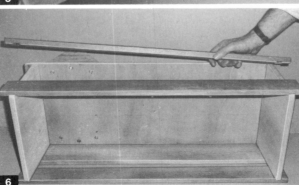

5. Trenching out one of the slats.

6. Slats added to the main body.

7. Underside of the front end.

Round Garden Tables

The two round tables shown and described here, whilst similar in design, are different in size and finishing treatment. Although they are designed for use in the garden they could also be useful in the house.

The principal table described here has been made at standard dining table height but with a fairly small diameter, envisaging it as a table for two on sunny summer Sunday mornings. The other table is a low version, smaller still in diameter and could equally well double as an occasional table indoors in the winter.

The construction of the main frame produces the required stability and the visual effect of this may be emphasised by staining or painting it, as on the low table. When designing for outdoor use, the effects of the weather must be taken into account, hence the division of the top into smaller parts, with spaces between for rain to run through. For the same reason the main 75 by 33 sections were used on edge to reduce the amount of exposed flat area, and Cascamite was used for all the joints as a strong waterproof glue. As to the choice of material we were fortunate enough to be provided with some excellent American oak by The National Hardwood Campaign, which should prove very durable. However, any timber which is going to be left outside should be treated with a preservative, such as Cuprinol, and also oiled or varnished regularly.

The main area of the construction which may look daunting is the tongued mitre joint. Mitres often seem to frighten people until they have actually tried them. However with careful setting out and accurate cutting, this should prove easier than it looks, especially if you have the use of a bench type circular saw. Time spent ensuring this is set up correctly should make the cutting of the joint quite straightforward. If you do have to make it by hand a bit more skill will be required but it is still quite possible. However if you really cannot face it the leg could be tenoned into a mortise under the top cross frame, although this would mean that the end grain would show on the vertical. The design should adapt well to being made up in a larger diameter but base stretchers would be advised over about one metre.

Construction

The first thing to do is to mark out the

timber. Ideally the grain should run with the central radius of each piece so that there will be a triangle of waste at the sides of the strip, if, in the most economical way, the top sections are cut from a wide board as shown. It would be

possible to waste less by cutting pairs diagonally across the plank, but this would result in the grain running parallel with one edge creating a visually distorting effect, and also leaving rather short grain at the tip, so the first method is to be preferred. The other components should be straightforward to mark out.

You can then cut the timber to manageable lengths, plane a flat face, side and thickness. For ease of working all

thicknesses remain constant throughout each table so all the timber can be prepared together. Following this the boards can be edged and the leg and frame components cut to width.

The next step is to cut the mitres at the top of each leg and at each end of the top frame. These could be dowelled, but a double tongue is a much stronger joint and has much greater gluing area. After cutting, the mitres should be checked for accuracy, and then the position of the two equally spaced 6mm ply tongues should be carefully marked out on one mitred face and 30mm along the inside edge. Use a mortise gauge to ensure they are exactly the same distance in from each side. These tongues are stopped short of the outside corner but appear through on the inside underneath. To cut the slots by hand, use a tenon saw to cut to the gauge lines and chisel out the waste working towards the outer corner.

To cut the joint by machine, use a piece of scrap material of the same dimensions and with the same gauge marks to set up and test the saw setting. Wind the blade up with the mitred component beside it to assess the correct height. Also check the distance the timber will need to travel into the blade to make the slot. Cramp a piece of waste timber approximately 80 by 5mm section to the rip fence to act as a stop at this point. Set the rip fence to the waste side of the first marked line, then using push sticks, feed the mitred end inner side down, into the saw until it reaches the stop and withdraw it thus creating a stopped groove. After all the components have been put through, the fence may then be moved across to widen the groove out to 6mm (use a spare piece of ply to check the fit) then reposition the fence to make the other groove. It is important to ensure accurate location on each side, as the faces which have been running against the fence will be on opposite sides when the joint is put together—inaccurate setting will cause misaligned slots.

The groove, of course, will be slightly rounded on the inside due to the curve of

the saw blade. A templet should therefore be made for the tongue by placing a piece of ply against the stop on the saw and

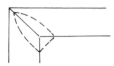

drawing round the blade. This shape, doubled, may then be used to cut eight ply tongues which should be checked for fit.

You can now cut the legs to length and chamfer the bottom of each. Follow this by cleaning up all the components and lightly chamfering the sharp edges.

Mix up some Cascamite using one part water to 3.5 powder by volume. When you have done this a few times you will recognise the correct consistency and be able to mix it 'by eye' as it were, but it is well worth measuring the propotions initially so as to experience the right viscosity. For a relatively small amount I generally put a little water in an old yoghurt pot and then add the quantity of powder which I think I will need, adding more if necessary, then stirring to a smooth paste with a piece of scrap timber with a nice flat tapered end to act as a spreader. Spread the glue on the tongues, a little in the base of the grooves and over one face of each mitre. Push the tongue into one section then locate the other onto it. Repeat with the other end. Three sash cramps will be needed for each frame plus an extra one to use diagonally if it needs pulling square. A spacer may be used between the legs at the bottom if necessary.

Clean off the excess glue with a damp rag and allow to dry for about six hours depending on the temperature of the workshop. When dry, clean up the joints and use a coping saw to cut off the excess tongue on the inside, trimming back with a sharp chisel.

Measure the centre of the top of the frame then mark out and cut a halving joint. So long as this is a tight fit it will no need to be housed as the corner block and the diagonal rails will stop the fram from twisting.

Mark the position of the diagonal rail i the side of the legs allowing for th thickness of the top which should com level with the top of the cross frame. Then cut a housing 40 by 25 by 6mm deep fo the diagonal rail in each side of each leg. router may be used if you have one t remove most of the waste, and th remainder squared out with a chisel.

Put the framework together dry an measure the shoulder length of th diagonal rails which should all be th same.

Cut the diagonal rails to length— shoulder length plus 6mm each end— 45 degrees.

Cut a shoulder at the back of the rail s that the front edge meets the corner of th leg.

Large table

All components 33mm thick

Legs	4 off 740 by	75mm
Top frame	2 off 760 by	75mm
Diagonal rails	4 off 525 by	40mm
Top*	16 off 360 by	130mm
Corner blocks*	4 off 150 by	75mm

Small table

All components 33mm thick

Legs	4 off 430 by	65mm
Top frame	2 off 555 by	65mm
Diagonal rails	4 off 385 by	35mm
Top*	16 off 260 by	95mm
Corner blocks*	4 off 105 by	50mm

* These components are triangular in shape and may be arranged for more economical cutting—see text.

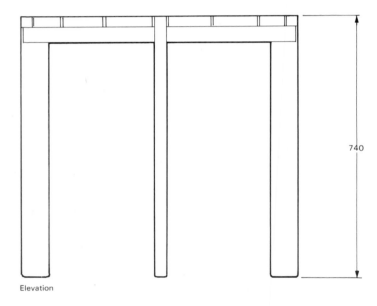

Elevation

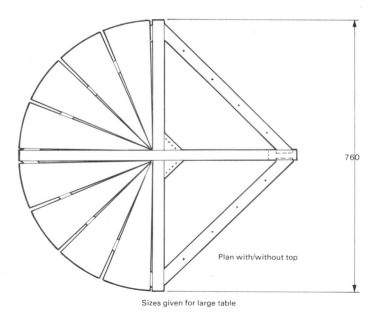

Plan with/without top

Sizes given for large table

1. The first thing to be done is mark out the timber. Note gra direction of circle segment
2. After sawing to manageab sizes, the boards should be plane and thicknesse
3. After edging, component piece for legs and frames can be cut size
4. With careful marking ou accurate mitring by hand possible, but check for accurac
5. For grooving the saw is set the correct height and a sto clamped to the fenc
6. Shaped plywood tongues fitte to the grooved joints made wi the sav
7. The bottoms of the legs a lightly chamfered all the wa roun
8. When gluing up the leg frame diagonal cramp can help to pull squar
9. At this stage the excess ply the tongues can be trimmed bac with saw and chise
10. Halving joint made in th centre of the leg frame an housings for diagonal rail
11. Forming the shouldered joi on the diagonal rails—trimmin back with a chise
12. Drilling the corner blocks f pins to hold them temporarily plac
13. Gluing the corner blocks place to give added strength to th structur
14. After bandsawing the circ segments, plane to a fine finish, inaccuracy will sho
15. Both tables are finished wi three coats of satin yach varnish

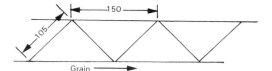

Put all four rails in position, dry, to check they are the correct length—the ends of the rails will project beyond the leg. Then take the frame apart and clean up. You can now glue up the centre joint and all four rails, cramping across each pair. Now make four corner blocks as shown in the drawing. Drill each for two temporary pins to hold them in position whilst aligning the cramps.

Mark 33mm down at the centre joint and cramp the blocks in position across each pair. When dry, trim the ends of the diagonal rails flush with the legs and clean up the whole thing. Remove the pins from the blocks and fill the pin holes.

To mark out the sections for the top you will need to make a templet. Take a piece of ply 360mm square, position it in one quadrant of the table and mark the ends of the legs. Draw the circumference of the circle from the centre point (internal corner of the ply). Mark out the segments on the ply allowing 10mm gaps at the circumference between the sections, tapering to nothing at the centre. Cut out one of these segments and use this as the templet to mark and cut the top pieces. If possible use a bandsaw and then plane up the edges afterwards. Sand the surfaces and chamfer the corners and edges and then position the pieces on the underframe. Mark out their position, drill the corner blocks and the diagonal rails so

that each segment is fixed centrally in two places. Countersink these holes and screw up from underneath using brass screws.

Unscrew the top pieces and apply two coats of Cuprinol preservative to all parts of the table. The second coat should be applied before the first is dry and special attention should be paid to the base of the legs which will be in contact with the ground. When this is quite dry it may be followed with one of International's paints or stains such as the black stain I used on the framework of the smaller table which I contrasted with an attractive white finish reminiscent of limed oak. This was done by applying micro-porous paint with a cloth rubber and rubbing it well into the grain. The other table was left with a natural finish with three coats of varnish applied with a brush at 24 hour intervals. Once the finish is satisfactory and quite dry, components may be rubbed down with a fine wire wool, and the top reassembled onto the base.

Screens and Decking

We have looked at the furniture and more functional items in our woodworker's garden at Chelsea, and now we turn our attention to two projects which enhance the garden for their decorative effect — the screens and decking. Gordon Warr, who worked to the designs of Lucinda Leech, describes how he built them.

THIS YEAR is the third year in which I have found myself involved in making items for the Chelsea Flower Show, this time with Lucinda Leech who had dreamed up the overall concept for the garden, and with whom I had had early discussions on the constructional details of the projects I was to make.

I commenced my share of the Woodworker's Garden with the screens. The Malaysian hardwood timber which I was to use had been supplied by arrangement with the National Hardwood Campaign, with the plywood by courtesy of the Panel Products' Association of The Timber Trades' Federation. The timber was in the form of hefty boards and planks up to 75mm (3in.) thick, while the plywood was 19mm ($\frac{3}{4}$in.) thick exterior quality sheathing grade of Canadian manufacture. The five panels making up each side of the screens were to be of different widths, but this was only to fit in with the other features making up the garden.

Plywood was used for the lower rail of the screen, for the top rails and end quadrants and the central archway. It was with the top rails which incorporated the quadrants that I commenced, and set out the shape on a sheet of ply. This I then cut with a combination of jigsaw and circular saw, leaving the edges as cut. This first piece I could then use as a templet for the remainder, remembering

in my case that I wanted two sets [o]f different lengths. The lower rails and th[e] straight top rails were simply ripped, the[n] crosscut from the ply, before giving [all] these components a generous coat [of] micro-porous paint.

This is a new type of paint which [is] easy to apply and maintain. The pai[nt] film has tiny pores in it allowing th[e] surface to breathe. Water is kept ou[t] but any moisture in the wood ca[n] escape through the paint. This elimi[n]ates two major problems with co[n]ventional gloss paint — blisters whic[h] are caused by moisture vapour expan[d]ing below the surface, and rot, so ofte[n] caused by moisture which is trappe[d] in the wood and which has difficul[ty] in escaping because of the seale[d] surface. The paint does not require [a] primer and produces a most interes[t]ing effect on the plywood, the fair[ly] coarse surface of which was tran[s]formed into one of interesting textu[re] by the paint.

Assembling the screens was to b[e] entirely by nailing, using galvanised nai[ls] of different lengths for this. I used a shee[t] of ply as an assembly base, which as we[ll] as providing support enabled the scree[n] to be easily kept square. The first stag[e] of the assembly was thus to nail togeth[er] the four pieces forming the basic fram[e].

I ripped a quantity of the 25mm (1in[.]

Made up as framed trellis work, the screens use both solid wood and painted ply which is more suited to the curved components of the arch and quadrant corners. The solid lauan decking is in the American tradition and demonstrates how the beauty of the timber itself can be used as a principle component in the design of any garden.

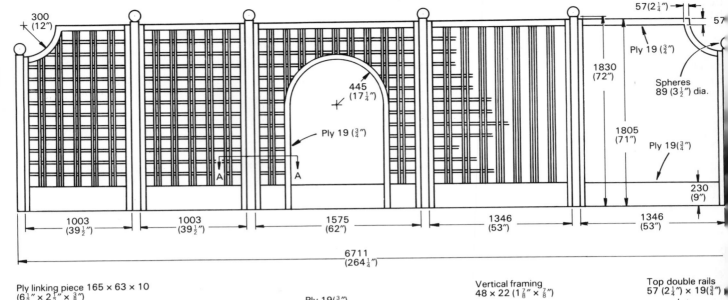

300
(12")

57 (2¼")

57

Ply 19 (¾")

445
(17¼")

Ply 19 (¾")

1830
(72")

Spheres
89 (3½") dia.

1805
(71")

Ply 19(¾")

230
(9")

A   A

| 1003 (39½") | 1003 (39½") | 1575 (62") | 1346 (53") | 1346 (53") |

6711
(264¼")

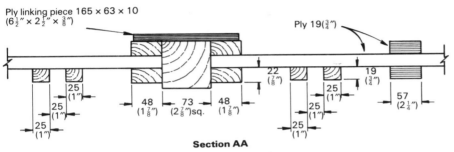

Ply linking piece 165 × 63 × 10
(6½" × 2½" × ⅜")

Ply 19(¾")

22 (⅞")   19 (¾")

25 (1")

48 (1⅞")   73 (2⅞")sq.   48 (1⅞")   25 (1")   25 (1")   57 (2¼")

25 (1")

25 (1")   25 (1")

Section AA

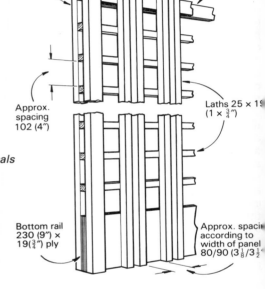

Vertical framing
48 × 22 (1⅞" × ⅞")

Top double rails
57 (2¼") × 19(¾")

Approx.
spacing
102 (4")

Laths 25 × 19
(1 × ¾")

Bottom rail
230 (9") ×
19(¾") ply

Approx. spacing
according to
width of panel
80/90 (3⅛/3½")

1. The first ply quadrant piece can be used as a templet to mark out the remainder.
2. The first stage of the assembly is to nail together the four components of the basic frame.
3. A rod is used to transfer the positions of the horizontal laths onto the uprights.
4. Fixing of the laths is simple enough using galvanised nails.

5. A rod is also used to locate the verticals when it comes to fixing in position.
6. Detail of the corner fixing.
7. To complete the panel the second top rail is added to abut against the first rail.
8. Setting out the radius for the arch using a lath and a pencil.

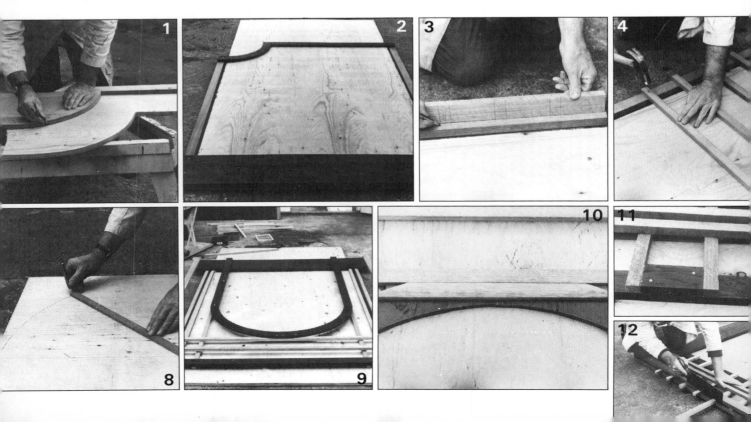

1
2
3
4
8
9
10
11
12

boards into the strips needed for the laths, and set out the horizontal spacing for these on a 'rod' from which I could transfer the position to the frame members. Nailing these in place was simple enough, and this was followed by fixing the second vertical framing members in position. The locations of the vertical laths were also set out on a rod—in fact I needed three to give the slightly different spacings to cover the three panel widths being made. The rod proved an easy way of locating the laths as the nails were driven in. Ends were fixed first, followed by nailing at the overlaps. All that was required now to complete the panel was the second top rail, which abutts immediately against the first rail on the opposite side to the vertical laths.

The centre panels incorporate the arches, a feature which is repeated on other items in the garden. Two laminations of the ply are used on the arches, with the joints staggered as shown on the drawings. I cut the arch pieces at the outset, using a lath of wood to act as a large compass for the marking out, and a jigsaw for the cutting. Both the width and height of the arch had been made to coincide with the laths, so that the spaces between all intermediate components in these centre panels remained the same.

The four frame members were secured together first, followed by the horizontal and vertical laths which are located outside the arch, these being the six which are either the full height or width of the panel. Next, one side of the arch was added, this being the lamination composing two pieces jointed at the top. As only the top part of the arch overlapped a lath, a packing piece was fitted below this lath to strengthen the butt joint at the crown of these two arch members. Shorter horizontal laths were nailed in place next,

between two of which were fixed packing pieces so as to coincide with the lower ends of the reverse upper arch lamination. These provided a firm support for the joints between the top semicircles of the arch, and the vertical parts which complete this feature. Now the remainder of the vertical laths could be fitted, as they all required to be scribed to the arch against which they were simply butted, there were adequate points at which they could be nailed in order to provide firm fixing. Adding the second lamination to the top rails completed these panels. Note that while two pieces of ply form the top rails to all the panels, only one is used at the lower end. The width of these bottom rails is such that it provides both strength and rigidity.

All the plywood components had been painted prior to assembly, so now on completion all untreated wood was given a couple of coats of clear preservative. It's applied by brush, and soon soaks in. Only at this stage were the outer frame members painted with micro-porous paint. I decided this was the easiest way of completing the painting as only the outer faces of the frames were in fact painted.

The posts had to be made from the thick planks which had been delivered to me, and after ripping these to square section, they were planed on all surfaces. Holes were bored in the tops of the posts into which the spheres could be dowelled, then the tops were splayed to prevent water from lodging. This was quickly accomplished on my DeWalt radial arm saw by canting over the blade by a few degrees. The posts too were given a coat of micro-porous paint.

The spheres have a diameter of 89mm ($3\frac{1}{2}$ in.), so for these I had to glue together two pieces 51mm (2in.) thick in order to gain the size needed. The lengths glued up were then cut into cubes, and had a

piece of 19mm ($\frac{3}{4}$ in.) dowel glued into a hole bored at one end. These were soon turned on the lathe, and apart from checking the diameter with a pair of callipers, the remainder of the outline was produced by eye. As the dowel was a good fit in the holes in the posts, I used paint as the adhesive and soon had the spheres tapped into place.

As a means had to be devised to secure the panels to the posts, I prepared a number of linking pieces from 10mm ($\frac{3}{8}$ in.) ply to the sizes shown. Two of these were screwed to each post, projecting outwards so as to support the panels and fixed to them also by screws.

With the work now completed on all ten panels forming the two screens, I thought it wise to try assembling one of the screens to ensure all was well. With the aid of several temporary stays to hold everything vertical, the panels were screwed to the linking pieces and a check with a long tape brought a sigh of relief from myself. The combined overall length was correct to within about 6mm ($\frac{1}{4}$ in.) —sufficiently accurate for any garden, including Chelsea!

Once re-erected at the Flower Show, the posts holding the screens would themselves be secured to steel post supports called Metposts. These are made of steel, and comprise a long spike at the lower end, and a socket at the top into which the wooden post is driven. Metposts are made in four lengths, and can accommodate posts from 50 by 50mm (2 by 2in.), up to 100mm by 100mm (4 by 4in.). The design of the socket is such that reasonable tolerance in timber size still allows for the wedge-grip to be fully effective. A 'Met-Tool' is also available to protect the posts as they are being driven in by hammer, as neither digging nor concreting is needed with this system.

9. Assembling the frame together with the full length laths.
10. A strengthening piece is added at the crown to reinforce the butt joint.
11. Further packing pieces are added at the joint between the straight and curved ply arch components.
12. After fitting the shorter laths in place the excess lengths can be trimmed.
13. The secondary ply of the arch frame is fitted in place over the laths.
14. Applying micro-porous paint to the posts – note the champered edges to the tops.
15. Turning one of the balls to shape on the lathe.
16. With a good fit, paint alone can be relied on as adhesive.

The decking

First, the good news about the timber which I had received for the Chelsea Flower Show. The boards intended for the decking were prime quality lauan, and had been planed to a finished thickness of 28mm (1⅛in.). Next the bad news—the lengths of all the boards were about 600mm (24in.) shorter than they should have been, as it had been intended that each board would be cut into four of the segments. There was sufficient timber to allow each of the boards to yield two segments only, and further supplies couldn't be arranged in time, so some re-planning of the original layout for the deck boarding was needed in order to make full use of the shorter than expected material which had been sent!

The problem was solved by the introduction of the three shorter boards making up the central shape. The arch theme was a feature which appeared in several of the other items making up the garden,

so it was a natural way of overcoming the difficulty presented by the timber itself.

I had had to stack the boards outside but kept them covered until I was ready to start. This I did by cutting a quantity of the wood into two, and how useful I found my Stanley bow saw for this. Next, I had to carry out a lot of careful setting out, to give me the exact layout of the boards, and more important, the widths at the wide and narrow ends. However accurate a drawing is when the scale of this is small then full-size setting out is essential, and especially so when tapered work is involved. Fortunately, plywood wanted for another part of the garden provided a temporary platform for the hardwood decking, and I was able to use this to establish the exact sizes needed.

As the arch feature formed the centre of the deck, the three boards needed for this part were the first to be prepared. After marking out the semi-circular

shape, the curved ends were sawn on the bandsaw, but were not smoothed any further. The ends which were left square were simply crosscut to their exact length. The six boards making up the rest of the front part of the deck, that is three on either side of the central arch feature, were quickly prepared. One edge was trued up, then they were sawn to width before these too were cut to length.

Rather more work was needed for the segments. One board was carefully marked to give the tapered shape required, then this was cut with a portable circular saw. After taking a few shavings off the edge to adjust the size very slightly, I could then use this first segment as a templet for cutting the remainder. By cramping this in turn to each board, it served as a guide for the sawing.

The outer end of these wedge-shaped boards did of course need to be cut to a curved shape corresponding to the outline of the semi-circle, but this was not necessary at the narrow end. As the boards were cut, they were laid out on the plywood to check that all was well. With 36 segments making up the full semi-circle, any slight inaccuracy would soon be magnified, but fortunately the gaps between each pair of boards provided for a little tolerance.

Chamfers are usually formed on the corners of wood for decorative purposes, and to give a lighter look to a project. However, they also have a functional role, as by removing the sharp corner they lessen the possibility of both bruising and splitting of vulnerable edges and especially those subjected to wear in one form or another. Upper corners of all the boards making up the deck were therefore chamfered, and this was carried out by router. I used an older industrial model from the Black and Decker range for this, combined with a chamfering cutter equipped with a pilot. Each

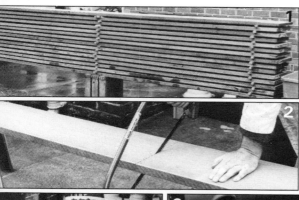

Setting up the decking on its base at Chelsea

iece of decking was in turn cramped to
he bench, and the router moved along
he edges and ends to create a uniform
ut easily and speedily.

The decking was naturally intended to
e raised several inches off the ground,
o a method had to be devised which
vould achieve this and which would be
easonably economical and suitable for
hort-term use at the Flower Show.
trips of ply were cut to form an under-
raming, and were cross-halved at their
nany points of intersection. This proved
ffective and practical when re-erected at
he garden at Chelsea, but is not recom-
nended as a long-term method of sup-
orting the decking.

The sketches show a suggested more
ermanent method of providing support
or the decking. A concrete base would
e needed, and dwarf walls built as
lustrated to carry timber wallplates.
hese in turn would support members
renched fully into the top edge so that
he upper surfaces of all components
vere flush. A damp-proof course would
e essential between the brickwork and
he timber, and the timber itself should be
ought as factory-treated against rot, or
iven several applications of a preserva-
ve. Note that this suggested method of
roviding support is shown in sketch
orm only, and the exact positions of the
valls and supporting timbers would need
o be established in relation to the deck-
ng boards.

As it was hoped that the decking
repared for Chelsea would be re-used
lsewhere after the Show, it was sensi-
le to treat this with preservative. Even
hough most hardwoods have a much
reater natural resistance to rot than do
he majority of softwoods, a good quality
reservative will extend whatever life
ature and the weather have destined for
hem. Two coats of clear wood preserver
vere therefore generously applied.

. Awaiting attention – the boards are
tacked clear of the ground with sticks
etween each.
. A start is made on cutting the boards
o more manageable sizes with a
owsaw.
. Crosscutting to more exact sizes on
he DeWalt radial arm saw.
. Truing up the edge of one of the
oards using the circular saw.
. After cutting the first board to
hape, it is used as a guide for cutting
he others.
. Checking the layout of the boards so
hat adjustments can be made where
ecessary.
. The upper edges of all the decking
oards are chamfered using a router
vith a pilot bit.
. Making up the ply underframing
vhich was used for setting up in the
Chelsea garden.

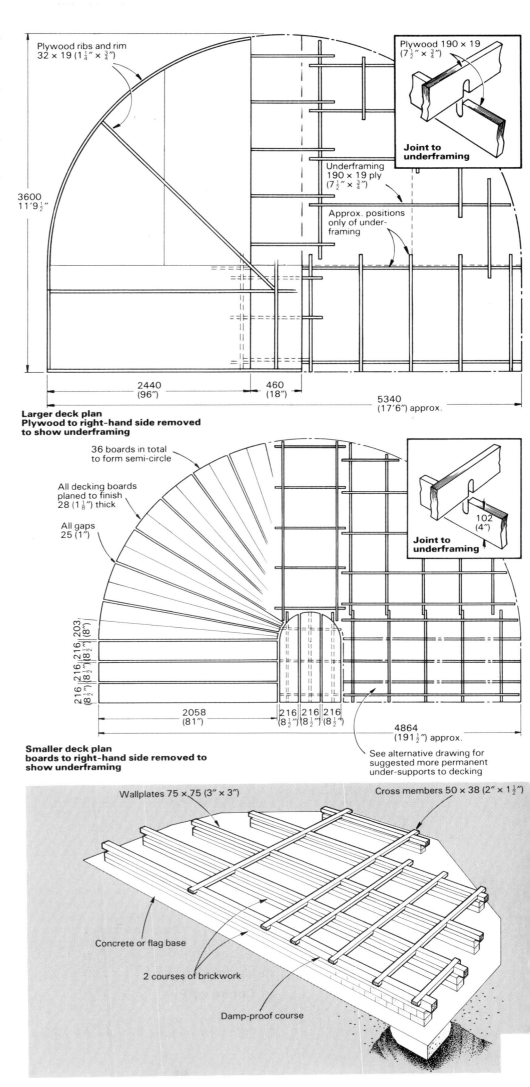

Plywood ribs and rim
32 × 19 (1¼" × ¾")

Plywood 190 × 19
(7½" × ¾")

Joint to
underframing

Underframing
190 × 19 ply
(7½" × ¾")

Approx. positions
only of under-
framing

3600
11'9½"

2440
(96")

460
(18")

5340
(17'6") approx.

Larger deck plan
Plywood to right-hand side removed
to show underframing

36 boards in total
to form semi-circle

All decking boards
planed to finish
28 (1⅛") thick

All gaps
25 (1")

102
(4")

Joint to
underframing

216, 216, 216, 203,
(8½")(8½")(8½")(8")

2058
(81")

216 216 216
(8½")(8½")(8½")

4864
(191½") approx.

Smaller deck plan
boards to right-hand side removed to
show underframing

See alternative drawing for
suggested more permanent
under-supports to decking

Wallplates 75 × 75 (3" × 3")

Cross members 50 × 38 (2" × 1½")

Concrete or flag base

2 courses of brickwork

Damp-proof course

Chelsea Arbour

The focal point of our woodworker's garden at Chelsea was undoubtedly the arbour, and it is a design which can easily be made to suit other gardens. Here Lucinda Leech describes the method of construction. Fuller details of the laminating process are given in the chaise longue section on pages 211–15.

THE arbour was the focal point of our garden at the Chelsea Flower Show in May, and would indeed provide a beautiful centrepiece for any plot, with clematis or wisteria climbing over it to give shade on a hot day. It seats a number of people comfortably, especially with the addition of cushions to soften the solid seats. The smaller of the two tables featured in the June issue was placed in the centre of the arbour, and at Chelsea provided us with a place for our celebratory glasses of champagne!

The National Hardwood Campaign gave us some lauan (also known as Phillipine mahogany), for the construction of the piece, which contrasted with the oak used for the furniture. The pale red tone was an excellent background to the plants. It laminated well and is said to be durable for outside use such as this, especially as it was also treated with timber preservative.

This is not, at first sight, an easy piece of woodwork to undertake. However, if it is considered in individual stages it should be a manageable project for those with some experience and it certainly provides a lovely place to relax in, once the hard work is over!

Construction

We have already looked in detail at the laminating process in the August issue in the article on how to make the chaise longue, and reference back to this may prove useful.

Two formers must be made up, one for the horizontal back rails, each made in four sections, and one for the top components. The curved sections of the former may be made up from three layers of 18mm chipboard glued and screwed together and cut out on a bandsaw or by hand. They should be accurately cleaned up to the line of the internal curve, then glued and screwed up from underneath onto a baseboard. The straight sections should then be fixed to the baseboard to complete the second former. Both should be made overlength.

Pencil marks should be made on each former indicating the finished length of each component. These should be transferred to each laminated piece before it is taken off, and squared across onto its face.

Constructional laminates may be used or you may prepare your own as previously described, remembering to clean up the finished faces before cutting into strips. The strips should be about 6mm wider than the finished width to allow for cleaning up.

When the laminates are ready they should be glued up using Cascamite. Grease the former with a candle and cramp the eight 2·5mm laminates in position, ensuring that they are flat to the base. Leave them to dry for about eight

Plan at BB

Slats

Seat supports

Back rails

Seat

Metal rod

2130

Plan at BB

Vertical section at AA

2185

B   B

Back rails

Seat

Seat support

Vertical section at AA

Materials list

Seats	12 off	400 by 400 by 30mm
Seat supports	12 off	600 by 195 by 30mm
Uprights	24 off	1460 by 40 by 20mm
Arm uprights	4 off	670 by 40 by 25mm
Arm top rails	2 off	350 by 40 by 25mm
Arm base rails	2 off	300 by 40 by 25mm

Laminates	
Top	sufficient for 24 off approx. 1800 by 40 by 20mm
Back rails	sufficient for 2 off approx. 5000 by 40 by 20mm

Former for back rails

Laminates

Baseboard

Former built up in sections

Former for top components

Centre point mark

Laminates

Former built up in sections

Cut off point mark

Baseboard

Plan of top

Gap between pairs of laminated sections

Spacers pinned and glued to ring

Ply ring

40

30

$22\frac{1}{2}$

$22\frac{1}{2}$

100

175

200

One pair at seat level left and right

Plan of top

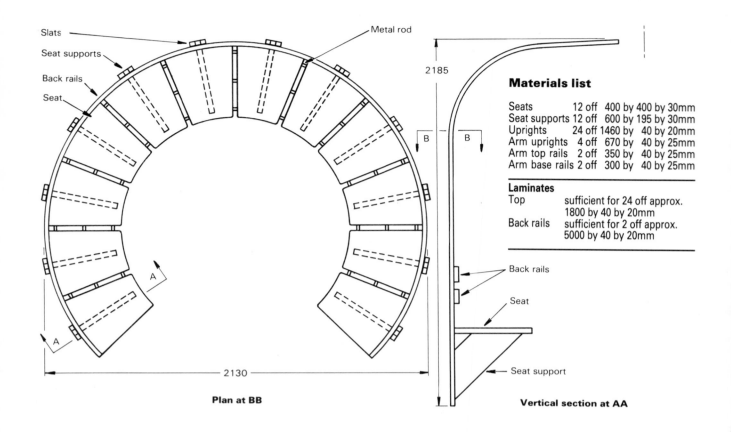

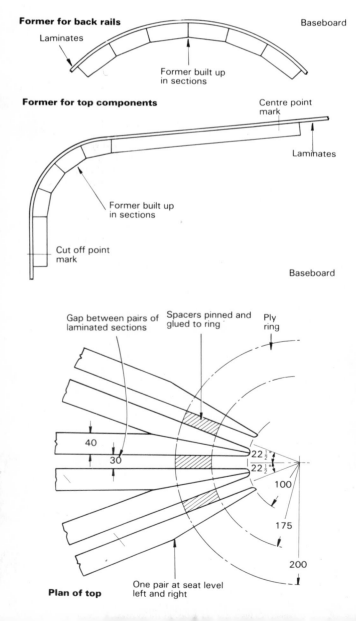

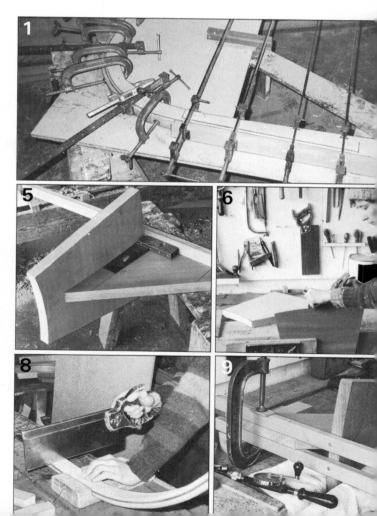

hours before removing from the mould.

Cut the laminated sections to width, either by hand planing or on a circular saw. The latter method is not the safest of operations with a curved workpiece, but the flat surface where it was in contact with the baseboard can be run against the rip fence for a first overwidth cut, and then the piece reversed and cut to the final width. Clean up the sawn edge with a smoothing plane.

Cut the top curved components to length at the vertical end allowing a 150mm straight section below the curve. You may find that the actual cross-section at this point varies a bit from laminate to laminate as the pressure may not have been applied completely evenly during the gluing process. Plane up by hand to make sure it is exactly 40 by 20mm and square for the area to be used for the halving joint.

Seats

Make a full-size templet in ply of the seat shape. Use a strip of wood with a hole drilled in it for a pencil and a panel pin knocked through as a rudimentary compass to draw part of a circle of radius 1050mm on a sheet of ply, and again at radius 650mm to give the internal curve. The straight sides of the seat are radii of the circle and the centre radius line should also be marked. Allowance should be made in the marking out for the final 15mm gap between seat sections.

Glue up blanks of sufficient size for each seat. The grain runs across the seat from side to side. When dry, mark the centre line and square across the seat blank. Lay the templet on matching centre lines, draw round it and cut out on the bandsaw, then clean up to the line.

Use the router to make a housing on the underneath of each seat, along the centre line 245mm long by 15mm deep by 12mm wide.

Vertical back

Prepare material 1460 long by 40 by 20mm section.

Seat supports

Prepare lengths of timber 195 by 30mm in section. It is more economical to cut several seat supports from each piece due to the 45 degree angle.

Cut off one end at an angle of 45 degrees, then tenon the edge to fit the housing in the seat. This may be done with a router using a straight piece of wood clamped on parallel with the end as a fence and the stop set to the depth of the shoulder. The process is repeated on each side. The end shoulders are cut off by hand with a tenon saw.

Tap the seat top into position onto the tenoned edge of the seat support with the angle in the right direction. Line up one vertical piece at the back of the seat, face to the back edge of the seat, edge to the support and at right angles to the top itself. Use this to mark the exact cut-off line on the support pieces. Remove the vertical and the seat top and cut the support as marked—the line should be at 45 degrees to the face edge. Cut 12 of these altogether, allowing for the tenon length. We cut them slightly overlength on the bandsaw, then hand planed back

to the line to keep the angle exact. This was one of the many times my Stanley plane proved invaluable.

Drill three holes in both long edges of each seat piece, except for the two outside ones which only need them on the inside edges.

The holes should be at right angles to the face, 10mm diameter by 30mm deep, one in the centre and the other two 50mm from each end. A jig may be made up to ensure the dowels are positioned centrally in the thickness, and the same distance apart in each piece.

Cut 33 75mm lengths of 10mm steel rod to fit these holes. These should be primed and painted black with the appropriate products.

The joint between the seat and its support is reinforced by screwing as well as gluing, as it is not really possible to apply cramping pressure at this angle.

Drill clearance holes in the seat section in the housing 25mm from each end, then counterbore for a 12mm plug in the face side.

Clean up the components and chamfer all edges and corners. Glue the supports to the seats with Cascamite, making sure they are square in elevation and that the tenon is tight into the housing. Plug the hole in the top and clean off flush.

Treat the whole component with two coats of clear wood preserver, and when dry with one or two coats of micro-porous paint.

Verticals

Cut a half lap joint 75mm long in the top

1. Cramping the laminates around the former.
2. Marking out the seat components using a templet.
3. Tongues on the seat supports are easily cut with a router.
4. Drilling the seat component for the connecting dowels.
5. Marking the vertical cut off line to the seat support.
6. All edges must be cleaned up prior to assembly.
7. The seat is also screwed to the supports and the holes plugged.
8. The top laminated pieces have half lap joints to the verticals.
9. Drilling through verticals prior to screwing up.
10. Temporarily cramping up top laminates to check length.
11. Checking that the verticals are at right angles to the seats.
12. Half lap joints on the back rails are made at the verticals.

ends of the vertical pieces and in the ends of the top laminated sections—the laminated section to be on the outside. Drill and countersink the uprights for screwing into the back of the seat top 435mm up from the bottom. Also drill the vertical pieces through the sides for two screws in each into the seat supports. These should be countersunk as half right and half left-handed members.

Screw the verticals to the seat components, squaring and lining up carefully in the process.

Top

Draw a full-size diagram of the top laminated sections coming together in the centre of the top as a plan view. This gives the angle and point at which to cut off the ends of the top components. These create a star-like effect wih the left-hand member of each pair meeting the right-hand member of the next pair by cutting the angle on the outside edge.

Cut a ring from 4mm ply of external radius 250mm, internal radius 175mm.

Transfer the position of the laminated sections onto this from the diagram, and glue and pin strips of wood of 30 by 20mm section across the ring to act as spacers between the laminated sections. If the angle is cut correctly the laminates will then wedge tightly between these.

As a temporary fixing cut 3 lengths of 9mm dowel 75mm long. Push the 12 seat sections together with 15mm space between each using the timber dowels (the metal ones are too tight to fit making it impossible to dismantle). The top laminates should have a line on them from the

former showing the centre point of the whole arbour. Cramp one of the top laminates to a vertical at the housing joint. Do the same to the one opposite it. Match up the centre point lines to check that the length is correct—i.e., that the piece is vertical, upright, etc. Measure 100mm back from the centre point and cut the top end of the laminate to length offering it up to the full-size diagram to get the angle. Repeat for the remaining top pieces.

Drill three clearance holes for No. 6 by $\frac{3}{4}$in. screws in the half lap joint of the laminated sections.

Screw these to the verticals, and screw down through the plywood ring to hold them in position at the top. Despite careful measurement the points will probably project through the ring unevenly, so draw round a 200mm plate or something similar and trim off the points to neaten them to a circle, rounding off the ends.

Back rails

Mark out the centre of the back rails on the vertical members, measuring up on the inside 130 and 200mm from the top of the seat. Drill and countersink on the outside. Tap the seat sections together to exactly the right position using 15mm scrap for spacers between each. Cramps may be used on the verticals to pull it all together. Make sure the verticals are parallel to each other. Cramp the first back rail section temporarily in position, allowing it to project beyond the end. Mark the position of the outside of the pairs of uprights 110mm apart and 297mm between each.

Make a half lap joint over a distance of 110mm where two seat sections meet at a pair of verticals, keeping the curve. Cramp in position and screw through from the back. Repeat for both rails.

Arms

Make up two rectangular frames 670mm high 350mm wide using 40 by 25mm section, with tongued mitre joints at the top (see chaise longue article), and mortise and tenon at the base. Clean up and glue with Cascamite. Round over the edges and front corners. Drill, countersink and screw through the frames into the sides of the end seats, and through the ends of the back rails into the frames. Cut off the back rails flush with the frame and radius the ends.

Dismantle the whole piece, numbering everything very carefully. Treat all the components with preservative except where gluing will be required. Paint the top ring with micro-porous paint.

Reassemble the whole piece using bright zinc or other non-rust screws, gluing the half lap joints and the laminates to the top ring. Apply preservative over the joints.

The arbour should be placed on a solid base on which a circle of radius 1050mm is drawn to aid assembly. It should then be fixed down to the base with brackets on the base of the verticals, and also through the bottom rail of the arm frames.

13. Leave the rails overlength when fixing to verticals.

14. The rectangular arm frame with tongued and tenoned joints.

15. The arm frame is screwed in place and the rails cut back.

16. Starting to assemble the outside after finishing.

17. View of the underside of top ring holding verticals in place.

18. Top view of ply ring showing the verticals screwed through.

19. A final going over with preservative and paint.

Traditional Garden Barrow

lm occurs widely in the Northern Hemisphere and is one of the native trees of Great Britain. The wood is usually of a rich light brown colour, rather coarse texture, and often with a wild and irregular grain pattern. It has a prominent growth ring, and dries fairly readily although stock with irregular grain is likely to distort.

Elm has a long and very varied history of use, particularly in the heyday of the "village carpenter," It is a wood which resists splitting, and because of this was always used for the naves (or hubs) of cart wheels, and also for the seat of the immortal Windsor chair. Elm also has a good resistance to rot, especially when in a permanently wet situation, and for this reason was employed for barge building, dock work, and piling. It is the wood used for the traditional wheelbarrow, and was one of only two woods—the other being oak—used in this country for coffins when burials were commoner than cremations.

Perhaps elm's greatest claim to fame lies in its use for London's early underground piped water scheme. Elm logs were bored out on a mechanical auger and one end tapered so as to engage in a corresponding recess in the end of the next pipe. Such a system was laid in London in 1613, and when these pipes were dug up over three hundred years later, they were found to be still in very good condition. Elm

logs anything up to ten feet long and twelve inches square were used for the water pumps, where the bore at the upper end was around five inches in diameter.

Sadly, Britain's elms have been dying in huge numbers in the last few years. Dutch elm disease, which arrived here in 1970 in consignments of rock elm from Canada, has resulted in an estimated three to four milion trees being killed. The disease is carried by a beetle which lives in the bark of the tree, and so far science has not produced a satisfactory way of stamping out the menace. "Epitaph for the Elm" by Gerald Wilkinson deals extensively with these lovely old trees and their disappearance from the landscape. While thus is a sad state of affairs as far as the countryside is concerned, the result has been a plentiful supply of elm, because providing the dead trees are not left standing too long, the timber itself is unaffected. Because of the relative abundance, the price of elm is currently fairly favourable, although is must be pointed out that it is a wood where knots are often prevalent, and these are frequently quite large. These can mean that material has sonetimes to be cut to waste, although this depends very much on the nature of the work it is for.

Dutch elm disease apart, elm was already enjoying a resurgence of favour, and one large furniture manufacturer had for years used this

timber very extensively. It is popular amongst turners for bowl making, and ply wallboard is available with elm veneer facing. Its combination of rich colour, and usually erratic grain, are the characteristics which give it its appeal.

Being aware of the present plentiful stocks of this material, I decided to embark on a series of projects which would make the most of its natural strength, beauty and weather resistance. The point was that even if these magnificent trees do disappear the projects will serve as a fitting epitaph with their natural strength to carry on.

I DECIDED TO START MY PROJECTS in elm with a job I had long had a strong desire to make, a traditional wheelbarrow. Somehow to me a wooden wheelbarrow brings together craftsmanship and the countryside, combines beauty and function, and has a life, vitality and character which are so utterly lacking in its modern steel counterpart. It is very questionable too, if the average metal wheelbarrow of today has a longer life than a well made wooden one, like many present day mass produced goods, there seems to be a measure of limited life built into them.

Making a barrow I regarded as something of a challenge. There are no drawings available, no literature or information as far as I can establish, although there are still a few old barrows around from which much can be learnt. I managed to track down about half a dozen old barrows, inspected and measured them carefully, and was surprised to find so much variation of constructional detail. One that I discovered had been in use in a railway works, was very large with particularly heavy construction, and with a huge all-metal wheel (photo 1). Another was perched on the roof of a pub, but alas this was one I was not able to inspect very closely!

I realised from the start that the wheel would present more problems than the body, as the traditional wheel was very much the combined product of the carpenter and the blacksmith, with the metal rim or tyre shrunk on as was the way with all cart wheels. After much deliberation, why not, I thought, have a crack at following in the footsteps of former craftsmen, and make my wheelbarrow truly traditional, and a faithful replica of this marvellous little workhorse? My mind was made up, I dismissed my earlier ideas of pneumatic alternatives or simplified wooden ones, I was going to have an attempt at the real thing.

I started work by preparing the five pieces which would form the chassis, selecting straight grained and knot-free material for these. The two outer members I marked to overall length, then set about shaping the handles. Sawing away the waste was followed by spokeshaving, with a file and glasspaper being used for final smoothing. Eyes are more important than pencil lines for this sort of work, but I was careful to ensure the handles were as identical as I could make them. A good way of ensuring this is to use a card templet and cut the handles as a pair.

In order to determine the shoulder lengths and exact angles for the three cross members, I laid out the five pieces on the floor with the shorter members resting on top of the two shafts (photo 3). By measuring and careful checking, I was able to determine positions of joints and all other information. I did, though, use a sliding bevel to ensure the slopes of the shoulders were identical, and the sliding bevel was again necessary in order to square off around the shoulders. The mortises, too, had to be cut on a slight angle, and again the same setting of the bevel enabled me to mark out the position of these mortises on both surfaces. Using the mortise gauge followed, and while the tenons are centrally placed on the ends of the cross pieces the setting for the mortises had to allow for the 19mm (¾in.) boards which form the floor.

Cutting the mortises was quite straightforward even allowing for the slight angle required, and the tenons too were quickly sawn. Some waste had been left on the ends of the cross pieces as, following tradition, my design allowed for the tenons to protrude through the mortises slightly, with the ends then rounded and chamfered as shown.

As the base or floor of the barrow was to be screwed in place, holes for this purpose were bored and countersunk in the underside of the cross members. Also at this stage the positions for the legs and side brackets were marked on the chassis sides, and shallow trenches cut in which these parts would engage. Holes were also bored on the underside of the shafts into the centres of the mortises, enabling the joints to be secured by screws.

1. **One old barrow used for comparison.**
2. **Spokeshave used to shape handle.**
3. **The individual parts of the chassis.**
4. **Cramping on one of the leg brackets.**
5. **The floor boards screwed into place.**
6. **Cutting leg trench on circular saw.**
7. **Leg and side supports now added.**
8. **Adding the front support brackets.**

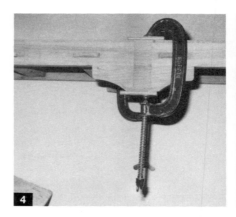

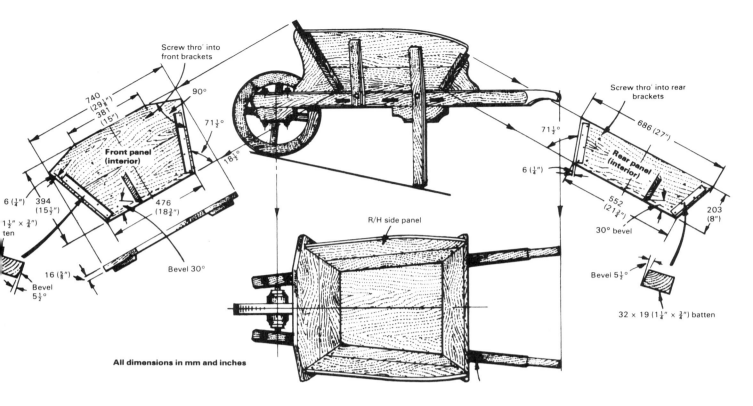

Screw thro' into
front brackets

740
(29⅛")

381
(15")

90°

71½°

18½°

Front panel
(interior)

6 (¼")   394
(15½")

1½" × ¾"
ten

476
(18¾")

Bevel 30°

16 (⅝")

Bevel
5½°

Screw thro' into rear
brackets

686 (27")

71½°

6 (¼")

Rear panel
(interior)

552
(21¾")

203
(8")

30° bevel

Bevel 5½°

32 × 19 (1¼" × ¾") batten

R/H side panel

All dimensions in mm and inches

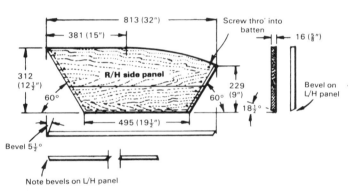

813 (32")

381 (15")

Screw thro' into
batten

16 (⅝")

312
(12¼")

R/H side panel

60°   60°

229
(9")

18½°

Bevel on
L/H panel

Bevel 5½°

495 (19½")

Note bevels on L/H panel

Dwg. 1 Side panel details

The front ends of the shafts were now gently ⋯nded, and the chamfers marked out along ⋯ edges. Only the top outer edge of each ⋯aft has the chamfer running from end to end, ⋯ remaining three have the chamfers starting ⋯d stopping at various points. The chamfer ⋯ps short 25mm (1in.) short from either side ⋯ leg bracket and 25mm (1in.) short of the ⋯e bracket. The top inside chamfer stops ⋯rt 25mm (1in.) from the edge of the base ⋯ards (dwg. 2). All these decorative corners ⋯re now worked by plane and spokeshave.

This brought progress to the point where I ⋯ld assemble the five components. I doubt if ⋯e was ever used on the barrows of old. As ⋯ as I know waterproof glue has appeared on ⋯ market since the time that wooden ⋯rows were available to buy, and the animal ⋯e much used in former years is useless for ⋯tdoor work. I decided that, where ap-⋯ppriate, I would use Cascamite One Shot ⋯e, although in practice this amounted to the ⋯assis and the wheel.

⋯Despite the tapering sides to the chassis, I ⋯ not experience any difficulty in gluing and ⋯mping up to this part of the barrow. I ⋯shed off the glue very thoroughly while still ⋯t, and before driving the screws into the ⋯nts I checked for squareness and freedom ⋯m twist. For the job to be 'square' in this ⋯se meant measuring the diagonals, as they ⋯st both be the same.

⋯The two leg brackets were made next, and ⋯re trenched to the same width and depth as

those already cut in the chassis. The simple shaping was followed by forming the chamfers, and four holes were bored for fixing the bracket in place. In addition, two holes were made in the trench of the bracket for securing the leg. I used a G-cramp to hold these brackets to the chassis while the screws were being driven in (photo 4).

Although the boards forming the sides of the barrow are 16mm (⅝in.) thick, I felt that the bottom boards would benefit from being a little stouter, and these were prepared to 19mm (¾in.). This thickness had of course been allowed for when jointing up the chassis, to enable the top surface of the base, once fixed, to be level with the upper edge of the shafts. Two boards made up the base, and I did not tongue and groove them as I felt any slight gap would help drain the barrow and prevent water being retained.

The base boards were cut to length so that they overhung the outer chassis cross members by 25mm (1in.), and the ends were then chamfered top and bottom. Once prepared they could be screwed in position straight away (photo 5).

I made a ply templet for the legs, and planed a piece of material to the thickness required and large enough for the two legs and also the two side brackets. I prepared the edge of this piece of wood to correspond to the inner surface of a leg as determined by the templet, this was done largely with an ordinary jack plane, because although it was shaped there were no

curves involved. My Burgess band saw was then brought into use to cut the outer surface, and smoothing here had to be carried out with spokeshave. The second leg was cut in similar fashion, as were the two brackets, and I was very careful to ensure that the angle of splay on all these four components was identical. At this stage I retained the excess waste at the upper ends, and also left the chamfering until later.

The legs had been shaped so far without the notch, or step, in the centre part, and the purpose of this is to provide a positive support for the legs to carry the weight of the loaded barrow. I cut this feature 6mm (¼in.) deep and used my circular saw (photo 6), and by leaving a small part un-cut at the upper end, was able to form it as if it were a trench.

Although work on the legs and brackets was not complete, they were ready to be temporarily added to the chassis. The main means of holding these securely in place is by tie bolts which go through from side to side. Not only do these bolts hold the legs and brackets in place, they add a great deal of strength to the chassis. If they are drilled in the position shown on the drawings they also support the floor boards.

I did have to make these tie bolts myself, and although an engineer's die and die holder are required, it is a fairly simple piece of metalworking. I used 10mm (⅜in.) steel rod, and formed in the ends a B.S.F. (British Standard Fine) thread. Because the holes for the bolts needed to be bored at an angle, I found the best way of achieving this was by the freehand use of a power drill. Photo 7 shows the chassis at this stage with the legs and brackets added.

Next, I set about making the four brackets which help to hold the front and back in place. Material 25mm (1in.) thick was used for these, and in all cases I planed the straight edges to the required profile and angle before cutting the shaped part. The base angle of 60 degrees is not at this stage critical within a degree or so, but it is also necessary to plane the upper sloping edge to a slight bevel. This is brought about by the tapering nature of the chassis, and I quickly attended to this bevelling and checked with a straight edge placed across both when in position.

The shaped outer edges were cut to the curved outline, the sawn surface smoothed and the arrises rounded. Holes were bored as indicated in the drawings for screw fixing, then the front ones only at this stage were fixed in place (photo 8).

Seven boards are used for the body sides, and these were initially cut with excess width and length. The boards forming the front and sides are tongued and grooved, so my next task was to plane the edges straight ready for jointing. I cut the tongues on my planing machine, and used my power tool rebating attachment for making the grooves.

The lower front board was bevelled so as to fit the base, then holes were made in both boards for screwing to the brackets. In addition, holes were bored at this stage in the base, so that screws could also be inserted from below into the front. The front boards were then temporarily screwed in position.

When fitting the sides up to the front, I initially cut the required angle only approximately, then obtained the exact fit by 'scribing' the joint. This is seen in photo 9, where a piece of wood is being used for the scribing process. The rear corners were tackled in a similar way, although the back boards and brackets remained loose during this time.

With the joints on the sides now prepared, cutting to final width and shaping followed and for this a compass plane was used. I was also now able to determine the exact extent of the front, and this too was removed and cut to its final shape. The sides of the front section are parallel with the body sides, and accommodate the battens on the outside (photo 10).

My attention now turned back to the legs and side brackets, as I now knew exactly how long these needed to be. They were cut to length, top ends rounded, and the chamfers made. When re-fixing these parts, I also added the screws through the leg brackets.

The sides could now be screwed back, and screws were also used through the sides and into the battens so as to lock the corners. Final shaping of the back next took place, and the brackets to hold this were fixed to the chassis. Adding the battens to the back was slightly different from the front, insofar as they were fixed after the back had been screwed to the brackets. I also found it easier to screw through the back into the battens, as otherwise the leg would have been in the way.

The axle brackets were next to be prepared, they were cut to length and the bolt holes marked and bored. The centre of one side of each was marked, and a hole bored 32mm (1¼in.) deep to suit the diameter of the axle bush. These holes had to be made at a slight angle because of the taper of the chassis, and I was careful to treat these blocks as an opposite handed pair on account of this. The simple shaping to these blocks was again followed by chamfering.

Now I was ready to tackle the wheel which I regarded as the most challenging part of the project. My elementary researches had revealed, apart from the all-metal ones, two main patterns of wheelbarrow wheel, but as

9. **Scribing the angle on the front end.**
10. **Angled battens added to the front.**
11. **One side section screwed into place.**
12. **Back piece ready for final fixing.**
13. **Mortises chopped into the nave.**
14. **Glasspapering between centres.**
15. **Complex axle assembly and bushes.**
16. **Checking accuracy of assembly.**
17. **The inner edge cleaned with a sander.**

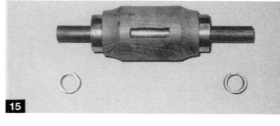
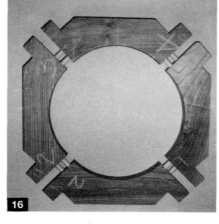

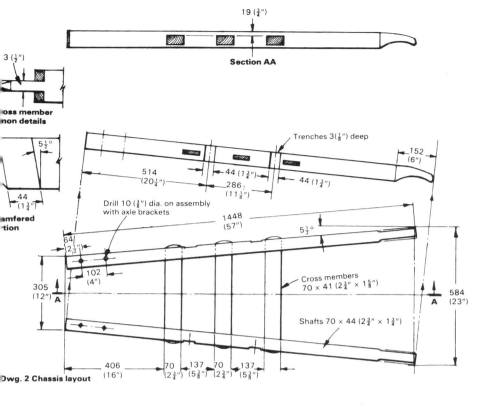

19 ($\frac{3}{4}$")

Section AA

3 ($\frac{1}{2}$")

oss member
non details

5$\frac{1}{2}$°

44
(1$\frac{3}{4}$")

amfered
tion

Trenches 3($\frac{1}{8}$") deep

152
(6")

514
(20$\frac{1}{4}$")

44 (1$\frac{3}{4}$")

44 (1$\frac{3}{4}$")

286
(11$\frac{1}{4}$")

Drill 10 ($\frac{3}{8}$") dia. on assembly
with axle brackets

1448
(57")

5$\frac{1}{2}$°

64
(2$\frac{1}{2}$")

102
(4")

305
(12")

Cross members
70 × 41 (2$\frac{3}{4}$" × 1$\frac{5}{8}$")

584
(23")

Shafts 70 × 44 (2$\frac{3}{4}$" × 1$\frac{3}{4}$")

406
(16")

70
(2$\frac{3}{4}$")

137
(5$\frac{3}{8}$")

70
(2$\frac{3}{4}$")

137
(5$\frac{3}{8}$")

Dwg. 2 Chassis layout

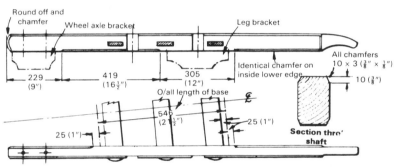

Round off and
chamfer

Wheel axle bracket

Leg bracket

All chamfers
10 × 3 ($\frac{3}{8}$" × $\frac{1}{8}$")

10 ($\frac{3}{8}$")

229
(9")

419
(16$\frac{1}{2}$")

305
(12")

Identical chamfer on
inside lower edge

**Section thro'
shaft**

O/all length of base

546
(2$\frac{1}{2}$")

25 (1")

25 (1")

(L/H shaft shown, R/H shaft chamfered
in identical manner)

Dwg. 2 Chamfering details

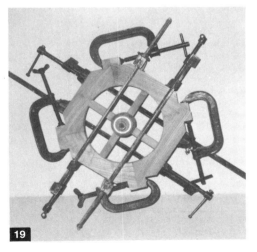

18. Tenons are cut at the spoke ends.
19. The wheel completely cramped up.
**20. Outside of wheel trimmed on
bandsaw.**

one of them depended very much on a blacksmith-made axle, I settled for the one which had the simpler metalwork.

A block was cut to 95mm (3$\frac{3}{4}$in.) square for the nave, this allowing for a finished diameter of 89mm (3$\frac{1}{2}$in.). The four mortises for the spokes were marked out centrally on each side, and these were chopped out until they met (photo 13). Note the slope at the ends of the mortises. The nave was now mounted between centres on the lathe, and initially turned down to cylindrical form. Two ferrules had been sawn from a piece of scrap steel tubing, so the next stage in the lathe was to turn a step at each end to accept the ferrules, checking at the same time I had the correct overall length. The concave shaping adjacent to the ferrules improves the appearance, and the whole nave at this stage was glasspapered while in the lathe (photo 14).

Using a 25mm (1in.) bit in a chuck mounted in the lathe headstock, and with the nave being fed on to the bit by the tailstock, a hole was bored halfway through from each end. The excess length on the outside of the ferrules was now removed, and the mild steel axle driven through. Both ferrules were drilled so that they could be secured by screws, and one of the holes was continued through the wood and part way into the axle. A self-tapping screw went into this hole and also the axle, in order to prevent lateral movement of the nave. A piece of old gas piping proved to have just the right inside diameter to provide bushes for the axle in the axle blocks, and these were cut in readiness (photo 15).

Again I made a ply templet, this time for the wheel felloes and to the shape shown in photo 16. Note that the felloes had extra width left on the outer edge, and also projections to enable G-cramps to be applied when assembling. They were cut out on the bandsaw, and the joints individually planed to form close fits. Dowel holes were next bored in the jointing surfaces and these were 'staggered'. Joints were then numbered, the dowels cut and a trial assembly made (photo 16). In order to level off the joints on the inner surface and smooth the whole of this edge, cramps were applied and a drum sander used very effectively for this purpose (photo 17).

I had already prepared two pieces of wood from which to make the four spokes, and these had been marked out for the tenons when the mortises were being attended to. Strictly speaking, the shoulders on these tenons should be slightly concave to match the curve of the nave. I know from experience, though, that if the shoulders are sawn at a slight angle, or undercut, then if carefully done this gives an almost perfect fit. The cheeks of the tenons were formed on the planer (photo 18). The double-length spokes were now sawn in half, and the taper formed on the edges. Each was mounted in turn on the lathe, and round tenons produced on their outer ends. Corresponding holes were bored in the centre of each felloe.

I was now at the stage when I could assemble the wheel. Joints were glued, and cramps applied. As well as the G-cramps, I also used sash cramps to ensure all joints were brought well home (photo 19).

I devised a simple jig to enable the excess around the outer edge of the wheel to be sawn away, and give a perfect circle. A piece of ply had a large vee-cut made in it, and this was then cramped to the table of the bandsaw. By allowing the nave to rest in the vee, I could then rotate the whole wheel against the blade of the saw (photo 20).

A piece of 38mm by 3mm (1$\frac{1}{2}$ by $\frac{1}{8}$in.) mild steel bar was used for the tyre, and my first job was to bend this as near as possible to the curvature of the wheel. Fortunately, I was able to borrow a simple bending machine, which consists in essence of two lower rollers, and an adjustable upper one, with feed provided from a

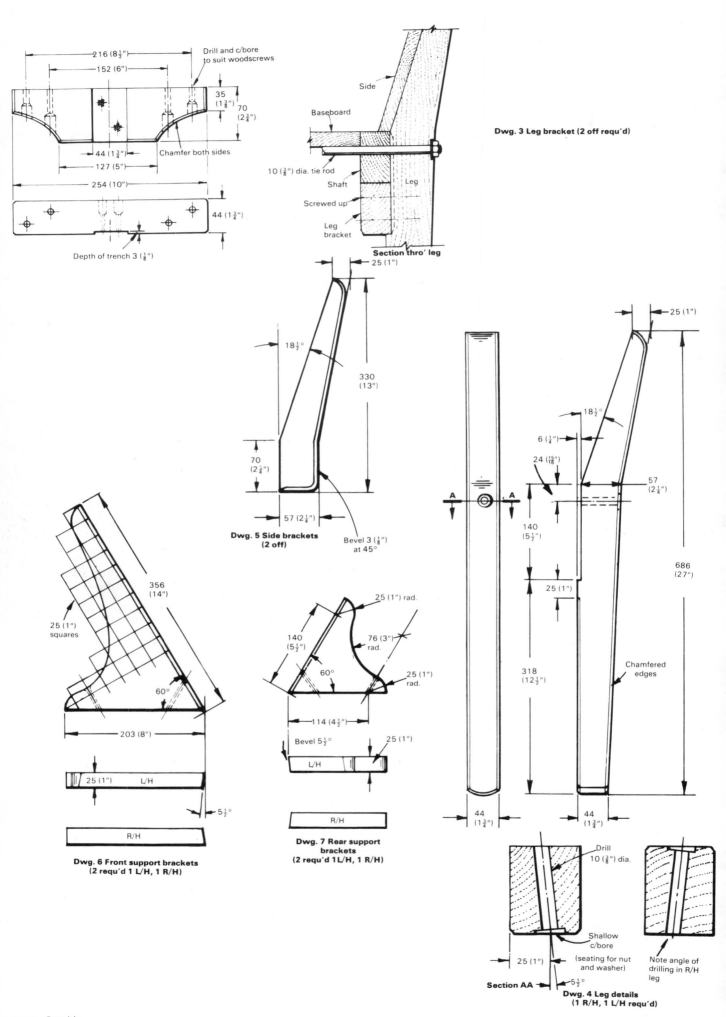

216 (8½")
152 (6")
Drill and c/bore to suit woodscrews
35 (1⅜")
70 (2¾")
44 (1¾")
Chamfer both sides
127 (5")
254 (10")
44 (1¾")
Depth of trench 3 (⅛")

Side
Baseboard
10 (⅜") dia. tie rod
Shaft
Screwed up
Leg bracket
Leg
Section thro' leg

Dwg. 3 Leg bracket (2 off requ'd)

25 (1")
18½°
330 (13")
70 (2¾")
57 (2¼")
Dwg. 5 Side brackets (2 off)
Bevel 3 (⅛") at 45°

25 (1")
18½°
6 (¼")
24 (15/16")
57 (2¼")
140 (5½")
25 (1")
686 (27")
318 (12½")
Chamfered edges
A ← → A
44 (1¾")
44 (1¾")

356 (14")
25 (1") squares
60°
203 (8")
25 (1") L/H
5½°
R/H
Dwg. 6 Front support brackets (2 requ'd 1 L/H, 1 R/H)

25 (1") rad.
140 (5½")
76 (3") rad.
60°
25 (1") rad.
114 (4½")
Bevel 5½°
25 (1")
L/H
R/H
Dwg. 7 Rear support brackets (2 requ'd 1L/H, 1 R/H)

Drill 10 (⅜") dia.
Shallow c/bore (seating for nut and washer)
25 (1")
5½°
Note angle of drilling in R/H leg
Section AA
Dwg. 4 Leg details (1 R/H, 1 L/H requ'd)

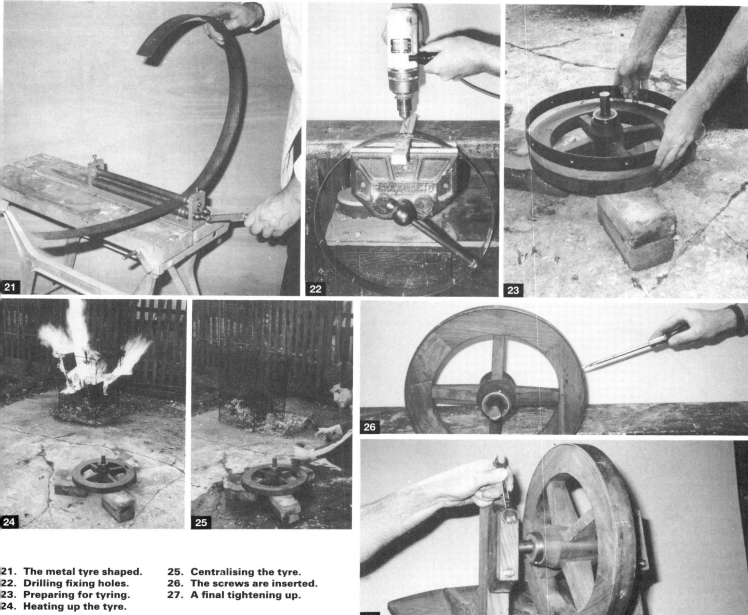

21. **The metal tyre shaped.**
22. **Drilling fixing holes.**
23. **Preparing for tyring.**
24. **Heating up the tyre.**
25. **Centralising the tyre.**
26. **The screws are inserted.**
27. **A final tightening up.**

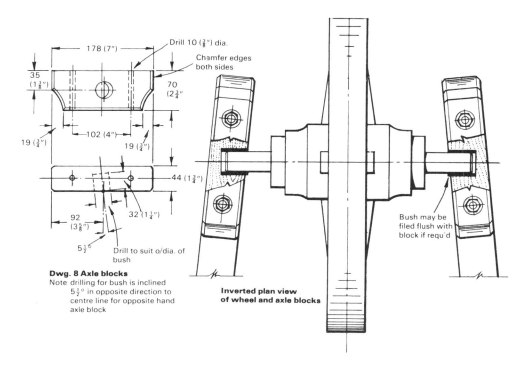

Drill 10 (³⁄₈") dia.

Chamfer edges
both sides

178 (7")

35
(1³⁄₈")

70
(2³⁄₄")

19 (³⁄₄")

102 (4")

19 (³⁄₄")

44 (1³⁄₄")

92
(3⁵⁄₈")

32 (1¼")

5½°

Drill to suit o/dia. of
bush

Dwg. 8 Axle blocks
Note drilling for bush is inclined
5½° in opposite direction to
centre line for opposite hand
axle block

**Inverted plan view
of wheel and axle blocks**

Bush may be
filed flush with
block if requ'd

handle (photo 21). By feeding the metal through the rollers, and adjusting the pressure from the upper one, the curvature was slowly increased until by checking on the wheel, it was possible to obtain a very close fit.

By a combination of calculation and estimation, I reckoned on making the tyre 3mm ($\frac{1}{8}$in.) shorter than the circumference of the wheel, and cut the metal accordingly. These ends I now brazed together, and bored and countersunk a series of holes around the tyre for screwing purposes. Incidentally, to have bored these holes while the metal was still flat would have resulted in unequal bending, with a slight tendency to kink where the holes had weakened the metal.

I now had reached the climax of the whole job, and also the moment of truth as to whether the tyre was going to expand and contract by the right amount. The wheel was set up on some bricks (photo 23), and my accumulated scrap of many months set afire to emulate the wheelwright of former years. With the tyre glowing somewhere between dull and bright red, it was lifted from the fire and lowered in place, and with a signal to my son, he played his part in re-enacting history with a couple of well aimed gallons from the watering can, while I used a cold chisel and hammer to centralise the tyre on the wheel (photo 25), and the fit was perfect.

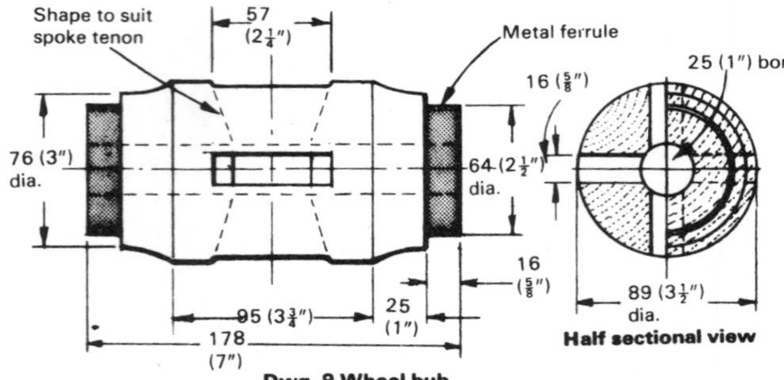

Dwg. 9 Wheel hub

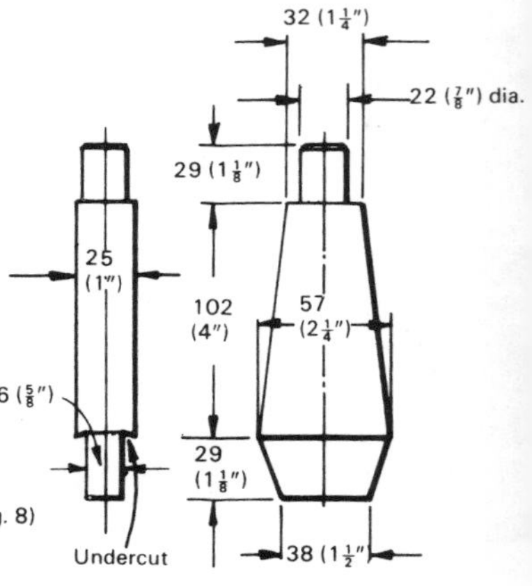

Dwg. 9 Spoke (4 off requ'd)

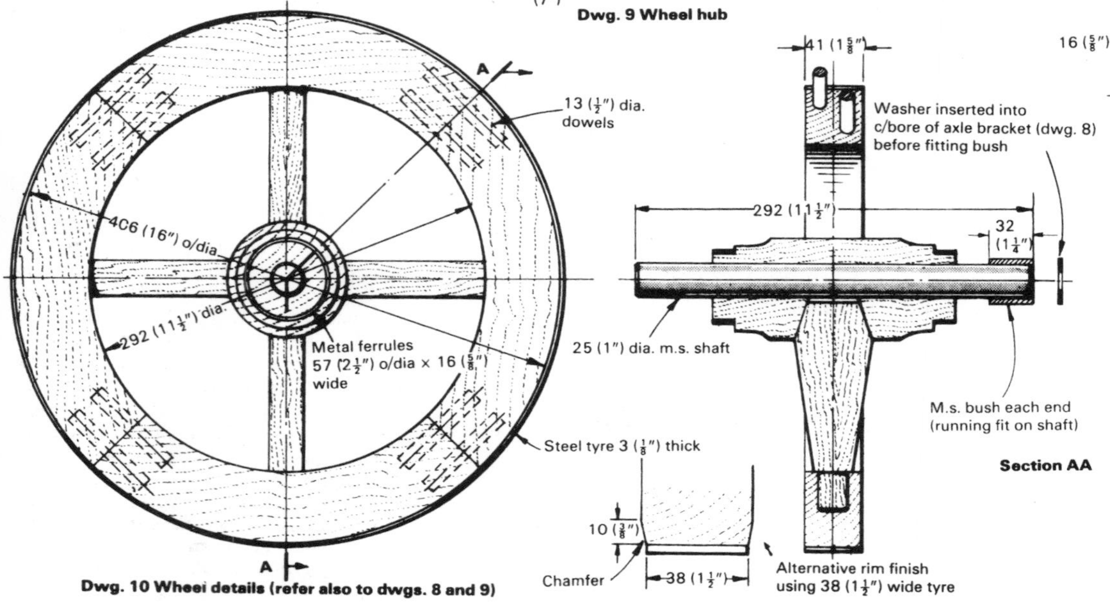

Dwg. 10 Wheel details (refer also to dwgs. 8 and 9)

(Sizes in mm and inches)

CUTTING LIST

(No allowance for waste)

Chassis sides	2 off	1448 by 70 by 44mm	(57 by $2\frac{3}{4}$ by $1\frac{3}{4}$in.)
Chassis cross member	1 off	483 by 70 by 41mm	(19 by $2\frac{3}{4}$ by $1\frac{5}{8}$in.)
Chassis cross member	1 off	444 by 70 by 41mm	($17\frac{1}{2}$ by $2\frac{3}{4}$ by $1\frac{5}{8}$in.)
Chassis cross member	1 off	406 by 70 by 41mm	(16 by $2\frac{3}{4}$ by $1\frac{5}{8}$in.)
Legs	2 off	686 by 89 by 44mm	(27 by $3\frac{1}{2}$ by $1\frac{3}{4}$in.)
Side brackets	2 off	330 by 76 by 44mm	(13 by 3 by $1\frac{3}{4}$in.)
Leg brackets	2 off	254 by 70 by 44mm	(10 by $2\frac{3}{4}$ by $1\frac{3}{4}$in.)
Front brackets	2 off	356 by 178 by 25mm	(14 by 7 by 1in.)
Rear brackets	2 off	165 by 127 by 25mm	($6\frac{1}{2}$ by 5 by 1in.)
Axle blocks	2 off	178 by 70 by 44mm	(7 by $2\frac{3}{4}$ by $1\frac{3}{4}$in.)
Body front	1 off	740 by 394 by 16mm	($29\frac{1}{8}$ by $15\frac{1}{2}$ by $\frac{5}{8}$in.)
Body sides	2 off	813 by 318 by 16mm	(32 by $12\frac{1}{2}$ by $\frac{5}{8}$in.)
Body rear	1 off	686 by 203 by 16mm	(27 by 8 by $\frac{5}{8}$in.)
Base	1 off	546 by 381 by 19mm	($21\frac{1}{2}$ by 15 by $\frac{3}{4}$in.)
Battens to front	2 off	330 by 38 by 19mm	(13 by $1\frac{1}{2}$ by $\frac{3}{4}$in.)
Battens to rear	2 off	178 by 32 by 19mm	(7 by $\frac{1}{4}$ by $\frac{3}{4}$in.)
Nave	1 off	178 by 89 by 89mm	(7 by $3\frac{1}{2}$ by $3\frac{1}{2}$in.)
Spokes	4 off	158 by 57 by 25mm	($6\frac{1}{4}$ by $2\frac{1}{4}$ by 1in.)
Felloes	4 off	292 by 114 by 41mm	($11\frac{1}{2}$ by $4\frac{1}{2}$ by $1\frac{5}{8}$in.)

Also required: Approx. 1321mm (52in.) of 38 by 3mm ($1\frac{1}{2}$ by $\frac{1}{8}$in.) "black" mild steel; approx. 1778mm (70in.) of 10mm ($\frac{3}{8}$in.) steel bar, and 12 nuts and washers to suit; approx. 330mm (13in.) of 25mm (1in.) dia. steel bar plus oddments for ferrules and bushes.

The tyre was now screwed in place (photo 26), mounted in the axle brackets which in turn were cramped to the chassis. Now holes could be made in the chassis, by boring through the holes already existing in the blocks. Tie rods for fixing these blocks were made from 10mm ($\frac{3}{8}$in.) rod in a similar way to the longer tie rods, and before re-mounting the wheel and tightening these up, grease was packed into the bushes.

Suddenly, my handiwork was completed—or nearly so. Anxious to give the barrow the maximun life span possible, and in spite of the prospects of a pampered future, I gave it a very generous coat of Cuprinol preservative. This was partly because of the staining effect of the 'light oak' variety I used, and I followed this when thoroughly dry with a couple of coats of varnish. Lastly, the small amounts of mild steel which were visible, apart from the tyre, had a coat of black paint.

Now the barrow has pride of place in the front porch of our house, my wife not being able to bear the idea of it being out in the garden getting wet, let alone used! I could not help wondering as I worked on it just when was the last one made in this country which was traditionally built and with a shrunk-on tyre? I had made a bit of history, as well as the barrow.

Garden shed

FEW PEOPLE find the house adequate for accommodating all their various needs, and one way to make more space is to have a garden shed. And, if the shed provides enough room for basic workshop facilities, as well as for storing garden tools, it is particularly useful.

Commercially made sheds I had seen seemed to offer poor value for money. Shoddy workmanship, combined with construction that can only be described as flimsy, made me determined to produce one to my own design. Though, I was aware from the outset that savings on cost would not be very great.

One weakness in all the ready-made sheds I inspected was the minimal headroom provided. So I planned to make my shed quite a bit higher, to allow for storage of timber immediately under the roof. A number of features not normally associated with structures of this nature were combined in the design. These included chipboard flooring panels, exterior grade plywood for the walls and pre-felted chipboard for the roof.

Some twelve years ago, I made a garden shed using 6mm ($\frac{1}{4}$ in.) plywood for the walls and it is still in good condition. However, as I wanted this new shed to have a maximum lifespan, I decided to use slightly thicker ply and settled for 10mm ($\frac{3}{8}$ in.). Plywood has a number

1. Assembling frame members for one side.

2. Cutting plywood panel with power saw.

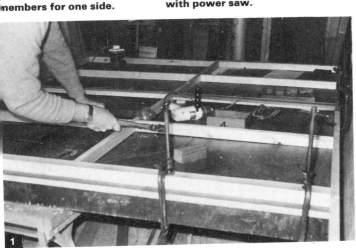

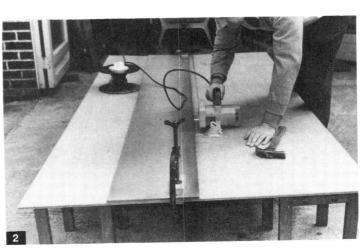

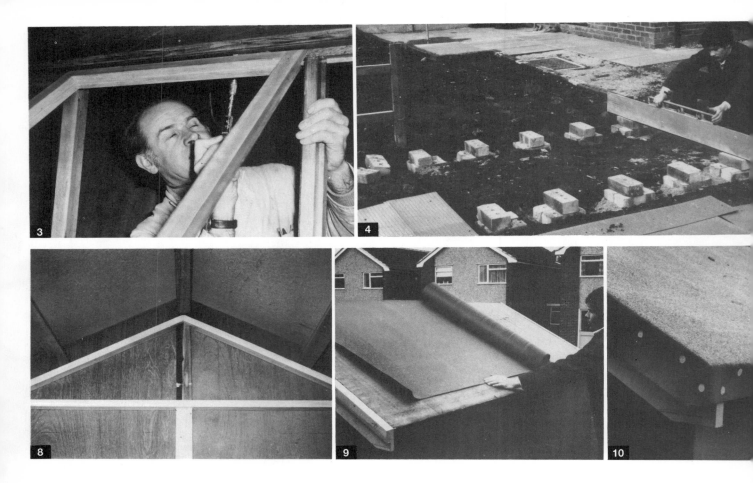

of advantages over both T and G and weather boarding, one of which is that because of its relative rigidity, framing members can be kept fairly small, and there is no need whatsoever for diagonal bracing.

The shed was to have a nominal overall size of 2440 by 1830mm (8 by 6ft.). This is about the smallest size that can be used as a workshop, but there is one advantage—most local authorities allow sheds below fifty square feet in plan to be free from rates. However, as the erection of a shed constitutes a "building operation", it would perhaps be as well to check with the local planning authority before starting.

In fact, the size of the shed was determined to some extent by the materials used. Its length was fixed by the standard size of pre-felted chipboard, used for the roof, and the width was simply the maximum I could obtain from three chipboard flooring panels.

Construction started on the floor, which was to have a finished size of 2280 by 1803mm (89¾ by 71in.). A substantial floor is needed if the shed is to serve as a workshop, so I decided to use 76 by 51mm (3 by 2in.) joists, and six of these were cut to this required length. They were made slightly shorter than the width of the floor, so that the shed wall would be kept well away from the ends. Thus there will be no danger of their being affected by rainwater.

Chipboard panels are usually tongued and grooved all round, so it is necessary to remove this feature on the outer edges. The panels were first of all cut to length and squared, then a tongue was sawn off one long edge and a groove off another. A cramp was used to ensure tight joints and, with the help of a handful of nails, the floor was soon completed. Subsequently the floor proved very useful as a platform for assembling the walls.

Timber for the main framework was next prepared to size and the first parts to be marked out were the ten uprights—eight for the corners and two for the doorway. In fact,

these needed very little preparation, just a mark for the overall length, and a simple trenched joint around the centre. When the joints had all been cut, the end waste was sawn off.

The long side without a window was tackled first. Corner posts were clamped to the floor which, as well as serving as a supporting platform, also enabled the exact positioning and squaring up of these two main parts to be easily achieved. Horizontal top and bottom

members were then added. These were secured by nailing into the ends of the corner posts and, to help prevent splitting, the waste was deliberately left on the rail ends. After nailing, waste was sawn off flush with the posts, and then the centre rail was cut and secured in the trenches.

Six vertical supports were now cut so that three fitted in the lower half and three in the upper. These were also simply nailed in place. The centre pair, however, were fixed flatways

CUTTING LIST

Floor joists	6 off	1778 by	76 by 51mm	(70 by 3 by 2in.)
Chipboard flooring panels	3 off	2440 by	610 by 22mm	(96 by 24 by ⅞in.)
Main uprights	10 off	1854 by	44 by 44mm	(73 by 1¾ by 1¾in.)
Horizontal rails (sides)	6 off	2287 by	44 by 25mm	(90 by 1¾ by 1in.)
Horizontal rails (ends)	5 off	1829 by	44 by 25mm	(72 by 1¾ by 1in.)
Horizontal rails (door end)	2 off	533 by	44 by 25mm	(21 by 1¾ by 1in.)
Horizontal rail (over window)	1 off	1753 by	44 by 25mm	(69 by 1¾ by 1in.)
Vertical members (lower sides)	6 off	864 by	44 by 25mm	(34 by 1¾ by 1in.)
Vertical members (upper sides)	5 off	1016 by	44 by 25mm	(40 by 1¾ by 1in.)
Sloping members (gables)	4 off	787 by	44 by 25mm	(31 by 1¾ by 1in.)
Vertical members (gables)	2 off	356 by	44 by 25mm	(14 by 1¾ by 1in.)
Vertical members (gable over door)	2 off	203 by	44 by 25mm	(8 by 1¾ by 1in.)
Sheets of ply cladding	7 off	2440 by	1220 by 10mm	(96 by 48 by ⅜in.)
Door battens	2 off	1829 by	70 by 19mm	(72 by 2¾ by ¾in.)
Door battens	3 off	559 by	114 by 19mm	(22 by 4½ by ¾in.)
Door packing piece	1 off	1956 by	48 by 11mm	(77 by 1⅞ by ⁷⁄₁₆in.)
Door capping piece	1 off	864 by	38 by 25mm	(34 by 1½ by 1in.)

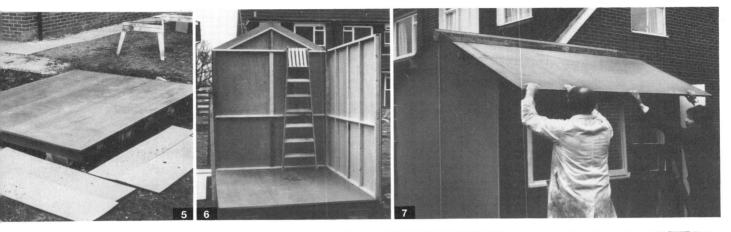

3. Hingeing sash in the window opening.
4. Making sure the foundations are level.
5. Locating the floor on its brick piers.
6. One side and one end bolted together.
7. Sliding roof panel into place.
8. Ridge and purlins for the roof support.
9. Getting ready to fix the roofing felt.
10. Detail of a corner with felt secured.
11. Putting in the final pane of glass.
12. Applying a coat of exterior varnish.

so that the broad surfaces would face the plywood. Because of this, there is quite a wide surface behind the point where the plywood is jointed, which facilitates nailing of the cladding material.

A similar arrangement was adopted throughout construction of the framing members. That is, the members were fixed edgeways, apart from at points where the plywood would be joined, and here the framing was secured flatways. The first side, with the

framing members in place, can be seen in photo 1.

Adding plywood to the members was quite straightforward. It required sawing to both length and width, before using 32mm (1¼in.) galvanised nails (with medium sized heads) to secure it in place.

The window side was the next part to be assembled. Corner posts and the three horizontal members were nailed up exactly as before, and the intermediate vertical supports were

then fixed to suit the window opening. The exact size of window is not critical, but it pays to be generous if you are going to use the shed as a workshop.

Vertical supports below the window were all fixed flatways, while those surrounding the window were secured edgeways. Plywood cladding was now added to the framework, but the window was not glazed at this stage.

Essentially the same methods were adopted for the rear of the shed but, as this had to include a gable end for the roof, three extra pieces of framing were required. That is, two sloping members and a vertical one in the centre. Reference to the drawings will show that, as the sloping pieces carry the purlins, the distance of the sloping pieces from the edge of the cladding must equal the width of the purlin.

Plywood was added immediately the framing was nailed up and, for cutting the ply to size, good use was made of a Shopmate portable power saw (photo 2). The ply was allowed to overlap the framing at the shed corners, so that when the cover strips were finally added there were no exposed edges.

Next, I started to construct the door end. This, apart from obvious variations to allow for a door, was basically the same as the rear end. However, two small extra pieces were needed below the sloping members to support joints in the plywood.

A piece of 10mm (⅜in.) plywood was used for the door, which was stiffened with battens 19mm (¾in.) thick. These also allowed for easier fixing of the T-hinges and lock. The door was designed to close onto the face of the shed end, so the battens were kept well in from edges of the door, and fixed from the inside by screws.

Before the door could be hinged in place, a packing strip was needed on the left-hand side of the door-opening—onto which the hinges could be fixed. The position and purpose of this packing strip should be clear from the drawings.

Hanging the door entailed no more than

Window sill	1 off	1829 by	83 by 44mm	(72 by	3¼ by	1¾in.)
Window head	1 off	1727 by	54 by 32mm	(68 by	2⅛ by	1¼in.)
Window stiles	2 off	813 by	54 by 32mm	(32 by	2⅛ by	1¼in.)
Window muntins	2 off	813 by	54 by 44mm	(32 by	2⅛ by	1¾in.)
Sash top rail	1 off	610 by	44 by 38mm	(24 by	1¾ by	1½in.)
Sash bottom rail	1 off	610 by	57 by 38mm	(24 by	2¼ by	1½in.)
Sash stiles	2 off	813 by	44 by 38mm	(32 by	1¾ by	1½in.)
Window side cover fillets	2 off	813 by	32 by 13mm	(32 by	1¼ by	½in.)
Window capping piece	1 off	1829 by	38 by 25mm	(72 by	1½ by	1in.)
Purlins and ridge	3 off	2457 by	89 by 48mm	(96¾ by	3½ by	1⅞in.)
Roof panels	2 off	2440 by	1220 by 19mm	(96 by 48	by	¾in.)
Barge boards	4 off	1220 by	102 by 19mm	(48 by 4	by	¾in.)
Verge pieces	4 off	1220 by	51 by 25mm	(48 by 2	by	1in.)

Allowance added to lengths. Widths and thicknesses are net.
Ply and chipboard are given as manufacturer's sizes.
Also required: Cover strips, cut from 17m (56ft.) of 22 by 10mm (⅞ by ⅜in.) material; 3 T-hinges (305mm/12in.); 1 rim lock; 1 pair sash hinges; 1 window stay; 12 coach bolts (114mm by 10mm/4½ by ⅜in.) complete with washers; 1 roll roofing felt; glass and putty; bricks for foundation.

screwing hinges in place. At this stage a capping piece was added just above the door. Its purpose was to prevent rain getting in at this point and it was identical in section to the one shown above the window.

The window was in fact the next part to receive attention. As with most structures of this nature, the window was to be built into the opening prepared for it—rather than made as an independent part. Outer parts, comprising of the head, sill and stiles, along with the two muntins, were cut to size and rebated to the sections shown. As with the main framework, joints between these members were trenches—the head and sill were marked out and cut accordingly.

To simplify matters, trenches were made the same depth as the rebates, and ends of the sill were notched so that they overlapped the plywood by about 38mm (1½in.). The sill was placed in position, and then this and the head were nailed to the main framework. All that was required for the four vertical parts of the window was to saw them to exact lengths before securing with nails.

Joints employed for the sash were slot (or open) mortise and tenons, and to further strengthen them screws were added on assembly. For a job like a sash, I always cut the joints first and set them out to allow for the rebates. Then, make the rebates for the glass and level off the inner tenon edges with the rebates. Assembling follows, and for this a waterproof glue is essential.

However, before gluing, rebates were formed on the outer edges and the fit of the sash was checked with the rest of the window. The sash was top hung, and hinges with a rustproof finish known as "stormproof sash hinges" were used. They were cranked to fit into the outer rebate of the sash. A window stay was added to the bottom rail, which both controls the extent of opening and holds the sash firmly closed.

As for the top of the door, a capping piece was fixed just over the window, and cover fillets added down each side to seal the joint between stile and framework. Cover fillets were also added at this stage to all plywood cladding joints.

This completed as much woodwork as could be done before assembly, but I decided to do some painting and varnishing before building. The exterior plywood used had a rich red face, so it seemed that varnish would be more attractive than paint on these surfaces. However, I decided to use paint on the door and windows. All the cladding was therefore given two coats of Cuprinol exterior varnish, while the door and windows were primed and then undercoated in white. In addition all underneath surfaces of the walls, including the lower edges of the ply, were given three coats of paint to seal and protect them. On the underside of the floor, wood preserver was used – again giving three applications.

The chosen site for this shed was reasonably level, so only a little spade-work was needed. Each end of the joists was supported on three bricks and it was of course essential that these should be true and level in each direction. A long straight edge, combined with a good sized level, ensured accuracy of the top bricks (photo 4).

To help space the bricks correctly, positions of the joists were marked in chalk on the straight edge—a simple dodge that proved very effective. Bricks were kept about 102mm (4in.) from the ends of the joists, which in effect reduced the span and made them more rigid. Ends of the joists will then form a small cantilever, which helps to keep the shed foundations protected from the elements.

When the floor was laid in position, a double thickness of roofing felt was inserted between bricks and joists to act as a damp-proof course.

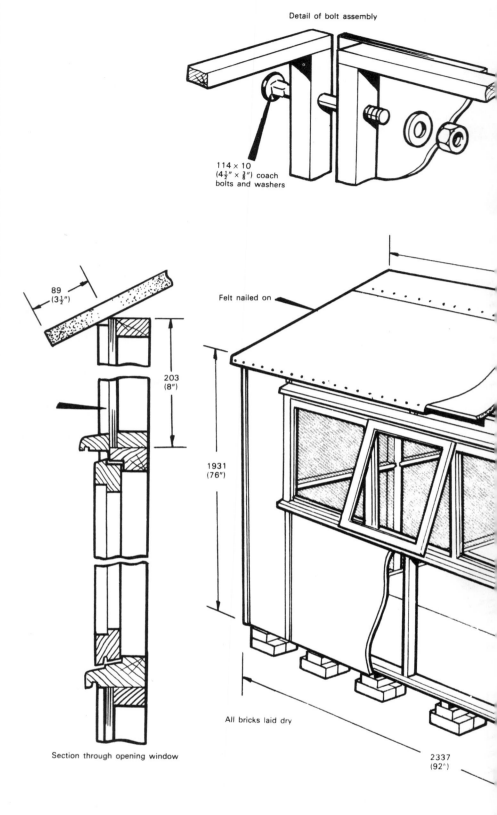

Detail of bolt assembly

114 × 10
(4½" × ⅜") coach
bolts and washers

89
(3½")

203
(8")

1931
(76")

Felt nailed on

2337
(92")

All bricks laid dry

Section through opening window

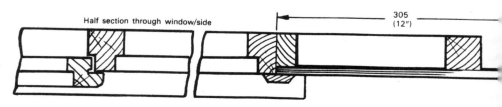

Half section through window/side

305
(12")

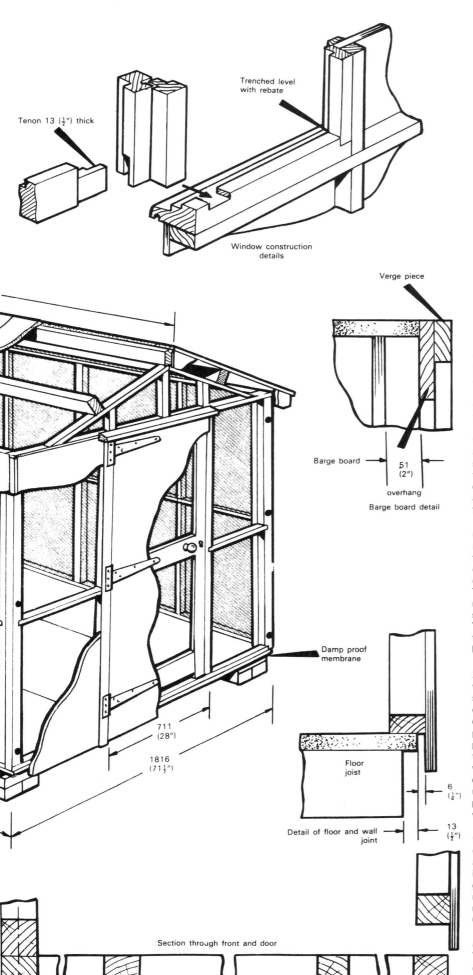

Tenon 13 (½") thick

Trenched level with rebate

Window construction details

Verge piece

2440 (96")

Barge board

51 (2")

overhang

Barge board detail

914 (36")

Damp proof membrane

711 (28")

1816 (71½")

Floor joist

6 (¼")

13 (½")

Detail of floor and wall joint

Section through front and door

illet

First to be located on the floor was the shed back, held upright by stays. This was quickly followed by one of the sides (photo 5). After checking that one wall was correctly aligned with the other, holes were bored through both and bolts were inserted. The window and door sides were added in like manner, and then the four sides were centralised on the floor so that overlap was equal all round. Finally, to ensure that there was no future movement, screws were inserted through the bottom rails into the floor.

Two purlins and a ridge were now prepared to size, and cut to the same length as chipboard to be used for the roof. The ridge had its upper edge formed with a double bevel to correspond with the slope of the roof. Only at this stage were slots cut in the plywood cladding for these three roof supports to fit into. The construction was such that, when the purlins and ridge were slipped into position, their upper surfaces were level with the plywood.

The advantages of pre-felted chipboard for the roof were simplicity of construction and competitive cost. Two sheets were required and were cut to width. Cutting was carried out to produce bevelled edges which would fit snugly together at the ridge.The roofing panels were then well nailed to the purlins, but only lightly nailed to the ridge. This was to help in any future dismantling of the shed.

Barge boards were the next parts to be tackled. They were cut and fitted at their ends to the shape shown in the elevation drawing. Nailing them in place was followed by fixing the verge pieces, which is a much better arrangement than on the average shed. It is the sort of construction that a builder might use on the edge of a flat roof to be felted. The purpose of the verge pieces is to carry the felt clear of all other components and thus allow rainwater to be safely drained away.

The use of pre-felted chipboard did not eliminate the need for felting the roof, but did result in double protection. A mineral surfaced felt of medium weight was chosen for the covering, and from the roll three pieces were cut to the length required including overhang. There is only one type of nail to use for fixing roofing felt—galvanised clout nails, made specially for the purpose with large heads. These were driven in about every 76mm (3in.), the lower piece on each side being the first to be secured (photo 10).

From the third piece of felt, a strip about 254mm (10in.) wide was cut lengthways. This was then nailed along the ridge, half being secured to each sloping surface. The remainder of the final piece of felt was also fixed to straddle the ridge, and the reduced width of this piece was still adequate to overlap the first two pieces by a generous amount. The idea behind the narrow strip at the ridge was that the whole of the roof would then have two layers of felt to protect it. Ends of the felt were trimmed so that they projected below the verge pieces by about 13mm (½in.), which forms what is referred to as a "drip".

With glass for the window obtained in advance, draught exclusion was quickly carried out. Two or three small panel pins were used around each edge of the glass to hold it firmly in place. I bought just enough putty for the glazing, as I fortunately remembered that, for rebates of average size, a half kilo of putty is needed for every two metres of glass perimeter (1 lb to every 6ft.).

Four cover strips were nailed in place at the corner, and a rim lock was fitted to the door. Then, a final coat of varnish was applied to the outside (photo 12), and the door and window were given a coat of white gloss paint. This completed the shed, but to get the best out of it a lot of shelving and racking is still needed on the inside.

Steak out

Ideal for parties in the open air, with food prepared in the garden. This combined barbecue/trolley can be made in appropriate species of either hardwood or softwood and involves some very elementary metalworking.

THIS REALLY is a splendid piece of equipment for those who enjoy parties in the open air, with the food prepared in the garden. The barbecue features a huge grilling area, with each half separately controlled from the panel on the front. One of the refinements is automatic ignition of the Calor gas.

The design is equally suitable for making in appropriate species of either hardwood or softwood, and some very elementary metal-working is involved. The trolley featured in this article is constructed from selected red deal, one of the better softwoods for a job like this.

The bulk of the timber needed for the trolley is either 55mm by 30mm, or 50mm by 28mm, and I prepared sufficient of this at the outset. I started with the base, and marked out the two main rails while they were held in the vice. While trenches are simple enough to cut by hand, my small circular saw is ideal for these and makes easy work of them. For greater accuracy, the two were cramped together for this stage, and were kept so

held while the holes for the dowel and axle rod were bored.

The slats for the base needed little attention. After cutting to length, screw holes were prepared at the ends, and a few shavings taken off all the corners. I felt that glue was worth adding to the joints, and used Cascamite-One-Shot, an adhesive well proven for outside work. Assembling the base was no more than screwing the parts together.

The axle blocks positioned under each end of the outer slat provide adequate anchorage for the stub-axles, and eliminate the alternative of a single but long axle. These were glued and screwed in place, and the hole for the axle bored through these blocks after fixing.

The design indicated that the parts of the leg frame be morticed and tenoned together, so much of the marking out for these were carried out in sets of legs and rails. The final marking of the joints was completed with the mortice gauge, before I brought my slot morticer into use. Slot

morticers work very quickly indeed, but they leave the mortice with rounded ends which require squaring-off by chisel. The tenons, though, were cut entirely by hand. Screw holes were made through the sides of the mortices, and the waste was sawn off the ends of the legs to the angle indicated.

Assembling the two frames was a straightforward operation, with the usual checks being made once in the cramps. It is always wise to remove the surplus glue while it's still wet, it is so much more difficult once set. When removed from the cramps, the screws were inserted into the joints to provide additional security.

The joints for the top frame were prepared and cut in a similar way as for the leg frames, with two of the joints being made as haunched mortice and tenons. I started forming the handles by cramping the two pieces together, and boring a hole so that half of this came in each member. The operation was of course repeated on the opposite edges before the waste was sawn away. I used a Surform to round over the handles, and this was followed by an abrasive 'flap wheel'. Actually, I had bought a couple of these flap wheels well over a year ago, and this was the first time I had used one. They proved to be ideal for a job like this.

I soon had the frame cramped up, and once dry the joggles were sawn off and the edge levelled. Because the four pieces making up this part of the trolley were all the same thickness, a little levelling off of the surfaces was needed. Again screws were inserted through the joints.

Progress had reached the stage when the main assemblies could be hinged together. The hinges I used were 38mm back flaps of a decorative pattern in pressed brass. While they had proved satisfactory, solid brass hinges would undoubtedly make a more robust job. The hinges were screwed to the leg frames first, before being secured to the top and bottom frames.

I broke off from woodworking activities at this stage, and switched crafts to tackle a little metalworking. I had bought a two metre length of 20mm by 3mm "black" mild steel from a small engineers' supply firm. This cost less than a pound, and I obtained it at the first place I enquired at. Two pieces were sawn to a length of 70mm, to provide the location brackets between the leg frames and the brace. Twisting these proved easier than I anticipated, although I almost made two identical ones instead of a "pair"! Each

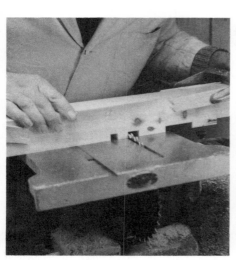

1. Cutting out the trenches on the circular saw.

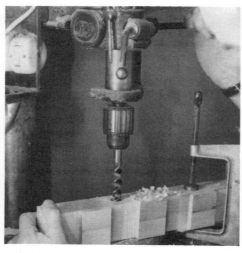

2. Boring out a hole for the dowel rod fixing.

...d of the metal was gripped in a sash
...amp, with a space of about 12mm
...etween them. One cramp was held in the
...ce, and the other rotated slightly so as to
...vist the metal. The angle was judged by
...al and error. A couple of holes were
...illed in the longer ends of the brackets
...r screws.

...The braces were prepared as shown in
...e drawings, with the lower ends cut at a
...vel, and the upper ends notched to take
...e cross rail. A piece of dowel was
...readed through the base frame, and
...re washers used as spacers between
...is and the brace. Locating the position of
...e metal bracket which engage with the
...tches in the brace members was es-
...blished by actually trying the parts
...gether. The cross rail linking the two
...aces was only added at this stage, and
...rews were also driven in at the lower
...ds to secure the braces to the dowel.

...In order to prevent a future calamity
...st when the sausages are sizzling, small
...lts were added to the inside of the leg
...as to engage with the brace. While the
...ace takes the weight of the trolley, the
...lts provide for the positive locking
...gether of the whole assembly.

...Although the wheels I used for the
...olley are perhaps a little small in
...ameter, they are of a wide bulbous type
...nd will thus cause negligible damage to a
...ell-kept lawn. Pieces were cut for the
...vo axles, hub caps added to one end,
...en inserted into place with a second hub
...ap ensuring positive retention in place.

...The two flaps do not have any joints
...ther than screwing, and so were quickly
...ade. As with all components, the pieces
...aking up the flaps had their arrises
...aned away, then they were assembled
...ith glue and screws. A pair of back flaps
...ecures each of these parts to the top
...ame.

...Clearly, support is needed for these
...aps, and this is provided by a bracket
...nder each. Because the brackets abut
...gainst the sloping legs, the brackets too
...ed to be angled which is why their top
...dges are bevelled. Again a pair of hinges
... each bracket provide for both securing
...nd folding flat, and the bracket when
...own are held against the legs by locating
...ins. These locating pins are the Scan
...rass Guide Dowel, as featured in the
..Woodfit'' catalogue, and they proved
...oth simple and effective for this applica-
...on.

...This completed the woodwork, but
...nore metalwork was needed. Because the
...arbecue obviously gets hot in use, it can-
...ot rest directly on the wood. Metal sup-
...orts are required, and the instructions
...vith the barbecue state a minimum
...learance all round of 50mm must be
...chieved. Careful measuring of the bar-
...ecue body was followed by making a full
...ize outline of the shape needed, which in
...urn gave me the length of metal required.
... was able to use a fairly large engineers'
...ice to hold the metal while banding it to
...hape, although sash cramps with
...ardwood packing make a very acceptable
...lternative. In fact, metal of the section
...eing used bends quite easily provided it
... positively held. Remember, though, that
...lack mild steel bends more readily than

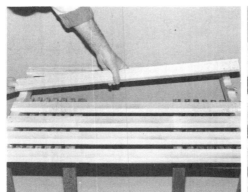

3. The simple assembly of the trolley base frame.

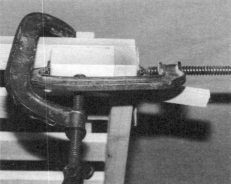

4. Adding the axle block to give extra support.

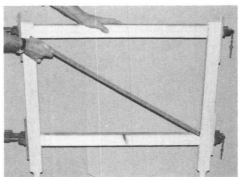

5. A good method of checking for squareness.

6. The leg frame is hinged to the trolley base.

Cutting List

Lower rails	2 off	670 by	55 by 30mm
Lower slats	7 off	890 by	50 by 20mm
Axle blocks	2 off	105 by	50 by 50mm
Legs	4 off	690 by	55 by 30mm
Rails to leg frames	3 off	870 by	70 by 20mm
Top frame handle members	2 off	870 by	55 by 30mm
Top frame cross rails	2 off	870 by	55 by 30mm
Rails to flaps	4 off	710 by	50 by 20mm
Slats to flaps	16 off	410 by	50 by 20mm
Brackets to flaps*	2 off	410 by	105 by 20mm
Braces	2 off	1010 by	55 by 30mm
Cross rail to braces	1 off	955 by	50 by 20mm

Allowance added to lengths, widths and thicknesses are net. Also required: 8 pairs of 38mm hinges; black mild steel 2 metres by 20mm by 3mm; wheels; axle rod and hub caps; 4 bolts 38mm by 6mm; length of 19mm dowelling. * Denotes that these two pieces can be cut side by side for economy.

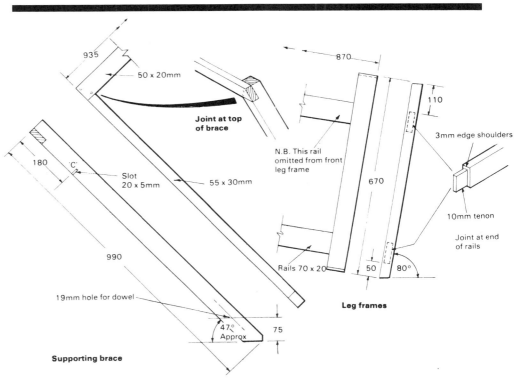

935

50 x 20mm

Joint at top of brace

870

110

3mm edge shoulders

N.B. This rail omitted from front leg frame

180

'C'

Slot 20 x 5mm

55 x 30mm

670

990

10mm tenon

Joint at end of rails

Rails 70 x 20

50   80°

19mm hole for dowel

47° Approx

75

Supporting brace

Leg frames

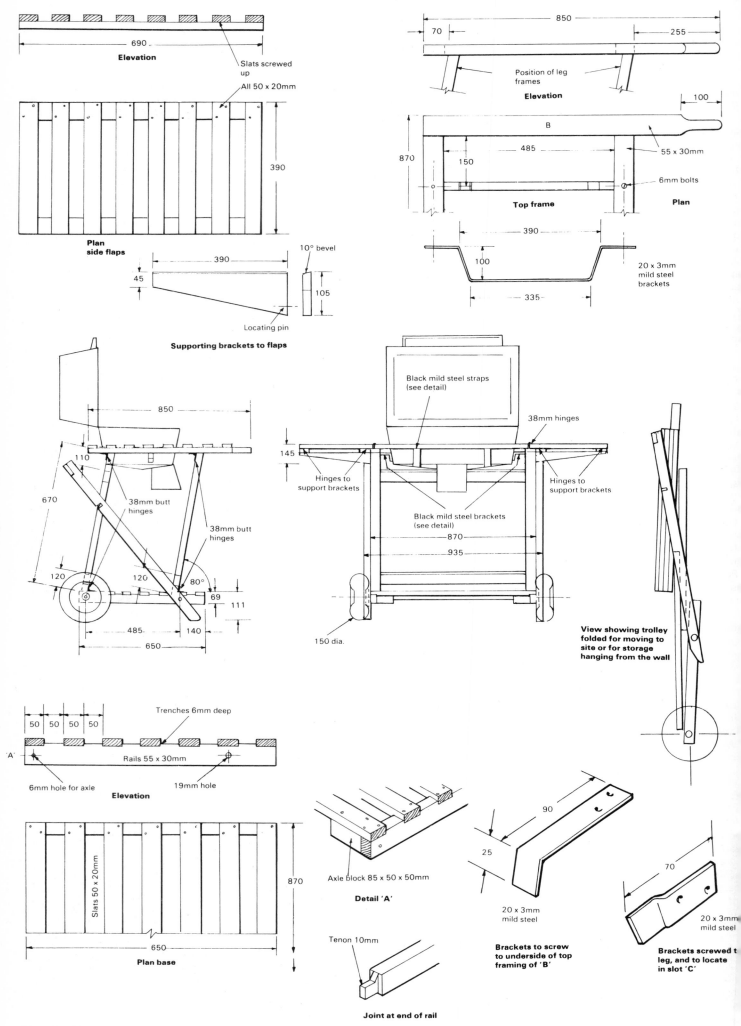

Elevation

690

Slats screwed up

All 50 x 20mm

390

Plan side flaps

390

45

10° bevel

105

Locating pin

Supporting brackets to flaps

850

70

255

Position of leg frames

Elevation

100

B

870

150

485

Top frame

55 x 30mm

6mm bolts

Plan

390

100

335

20 x 3mm mild steel brackets

850

110

670

120

38mm butt hinges

120

38mm butt hinges

80°

69

111

485

140

650

Black mild steel straps (see detail)

38mm hinges

145

Hinges to support brackets

Hinges to support brackets

Black mild steel brackets (see detail)

870

935

150 dia.

View showing trolley folded for moving to site or for storage hanging from the wall

Trenches 6mm deep

50 50 50 50

'A'

Rails 55 x 30mm

6mm hole for axle

19mm hole

Elevation

Slats 50 x 20mm

870

650

Plan base

Axle block 85 x 50 x 50mm

Detail 'A'

90

25

20 x 3mm mild steel

Brackets to screw to underside of top framing of 'B'

70

20 x 3mm mild steel

Brackets screwed t leg, and to locate in slot 'C'

Tenon 10mm

Joint at end of rail

right", which is a little harder. A few
strokes from a file removes the burrs and
rough corners from the metal. Holes of
□mm diameter were bored at each end of
□ese supports, corresponding holes made
□ the top frame, and mushroom headed
□lts used to secure them in place.

In order to prevent lateral movement of
□e barbecue when on its supports, two
□ther metal components are required.
□tails of these are shown in the draw-
□s, and a couple of screws hold each of
□ese to the underside of the top frame.

In order to protect the woodwork, I
□ve it a couple of coats of Cuprinol
□d Cedar Preserver — the pleasant
□lour adding to the attractiveness
□ the finished trolley. It is bound
□ get wet from time to time, even
□ough it is not intended to live in
□e garden.

□A gas cylinder borrowed from my
□ravan was soon installed in place, and
□al safety checks made that all was well
□arding the fuel supply. The moment of
□th had arrived, and despite the weather
□t being too kind at what would be the
□ristening ceremony, steaks were
□ught to be grilled in the open air. Uncer
□n as to the culinary adjustments which
□ght be needed to this new-style of
□oking, success was achieved first time
□d the food prepared tasted different and
□citing despite the chill in the air. Never
□ve steaks been enjoyed so much—
□ually they were only steakburgers, but I
□s nearly fooled!

□Perhaps the most ingenious aspect of
□s design is the way it folds flat for storing
□ a couple of hooks on the garage wall.

9. Fixing the cross brace to the pivot dowel.

10. Checking the position of the location plate.

11. The bolt ensures a positive locking.

12. Checking the flap assembly for accuracy.

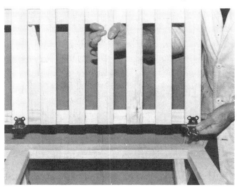
13. The flap is added to the top frame.

14. A shaped hinged bracket supports the flap.

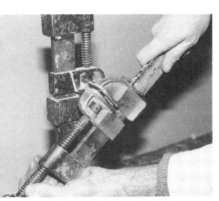
□utting a twist into the mild steel rod.

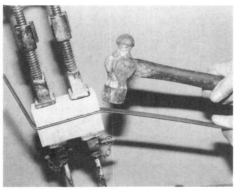
15. An alternative way of bending your metal.

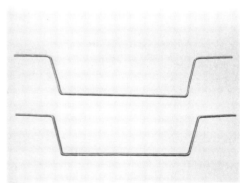
16. The completed main supports for the burner.

□Drilling the location plate on a pillar drill.

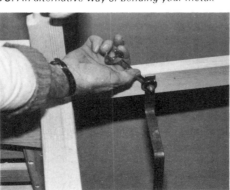
17. Bolting the supports to the top frame.

18. A coat of preservative finished the project

1. When in the folded position the trolley is completely mobile.

2. Up she comes! Simplicity itself the trolley unfolds just like a deckchair.

3. The next stage in the erection is the unfolding of the side flaps.

4. Set the support prop to take the weight of the flap in the open position.

5. The all-important supply of Calor gas is now placed on the lower level.

6. All set up and ready to go for a meal in the great outdoors.

Garden seat for two

If sometimes you feel you would like a break from your workshop routine, then why not put your skills to good use and make a garden seat.

ANYONE who says a garden seat is only something for old people should think again; people of all generations enjoy a seat in the sun or even, weather permitting, in a cool corner of the garden.

The one we feature here is also suited to sitting at a table for taking meals out of doors, and the way that the seat slats are arranged means that it is possible to sit for an even longer time in an upright or slightly leaning position without it becoming uncomfortable.

Making this little two seater is not particularly difficult so long as you work fairly accurately and follow the instruction sequence which is illustrated in the photographs. The construction has been designed to be simple and complicated joints are avoided by working on a built-up sandwich method. Thus it is much simpler to cut a notch than it is to chop out a mortise, as is the case where the front rails are jointed to the legs.

Whilst the drawing gives general overall sizes for the seat, the materials list further indicates sizes of component parts. The old maxim of measure twice before you cut is worth remembering particularly in relation to the angled back slats which should be marked off against the part-constructed bench when you have reached that stage.

If the bench is to be left out of doors for any length of time then waterproof glue and the use of brass screws is important. A tip here is to screw up first with steel screws and thus cut the correct thread in the wood so that there is no danger of the brass screws breaking when you drive them in.

It is equally important to protect the bench against the weather. Clear varnish can crack and does not permanently prevent a greying of the wood. The new micro-porous stains, such as Cuprinol Wood Stain, are excellent as they give a natural wood appearance and resist cracking and peeling.

1. All corners of this seat are rounded using a milling cutter or router. This is done after the pieces have been sawn, and before they are either screwed down or glued together.

2. The curve on the backrest is cut out using a jigsaw. First of all saw to the middle, and then use the piece that as been cut away as a pattern for the second half. Finally use the front board as a pattern for the back one, which doubles up on the front one except that it measures 110mm instead of 95mm in height.

3. The bench legs are each made up of one board and one facing piece. Follow the drawing: this shows where to cut the mortise joints for the top of the backrest, and how to fit the various parts together. The facing piece is glued either in front of or behind the plank depending on whether it is a front or rear leg

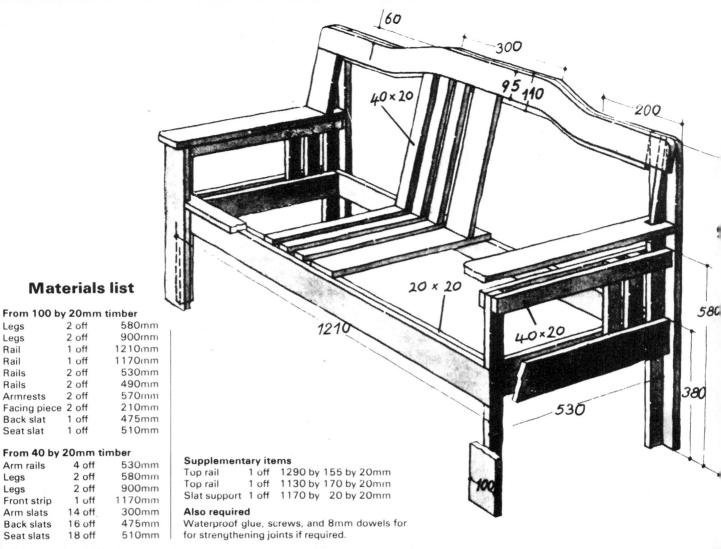

Materials list

From 100 by 20mm timber

Legs	2 off	580mm
Legs	2 off	900mm
Rail	1 off	1210mm
Rail	1 off	1170mm
Rails	2 off	530mm
Rails	2 off	490mm
Armrests	2 off	570mm
Facing piece	2 off	210mm
Back slat	1 off	475mm
Seat slat	1 off	510mm

From 40 by 20mm timber

Arm rails	4 off	530mm
Legs	2 off	580mm
Legs	2 off	900mm
Front strip	1 off	1170mm
Arm slats	14 off	300mm
Back slats	16 off	475mm
Seat slats	18 off	510mm

Supplementary items

Top rail	1 off	1290 by 155 by 20mm
Top rail	1 off	1130 by 170 by 20mm
Slat support	1 off	1170 by 20 by 20mm

Also required

Waterproof glue, screws, and 8mm dowels for for strengthening joints if required.

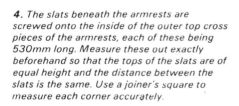

4. The slats beneath the armrests are screwed onto the inside of the outer top cross pieces of the armrests, each of these being 530mm long. Measure these out exactly beforehand so that the tops of the slats are of equal height and the distance between the slats is the same. Use a joiner's square to measure each corner accurately.

5. The inner cross pieces (the lower one on each armrest being only 490mm long) of the armrests, then only need to be glued onto the slats. In this way the screws will be completely hidden.

6. When sticking the side pieces to the legs you do not need to pay so much attention to the different parts since both rear legs and both front legs are the same. Instead make sure that the mortise holes for both of the long cross pieces remain clean and free of glue.

7. When gluing in the long cross pieces of the bench, pay special attention to the corner angles of the bench and also check that the legs are standing vertically.

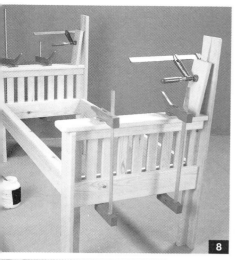

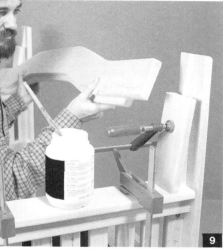

8 & 9. The bench is now completed with the addition of the planks on top of the armrests (each with a mortise joint at the back), the backrest, and the two short pieces between the back of the armrests and the horizontal backrest piece.

10. The slats for the seat are then glued onto the front cross piece and then screwed from the underneath as well. Screw the slats directly onto the rear cross piece.

11. When aligning the slats small wood spacers 20mm wide are a help. The slats on the backrest of the bench should fit in exactly and are then screwed in from the back.

Bird Table

Designed to encourage the birds which visit your garden to stay but high enough to discourage the cat, this bird table is sturdily built.

THERE CAN BE FEW PEOPLE who do not welcome birds into their gardens, and most of us encourage them by putting out food scraps onto the lawn. It was my wife's passion for insisting that our feathered friends have a generous share of our pantry that led to my making this bird table, with the result that we are now rarely without our little visitors.

I started work on the platform and prepared the two wide boards and the two outer battens. The centre batten is secured to the main post, and is not fixed to the platform until later. With the four pieces cut to length, chamfers were formed where shown, and holes made in the battens for screwing up. Strictly speaking the battens should be slot screwed to allow for shrinkage and swelling, but I compromised in this case by making the screw holes slightly oversize to allow for any movement. The two large boards are not jointed together in any way, and the parts were simply screwed together (photo 1).

The next step was to cut six pieces from boards 16mm ($\frac{5}{8}$in.) thick to provide material for the ends of the house. The vertical pieces were cut so that their outer edges were tapered, and to the correct overall width, and the gable ends were trimmed to their final shape, apart from the steps on the upper edges. These parts were then screwed together, the work at this stage appearing as in photo 2. The excess length at the top was then

sawn off, and the archway marked out ready for removal of the waste. This was quickly done on my bandsaw (photo 3), and the arrises were then smoothed and rounded by file (photo 4).

With this done the notches for the roof slats or boards were marked out. They were made 44mm (1$\frac{3}{4}$in.) apart, starting at the top, and I cut them with a tenon saw (photo 5).

The location of the ends was marked out on the platform, and a total of eight holes bored and countersunk for screwing these parts together. Two narrow pieces were next prepared for the eaves, and these required the edges bevelling so as to conform to the section needed. Their length is equal to the outside dimension of the house, and after cutting to this exact length, the ends were prepared for screwing up. A sash cramp conveniently held them in place while I drilled pilot holes in readiness for the screws (photo 6). Screws were also added through previously made holes in the gables, and I had carefully arranged the positions of the screws at the ends of these eaves pieces so that they did not foul one another.

Now I was ready to proceed with the roof. This was a good opportunity to use up all the offcuts of elm accumulated so far, as an essential feature of my design was the use of waney edged material for the roof. I cut the boards rather longer than needed, planed them to a

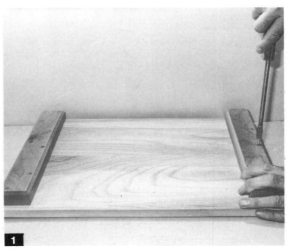

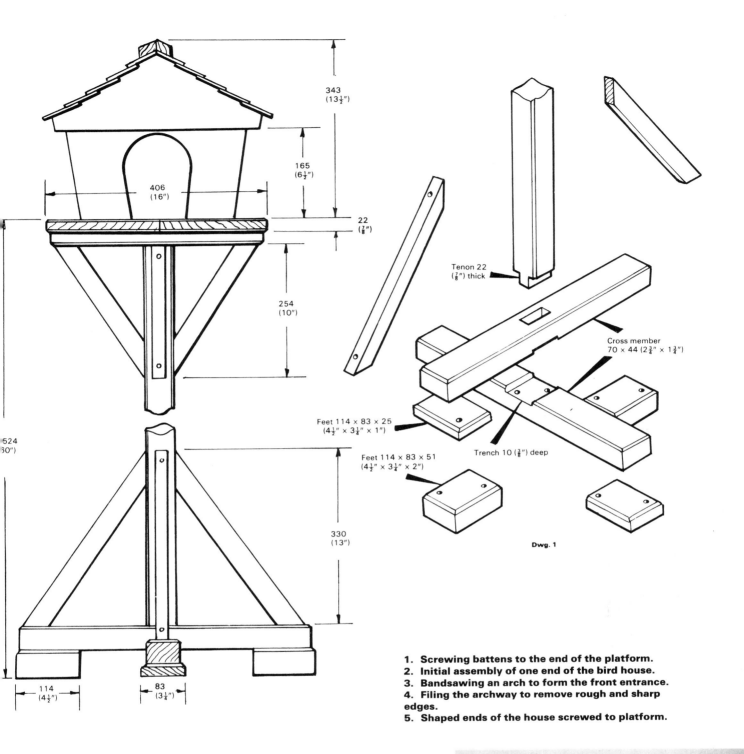

343
(13½″)

165
(6½″)

22
(⅞″)

406
(16″)

254
(10″)

524
(30″)

330
(13″)

114
(4½″)

83
(3¼″)

Tenon 22
(⅞″) thick

Cross member
70 × 44 (2¾″ × 1¾″)

Feet 114 × 83 × 25
(4½″ × 3¼″ × 1″)

Feet 114 × 83 × 51
(4½″ × 3¼″ × 2″)

Trench 10 (⅜″) deep

Dwg. 1

1. **Screwing battens to the end of the platform.**
2. **Initial assembly of one end of the bird house.**
3. **Bandsawing an arch to form the front entrance.**
4. **Filing the archway to remove rough and sharp edges.**
5. **Shaped ends of the house screwed to platform.**

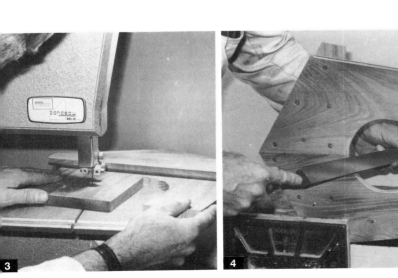

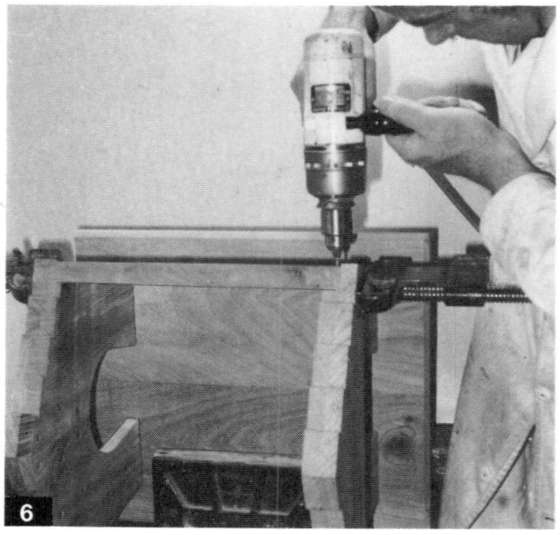

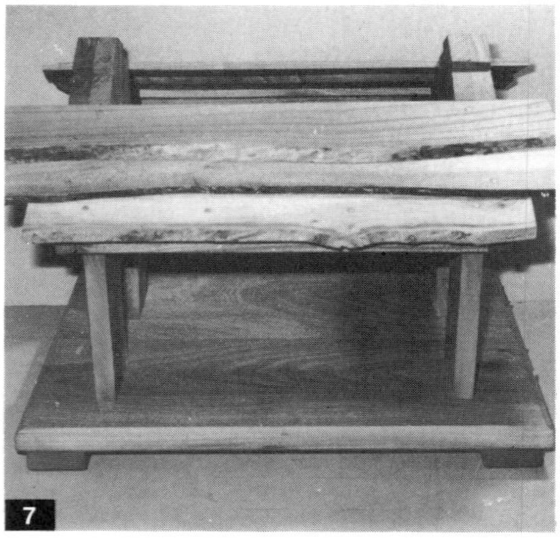

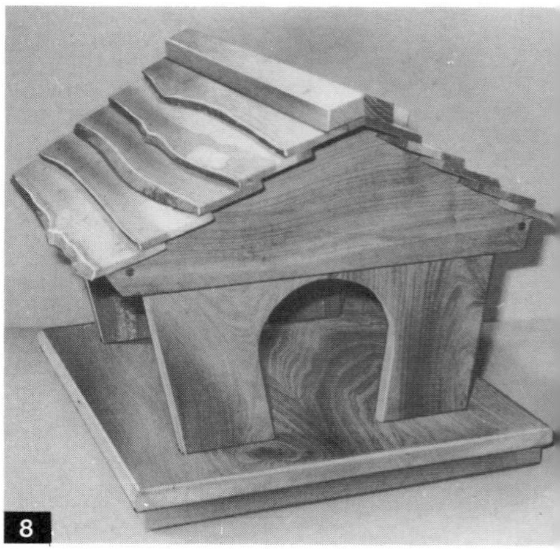

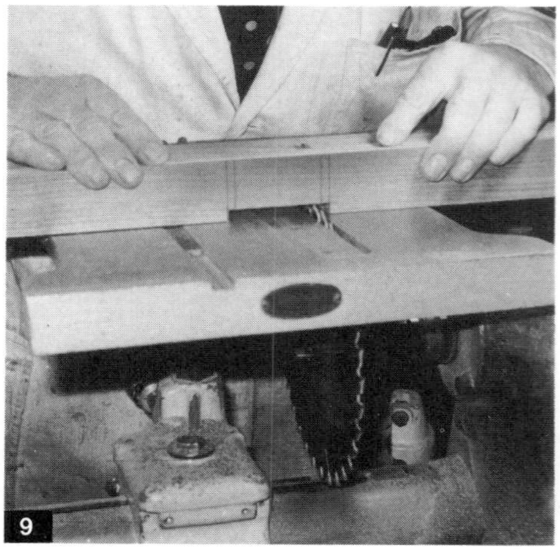

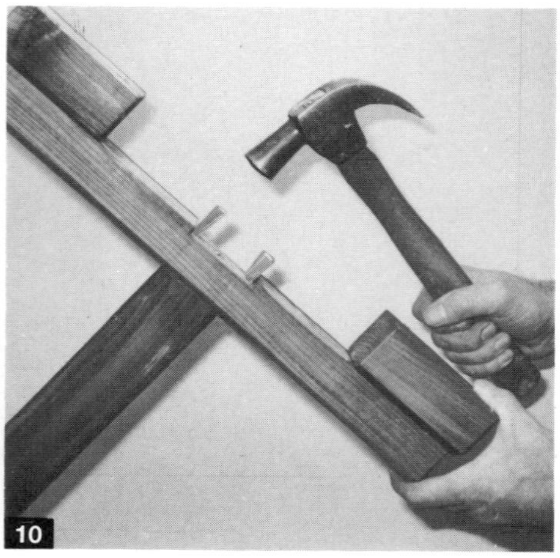

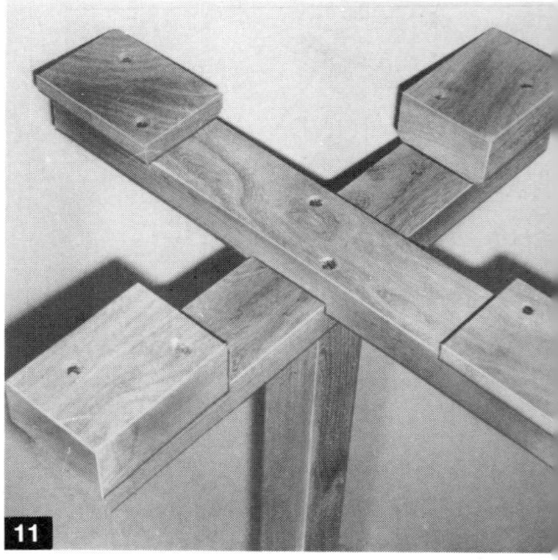

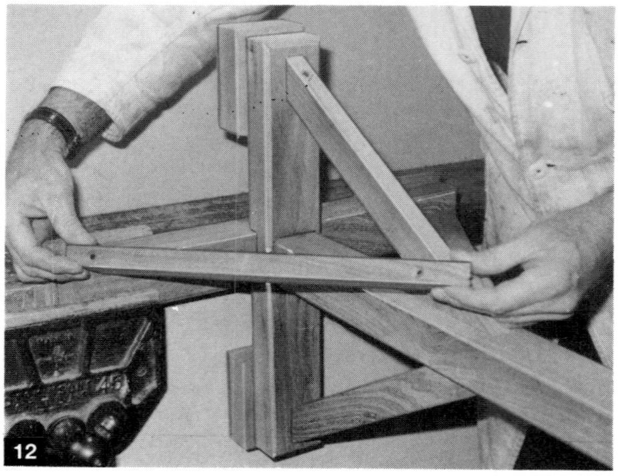

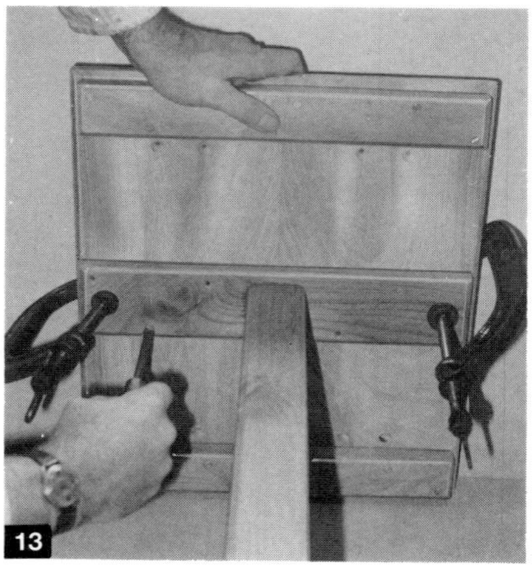

6. Marking through screw positions for the eaves.
7. Slats added to the roof from bottom upwards.
8. Upper portion of the bird table without stand.
9. Trenches for jointing feet made on circular saw.
10. Wedging joint between the foot and main post.
11. Feet cross members are screwed and jointed.
12. Checking the fit of the stays against the base.
13. Bird table platform is added to top of post.

CUTTING LIST

(Sizes in mm and inches) (No allowance for waste)

Main post	1 off	1448 by 57 by 57mm	(57 by 2¼ by 2¼in.)
Base cross members	2 off	533 by 70 by 44mm	(21 by 2¾ by 1¾in.)
Feet	2 off	114 by 83 by 25mm	(4½ by 3¼ by 1 in.)
Feet	2 off	114 by 83 by 51mm	(4½ by 3¼ by 2 in.)
Lower stays	4 off	406 by 38 by 19mm	(16 by 1½ by ¾in.)
Upper stays	4 off	305 by 38 by 19mm	(12 by 1½ by ¾in.)
Battens to platform	2 off	406 by 64 by 25mm	(16 by 2½ by 1 in.)
Batten to platform	1 off	406 by 76 by 25mm	(16 by 3 by 1 in.)
House ends	2 off	305 by 343 by 16mm	(12 by 13½ by ⅝in.)
Gable boards	2 off	381 by 140 by 16mm	(15 by 5½ by ⅝in.)
Eaves pieces	2 off	330 by 41 by 22mm	(13 by 1⅝ by ⅞in.)
Slats to roof	10 off	508 by 64 by 8mm	(20 by 2½ by 5/16 in.)
Ridge	1 off	508 by 57 by 32mm	(20 by 2¼ by 1¼in.)
Platform	1 off	457 by 406 by 22mm	(18 by 16 by ⅞in.)

finished thickness of 8mm (5/16 in.), and with a average width of 64mm (2½in.). These I starte fixing from the eaves, to which the first boa was fixed as well as to the gables. I used 1¼i galvanised nails for fixing, and two at each e (photo 7). Five pieces were required for eac side, the top two being bevelled on th meeting edges so that they fitted neat together. Only when all the roof boards we fixed did I trim them to length with a saw. A the roof ends are themselves at an angl sawing them to length after fixing meant it w easy to get the correct splay required.

The piece for the ridge was first of all cut t rectangular section, then the slope on the up per surface planed. This corresponds to th slope of the top two boards of the roof, and sliding bevel proved useful to check this angl The lower internal cut was then quick produced on my circular saw, with the blad

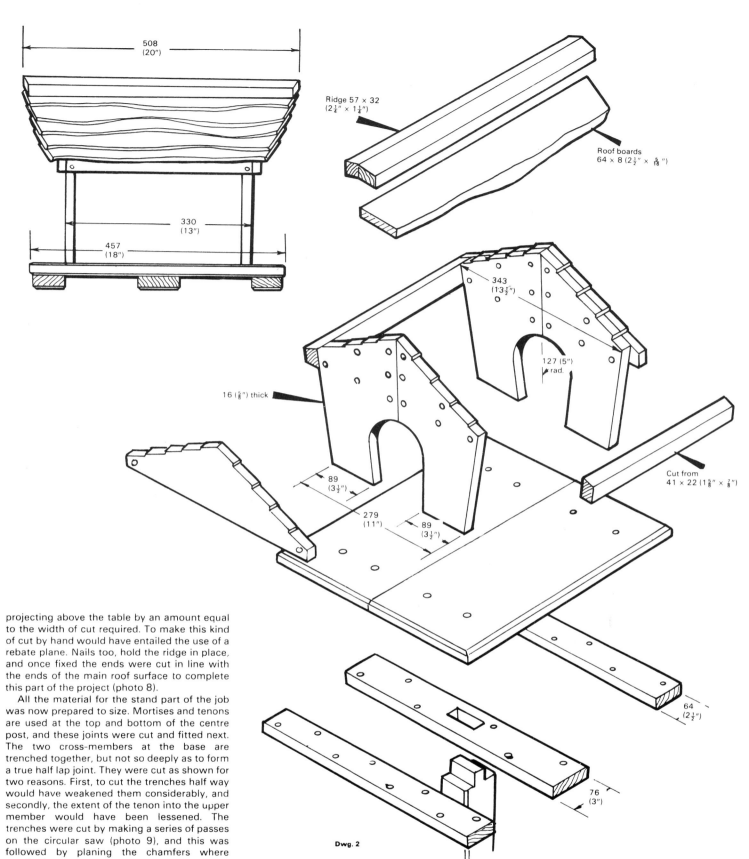

Ridge 57 × 32
(2¼" × 1¼")

Roof boards
64 × 8 (2½" × ⁵⁄₁₆")

508
(20")

330
(13")

457
(18")

343
(13½")

127 (5")
rad.

16 (⁵⁄₈") thick

89
(3½")

279
(11")

89
(3½")

Cut from
41 × 22 (1⁵⁄₈" × ⁷⁄₈")

64
(2½")

76
(3")

Dwg. 2

projecting above the table by an amount equal to the width of cut required. To make this kind of cut by hand would have entailed the use of a rebate plane. Nails too, hold the ridge in place, and once fixed the ends were cut in line with the ends of the main roof surface to complete this part of the project (photo 8).

All the material for the stand part of the job was now prepared to size. Mortises and tenons are used at the top and bottom of the centre post, and these joints were cut and fitted next. The two cross-members at the base are trenched together, but not so deeply as to form a true half lap joint. They were cut as shown for two reasons. First, to cut the trenches half way would have weakened them considerably, and secondly, the extent of the tenon into the upper member would have been lessened. The trenches were cut by making a series of passes on the circular saw (photo 9), and this was followed by planing the chamfers where required.

The blocks which form the actual feet were made next. Because of the way in which the two main cross-members are trenched, two different thicknesses were needed for these feet. They were prepared in pairs, chamfered and bored and then cut to length. Screwing them in place followed directly. At this stage I could assemble the main post with the upper and lower cross pieces, and for this I used Cascamite One Shot glue, and wedges (photo 10). I was very careful here to check that the cross-members were square to the post, as an error during assembly would have been difficult to correct. Wedges were levelled off

once the glue had set, and the second cross-member added (photo 11).

The stays add a lot of strength to a job of this type, and material for the two sets required were prepared to size, and the edges lightly chamfered. The angle cuts needed at each end were cut by saw and trimmed to an exact fit with a small plane. Holes were bored at the ends of the stays for screws, and then fixed in place (photo 12).

Only at this stage did I add the upper structure to the base part. I found the use of a

couple of G-cramps very helpful to initially hold the two parts together, while the screws were being inserted through the centre batten. This was of course, jointed onto the main post (photo 13). The stays at the top were added in a similar manner to those at the bottom.

As with an earlier project made of elm and intended to spend its life in the garden, I gave my bird table two coats of Cuprinol wood preservative, and once this had thoroughly dried an inaugural feast was laid for our expected visitors.

Adventure playhouse

Detail of underside construction.

The apex showing lapping method.

The steps and climbing frame bars.

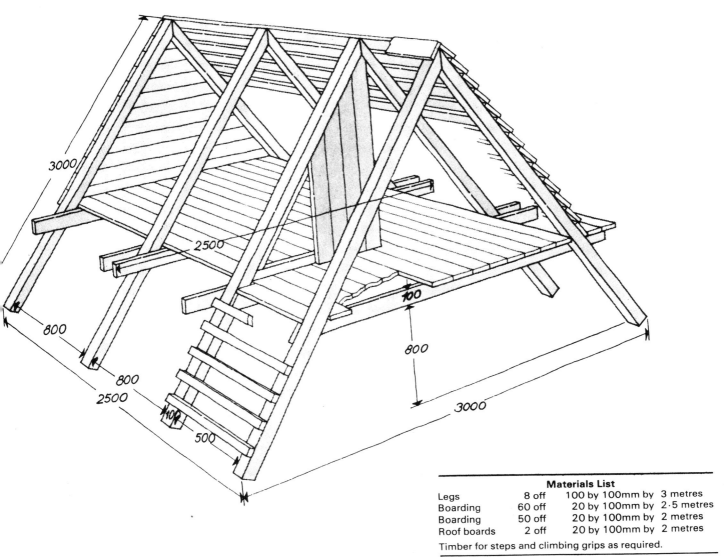

3000

2500

800

800

2500

100

500

100

800

3000

Materials List			
Legs	8 off	100 by 100mm by	3 metres
Boarding	60 off	20 by 100mm by	2·5 metres
Boarding	50 off	20 by 100mm by	2 metres
Roof boards	2 off	20 by 100mm by	2 metres

Timber for steps and climbing grips as required.

MOST OF US LOSE the joy and wonder of our childhood but we seldom completely forget it. Who can't remember those endless summer days when time meant nothing and the only thing that was really important was what we were going to have for tea. Times may change but seemingly everything remains the same, specially children. I think as a boy I would have given my right arm for this children's playhouse to use at will as a castle, fort, spaceship or galleon, in which to roam the skies or to fight off fierce pirates. Or perhaps as an outlaw camp deep among the geraniums where brave men would shudder to go.

Nowadays of course the only contact I'm likely to have with these things is being pestered to make them by the new generation of desperados. This particular design we found in a German DIY Magazine and although it may be a little expensive to make we couldn't resist it. The most obvious saving on cost would be of course to use secondhand timber although a good deal of care would be needed to ensure that it was free from nails. Similarly, although we don't show it in the photographs, it might be as well to spend a little time finishing the timbers to avoid splinters in the kids hands.

One thing that readily occurred to us was that the structure itself would be easily converted to something useful such as a garden shed or greenhouse when the kids are grown up, or even with modifications a summerhouse for adults. It could even in fact be built primarily as a summerhouse with the needs of the kids as a secondary consideration. In any event we felt it

to be a worthwhile project and suspect that with the summer days ahead many of you will too.

Construction
It will be obvious from the drawing that the whole structure is based on equilateral triangles; thus the apex angles as well as those formed by the legs with the ground will all be 60 degrees. The first job then is to cut the eight legs to size and cut the top angles accordingly. The bottoms of the legs can of course be angled off as well but we have chosen not to do this but instead to sit them on concrete blocks to prevent them from sinking in soft ground.

The next step is to cut the six cross beams which support the floor. Two of these are cut shorter than the rest at each end of the house to prevent fouling the stairs (see drawing).

The other two are cut 2500mm long and all are set across the legs at a height of 800mm from the base line formed by the triangles. Reference to the drawing should make this quite clear. The four individual frames are assembled in this way and all screwheads slightly countersunk.

You will almost certainly need a little assistance with the next stage since it basically entails standing all four frames upright at the specified distances apart, and temporarily holding them in place with one or two battens until sufficient floorboards can be screwed in place to make the whole structure rigid. This is where you commandeer the inquisitive

neighbour with his head already over the fence or grab the milkman off the garden path and refuse to pay the bill until the job is done. Be sure to countersink the floorboard screws since bare feet will almost certainly be on them at sometime or other.

There is really nothing to the rest of it. The rear gable end is boarded up as shown, making sure that a spirit level is used on the first board to ensure its running true. It's probably just as easy and certainly quicker to use nails for these fixings. As for the roof the drawing and photos are almost self explanatory. Begin from the bottom by fixing one board flat against the frames and work upwards using the lapping method shown. Ordinary feather-edge boarding used for fences would be cheaper than the timber we have used although not so strong. On either side of the playhouse we nailed walkways running on the projections of the crossbeams, but these are stopped short on the left hand side at each end where they meet the steps. The steps themselves are equidistantly spaced and pre-drilled and screwed to the frame.

Just to add a little more excitement and interest to the project we included climbing grips over the roof and a partition towards the front for greater secrecy.

There are many ways of finishing the project to make it weatherproof, the cheapest of which is creosote (with all the attendant mess and smell) so it might be better to confine this just to the bottom of the legs. For the rest of the house a general wood preservative such as Cuprinol is probably best.

Garden lounger

With three or four comfortable positions for relaxing in the summer sun who could resist carting themselves off into the garden with this one.

Left: the finished recliner minus the foam cushions, note the slats are fitted in alternate widths of 80 and 170mm.

Centre: detail of the adjuster assembly in this case with four positions as opposed to the optional three shown in the drawing.

Right: the shaping of the handles and the ground supports is worth taking a little time and care over.

With spring passing we look forward to the long hot summer days spent dreamily in the garden. Relaxing hours with time to think and to reflect upon the past and future emerge along with the summer blooms and lengthening days. Now is the time to make the most of leisure by having the facilities for relaxation in the open air Garden furniture comes in all shapes and sizes but why not add a little charm and invention to give a bit more character to these pieces.

This recliner is reminiscent of an old farm cart or barrow evoking the memories of an earlier and more placid time when life had a pace that made rather more sense than the frantic scurrying about that we now all seem to take so much for granted. It's not hard to make, and a day or so in the workshop is in itself sufficiently relaxing to put you in the mood to use it.

Begin by cutting the two long rails to length and shaping the ends and the handles. Even working without power tools this is not difficult but it's worth taking your time to get a nice matching pair. Repeat the procedure with the two upright rails and drill the holes in all four pieces for the pivoting action. The two long rails now have extra spacing pieces added at the front ends similarly shaped. These are to add support for the axle.

The next step is to cut out the housings for the crossmembers on all four pieces and note that these are alternately 80 and 170mm wide. The crossmembers are now cut to length and dowelled and glued in position. Spacing pieces are now added to the inside faces of the adjusting back at the points where the toothed height adjusters pivot (see drawing). These are drilled to take the pivot screws. The height adjusters can now be cut to size, shaped up at the ends and the three notches cut out. Drill each to take the pivot screws and fit them to the adjusting back.

Returning to the main chassis cut out and shape the ground rests which are located just in front of the handles in line with the housing for the first slat. These can be either screwed or dowelled in position. Similarly cut out and fit the folding legs situated just behind the wheel (these are for additional support).

The holes to take the axle can now be cut and these should be a clearance fit for the 5mm hardwood dowel to be used.

Making the wheel requires more patience than skill, and for all practical purposes a bandsaw or at least a jigsaw is necessary. Photos 1 to 4 show how the wheel and hub are built up from a series of circles, half circles and quadrants with the spokes simply laid between. Nobody would suggest making a proper cartwheel in this way but in this case its function is mainly ornamental. Similarly we are working here in softwood which for the real thing would certainly not be adequate.

It's probably best to make up templates first to check your fits and from them do all the marking out before cutting. With the large semicircles inevitably you will end up with some very short grain in places so be careful until the whole wheel is glued up. The axle washers are best cut from a hardwood or even metal for durability.

The sequence of assembly for the wheel

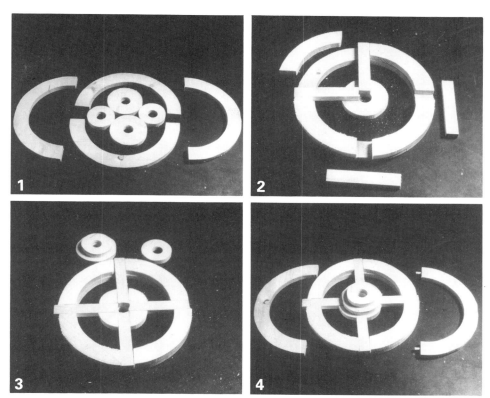

Photos 1 to 4 above show the sequence used in laminating the wheel.

is clearly shown in photos 1 to 4 with the two outer rings being held by dowels as shown. When making the final assembly be sure to wipe off all excess glue that will

inevitably ooze out with the cramping up. The wheel will probably take quite a bit of cleaning up with glasspaper for a nice smooth and symmetrical finish.

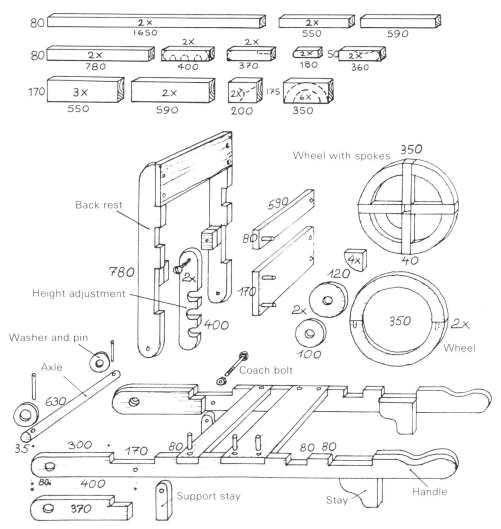

Lantern greenhouse

Fun to make, but also highly practical and inexpensive. The materials used are freely available.

The concept of "self help" was one well understood by our Victorian forebearers for reasons that they could hardly be proud of, but it did have its more acceptable side and it still does today. Many people never consider making things for themselves, preferring it seems to be content with what the manufacturers supply. In good times this is an easy attitude to adopt, and one which we as a magazine would not care to moralise about. However, inflation bites even deeper and many of us are now forced to be a little more inventive if we want to retain our standard of living. This is no bad thing because we usually find that we are not only more skilled than we thought but that we actually begin to enjoy our efforts in making what we want rather than simply going out and buying it. All this is even more true if we are talking about luxuries or things which might be described as marginal necessities.

The greenhouse project here falls into the above category and is not only fun to make but highly practical and inexpensive. The design has sufficient novelty to stimulate interest without being unnecessarily complex, and the materials used are freely available. So pleased were we with the results in this case that we thought it might be of interest to you, the readers, to suggest similar projects for the garden using Novolux sheets as we used here. We thought the way to do this would best be in the form of a competition to tax your ingenuity and bring out the practical qualities in you. The entry form for the competition is on the page following this article and all details can be found in it. So, down to work, make this delightful addition to your back garden, find out the working qualities of the Novolux sheets and then send in a prize-winning design for another project. If, of course, you already have a greenhouse enter the competition anyway, who knows, a little "self help" might pay off in a big way!

1. Cutting the bevel on a hip member on the Kity combination machine.

2. The next step is to cut the rebate on the member (guard removed for clarity).

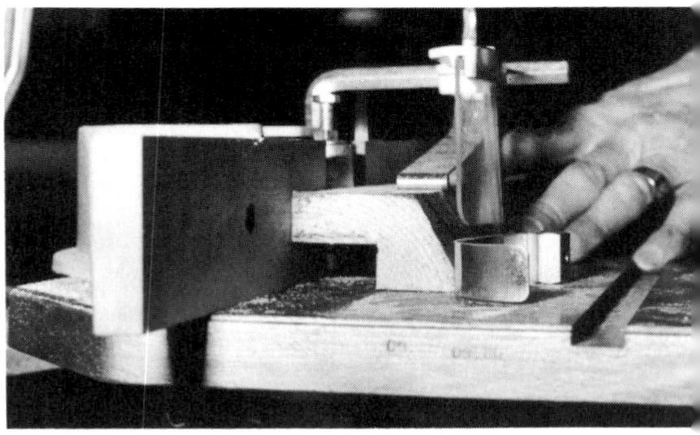

3. Alternatively, the rebate could be cut away on the spindle moulder.

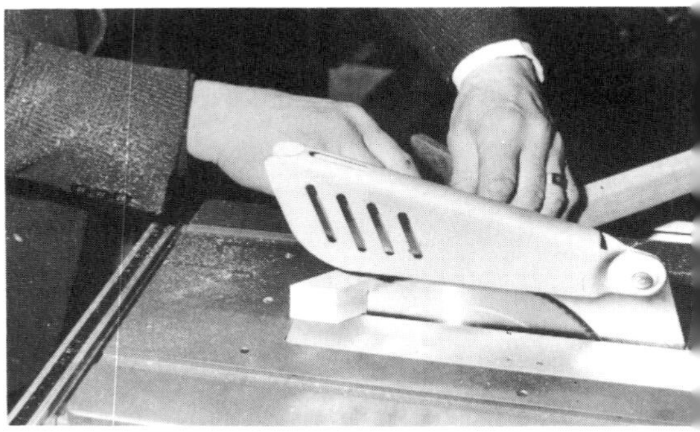

4. The bevelled bracing rails were again cut on the circular saw but hand methods could quite easily be employed for this.

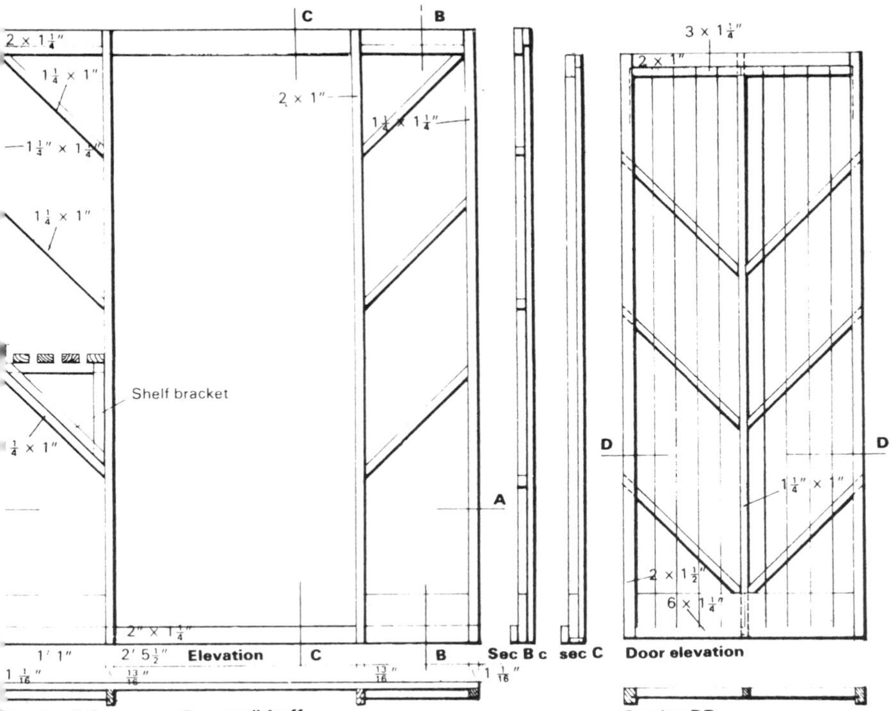

C
B
2 x 1¼"
1¼ x 1"
1¼" x 1¼"
1¼ x 1"
2 x 1"
1¼ x 1¼"
Shelf bracket
¼ x 1"
A
2" x 1¼"
1' 1"
2' 5½"
Elevation
C
B
Sec B c
sec C
3 x 1¼"
2 x 1"
D
D
1¼" x 1"
2 x 1½"
6 x 1¼"
Door elevation
Section A A
Door wall 1 off
Section DD

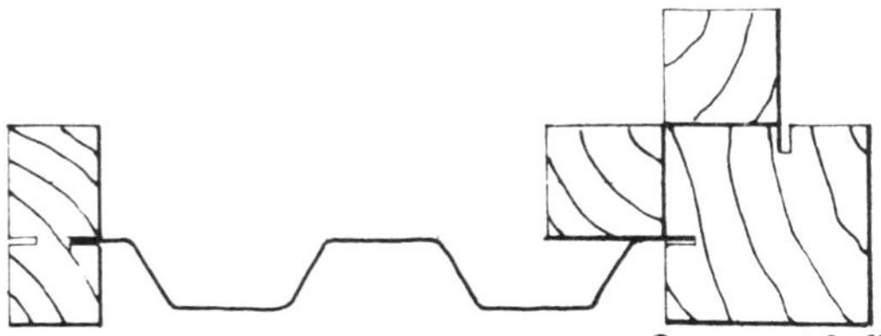

Corner post 4 off

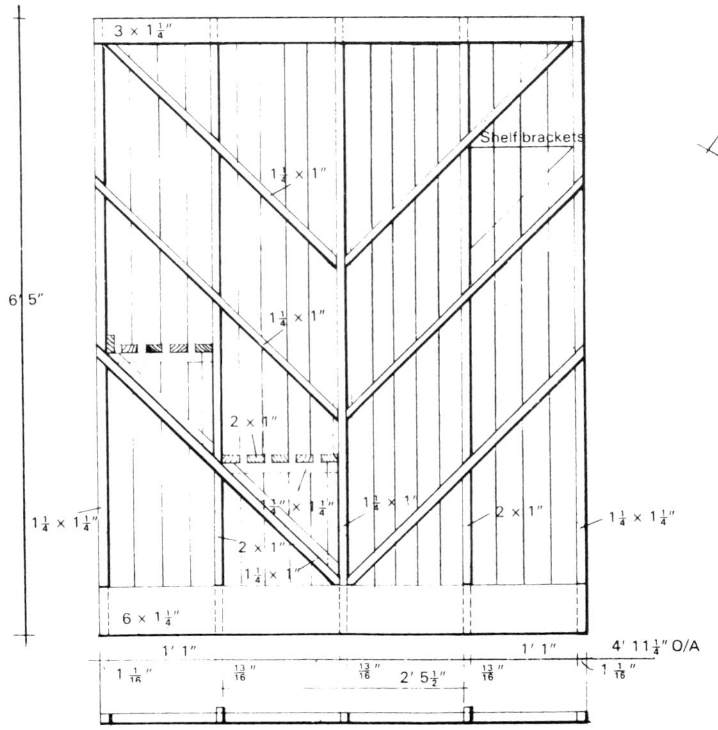

3 x 1¼"
Shelf brackets
1¼ x 1"
1¼ x 1"
6' 5"
2 x 1"
1¼" x 1¼"
1¼ x 1"
2 x 1"
1¼ x 1¼"
1¼ x 1¼"
2 x 1"
1¼ x 1"
6 x 1¼"
1' 1"
1' 1"
4' 11¼" O/A
2' 5½"

Walls 3 off

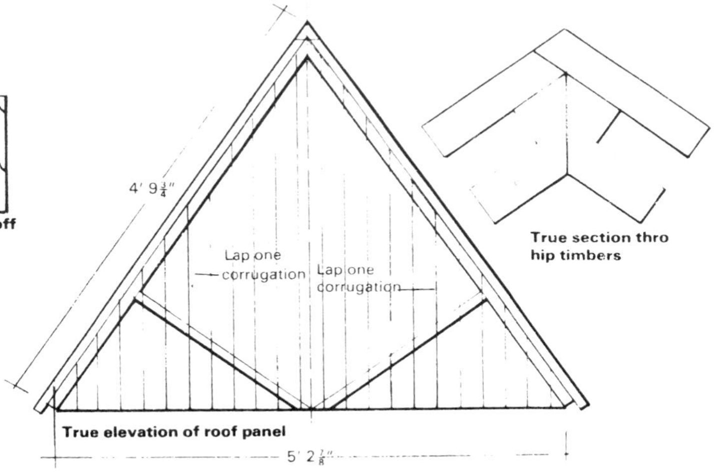

4' 9¾"
Lap one corrugation
Lap one corrugation
5' 2⅞"

True elevation of roof panel

True section thro hip timbers

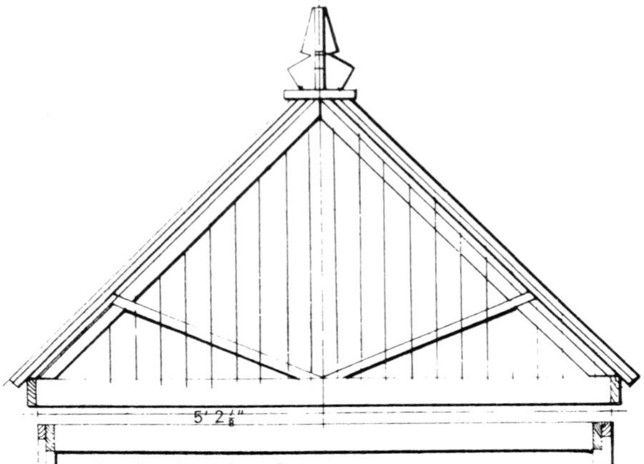

5' 2⅞"

Section through roof

5. Cutting the bevelled housings and halving joints with a spacing timber to give the correct depth of cut.

6. The uprights are halved on the top and bottom rails and screw fixed.

7. Diagonal bracing rails are set in at 45 degrees. They are halved and notched in position.

8. Fixing the Novolux into the groove made into the uprights and into the corresponding groove in the corner post. The setting out allows for a full size sheet of Novolux to be used in the centre, and five corrugations wide on either side. Note: the top batten fixed to the outside of the top rail to form a rebate and seal the top edge of the sheet.

9. Springing in the central sheet so that the edges engage in the grooves.

10. Fix the sheet tight into the top rebate and finish with Novolux sealing caps.

11. The corner posts with the two inner faces grooved with a sawcut to pick up the edges of the sheets. The dimensions from the inside face to the inside of the groove is equal to that of the side frame in both cases.

CUTTING LIST

Corner posts	4 off	77	by 2 by 2in
Infill frame upright	11 off	77	by $1\frac{1}{4}$ by $1\frac{1}{4}$in.
Intermediate uprights	8 off	77	by 2 by 1in.
Diagonal braces*	18 off	43	by $1\frac{1}{4}$ by $1\frac{1}{4}$in.
Infill frame bottom rail	3 off	$59\frac{1}{4}$	by 6 by $1\frac{1}{4}$in.
Infill frame (door panel), bottom rail	2 off	$14\frac{7}{8}$	by 6 by $1\frac{1}{4}$in.
Infill frame top rail	4 off	$59\frac{1}{4}$	by 3 by $1\frac{1}{4}$in.
Infill frame (door panel) braces*	6 off	20	by $1\frac{1}{4}$ by $1\frac{1}{4}$in.
Infill frame top rail	8 off	$14\frac{1}{16}$	by 2 by 1in.
Infill frame top rail (central)	6 off	$14\frac{5}{16}$	by 2 by 1in.
Infill frame top rail (over door)	1 off	$19\frac{1}{2}$	by 2 by 1in.
Door frame threshold	1 off	$59\frac{1}{4}$	by 2 by 1in.
Door styles	2 off	$73\frac{1}{4}$	by 2 by $1\frac{1}{4}$in.
Door centre upright	1 off	$73\frac{1}{4}$	by $1\frac{1}{4}$ by $1\frac{1}{4}$in.
Door bottom rail	1 off	$29\frac{1}{2}$	by 6 by $1\frac{1}{4}$in.
Door top rail	1 off	$29\frac{1}{2}$	by 3 by $1\frac{1}{4}$in.
Door top rail facing	1 off	$24\frac{1}{8}$	by 2 by 1in.
Door braces*	6 off	21	by $1\frac{1}{4}$ by $1\frac{1}{4}$in.
Shelf rails	20 off	$61\frac{1}{4}$	by 2 by 1in.
Triangular brackets*	8 off	48	by 2 by 1in.
Roof frames	4 off	$64\frac{1}{2}$	by 3 by 1in.
Roof ridges*	8 off	58	by $2\frac{1}{2}$ by $1\frac{1}{4}$in.
Roof ridge facings*	4 off	60	by 5 by $\frac{3}{4}$in.
Roof braces*	8 off	27	by 2 by $\frac{3}{4}$in.

Also required: 14 sheets Novolux box section 6ft.; Novolux screws and washers; timber preservative; wood screws.

* Denotes to be cut to size and fitted.

12. Fix a corner post to the left-hand side of each frame then glaze up. This is easiest to do with the frame lying flat in the workshop. If, however, you do it in the open be sure to fix each sheet securely before leaving.

13. Fixing the last panel, the door frame to complete the central box. The overall size is identical to the others, the only difference being that the central upright and bracings are removed and the bottom rail is cut to form a threshold.

14. Hanging the door made to match the existing structure to the 2 by 1 uprights.

15. A base frame for the roof lantern is made with the internal size of the previously assembled side frames. Having prepared all the timbers it is sensible to treat them with a preservative before assembly and then perhaps another coat when the structure is finished.

16. The hip timbers are machined from 1¾in. board, a straight rebate ⅝in. deep and then bevelled so that each pair form a common hip. The bottom end of each is rebated to form a bird's mouth to fit over the corner of the bottom frame.

17. The top corners are mitred so that the four hips join to form a central point, the top facet then being cut off to form a fixing for the decorative finial.

18. The fourth hip member being fixed into its position before the finial is fitted.

19. Screw fixing the hip members to main lantern base frame to take the Novolux.

20. Diagonal braces cut with a bevel to fit the frame and halved into the rebate of the hip members. These braces come out square from the hip member and meet at the centre point.

21. Fixing the diagonal braces halved into the rebated hip timber.

22. Right: glazing of the lantern is done with three pieces on each side, a centre section, a full width sheet and two triangular pieces. The only fixing necessary is through every third ridge into the bottom frame.

3. After glazing each ridge is capped with in. timbers bevelled and mitred to fit.

24. Fixing the finial. This was made simply by halving pieces of exterior grade ply, fixing to a base and then screwing down to the hip members.

25. The lantern is dropped into position; and secured with screws.

Garden Frame

THE NATURAL strength and resilience of elm makes it a natural choice of timber for a garden frame where the quality of weather resistance is also important.

Keen gardeners will need little reminding of the usefulness of such a frame, and although it tends to be associated with promoting the early growth of plants in the spring, in practice it can be put to very good use for a large part of the year.

Overall sizes for a job of this type are not critical, except perhaps the height which needs to be reasonably generous to allow for plant growth. The elm boards I was using had been planed down to finish 16mm ($\frac{5}{8}$in.), and after truing the edges by hand, they were cross cut to length. I felt it was worthwhile to form tongued and grooved joints on each pair of boards, and cut both parts of these joints with my power tool rebating attachment (photo 1). Next, the upper boards forming the ends had

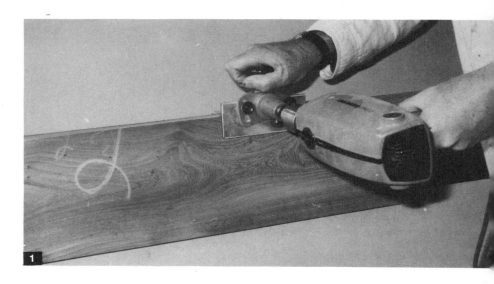

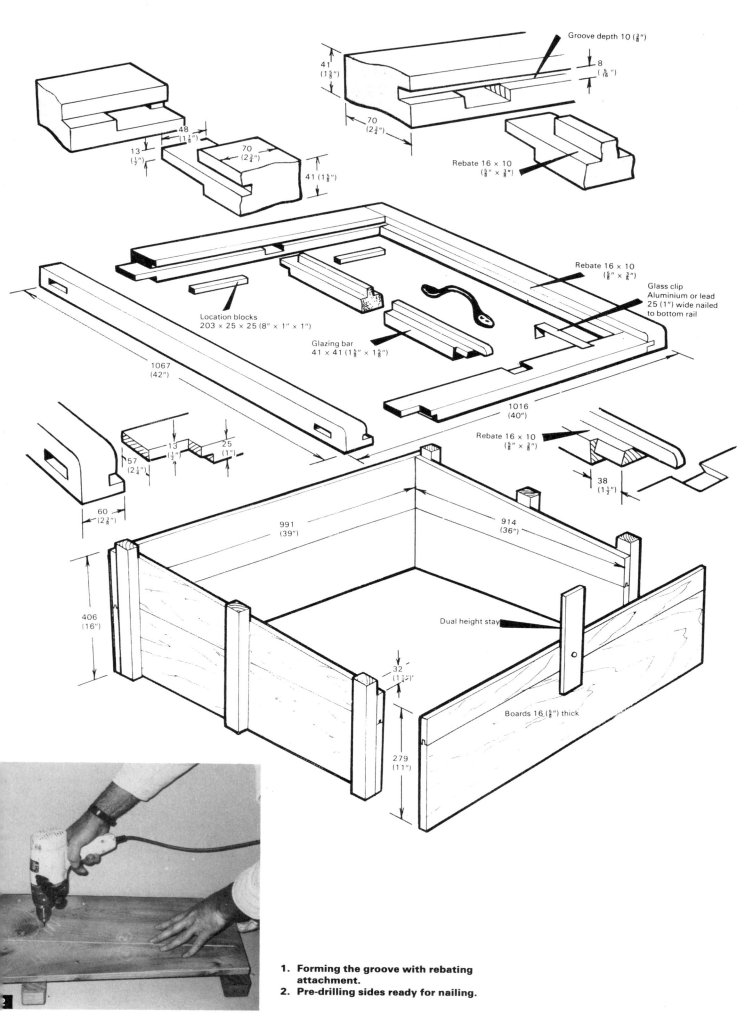

Groove depth 10 ($\frac{3}{8}$")

41
($1\frac{5}{8}$")

8
($\frac{5}{16}$")

70
($2\frac{3}{4}$")

Rebate 16 × 10
($\frac{5}{8}$" × $\frac{3}{8}$")

48
($1\frac{7}{8}$")

13
($\frac{1}{2}$")

70
($2\frac{3}{4}$")

41 ($1\frac{5}{8}$")

Rebate 16 × 10
($\frac{5}{8}$" × $\frac{3}{8}$")

Glass clip
Aluminium or lead
25 (1") wide nailed
to bottom rail

1067
(42")

Location blocks
203 × 25 × 25 (8" × 1" × 1")

Glazing bar
41 × 41 ($1\frac{5}{8}$" × $1\frac{5}{8}$")

1016
(40")

Rebate 16 × 10
($\frac{5}{8}$" × $\frac{3}{8}$")

13
($\frac{1}{2}$")

25
(1")

57
($2\frac{1}{4}$")

38
($1\frac{1}{2}$")

60
($2\frac{3}{8}$")

406
(16")

991
(39")

914
(36")

Dual height stay

32
($1\frac{1}{4}$")

279
(11")

Boards 16 ($\frac{5}{8}$") thick

1. **Forming the groove with rebating attachment.**
2. **Pre-drilling sides ready for nailing.**

3 4

5

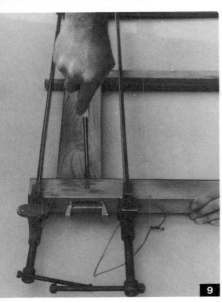

9 10

11

the taper marked on them, then the waste was sawn and planed away to produce the necessary pitch to the frame top (photo 2).

The three battens down each end not only hold the two boards of the end sections together, they also provide the means of creating the nailed corner joints, and their projecting upper ends serve to locate the top sash and prevent it from moving sideways. These battens I first planed to size, then cut to length. I cut them so that their upper ends had the same slope as the side boards, and in such a way that they all had a 32mm (1¼in.) projection above the ends.

At this stage I removed the arrises from the outer edges of the boards, and battens, including their upper ends.

With the material thus prepared, I was ready for the assembly. This was to be entirely by nailing and I used 51mm (2in.) galvanised nails of a fairly heavy gauge. As they had large heads, they were strictly speaking clout nails. In order to lessen the risk of the wood splitting, or the nails bending, all nail positions were predrilled (photo 3). The ends were assembled first, and in all cases I arranged the boards with the tongues upwards, as to have put the groove that way round would have meant that any water seeping into the joint would lodge.

The width of the boards making up the front and back had been made to correspond with the sloping ends, so all that remained to complete the assembly was to nail these boards in place (photo 4). Not only did I nail into the bat-

tens but nails were also driven into the boards forming the ends. As these nails were driven into end grain they have limited holding power, but I used the age-old method of knocking them in at a slight angle, or dovetail nailing as it is called. A shaving or two along the outer corners completed this part (photo 5).

The mode of construction I adopted for the sash was on the lines of a traditional skylight. With the material prepared to size, I set about marking out the sash. Note, that while there is a fairly generous overlap at the upper and lower ends of the sash to gain the maximum amount of glass area, the width is about 6mm (¼in.) less than the distance between the battens, so as to allow for easy movement.

Construction is based on the mortise and tenon joint although those at the lower end are the bare-faced variety. This is because the lower rail is much thinner than the rest of the framework, to allow the glass to completely overlap this rail. I used a square and a mortise gauge to mark out the correct positions of all the necessary joints (photos 6 and 7).

These were quickly cut by hand (photo 8), and the waste removed from the mortises by first using a brace and bit, then a chisel. The joint at the lower end of the glazing bar is a dovetail, and this was cut to the form shown in the drawings.

One feature always adopted on skylights is that while the stiles and glazing bars are rebated in order to accommodate the glass, the upper rail is grooved. Both the grooves and

rebates were again cut out with the use of th rebating attachment, and at this stage I bore from the underside into the mortises, so tha screws could be inserted later for locking thes joints. I made a trial fit of all the joints and was ready for gluing up.

I used Cascamite One Shot glue for th joints, cramping the frame together and check ing for squareness and flatness. Wedges wer driven into the joints alongside the tenon where the mortises had been deliberate made wider to allow for this—indeed it known as 'wedge-room'. The screws were the also inserted into the joints (photo 10).

Although the degree of cleaning up on a outdoor project of this type need only b minimal, I did go to the trouble to level off th joints with the smoothing plane (photo 11 The joggles on the stiles were sawn off, were the tenon ends and wedges, and the these parts too received a little attention fro the plane (photo 12).

To help to shed water at the lower end brought my throating plane into use to form shallow trench referred to as a drip groov This is not really essential for a job of th nature, and in any case a square groove cou be formed with the rebating attachment.

In order that the sash does not slide too f forward, a couple of location blocks were ad ded to the underside of the top rail. These a no more than oddments of wood screwed place. Another offcut I prepared as a stay allow the sash to be propped up clear of th

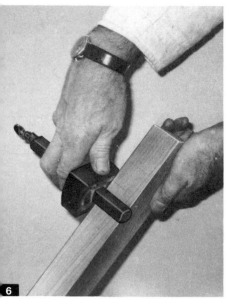

6

7

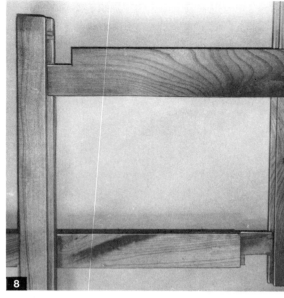

8

2

13

14

base. By boring the hole for the securing bolt off-centre the stay can be used at two different heights. Alternatively if it is left horizontal it will allow the sash to be completely lowered.

Although elm has a remarkable natural resistance to rot, I felt that treatment with preservative would improve it still further. Two coats of Cuprinol were applied, and I paid particular attention to joints and to end grain (photo 14). Before glazing I left my garden frame for about a week, by which time all traces of the slight surface oiliness from the preservative had disappeared.

Even though the slope of the sash is only fairly slight, there is always the possibility that the glass could at some future time slip. I therefore took the precaution of making a couple of glazing clips. These are no more than strips of soft aluminium, cut approximately 25mm (1in.) wide, and with initially one end bent over at right angles as seen in the drawing. These clips were then nailed to the inner edge of the sash.

Glazing was simple enough and, although the glass was bedded in putty, I did not think it necessary to putty-point the outer edges. The metal clips had been made sufficiently long for them to protrude about 25mm (1in.) beyond the edge of the glass, and these were now bent over to complete the glazing.

Only one small job now remained to be done, that was fix a handle to the lower end of the sash to enable it to be easily lifted. Screwing this in place completed my garden frame.

3. Clout nailing into a corner batten.
4. Levelling the corners with a plane.
5. Marking out stiles with a square.
6. The mortise joints are gauged out.
7. Cutting cheeks of tenon by hand.
8. Joints and rebates cut for assembly.
9. Reinforcing joint with a wood screw.
10. The corner joints are planed level.
11. Trimming up the edges of the sash.
12. Forming a throating on the rail.
13. Applying Cuprinol Wood Preserver to all parts.
14. Carefully bedding in the glass.
15. The completed frame ready for use.

15

GARDEN FRAME

(All sizes in mm and inches)   **GARDEN FRAME**   (No allowance for waste)

Ends	2 off	914 by 406 by 16mm	(36 by 16 by $\frac{5}{8}$in.)
Front	1 off	1098 by 279 by 16mm	(43$\frac{1}{4}$ by 11 by $\frac{5}{8}$in.)
Back	1 off	1098 by 406 by 16mm	(43$\frac{1}{4}$ by 16 by $\frac{5}{8}$in.)
Battens	2 off	438 by 51 by 38mm	(17$\frac{1}{4}$ by 2 by 1$\frac{1}{2}$in.)
Battens	2 off	381 by 51 by 38mm	(15 by 2 by 1$\frac{1}{2}$in.)
Battens	2 off	311 by 51 by 38mm	(12$\frac{1}{4}$ by 2 by 1$\frac{1}{2}$in.)
Stiles	2 off	1067 by 60 by 41mm	(42 by 2$\frac{3}{8}$ by 1$\frac{5}{8}$in.)
Top rail	1 off	1016 by 70 by 41mm	(40 by 2$\frac{3}{4}$ by 1$\frac{5}{8}$in.)
Bottom rail	1 off	1016 by 89 by 25mm	(40 by 3$\frac{1}{2}$ by 1 in.)
Glazing bar	1 off	1041 by 41 by 41mm	(41 by 1$\frac{5}{8}$ by 1$\frac{5}{8}$in.)
Location blocks	2 off	203 by 25 by 25mm	(8 by 1 by 1 in.)
Stay	1 off	381 by 76 by 16mm	(15 by 3 by $\frac{5}{8}$in.)

Also required: glass; oddments of metal for glazing chips; handle.

A blooming good idea

THE IDEA behind these two projects was to provide containers for favourite plants which we could then put in special places—flanking the front door, or in the porch, or on the rear patio. Indeed, one of the advantages of plants housed in this way is that they can be moved around according to their state of bloom, or our particular needs. Being made of elm the troughs will withstand all the hazards of an outdoor life for many many years.

The first of the two designs is based on the use of a plastic plant container of the type readily available at garden centres and multiple stores, and they come in several sizes. The one I bought is medium size and measures 610 by 165 by 140mm deep (24in by 6½in by 5½in). It is important to buy the plant container first, and make the trough to suit this since small adjustments to the size given will not alter the construction details.

Initially I planed all the wood to size, then marked out the legs to length, along with the shape needed for the centre part which was to be cut away. Next, the locations of the mortises in these legs were pencilled in, and at this stage the shoulder lines were squared for the tenons all round on the lower rails. Using the mortise gauge I completed the marking out of the joints. The mortises were cut by first boring out the waste (photo 1), and completing this

half of the joint by chiselling out (photo 2). They were made slightly wider on the outer surface of the legs by sloping their ends, a feature known as "wedge room". The tenons were carefully cut to size and two saw kerfs were let in on each one to accommodate the wedges.

The waste from the middle of the legs was sawn away, and the edges smoothed over with a file, although I did not go to great pains over this operation. The tops of the legs were marked out for 4mm chamfers, and these were then formed with a smoothing plane. Chamfering the ends in this way was a feature adopted for all the upper components.

Marking out for the upper rails took very little time, the trenches were gauged in at one third the thickness of the material. I was careful to check that the inside line for the trenches corresponded with the shoulder line of the lower rails. A saw and chisel soon removed the bulk of the waste from the trenches, and I used a router for levelling off (photo 3). Two holes were bored and countersunk in each trench for the screw fixings and the ends of the rails were chamfered in a similar way to the tops of the legs.

At this stage I was ready to start the assembling. As the particular troughs I was making were going to finish up outside, I did not feel

that cleaning up and glasspapering would be appropriate and all I did in this connection was to take a few shavings off the arrises to remove their extreme sharpness.

The first parts to be assembled were the legs and lower rails. For these joints I used waterproof glue, and cramped the work up so that the shoulders were quite tight. In order to hold the legs parallel, an upper rail was slid loosely into place, as seen in photo 4. Wedges were glued and driven into the saw kerfs in the tenons, the operation repeated for the other rail, and the work put aside for the glue to dry. Once the glue had set, the protruding tenon ends and wedges were sawn off, then levelled with a few shavings from the plane.

The second stage of assembling was quickly done, as all that was needed was to screw the side battens in place. However, both to make the job of screwing easier, and to minimise the chance of the legs splitting, I carefully predrilled small holes before driving in the screws.

The three cross battens which actually support the plant container needed little preparation, all that was required was to cut them to length, bore the holes for the screws, and chamfer the ends. Screwing them in place completed the work on the first trough.

The second design of trough differs from the first in a number of ways, one of these being

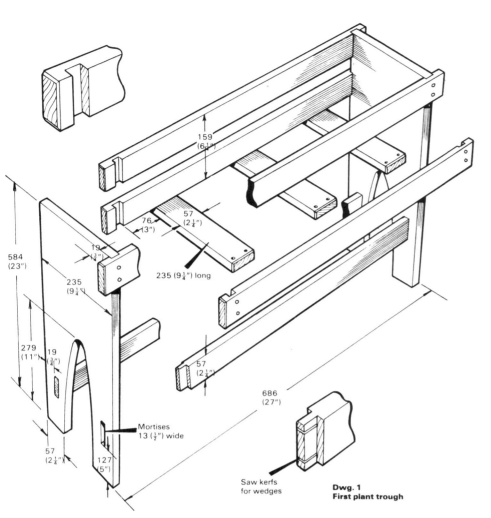

159
(6¼")

76
(3")

57
(2¼")

235 (9¼") long

19
(¾")

584
(23")

235
(9¼")

279
(11")

19
(¾")

57
(2¼")

57
(2¼")

127
(5")

686
(27")

Mortises
13 (½") wide

Saw kerfs
for wedges

Dwg. 1
First plant trough

that it is made as two separate parts, another that the box section at the top is intended to be the actual plant container and therefore loaded with soil. I started work on the upper part.

The four pieces forming the box were cut to length with their ends dead square ready for dovetailing. The pins were marked out on the smaller pieces, and the waste sawn and chiselled away (photo 6). Using the pins as a templet, the sockets, or tails, were then marked on the longer sides of the box (photo 7). Some craftsmen prefer to cut the sockets first, and mark the pins from these, but I believe the method I adopt is the one generally employed. Face marks, and individual joint identification marks, are particularly important when dovetailing.

The ends of the box had been made deliberately wider than the sides in order that they could be rounded, This curve was marked out, the waste sawn away, and smoothed with a compass plane (photo 8). A spokeshave would have done the job just as well.

I removed the arrises on the upper edges of all four pieces, and I was then ready for gluing up. With waterproof glue on both parts of the joints, assembly was fairly rapid, and again the work was left overnight. Only the minimum of planing was then needed on the outer surfaces primarily to ensure that the joints were levelled.

The piece for the bottom of the box was cut

1. **Boring out waste from the mortises.**
2. **The joints cleaned up with a chisel.**
3. **Levelling the trench with a router.**
4. **Wedging tenons while still cramped.**
5. **The supporting battens are added.**

1

2

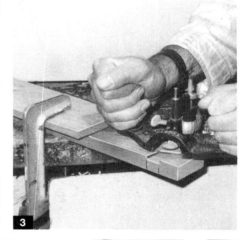

3

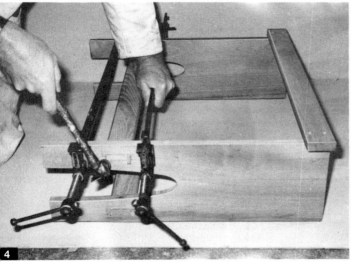

4

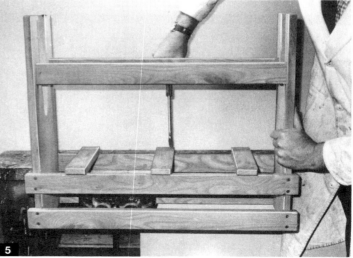

5

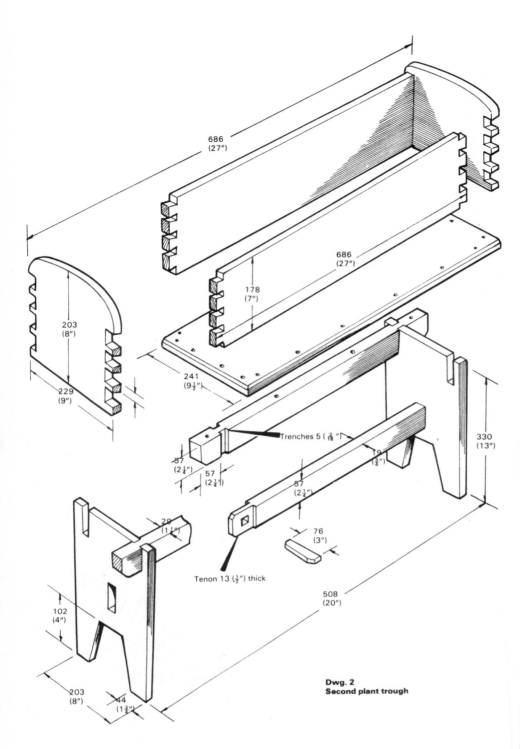

686
(27")

686
(27")

178
(7")

203
(8")

229
(9")

241
(9½")

330
(13")

57
(2¼")

57
(2¼")

57
(2¼")

Trenches 5 (3/16 ")

19
(¾")

29
(1⅛")

76
(3")

Tenon 13 (½") thick

508
(20")

102
(4")

203
(8")

44
(1¾")

**Dwg. 2
Second plant trough**

to overlap the sides by 6mm (¼in.) all round.
Holes were prepared for screwing up, edges
chamfered on both sides, and this part added
to the rest of the box (photo 9).

I could now turn my attention to the under
framing, or stand, and started this by cutting all
the material to exact size. The joints on the top
rails and the upper end of the legs were then
marked out. As these are bridle joints, the
marking out needed is very similar to a mortise
and tenon, and indeed the mortise gauge was
used for the purpose. The joints on the lower
rail are mortise and tenons, and these too were
marked out at this stage. To complete the
marking out on the legs, the simple shaping a

6

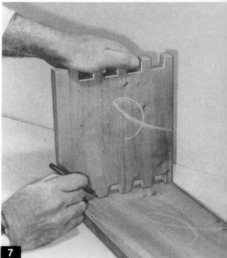

7

8

CUTTING LIST

(Sizes in mm and inches)   (No allowance for waste)

Trough 1

Legs	2 off	584 by 197 by 19mm	(23 by 7¾ by ¾ in.)
Lower rails	2 off	686 by 57 by 19mm	(27 by 2¼ by ¾ in.)
Side rails	4 off	724 by 57 by 19mm	(28½ by 2¼ by ¾ in.)
Cross battens	3 off	235 by 57 by 19mm	(9¼ by 2¼ by ¾ in.)

Trough 2

Box sides	2 off	686 by 178 by 19mm	(27 by 7 by ¾ in.)
Box ends	2 off	229 by 203 by 19mm	(9 by 8 by ¾ in.)
Box base	1 off	699 by 241 by 19mm	(27½ by 9½ by ¾ in.)
Legs	2 off	330 by 203 by 19mm	(13 by 8 by ¾ in.)
Upper rails	2 off	622 by 57 by 29mm	(24½ by 2¼ by 1⅛ in.)
Lower rail	1 off	584 by 57 by 19mm	(23 by 2¼ by ⅜ in.)

Also required: oddments for wedges; plastic plant container.

the bottom end was pencilled in .The waste to these joints was then cut out and the shaping at the bottom carried out first by bandsawing, then filing (photo 10). I decided to cut the trenches on the upper rails on my circular saw (photo 11), several passes over the blade being needed to gain the required width.

Before cutting the tenons on the lower rail, the small mortises needed for the wedges which are driven through the tenons are marked and cut. The outer ends of the mortises were formed with a slope to match the slope of the wedges, and the inner ends of them were slightly overcut. This latter feature was to ensure that the wedges would have the desired effect of pulling the joint together, and thus ensuring that the shoulders would be tight. With the mortises cut in this way within the tenons, the cheeks and shoulders were sawn.

To enable the underframing to be secured to the box, four holes were bored for screws in each of the upper rails. Because of the width of the rails, these holes were actually counterbored. The lower corners of these rails were removed as shown, as were the corners of the tenons on the lower rail. Two wedges were also made prior to assembling.

With all the joints cut, and the parts prepared ready for gluing up, this was obviously the next step. Cramps were sufficient to hold the upper rails in place (photo 12), while with the lower rails the wedges were driven in with the desired effect. All joints, including the wedges, were coated with waterproof glue.

Once the cramps were removed the underframing was immediately ready for adding to the box (photo 13), and with the two parts together the plant trough was completed.

Again I felt it worthwhile to give my two latest projects a coat of preservative (photo 14), as however long lasting elm may be I felt the preservative must add to the life of the troughs. The application also left the troughs a rich brown colour, but it was filling them both with plants that really brought them to life.

6. Cutting away waste from the pins.
7. Marking out for the dovetail sockets.
8. Both of the ends are smothly curved.
9. Screwing on the bottom of the box.
10. File takes the rough off the edges.
11. Trenching the rails on the saw bed.
12. Finished piece glued and cramped up.
13. Screwing the underframe to the box.
14. Finally a coat of wood preservative.

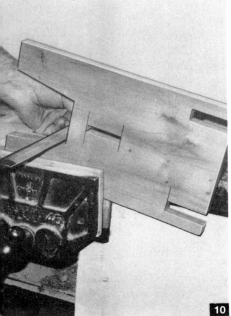

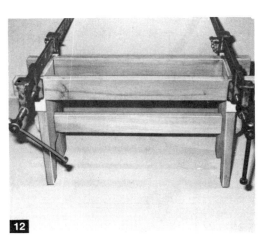

Garden gate

in a traditional style

RECENTLY I WAS ASKED if I would make a replacement garden gate for a friend and when I received the measurements I realised it was larger than average although in a traditional style. I believe this type of gate is the ideal project for the enthusiast woodworker with a well equipped workshop; with some light machinery; or by hand. It gives a good range of joints and woodworking techniques. Here I am trying to show some interesting principles of cutting joints using power tools, but don't be put off by not owning the type of machines shown, hand tools are quite adequate for this project. The size I am making is 60in. (152½cm) high by 38½in (98cm) wide. These dimensions of course can be adjusted to suit your own requirements. If it is much bigger than this the addition of a diagonal bearer

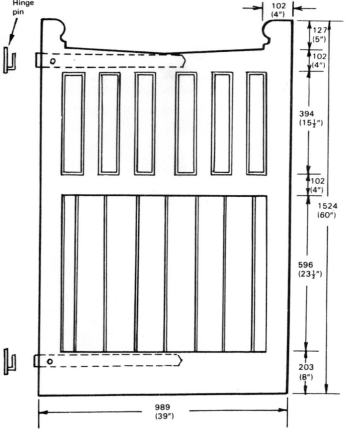

Hinge pin

102 (4")

127 (5")

102 (4")

394 (15½")

102 (4")

1524 (60")

596 (23½")

203 (8")

989 (39")

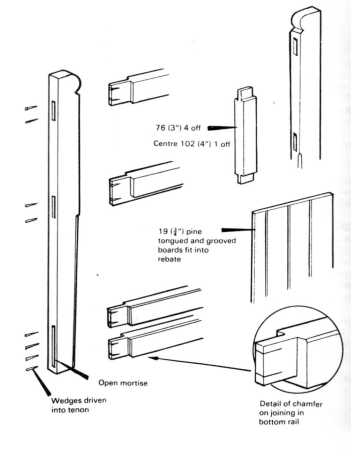

76 (3") 4 off
Centre 102 (4") 1 off

19 (¾") pine tongued and grooved boards fit into rebate

Open mortise

Wedges driven into tenon

Detail of chamfer on joining in bottom rail

1. Cross cutting with the radial arm saw.

2. The major pieces are cut to length.

3. Marking out the mortises on the stiles.

4. The principle of wedging the cut tenons.

5. Marking the mortises on the cross rails.

6. Mortises are cut with a hollow chisel.

behind the lower panelling will give more stability. Photos 1 and 2 show cutting the lengths to the correct sizes, allowing approximately 3in. (76mm) on the stiles for haunches. Note that the cross rails consist of 4 pieces, two of which go to make up the bottom rail. I choose to construct the wider bottom rail this way for two reasons. Firstly you need only buy the wood in one section, secondly I find wider planks tend to bow slightly, even when they have been run though a thicknesser. Before assembling put a small chamfer on the face edge where the two meet, gluing at the same time.

Mark out the mortises on the stiles leaving 3in. at the bottom for the haunches. The central mortise is determined in my case by the original hinge studs that are leaded into the wall. If however you have, or are putting in posts you will be able to hang from the top and bottom rails, making the placing of the centre rail less critical.

The mortises on the stiles are cut right through, and opened either side $\frac{1}{4}$in. (6mm). This will allow the tenon to be wedged to form a dovetail inside the mortise, as shown in photo 4.

Mark out all mortises on the underside of the top rail, and the top of the centre rail to take the five vertical bars. Note the middle bar is a little wider than the other four. The mortises only go $1\frac{1}{4}$in. (32mm) deep.

Cut out all mortises to $\frac{1}{2}$in. (13mm) wide.

Photo 6 shows this operation being carried out using a hollow chisel on a universal machine.

A $\frac{5}{8}$ by $\frac{1}{2}$in. rebate has to be made in the bottom half of the gate. This is to recess the panelling flush with the frame. The rebate on the stiles is stopped at the middle mortise as shown in photo 9.

To make the rebate in the right stile I use the small planer. The left one was made on the saw bench making two separate cuts one $\frac{1}{2}$in. and one $\frac{5}{8}$in., both can be done on the saw bench, or with a power drill saw attachment.

Shape the top of the stiles to the design you want and sand to a smooth finish. Photo 10 shows shaping with a jigsaw. This is just as easily done by hand using coping saw albeit a little more slowly. The top rail is curved slightly, this can be cut either before or after the tenons have been cut. Photo 11 shows cutting the curve using a bandsaw but a coping saw is adequate.

Now we come to the tenons, these can be cut traditionally with tenon saw, or there are a number of different ways using power tools. The one I used was a radial arm saw. First mark out the tenon with a mortise gauge, lower the blade to the depth of the shoulder and mark a pencil line on the fence the length of the tenon. (Note the top has parallel shoulders, but the middle and bottom rail have $\frac{1}{2}$in. (13mm) stepped to alow for the rebate). The saw is drawn across the joint several times to remove most of the waste. Two or three

joints can be cut at the same time using this principle, but be careful to keep the wood square with the fence as shown in photo 12.

The tenons are cleaned up by paring the rest of the waste with a sharp chisel.

This technique of cutting tenons by slicing can be done on a conventional saw bench by using the mitre fence. All curves are finally glasspapered smooth, and the inside edges sanded with a finish sander, or belt sander, prior to assembling. First clamp the vertical rails to the top and centre rail gluing with a waterproof glue. I find the aluminium star sprigs useful for holding these tight, so one can get the rest of the frame assembled not having to wait for the glue to set. Photo 14 shows me driving the wedges home.

The tongued and grooved and V jointed boards are then cut and fitted into the rebate. Photo 15 shows a bevel (45°) being made round the openings between the verticals, this is run right round and gives a continuous flow to the finished project. This is a personal preference, alternatively a sloped chamfer could be substituted or it could even be left plain.

Photo 16 shows the finished gate ready to paint or stain. If you decide to paint, I strongly recommend a good wood preserver to protect it from rot. If you prefer a natural finish use a micro-porous wood stain, such as Cuprinol Wood Stain, which resists cracking and peeling.

7. Making the rebate with a small planer.

8. Rebate can be made on the saw bench.

9. Note rebate stops at centre mortise.

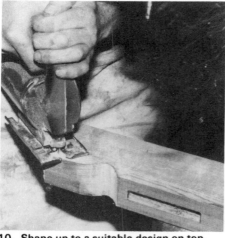
10. Shape up to a suitable design on top.

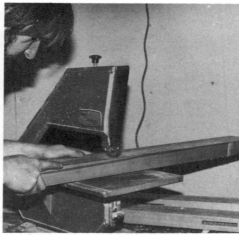
11. Cutting the curved rail on the bandsaw.

12. Several passes made to cut the tenons.

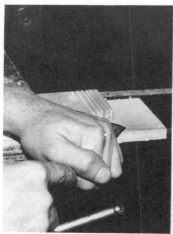
13. Chiselling off the waste.

14. Driving home the tenon wedges in toprail.

15. A 45 degree bevel is made around the inside of the edges with a router.

16. The finished job before the addition of paint.

Garden recliner

This is a really comfortable piece of garden furniture being a chair and a lounger combined. It's simplicity itself to make but it does include some elementary metalwork. Most of the fixtures and fittings can be bought at any ironmongers and it's just a question of making a few minor alterations to their shapes.

A GARDEN lounge-chair in our climate needs not only to be comfortable, but to be resistent to the unpredictability of our summer weather. For this reason, particular attention has been paid to making this chair weatherproof in the long term by permanent wood protection.

To ensure that all the surfaces are properly protected, the chair is dismantled after a trial assembly and the individual parts — back-rest, seat, footrest and framework — are then sealed with a multi-layer wood protection, beginning with a primer. In addition to the primer, wood such as pine should be given two or three coats of wood-protecting glaze; for hard woods you should apply three coats.

This ensures that the wood is protected at the hinge-points and, above all, in the rack fixing. The seat and footrest sections naturally do not need to be taken apart again, as here the wood is firmly screwed down.

If you are this careful in the construction of the lounge-chair, you will have a piece of garden furniture which can stand outside all summer. When it comes on to rain you will only need to take indoors the cushions, your sun-tan oil and of course yourself.

There are only two sizes of timber, 50 × 25mm for the slats, and 60 × 20mm for the frame. The lengths of the hinged pieces are given to the hinge centres so add 30mm to allow for the rounded ends. Rack dimensions are shown bottom right.

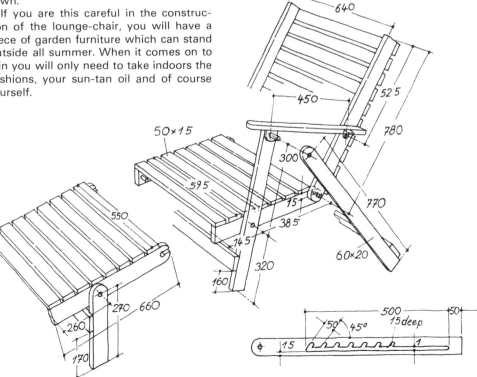

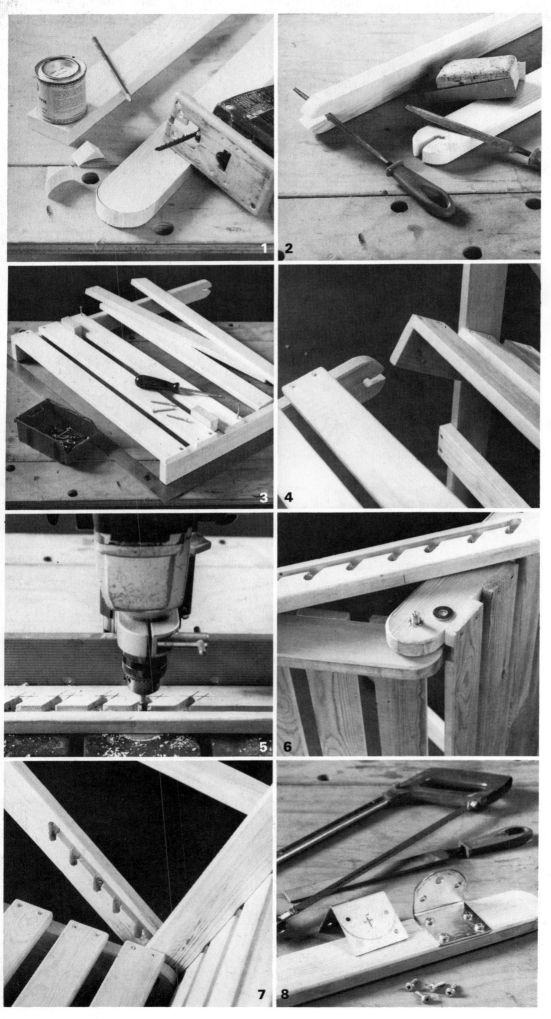

1. Using a jigsaw the round ends are quickly cut. A small tin or glass is ideal for marking out the curves. When finishing off the curves clamp them together in the vice and finish as if they were one piece.

2. The slots in the footrest are also cut with the jigsaw and finished with a wood file as shown. Now is a good time to glasspaper the edges of the components to ensure that they are free from splinters.

3. The slats are screwed to the side pieces 20mm apart. Two offcuts from the side pieces will make excellent spacers and ensure a constant distance. Here we are using a large set square to keep the right angle but if you don't have one it's easy enough to make one up or improvise with the corner of a table.

4. The footrest hooks under the seat of the chair. To ensure that it does not slip off, the slots are cut into an "L" shape to fit over the 8mm dowel pegs in the seat frame.

5. The rack for adjusting the setting of the chair back can be cut with a milling cutter on a vertical drill stand, dimensions are shown on the previous page. These are 10mm wide. It's worth taking some time over them to ensure that they are all accurate and even.

6. The hinge bolt also acts as the rod for the height adjustment so the nut must be countersunk into the rail before the washer is added. Note the bottom slat of the chair is notched to accommodate the swing.

7. When the chair is assembled the slots in the rack must point downwards as shown.

8. The link for the arm rest is made up from an angle bracket. Saw the curve with a hacksaw and finish with a file to take off the rough edges and drill the hole to suit.